The New Local Government Series
No. 8

TOWN AND COUNTRY PLANNING IN BRITAIN

The New Local Government Series

GENERAL EDITOR

PROFESSOR
PETER G. RICHARDS

TOWN AND COUNTRY
PLANNING IN BRITAIN

BY

J. B. CULLINGWORTH

Professor of Urban and Regional Studies
University of Birmingham

Fifth Edition

London
GEORGE ALLEN & UNWIN LTD
RUSKIN HOUSE   MUSEUM STREET

FIRST PUBLISHED 1964
REVISED SECOND EDITION 1967
REPRINTED 1969
REVISED THIRD EDITION 1970
REVISED FOURTH EDITION 1972
REVISED FIFTH EDITION 1974

© *J. B. Cullingworth* 1964, 1967, 1970, 1972, 1974
ISBN 0 04 352055 3 hardback
0 04 352054 5 paper

PRINTED IN GREAT BRITAIN
in 10 *on* 11 *pt. Times type*
BY T. AND A. CONSTABLE
HOPETOUN STREET, EDINBURGH

'Planning policies depend more on political than on technical objectives; and they are always in a state of evolution. Planning is essentially a service rather than a science in its own right.'

BARONESS SHARP, former Permanent Secretary to the Ministry of Housing and Local Government*

* E. Sharp, *The Ministry of Housing and Local Government*, Allen & Unwin, 1969

The fourth edition of this book was written in the summer of 1971 and published in 1972. Since then, major changes have taken place in the institutional framework of planning and, to a lesser extent, in planning policy. Some of the changes are so dramatic that certain sections of this book are in process of becoming totally outdated. This applies particularly to Chapter V on 'The Local Planning Machine'. Nevertheless, at the time of writing (December 1973), the situation was too fluid to permit a clear statement to be given of the new local government structures. Though some trends are clear, the overall position is one of confusion and rapid change. The reorganization of local government involves far more than the passing of an Act of Parliament: it takes a considerable time to implement and is both the cause of, and the opportunity for, more radical changes in the operation of the planning system. A thorough revision of this book must await the establishment of the new authorities (1974 in England and Wales, and 1975 in Scotland).

In the meantime, an appendix has been included in this edition which attempts to outline a selection of the more important changes in planning organization and policy over the period 1971 to 1973.

The main body of the book remains the same as in the last edition. Chapter I provides a background account of the evolution of town and country planning, the inadequacies of the embryonic instruments of the inter-war years, and the now largely forgotten enthusiasm and confidence of the architects of post-war planning. Chapter II describes how this idealism battled against the facts of political and administrative life: a battle which is still unresolved – if it ever can be.

Chapters III to V give an account of the structure of the planning machine and the general powers at its disposal. Chapter III takes account of the machinery of central government reorganization made by the Conservative Government late in 1970. Chapter IV attempts to incorporate a description of the changes made following the 1968 Planning Act, but the picture is inevitably out of focus, since the 'new' system is operating side by side with the 'old' one. If the reader is confused, he may be comforted by the thought that he has the company of many who are working in this quicksand of change.

Chapter V includes a discussion of the proposals for the reorganization of local government as at mid-1971. It now needs to be read in conjunction with the new appendix.

Chapter VI, on land values, is largely of historical interest:

hopefully a later edition may be able to describe a further attempt by Government to cope with the problems which, at the time of writing, are all too obvious.

Issues of amenity and the protection of the environment which are discussed in Chapters VII and VIII, have become of greater and more widespread concern. Though the text has not been altered, the new appendix highlights the reactions of the legislature to this.

The following three chapters deal with planning for leisure, new and expanded towns, and regional planning. The final chapter discusses the relationship between the planners and the planned in a democratic society. A more extended discussion is to be found in Volume II of the author's *Problems of an Urban Society*.

Grateful acknowledgement is made to the many people, mostly within the planning profession, who have assisted in various ways in the writing of this book. Though anonymity must be preserved in accordance with convention, my debt is great – and, to the discerning, obvious. Thanks are due to the Controller of HM Stationery Office for permission to quote extensively from official publications. My largest debt, as always, is to my wife, who has borne a large part of the social cost of this composition.

J. B. Cullingworth

The Planning Exchange
Glasgow
December 1973

Contents

Chapter I

THE EVOLUTION OF TOWN AND COUNTRY PLANNING

THE PUBLIC HEALTH ORIGINS

Town and Country Planning as a task of government has developed from public health and housing policies. The nineteenth-century increase in population and, even more significant, the growth of towns led to public health problems which demanded a new role for government. Together with the growth of medical knowledge, the realization that overcrowded insanitary urban areas resulted in an economic cost (which had to be borne at least in part by the local ratepayers) and the fear of social unrest, this new urban growth eventually resulted in an appreciation of the necessity for interfering with market forces and private property rights in the interest of social well-being. The nineteenth-century Public Health legislation was directed at the creation of adequate sanitary conditions. Among the measures taken to achieve these were powers for Local Authorities to make and enforce building by-laws for controlling street widths and the height, structure and layout of buildings. Limited and defective though these powers proved to be, they represented a marked advance in social control and paved the way for more imaginative measures. The physical impact of by-law control on British towns is depressingly still very much in evidence; and it did not escape the attention of contemporary social reformers.

'. . . much good work has been done. In the ample supply of pure water, in the drainage and removal of waste matter, in the paving, lighting and cleansing of streets, and in many other such ways, probably our towns are as well served as, or even better than, those elsewhere. Moreover, by means of our much abused building bye-laws, the worst excesses of overcrowding have been restrained; a certain minimum standard of air-space, light and ventilation has been secured; while in the more modern parts of towns a fairly high degree of sanitation, of immunity from fire, and general stability of construction have been maintained, the importance of which can hardly be exaggerated. We have, indeed, in all these matters laid a good foundation and have secured many of the necessary elements for a healthy condition of life; and yet the remarkable fact remains that there are growing up around our big towns vast districts, under these very bye-laws, which for dreariness and sheer ugliness it is difficult to match anywhere, and compared with which many of the old unhealthy slums are, from the point of view of picturesqueness and beauty, infinitely more attractive'.[27]

It was on this point that public health and architecture met. The enlightened experiments at Saltaire (1853), Bournville (1878), Port Sunlight (1887) and elsewhere had provided object lessons. Ebenezer Howard and the Garden City Movement were now exerting considerable influence on contemporary thought. The National Housing Reform Council (later the National Housing and Town Planning Council) were campaigning for the introduction of town planning. Even more significant was a similar demand from local government and professional associations such as the Association of Municipal Corporations, the Royal Institute of British Architects, the Surveyors' Institute, and the Association of Municipal and County Engineers. As Ashworth has pointed out,[3] 'the support of many of these bodies was particularly important because it showed that the demand for town planning was arising not simply out of theoretical preoccupations but out of the everyday practical experience of local administration. The demand was coming in part from those who would be responsible for the execution of town planning if it were introduced.'

THE FIRST PLANNING ACT

The movement for the extension of sanitary policy into town planning was uniting diverse interests. These were nicely summarized by John Burns, the President of the Local Government Board, when he introduced the first legislation bearing the term 'town planning' – the Housing, Town Planning, Etc., Act, 1909:

'The object of the Bill is to provide a domestic condition for the people in which their physical health, their morals, their character and their whole social condition can be improved by what we hope to secure in this Bill. The Bill aims in broad outline at, and hopes to secure, the home healthy, the house beautiful, the town pleasant, the city dignified and the suburb salubrious.'[16]

The new powers provided by the Act were for the preparation of 'schemes' by local authorities for controlling the development of new housing areas. Though novel, these powers were logically a simple extension of existing ones. It is significant that this first legislative acceptance of town planning came in an Act dealing with health and housing. And, as Ashworth has pointed out, the gradual development and the accumulated experience of public health and housing measures facilitated a general acceptance of the principle of town planning. 'Housing reform had gradually been conceived in terms of larger and larger units. Torrens' Act (Artizans and Labourers Dwellings Act, 1868) had made a beginning with individual houses; Cross's Act (Artizans and Labourers Dwellings Improvement Act, 1875) had introduced an element of town planning by concerning itself with the reconstruction of insanitary areas; the framing of bye-laws in accordance with the Public Health Act of 1875 had accustomed local authorities to the imposition of at least a minimum of regulation on new building, and such a measure as the London Building Act of 1894 brought into the scope of public control the formation and widening of streets, the lines of buildings frontage, the extent of open space around buildings, and the height of buildings. Town planning was therefore not altogether a leap in the dark, but could be represented as a logical extension, in accordance with changing aims and conditions, of earlier legislation concerned with housing and public health.'[3] The 'changing conditions' were predominantly the rapid growth of suburban development – a factor which increased in importance in the following decades.

'In fifteen years 500,000 acres of land have been abstracted from the agricultural domain for houses, factories, workshops and railways. . . . If we go in the next fifteen years abstracting another half a million from the agricultural domain, and we go on rearing in green fields slums, in many respects, considering their situation, more squalid than those which are found in Liverpool, London and Glasgow, posterity will blame us for not taking this matter in hand in a scientific spirit. Every two and a half years there is a County of London converted into urban life from rural conditions and agricultural land. It represents an enormous amount of building land which we have no right to allow to go unregulated.'[16]

The emphasis was entirely on raising the standards of *new* development. The Act permitted local authorities (after obtaining the permission of the Local Government Board) to prepare town planning schemes with the general object of 'securing proper sanitary conditions, amenity and convenience', but only for land which was being developed or appeared likely to be developed.

Strangely it was not at all clear what town planning involved. It certainly did not include 'the remodelling of the existing town, the replanning of badly planned areas, the driving of new roads through old parts of a town – all these are beyond the scope of the new town planning powers'.[2] The Act itself provided no definition: indeed, it merely listed nineteen 'matters to be dealt with by General Provisions Prescribed by the Local Government Board'. The restricted and vague nature of this first legislation was associated in part with the lack of experience of the problems involved: Nettleford even went so far as to suggest that 'when this Act was passed, it was recognized as only a trial trip for the purpose of finding out the weak spots in local government with regard to town and estate development so that effective remedies might be later on devised'.[15]

Nevertheless the cumbersome administrative procedure devised by the Local Government Board – in order to give all interested parties 'full opportunity of considering the proposals at all stages' – might well have been intended to deter all but the most ardent of local authorities. The land taxes threatened by the 1910 Finance Act, and then the First World War added to the difficulties. It can be the occasion of no surprise that very few schemes were actually completed under the 1909 Act.

INTER-WAR LEGISLATION

The first revision of town planning legislation which took place after the first world war (the Housing and Town Planning Act of 1919) did little in practice to broaden the basis of town planning. The preparation of schemes was made obligatory on all Borough and Urban Districts having a population of 20,000 or more, but the time limit (January 1, 1926) was first extended (by the Housing Act, 1923) and finally abolished (by the Town and Country Planning Act, 1932). Some of the procedural difficulties were removed, but no change in concept appeared. Despite lip-service to the idea of town planning, the major advances made at this time were in the field of housing rather than in planning. It was the 1919 Act which began what Marion Bowley has called 'the series of experiments in State intervention to increase the supply of working-class houses'.[6] The 1919 Act accepted the principle of State subsidies for housing and thus began the nation-wide growth of council house estates. Equally significant was the entirely new standard of working-class housing provided: the three-bedroom house with kitchen, bath and garden, built at the density recommended by the Tudor Walters Report[26] of not more than twelve houses to the acre. At these new standards development could generally take place only on virgin land on the periphery of towns, and municipal estates grew alongside the private suburbs – 'the basic social products of the twentieth century', as Asa Briggs has termed them.[7]

This suburbanization was greatly accelerated by rapid developments in transportation – developments with which the young planning machine could not keep pace. The ideas of Howard and the Garden City Movement, of Geddes and of those who, like Warren and Davidge, saw town planning not just as a technique for controlling the layout and design of residential areas, but as part of a policy of national economic and social planning, were receiving increasing attention, but in practice town planning often meant little more than an extension of the old public health and housing controls.

Various attempts were made to deal with the increasing difficulties. Of particular significance were the Town and Country Planning Act of 1932, which extended planning powers to almost any type of land, whether built-up or undeveloped, and the Restriction of Ribbon Development Act, 1935, which, as its name suggests, was designed to control the spread of development along major roads. But these and similar measures were inadequate. For instance, under the 1932 Act planning schemes took about three years to prepare and pass through all their stages. Final approval had to be given by Parliament and schemes then had the force of law – as a result of which variations or amendments were not possible except by a repetition of the whole procedure. 'Interim development control' operated during the time between the passing of a resolution to prepare a scheme and its date of operation (as approved by Parliament). This enabled – but did not require – developers to apply for planning permission. If they did not obtain planning permission and the development was not in conformity with the scheme when approved the planning authority could require the owner (without compensation) to remove or alter the development. But all too often developers preferred to take a chance that no scheme would ever come into force, or that if it did no local authority would face pulling down existing buildings. The damage was therefore done before the planning authorities had a chance to intervene. Once a planning scheme was approved, on the other hand, the local authority ceased to have any planning control over individual developments. The scheme was in fact a zoning plan: land was zoned for particular uses – residential, industrial and so on – though provision could be made for limiting the number of buildings, the space around them, etc. In fact, so long as the developer did not try to introduce a non-conforming use he was fairly safe. Furthermore, most schemes in fact did little more than accept and ratify existing trends of development, since any attempt at a more radical solution would have involved the planning authority in compensation they could not afford to pay. In most cases the zones were so widely drawn as to place hardly more restriction on the developer than if there had been no scheme at all. Indeed in the half of the country covered by draft planning schemes in 1937 there was sufficient land zoned for housing to accommodate 350 million people.

ADMINISTRATIVE SHORTCOMINGS

A major weakness was, of course, the administrative structure itself. At the local level the administrative unit outside the county boroughs was the district council. Such authorities were generally small and weak. This was implicitly recognized as early as 1919, for the Act of that year permitted the establishment of joint planning committees. The 1929 Local Government Act went further, by empowering county councils to take part in planning, either by becoming constituent members of joint planning committees or by undertaking powers relinquished by district councils. A number of regional advisory plans were prepared, but these were generally ineffective and, indeed, conceived as little more than a series of suggestions for controlling future development, together with proposals for new main roads. The noteworthy characteristic of a planning scheme was its regulatory nature. It did not secure that development would take place: it merely secured that if it did take place in any particular part of the area covered by the scheme it would be controlled in certain ways. Furthermore, as the Uthwatt Report stressed, the system was 'essentially one of local planning, based on the initiative and financial resources of local bodies (whether individual local authorities or combinations of such authorities) responsible to local electorates. . . . The local authorities naturally consider questions of planning and development largely with a view to the effect they will have on the authorities' own finances and trade of the district. Proposals by landowners involving the further development of an existing urban area are not likely in practice to be refused by a local authority if the only reason against the development taking place is that from the national standpoint its proper location is elsewhere, particularly when it is remembered that the prevention of any such development might not only involve the authority in liability to pay heavy compensation but would, in addition, deprive them of substantial increases in rate income.'

The central authority – the Ministry of Health – had no effective powers of initiation and no power to grant financial assistance to local authorities. Indeed its powers were essentially regulatory and seemed to be designed to cast it in the role of a quasi-judicial body to be chiefly concerned with ensuring that local authorities did not treat property owners unfairly.

The difficulties were not, however, solely administrative. Even the most progressive authority was greatly handicapped by the inadequacies of the law relating to compensation. The compensation paid either for planning restrictions or for compulsory acquisition had to be determined in relation to the most profitable use of the land, even if it was unlikely that the land would be so developed, and without regard to the fact that the prohibition of development on one site usually resulted in the development value (which had been purchased at high cost) shifting to another site. Consequently in the words of the Uthwatt Committee, 'an examination of the Town Planning maps of some of our most important built-up areas reveals that in many cases they are little more than photographs of existing users and existing lay-outs, which, to avoid the necessity of paying compensation, become perpetuated by incorporation in a statutory scheme irrespective of their suitability or desirability'.

These problems increased as the housing boom of the 'thirties developed. 2,700,000 houses were built in England and Wales between 1930 and 1940. At the outbreak of war one-third of all the houses in England and Wales had been built since 1918. The implications for urbanization were obvious, particularly in the London area. Between 1919 and 1939 the population of Greater London rose by about $\frac{3}{4}$ million on account of natural increase but by over $1\frac{1}{4}$ million by migration.[1] This growth of the metropolis was a force which existing powers were incapable of halting, despite the large body of opinion favouring some degree of control.

THE DEPRESSED AREAS

The crux of the matter was that the problem of London was closely allied to that of the declining areas of the North and of South Wales – and both were part of the much wider problem of industrial location. In the South-East the insured employed population rose by 44 per cent between 1923 and 1934, but in the North-East it fell by $5\frac{1}{2}$ per cent and in Wales by 26 per cent. In 1934 8·6 per cent of insured workers in Greater London were unemployed, but in Workington the proportion was 36·3 per cent, in Gateshead 44·2 per cent and in Jarrow 67·8 per cent. In the early stages of political action these two problems were divorced. For London various advisory committees were set up and a series of reports issued – the Royal Commission on the Local Government of Greater London (1921–3); the London and Home Counties Traffic Advisory Committee (1924); the Greater London Regional Planning Committee (1927); the Standing Conference on London Regional Planning (1937); as well as *ad hoc* committees and inquiries, e.g. on Greater

London Drainage (1935) and a Highway Development Plan (the Bressey Report, 1938). For the depressed areas attention was first concentrated on encouraging migration, on training schemes and on schemes for establishing the unemployed in smallholdings. Increasing unemployment accompanied by rising public concern (especially after hunger marches on the one hand and articles in *The Times* on the other)[23] necessitated further action. Government 'investigators' were appointed and, following their reports,[19] the Depressed Areas Bill was introduced in November 1934 – to pass (after the Lords had amended the title) as the Special Areas Act. Under the Act a Special Commissioner for England and Wales (and one for Scotland) was appointed, with very wide powers for 'the initiation, organization, prosecution and assistance of measures designed to facilitate the economic development and social improvement' of the Special Areas. The Areas were defined in the Act and included the North-East Coast, West Cumberland, industrial South Wales – and, in Scotland, the industrial area around Glasgow. By September 1938, the Commissioners had spent, or approved the spending of, nearly £21 million, of which £15 million was for the improvement of public and social services, £3 million for smallholdings and allotment schemes, and £½ million on amenity schemes such as the clearance of derelict sites. Physical and social amelioration, however, was intended to be complementary to the Commissioner's main task: the attraction of new industry. Appeals to industrialists proved inadequate; in his second report, Sir Malcolm Stewart, the Commissioner for England and Wales, concluded 'there is little prospect of the Special Areas being assisted by the spontaneous action of industrialists now located outside these Areas'. On the other hand the attempt to actively attract new industry by the development of trading estates achieved considerable success, which at least warranted the comment of the Scottish Commissioner that there had been 'sufficient progress to dispel the fallacy that the Areas are incapable of expanding their light industries'. Nevertheless there were still 300,000 unemployed in the Special Areas at the end of 1938, and though 123 factories had been opened between 1937 and 1938 in the Special Areas, 372 had been opened in the London area. Sir Malcolm Stewart concluded, in his third annual report, that 'the further expansion of industry should be controlled to secure a more evenly distributed production'. Such thinking might have been in harmony with the current increasing recognition of the need for national planning, but it called for political action of a character which would have been sensational. Furthermore, as Neville Chamberlain (then Chancellor of the Exchequer) pointed out, even if new factories were excluded from London it did not follow that they would forthwith spring up in South Wales or West Cumberland. The immediate answer of the Government was to appoint the Barlow Commission.

THE BARLOW REPORT

The Barlow Report is of significance not merely because it is an important historical landmark, but also because some of its major policy recommendations have been accepted by all post-war governments as a basis for planning policy. Only recently have these policies been questioned.

The terms of reference of the Commission were 'to inquire into the causes which have influenced the present geographical distribution of the industrial population of Great Britain and the probable direction of any change in that distribution in the future; to consider what social, economic or strategic disadvantages arise from the concentration of industries or of the industrial population in large towns or in particular areas of the country; and to report what remedial measures if any should be taken in the national interest.'

These very wide terms of reference represented, as the Commission pointed out, 'an important step forward' in contemporary thinking. Reviewing the history of town planning they noted that:

'Legislation has not yet proceeded so far as to deal with the problem of planning from a *national* standpoint; there is no duty imposed on any authority or Government Department to view the country as a whole and to consider the problems of industrial, commercial and urban growth in the light of the needs of the entire population. The appointment, therefore, of the present Commission marks an important step forward. The evils attendant on haphazard and ill-regulated town growth were first brought under observation; then similar dangers when prevalent over wider areas or regions; now the investigation is extended to Great Britain as a whole. The Causes, Probable Direction of Change and Disadvantages mentioned in the Terms of Reference are clearly not concerned with separate localities or local authorities, but with England, Scotland and Wales collectively: and the Remedial Measures to be considered are expressly required to be in the national interest.'

After reviewing the evidence, the Commission concluded that 'the disadvantages in many, if not in most of the great industrial concentrations, alike on the strategical, the social and the economic side, do constitute serious handicaps and even in some respects dangers to the nation's life and development, and we are of opinion that definite action should be taken by the Government towards remedying them.' The advantages of concentration were clear – proximity to market, reduction of transport costs and availability of a supply of suitable labour. But these, in the Commission's view, were accompanied by serious disadvantages such as heavy charges on account mainly of high site values, loss of time through street traffic congestion, and the risk of adverse effects on efficiency due to long and fatiguing journeys to work. The Commission maintained that the development of garden cities, satellite towns and trading estates could make a useful contribution towards the solution of this problems of urban congestion.

The London area, of course, presented the largest problem, not simply because of its huge size, but also because 'the trend of migration to London and the Home Counties is on so large a scale and of so serious a character that it can hardly fail to increase in the future the disadvantages already shown to exist'. The problems of London were thus in part related to the problems of the Depressed Areas:

'It is not in the national interest, economically, socially or strategic-ally, that a quarter, or even a larger, proportion of the population of Great Britain should be concentrated within 20 to 30 miles or so of Central London. On the other hand, a policy:

(i) of balanced distribution of industry and the industrial popu-lation so far as possible throughout the different areas or regions in Great Britain;

(ii) of appropriate diversification of industries in those areas or regions;

would tend to make the best national use of the resources of the country, and at the same time would go far to secure for each region or area, through diversification of industry and variety of employ-ment, some safeguard against severe and persistent depression, such as attacks an area dependent mainly on one industry when that industry is struck by bad times.'

Such policies could not be carried out by the existing administra-tive machinery: it was no part of statutory planning to check or to encourage a local or regional growth of population. Planning was essentially on a local basis; it did not, and was not intended to, influence the geographical distribution of the population as between one locality and another. The Commission unanimously agreed that the problems were national in character and required a central authority to deal with them. They argued that the activities of this authority ought to be distinct from and extend beyond those of any existing Government Department. It should be responsible for formulating a plan for dispersal from congested urban areas – determining in which areas dispersal was desirable; whether and where dispersal could be effected by developing garden cities or garden suburbs, satellite towns, trading estates or the expansion of existing small towns or regional centres It should be given the right to inspect town-planning schemes and 'to consider, where necessary, in co-operation with the Government Departments concerned, the modification or correlation of existing or future plans in the national interest'. It should study the location of industry throughout the country with a view to anticipating cases where depression might probably occur in the future and encouraging industrial or public development before a depression actually occurred.

But though the Commission were agreed on the 'objectives of national action' and on the necessity for a central authority, they were not agreed on the powers to be given to this authority. The majority recommended that it should be a National Industrial Board consisting of a chairman and three other members appointed by the President of the Board of Trade after consultation with the Ministers of Health, Labour and Transport, and the Secretary of State for Scotland. This Board should have research, advisory and publicity functions, but also (in view of the necessity for immediate action in the London area) executive powers to regulate additional industrial building in London and the Home Counties. These 'negative powers' should be extendable by Order in Council to other areas. Finally the Board should be required to decide what additional powers it needed to carry out its functions.

Three members of the Commission (Professor J. H. Jones, Mr George W. Thomson and Sir William E. Whyte), though signing the majority report, prepared a 'Note of Reservations'. They argued that the control of industrial development in the London area was an inadequate measure to achieve the 'objectives of national action'. Such controls needed to be operated over the whole country. Furthermore, they believed that it was even more important for the Government 'to create more favourable conditions of life and work in other parts of the country and thereby weaken the inducement to seek work in or near London'. In their view the powers of the Commissioners for the Special Areas should be largely transferred to the new Board which would be given powers to enable them to offer such inducements as they thought necessary to make effective the policy of securing a better balance and a greater diversification of industry throughout the country. Regional administration was essential, and a series of Divisional Boards should be set up as an integral part of the new Authority.

A minority of the Commission (Professor Patrick Abercrombie, Mr H. H. Elvin and Mrs H. Hichens) felt unable to put their signatures to the main recommendations. They went even further in their criticisms of the inadequacy of these than the three members who signed the Note of Reservations. In their view the problems were of immediate urgency, particularly since an unprecedented amount of new factory building was under way in connection with the rearmament programme. They felt that the Majority Report seemed to imply that there was ample time for preparation and research, whereas in fact the problem was an immediate one. The urgency of the situation demanded the setting up of a powerful body with executive powers. The Board proposed by the Majority was not strong enough: what was required was a new Ministry exercising full executive powers. This Ministry would 'need to be fitted into the scheme of central and local government if it is to function properly'. It would obviously have to take over the planning functions of the Ministry of Health (and possibly some of its housing functions), as well as some of the planning powers of the Ministry of Transport. The work of the Commissioners for the Special Areas should be transferred to it – and at the same time extended to the whole country.

The differences between the three sets of recommendations were less striking than their unanimous condemnation of the existing situation and the inadequacy of both policy and machinery for dealing with it. All were agreed that a far more positive role for government was required, that control should be exercised over new factory building at least in London and the Home Counties, that dispersal from the larger urban concentrations was desirable, and that measures should be taken to anticipate regional economic depression. The differences centred largely on how such policies should be translated into terms of administrative machinery.

THE IMPACT OF WAR

The Barlow Report was published in January 1940 – some four months after the start of the Second World War. The problem which precipitated the decision to set up the Barlow Commission – that of the Depressed Areas – rapidly disappeared. The unemployed of the Depressed Areas now became a powerful national asset. A considerable share of the new factories built to provide munitions or to replace bombed factories were located in these areas. By the end of 1940 'an extraordinary scramble for factory space had developed'; and out of all this 'grew a war-time, an extempore, location of industry policy covering the country as a whole'.[13] This emergency war-time policy – paralleled in other fields, such as hospitals – not only provided some 13 million square feet of munitions factory space in the Depressed Areas which could be adapted for civilian industry after the end of the war; it also provided experience in dispersing industry and in controlling industrial location which showed the practicability (under war-time conditions at least) of such policies. The Board of Trade became a central clearing-house of information on industrial sites:

'We have collected a great deal of information regarding the relative advantages of different sites in different parts of the country, and of the facilities available there with regard to local labour supply, housing accommodation, transport facilities, electricity, gas, water, drainage and so on . . . we are now able to offer to industrialists a service of information regarding location which has never been available before.'[17]

Hence, though the Barlow Report (to use a phrase of Dame Alix Meynell) 'lay inanimate in the iron lung of war', it seemed that the conditions for the acceptance of its views on the control of industrial location were becoming very propitious: there is nothing better than successful experience for demonstrating the practicability of a policy.

The war thus provided a great stimulus to the extension of town and country planning into the sphere of industrial location. And this was not the only stimulus it provided. The destruction wrought by bombing transformed 'the rebuilding of Britain' from a socially desirable but somewhat visionary and vague ideal into a matter of practical and defined necessity. Nor was this all: the very fact that rebuilding was clearly going to take place on a large scale provided an unprecedented opportunity for comprehensive planning of the bombed areas and a stimulus to overall town planning. In Exeter: 'to rebuild the city in the old lines . . . would be a dreadful mistake. It would be an exact repetition of what happened in the rebuilding of London after the Fire – and the results, in regret at lost opportunity, will be the same. While, therefore, the arrangements for rebuilding to the new plan should proceed with all possible speed, some patience and discipline will be necessary if the new-built city is to be a city that is really renewed.'[22] In Hull: 'there is now both the opportunity and the necessity for an overhaul of the urban structure before undertaking this second refounding of the great Port on the Humber. Due consideration, however urgent the desire to get back to working conditions, must be given to every aspect of town existence.'[12] The note was one of optimism of being able to tackle problems which were of long standing. In the Metropolis: 'London was ripe for reconstruction before the war; obsolescence, bad and unsuitable housing, inchoate communities, uncorrelated road systems, industrial congestion, a low level of urban design, inequality in the distribution of open spaces, increasing congestion of dismal journeys to work – all these and more clamoured for improvement before the enemy's efforts to smash us by air attack stiffened our resistance and intensified our zeal for reconstruction.'[9]

This was the social climate of the war and early post-war years. There was an enthusiasm and a determination to undertake social reconstruction on a scale hitherto considered utopian. The catalyst was, of course, the war itself. At one and the same time war occasions a mass support for the way of life which is being fought for and a critical appraisal of the inadequacies of that way of life. Modern total warfare demands the unification of national effort and a breaking down of social barriers and differences. It 'presupposes and imposes a great increase in social discipline; moreover, this discipline is only tolerable if – and only if – social inequalities are not intolerable'.[25] On no occasion was this more true than in the Second World War. A new and better Britain was to be built. The feeling was one of intense optimism and confidence. Not only would the war be won: it would be followed by a similar campaign against the forces of want. That there was much that was inadequate, even intolerable, in pre-war Britain had been generally accepted. What was new was the belief that the problems could be tackled in the same way as a military operation. What supreme confidence was evidenced by the setting up in 1941 of committees to consider post-war reconstruction problems – the Uthwatt Committee on Compensation and Betterment, the Scott Committee on Land Utilization in Rural Areas, and the Beveridge Committee on Social Insurance and Allied Services. Perhaps it was Beveridge who most clearly summed up the spirit of the time – and the philosophy which was to underlie post-war social policy:

'The Plan for Social Security is put forward as part of a general programme of socal policy. It is one part only of an attack upon five great evils: upon the physical Want with which it is directly concerned, upon Disease which often causes Want and brings many other troubles in its train, upon Ignorance which no democracy can afford among its citizens, upon the Squalor which arises mainly through haphazard distribution of industry and population, and upon Idleness which destroys wealth and corrupts men, whether they are well fed or not, when they are idle. In seeking security not merely against physical want, but against all these evils in all their forms, and in showing that security can be combined with freedom and enterprise and responsibility of the individual for his own life, the British community and those who in other lands have inherited the British tradition, have a vital service to render to human progress.'[5]

It was within this framework of a newly acquired confidence to tackle long-standing social and economic problems that post-war town and country planning policy was conceived. No longer was this to be restricted to town planning 'schemes' or regulatory measures. There was now the same breadth in official thinking as had permeated the Barlow Report. The attack on Squalor was conceived as part of a comprehensive series of plans for social amelioration. To quote the 1944 White Paper *The Control of Land Use*:

'Provision for the right use of land, in accordance with a considered policy, is an essential requirement of the Government's programme of post-war reconstruction. New houses, whether of permanent or emergency construction; the new layout of areas devastated by enemy action or blighted by reason of age or bad living conditions; the new schools which will be required under the Education Bill now before Parliament; the balanced distribution of industry which the Government's recently published proposals for maintaining active employment envisage; the requirements of sound nutrition and of a healthy and well-balanced agriculture; the preservation of land for national parks and forests, and the assurance to the people of enjoyment of the sea and countryside in times of leisure; a new and safer highway system better adapted to modern industrial and other needs; the proper provision of airfields – all these related parts of a single reconstruction programme involve the use of land, and it is essential that their various claims on land should be so harmonized as to ensure for the people of this country the greatest possible measure of individual well-being and national prosperity.'

THE NEW PLANNING MACHINERY

This broad historical approach must now give way to a series of discussions on particular issues – administration, planning powers and policies, the problem of land values, and so on. Before embarking upon this, however, it is useful to provide a brief outline of the new planning machinery. This will provide a general background which will be detailed and brought up to date in later chapters.

The pre-war machinery of planning was defective in several ways. It was optional on local authorities; planning powers were essentially regulatory and restrictive; such planning as was achieved was purely

local in character; the central government had no effective powers
of initiative, or of co-ordinating local plans; and the 'compensation
bogey' – with which local authorities had to cope without any
Exchequer assistance – bedevilled the efforts of all who attempted to
make the cumbersome planning machinery work.

By 1942, 73 per cent of the land in England and 36 per cent of the
land in Wales had become subject to 'interim development control',
but only 5 per cent of England and 1 per cent of Wales was actually
subject to operative schemes; and there were several important
towns and cities as well as some large country districts for which not
even the preliminary stages of a planning scheme had been taken.
Administration was highly fragmented and was essentially a matter
for the lower tier authorities: in 1944 there were over 1,400 planning
authorities. Some attempt to solve the problems to which this gave
rise was made by the (voluntary) grouping of planning authorities
in joint committees for formulating schemes over wide areas, but,
though an improvement, this was not sufficiently effective.

The new conception of town and country planning underlined the
inadequacies. It was generally (and perhaps uncritically) accepted
that the growth of the large cities should be restricted. Regional
plans for London, Lancashire, the Clyde Valley and South Wales
all stressed the necessity of large-scale overspill to new and expanded
towns. Government pronouncements echoed the enthusiasm which
permeated these plans. Large cities were no longer to be allowed to
continue their unchecked sprawl over the countryside. The explosive
forces generated by the desire for better living and working conditions would no longer run riot. Suburban dormitories were a thing
of the past. Overspill would be steered into new and expanded towns
which could provide the conditions people wanted – without the disadvantages inherent in satellite suburban development. When the
problems of reconstructing blitzed areas, redeveloping blighted areas,
securing a 'proper distribution' of industry, developing national
parks, and so on, are added to the list, there was a clear need for a
new and more positive role for the central government, a transfer
of powers from the smaller to the larger authorities, a considerable extension of these powers and – most difficult of all – a solution
to the compensation-betterment problem.

The necessary machinery was provided in the main by the Town
and Country Planning Acts, the Distribution of Industry Acts, the
National Parks and Access to the Countryside Act, the New Towns
Act and the Town Development Act.

The 1947 Town and Country Planning Act brought almost all
development under control by making it subject to planning permission. But planning was to be no longer merely a regulative function.

Development plans were to be prepared for every area in the country. These were to outline the way in which each area was to be developed or, where desirable, preserved. In accordance with the wider concepts of planning, powers were transferred from district councils to county councils. The smallest planning units thereby became the counties and the county boroughs. Co-ordination of local plans was to be effected by the new Ministry of Town and Country Planning. Development rights in land and the associated development values were nationalized. All owners were thus placed in the position of owning only the existing (1947) use rights and values in their land. Compensation for development rights was to be paid 'once and for all' out of a national fund, and developers were to pay a 'development charge' amounting to 100 per cent of the increase in the value of land resulting from the development. The 'compensation bogey' was thus at last to be completely abolished: henceforth development would take place according to 'good planning principles'.

Responsibility for securing a 'proper distribution of industry' was given to the Board of Trade. New industrial projects (above a minimum size) would require the Board's certification that the development would be consistent with the proper distribution of industry. More positively, the Board was given powers to attract industries to Development Areas by loans and grants, and by the erection of factories.

New Towns were to be developed by *ad hoc* development corporations financed by the Treasury. Somewhat later (in 1952) new powers were provided for the planned expansion of towns by local authorities. The designation of national parks and 'Areas of Outstanding National Beauty' was entrusted to a new National Parks Commission, and local authorities were given wider powers for securing public access to the countryside. A Nature Conservancy was set up to provide scientific advice on the conservation and control of natural flora and fauna, and to establish and manage nature reserves. New powers were granted for preserving amenity, trees, historic buildings and ancient monuments. Later greater controls were introduced over river and air pollution, litter and noise. Indeed, the flow of legislation has been unceasing.

It would, however, be misleading even in a brief sketch to give an impression of continued progress. Certainly there have been some remarkable achievements (which the social commentator tends to forget in his analysis of shortcomings and needed reforms), but many of the problems for which this wealth of legislation was designed have themselves changed in character and become more difficult. Experience of dealing with industrial location, urban growth, amenity and so on, has shown that they present far greater

B

problems than was originally anticipated. Above all, instead of having to plan for a static or slowly growing population, the planners have had to wrestle with the problem created by an unexpected population increase – one which on current indications will result by the end of the century in a total England and Wales population of 59 million and a Great Britain population of around 65 million.*

* Population projections are published each year in the Registrar Generals' Quarterly Returns. Annual revisions can make a huge difference as is illustrated in the table below.

Base year of projection	Projected population for England and Wales			
	Year	Million	Year	Million
1955	(1975)	46·4	(1995)	46·3
1958	(1978)	49·0	(1998)	52·0
1961	(1981)	52·1	(2001)	58·3
1965	(1981)	54·3	(2001)	66·4
1966	(1981)	53·5	(2001)	64·8
1967	(1981)	53·0	(2001)	62·9
1968	(1981)	52·6		
	(1991)	56·1		
1969	(1981)	51·9	(2001)	58·6
	(1991)	54·9		

These projections demonstrate one of the difficulties of long-term planning.

REFERENCES AND FURTHER READING

1 Abercrombie, P., *Greater London Plan*, HMSO, 1945.
2 Aldridge, H. R., *The Case for Town Planning*, National Housing and Town Planning Council, 1915.
3 Ashworth, W., *The Genesis of Modern British Town Planning*, Routledge, 1954.
4 Barlow Report, *Report of the Royal Commission on the Distribution of the Industrial Population*, Cmd. 6153, HMSO, 1940.
5 Beveridge Report, *Social Insurance and Allied Services*, Cmd. 6404, HMSO, 1942.
6 Bowley, M., *Housing and the State 1919–1944*, Allen & Unwin, 1945.
7 Briggs, A., *History of Birmingham*, Vol. 2, Oxford University Press, 1952.
8 Davison, R. C., *British Unemployment Policy: The Modern Phase Since 1930*, Longmans Green, 1938.
9 Forshaw, J. H. and Abercrombie, P., *County of London Plan*, Macmillan, 1943.
10 Geddes, P., *Cities in Evolution*, London, 1915.
11 Howard, E., *Garden Cities of Tomorrow*, edited by F. J. Osborn, Faber, 1946.
12 Lutyens, E. and Abercrombie, P., *A Plan for Kingston upon Hull*, A. Brown & Sons, 1945.
13 Meynell, A., 'Location of Industry', *Public Administration*, Vol. 37, Spring 1959.
14 Mowat, C. L., *Britain Between the Wars, 1918–1940*, Methuen, 1955.
15 Nettleford, J. S., *Practical Town Planning*, St Catherine Press, London, 1914.
16 Parliamentary Debates on the Housing, Town Planning, Etc. Bill, *H.C. Debates*, Vol. 188, May 1908.
17 Parliamentary Debates on the Distribution of Industry Bill, *H.C. Debates*, Vol. 409, March 1945.
18 Political and Economic Planning, *Location of Industry*, PEP, 1939.
19 *Reports of Investigations into the Industrial Conditions in Certain Depressed Areas*, Cmd. 4728, HMSO, 1934.

20 *Reports of the Commissioner for the Special Areas* (*England and Wales*), HMSO, 1935–8.
21 *Reports of the Commissioner for the Special Areas in Scotland*, HMSO 1935–8.
22 Sharp, T., *Exeter Phoenix*, Architectural Press, 1946.
23 The Times, 'Places without a Future', *The Times*, March 20, 21 and 22, 1934.
24 Titmuss, R. M., *Problems of Social Policy*, HMSO and Longmans, 1950.
25 Titmuss, R. M., 'War and Social Policy', *Essays on 'The Welfare State'*, Allen & Unwin, 1958.
26 Tudor Walters Report, *Report of the Committee on Questions of Building Construction in Connection with the Provision of Dwellings for the Working Classes*, Cd. 9191, HMSO, 1918.
27 Unwin, R., *Town Planning in Practice: An Introduction to the Art of Designing Cities and Suburbs*, T. Fisher Unwin, 1909.
28 Warren, H. and Davidge, W. R. (eds), *Decentralization of Population and Industry: A New Principle in Town Planning*, P. S. King & Son, 1930.
29 Wood, E., *Planning and the Law*, Percival Marshall, 1949.

Chapter II

THE NEW AGENCIES OF PLANNING

THE CENTRAL AUTHORITY

The new conception of town and country planning raised the difficult problem as to how the extended responsibilities were to be fitted into the organization of central government. Was the Ministry of Health – the department responsible for housing and other local government matters – to retain its existing executive powers in relation to town and country planning, and, at the same time, expand its activities into the broad policy fields of regional and national planning? Should there be a separate Ministry of Town and Country Planning, and, if so, should it be responsible both for the framing of policies and for their implementation? Would it be preferable to leave the latter with the Ministry of Health and set up a separate National Planning Authority which could also have certain responsibilities in the field of industrial location and transport? Should Scotland be dealt with in the same way as England and Wales?

Such questions were not quickly answered. Indeed the problems they pose are still with us, and it is doubtful whether any ideal solution exists. Town and country planning in its wider sense embraces a large part of the activities of government. A separate all-embracing Ministry is a contradiction in terms. An all-powerful 'grand co-ordinating' Ministry does not square with the facts of administrative and political life. There must be some division of responsibilities and, at the same time, some means of co-ordination which is acceptable to the individual Ministries. The *modus operandi* devised at any one point of time will reflect not only the particular urgencies of the existing situation, but also the views and personalities of the politicians and administrators whose task it is to interpret them. The importance of these factors is highlighted by the story of the setting up of the Ministry of Town and Country Planning.

The new town and country planning was born in the ancient Office of Works – a department which had become increasingly active with

Government building since the rearmament programme started. In September 1940 this Office became the Ministry of Works and Buildings – responsible for 'the proper co-ordination of building work, the carrying out of Government building programmes, the control of building materials, and research into building and conservation of materials'. At the invitation of Ernest Bevin, then Minister of Labour, Sir John (later Lord) Reith became the first Minister of this Department – an appointment which exercised considerable influence on later developments in the organization of planning. Reith was not only enthusiastic about the new post: he was already 'looking beyond the war to the problems of planning and reconstruction'[6] and was hoping that however much responsibility the Ministry of Works and Buildings might initially be given, 'it would acquire still more – by doing things that had not been thought of and for which no one else had staked claims'. Indeed almost immediately he proposed that his Ministry 'should be ready to take up responsibility for . . . planning and reconstruction arising out of the war and post-war period'. This met with objection from the Ministry of Health (the department then responsible for town and country planning). This dispute was only settled after the Lord Privy Seal (Mr Attlee) had acted as arbiter:

'It is clear that the reconstruction of town and country planning after the war raises great problems and gives a great opportunity. The Minister of Works has, therefore, been charged by the Government with the responsibility for consulting the departments and organizations concerned with a view to reporting to the Cabinet the appropriate methods and machinery for dealing with the issues involved.'[6]

Thus the Ministry of Health retained its normal town and country planning functions while Lord Reith was to plan for the future. This he did by means of a Reconstruction Group in his Department, as well as by setting up two committees – the Uthwatt Committee on Compensation and Betterment and the Scott Committee on Land Utilization in Rural Areas. The reports of these committees together with that of the Barlow Commission constituted the famous trilogy which had a great influence on post-war planning.

Relationships between Lord Reith and Mr Arthur Greenwood (who had been appointed as Minister without Portfolio with special responsibility for all post-war reconstruction problems) and with the Ministry of Health were not easy. The boundaries between town and country planning on the one hand and general social and economic planning were not always clear. Lord Reith, however, was authorized to proceed on the assumptions:

'(1) That the principle of planning will be accepted as national policy and that some central planning authority will be required;

(2) that this authority will proceed on a positive policy for such matters as agriculture, industrial development and transport;

(3) that some services will require treatment on a national basis, some regionally and some locally.'[4]

For a while Lord Reith retained his personal responsibility for long-term planning while the Minister of Health retained his statutory planning functions. Following an interim report of the Uthwatt Committee, and 'to ensure that the administration of the Town and Country Planning Act and any legislation implementing the recommendations made in the first report of the Uthwatt Committee shall proceed in conformity with long-term planning policy as it is progressively developed' a Committee of the Privy Council was appointed – Lord Reith (as chairman), the Minister of Health, and the Secretary of State for Scotland.

The next development was the fusion of Lord Reith's Reconstruction Group and the Town and Country Planning Division of the Ministry of Health. This created some misgivings, particularly on the part of the Minister without Portfolio. A proposal to create both a new department for town and country planning and a new executive council for policy and development was rejected by the Cabinet: instead all the town and country planning functions of the Ministry of Health were transferred to a reorganized Ministry of Works and Planning. Lord Reith's apparent victory proved to be a hollow one: within a fortnight of the Cabinet decision he was asked to resign.* With the exit of Lord Reith (and his replacement by Lord Portal who 'disliked planning') the sands shifted. Furthermore, the Ministry of Health was now overburdened. The alternatives were now to create a new department or a non-departmental body. The latter proposal – on which a four-man committee set up under Lord Samuel's chairmanship could not agree – was rejected by the Cabinet on the ground that planning policy was essentially political and could not be removed from parliamentary control. Furthermore, experience which had been gained with the Ministry of Works and Planning, showed that the subject required 'the whole time services of a front-rank Minister'[5] and also that this Minister 'should not only be, but should

---

* According to Reith's autobiography Churchill had apparently been told 'that the Conservatives demanded my expulsion and that I be replaced by a good Tory. Moving too fast, too much planning all round; even fear of land nationalization perhaps. And this was at the time when Churchill was "yielding to public pressure".' *Into the Wind*, pp. 445–6.

also appear to be, entirely impartial in his judgment as to the right use of any particular piece of land: if he can be regarded as a Minister already predisposed by reason of his other Ministerial duties to lean to a particular type of land use he will for that very reason be less able to exercise his influence'.

In short, the decision was taken to set up a separate Ministry of Town and Country Planning.

The decision was not unanimously applauded, especially since the legislation merely dealt with machinery: 'the way in which it will be used will depend on the powers which the House confers on the Minister hereafter'. Mr Greenwood was particularly concerned about what he considered to be the implicit assumption that town and country planning could neatly be made the responsibility of a single department:

'I cannot overemphasize what I think Government inquiries and enlightened public opinion . . . have undoubtedly proved, namely the complexities of the issues involved and the paramount importance of collective responsibility for policy by the Ministers whose departments will have to take a hand in carrying the plans into effect. You cannot make a super-department which will take the life blood of the Ministry of Agriculture, the Board of Trade and the Ministry of Health and so on.'[5]

But the general discussion was inconclusive – as it had to be, since the legislation did little more that establish the new Department, with a Minister charged with the study of 'securing consistency and continuity in the framing and execution of a national policy with respect to the use and development of land throughout England and Wales'.

The new Ministry had responsibilities only for England and Wales. In Scotland central responsibility remained with the Department of Health for Scotland. Neither of these two Departments was responsible for the location of industry. The 'Barlow policy' for industrial location was accepted, as was the Beveridge principle of full employment, but

'no single Department could undertake the responsibility for formulating and administering the policy for the distribution of industry. . . . This is essentially a policy of the Government as a whole, and its application in practice will involve action by a number of different Departments, each of which will adapt its administration to conform with the general Government policy. The main responsibility will rest with the Board of Trade, the Ministry of Labour and

National Service, the Ministry of Town and Country Planning and the Scottish Office. Standing arrangements will be made for supervising and controlling, under the Cabinet and as part of the central Government machinery, the development and execution of the policy as a whole. . . . It is necessary, however, that there should be a single channel through which Government policy on the distribution of industry can be expressed. . . . (This) shall be the Board of Trade.'[12]

In short, the Ministry of Town and Country Planning was to be responsible for town and country planning, the Ministry of Health for housing and the Board of Trade for industrial location, but there would be 'standing arrangements' for co-ordination where necessary.

LOCAL PLANNING AUTHORITIES

The shaping of a local government structure to meet new needs raises problems of an acute nature. There are inherent problems of devising units which are viable in terms of size and financial resources for the administration of different services.[3] But of even greater practical importance is the problem of securing political agreement for change – at the level of both national and local politics. The need for reform at any one point of time may be clear to the reformers, but to demonstrate and prove the beneficial effects (which are often of a long-term nature) is quite a different matter. Usually local government reform is a matter of real interest only to academics, politicians and local government officers. Since these cannot agree (even on the necessity for change) the result is commonly a deadlock. Local government may then be bypassed, and services transferred to government departments or *ad hoc* authorities – as has happened, for example, with the licensing of passenger road services, trunk roads, hospitals, public assistance, valuation for rating, and the major 'public utilities of gas and electricity. Post-war attempts to reorganize local government have generally been abortive and it is only in the last few years that the problem has been tackled. The tone was set in 1944 when the then Minister of Health stated that it was clear from the views put forward by the various Local Government Associations and 'other authoritative sources' that there was no general desire to disrupt the existing structure of local government: in the view of the Government no case had been made out for any drastic change. However, there was scope for improvements, and a White Paper (*Local Government in England and Wales during the Period of Reconstruction*) published the following year outlined the Government's proposals for a Local Government Boundary Commission. This was set up in the same year, but in fact achieved nothing more than the publication of three annual reports. The Commission was set up to consider the *boundaries* of local authorities – in spite of the general agreement that the question of boundaries could be usefully considered only in relation to *functions*. In their second report, they argued cogently that they could not, within their terms of reference, make proposals which would result in 'effective and convenient units of local government administration'. Such units 'cannot everywhere be produced without a fresh allocation of functions among the various types of local authorities, particularly where the larger towns are concerned.' They therefore had to decide whether to make second-best alterations to the existing structure (i.e. boundary adjustments) within the limits of their powers or to outline the case for radical reorganization in the hope that this would be followed by legislation widening their powers. They chose the latter.

Briefly, their plan envisaged three types of local authorities. The whole of England and Wales *including the areas of existing county boroughs*, would be divided into new counties. These would be formed on the basis of existing counties (combined or divided where necessary) and county boroughs (combined or extended as necessary). The smaller of the new counties would be administered on the one-tier system and the larger on the two-tier system. Second tier authorities would be either 'new county boroughs' ('most-purpose' authorities) or county districts ('minor-purpose' authorities).

So far as town and country planning was concerned responsibility for preparing overall development plans would rest with the counties. They would thus be responsible for general policy issues such as determining main lines of communication, and the location of new developments, green belts and major open spaces. Within the framework of the county plan, the new most-purpose authorities would be responsible for the preparation of the detailed plans for their areas.

To the advocates of local government reform these proposals were regarded as a step forward, but the absence of a 'regional outlook' was criticized. Robson, for example, complained that 'the Commissioners never for a moment turned their eyes towards the regional movement which has wrought havoc with local government. They did not ask why responsibility for electricity and gas supply, civil airfields, hospitals, trunk roads, passenger road services, and other services, has recently been taken away from local authorities and given to regional or central bodies; or under what conditions it might be practicable for these functions to be restored to the realm of local self-government.'[7] Though the proposals did 'abolish the fatal

separation of town and country in watertight compartments which
was made in 1888', they gave too little attention to the size of areas
and types of authorities needed to carry out services which require
large scale planning and administration.

But to the Government of the day the proposals were either too
radical or too embarrassing. There was little political support for
them and the Government took the easy way out by simply abolishing
the Commission.

Since local government was not to be reorganized the question
of the local administration of planning resolved itself into a choice
between giving responsibility to the existing local government units
or setting up *ad hoc* planning bodies on the lines followed in the case
of hospitals or the nationalized utilities. The latter would have had
the advantage of allowing the boundaries of planning authorities
to be drawn on a rational basis, but in fact it was never seriously
entertained. The 1947 Town and Country Planning Act gave
responsibility to the major authorities – the counties and county
boroughs. This reduced the number of local planning authorities
from 1,441 to 145 – a reduction of 90 per cent. This obviously
greatly enlarged the area over which local planning was to be
effected, but two further steps were required.

First, as the Scott Committee pointed out:

'the local planning authority should be the same authority or
combination of authorities as executes the principal local government functions involving the use of land. Within this framework the
extremely important functions will devolve on the smaller authorities
of affording the county planning authorities the benefit of their local
knowledge in the formulation of plans, and the county authorities
must consult the district councils accordingly; whilst in due course
the responsibility for the execution of works within the approved
scheme may fall on the district councils.'

Accordingly the 1947 Act required county councils to consult with
district authorities in the preparation of their plans and enabled them
to delegate powers of controlling development to district councils
(or to decentralize these powers to sub-committees charged with
responsibility for certain areas).

Secondly, though the Act enlarged the areas over which planning
powers were to be exercised by single authorities, the need still
existed, in some parts of the country (particularly in the case of
conurbations) for larger planning areas. The Act therefore gave the
Minister power to set up Joint Planning Boards for combined areas.
This could be done either with the agreement of the local authorities

concerned, or following a local inquiry, by the Minister. In fact this power has never been used. A similar power to establish joint advisory committees, on the other hand, has been used.

REGIONAL ADMINISTRATION

Within the new structure there was no formal place for regional authorities. The need for wider planning areas was recognized in the provision made for joint planning boards and joint advisory committees, but these constituted a typical English compromise which excited little enthusiasm. Mr Bevan, when Minister of Health, echoed the general feeling: a joint board, he said 'has no biological content; it has no mother and it has no progeny; it is a piece of paper work'.[7] In the absence of a formal creation of executive, financially responsible, organs of regional government it was left to the Ministry itself to undertake such regional planning as was to be effected – by co-ordinating the efforts of the separate planning authorities and reconciling and amending the plans prepared by them and submitted to the Ministry for approval. This, indeed, was one of the functions implied by the duty with which the Ministry was charged of 'securing consistency and continuity in the framing and execution of a national policy with respect to the use and development of land throughout England and Wales'.

What might at first sight have been regarded as a clear advance towards regionalism was the war-time establishment of civil defence regions and the appointment of Regional Commissioners. These were set up to deal with the conditions which might have arisen had communications been disrupted. This organization – into eleven regions – was retained after the war, but the regions were (and still are) 'no more than civil service creations, established for the dispatch of business; they are not, in any sense, "organic" units'. The Ministry of Town and Country Planning appointed regional planning officers as early as 1943. As the scope and complexity of planning legislation grew the regional machinery was expanded. By 1948 there was an office in each region under the control of a Regional Controller. The initial object of the regional offices was to give advice to local authorities, but the establishment of Regional Controllers marked a new step towards solving the increasing number of conflicting claims over land use from Government Departments. The Regional Controllers presided over Regional Planning Committees composed of representatives from the various other Government Departments in the region. But this was simply an administrative device to cope with inter-departmental frictions.

In view of the absence of regional machinery in the final outcome it is interesting to note Reith's original proposals (submitted to Churchill in 1940) for:

'a central authority to frame and be responsible for the execution of a national plan covering the basic objectives; to lay down the general principles of planning; to supervise planning, design, finance, execution; regional machinery to apply the national plan and to co-ordinate and control the work of local authorities; Exchequer assistance to supplement local funds in approved development.'[6]

Since there was now no middle tier it followed that the central authority would be greatly concerned with the day-to-day work of local authorities (and the time-consuming business of appeals against local authorities), and thus face the danger of paying insufficient attention to 'basic objectives' and 'general principles' – a point to which we return in later chapters.

References and Further Reading

1 Chester, D. N. and Willson, F. M. G., *The Organisation of British Central Government, 1914–1964*, Allen & Unwin, 2nd edition, 1968.
2 Cole, G. D. H., *Local and Regional Government*, Cassell, 1947.
3 Lipman, V. D., *Local Government Areas 1834–1945*, Basil Blackwell, 1949.
4 Parliamentary Debates, *H.L. Debates*, Vol. 118, February 26, 1941.
5 Parliamentary Debates on the Minister of Town and Country Planning Bill, *H.C. Debates*, Vol. 386, January 1943.
6 Reith, Lord, *Into the Wind*, Hodder & Stoughton, 1949.
7 Robson, W. A., *The Development of Local Government*, Allen & Unwin, 2nd edition, 1948; 3rd edition, 1954.
8 Scott Report: *Report on the Committee on Land Utilisation in Rural Areas*, Cmnd. 6378, HMSO, 1942.
9 Self, P., *Regionalism*, Fabian Publications and Allen & Unwin, 1949.
10 Smith, B. C., *Regionalism in England I: Regional Institutions – A Guide*, Acton Society, 1964.
11 Smith, B. C., *Regionalism in England II: Its Nature and Purpose 1905–1965*, Acton Society, 1965,
12 White Paper, *Employment Policy*, Cmd. 6527, HMSO, 1944.

Chapter III

THE ROLE OF CENTRAL GOVERNMENT

CENTRAL GOVERNMENT ORGANIZATION

In *Beyond the Stable State*, Donald Schon argues that 'if government is to learn to solve new public problems, it must also learn to create the systems for doing so and to discard the structure and mechanisms grown up around old problems. The need is not merely to cope with a particular set of new problems, or to discard the organizational vestiges of a particular form of governmental activity which happen at present to be particularly cumbersome. It is to design and bring into being the institutional processes through which new problems can continually be confronted and old structures continually discarded.'[36]

How far recent years have seen the development of really new and relevant 'institutional processes' is a big question which cannot be adequately examined here, but certainly there have been a remarkable number of organizational changes. Indeed, while the structure of local government is painfully slow to change, the machinery of central government can alter at a rate which defeats the chronicler who attempts to provide an up-to-date picture.

Throughout the 'fifties town and country planning was the responsibility of the Ministry of Housing and Local Government – the central department also responsible (as the name suggests) for housing and a range of local government services. These included water and sewerage, refuse collection and disposal, burial grounds and crematoria, clean air and river pollution, together with the general structure (including reorganization) and finance of local government. In April 1965, certain functions (e.g. in relation to water resources, national parks and responsibility for the Land Commission and Leasehold Enfranchisement Bills) were transferred to a new Ministry of Land and Natural Resources. This Ministry was, however, short-lived:

its functions were transferred back to the Ministry of Housing and Local Government in February 1967.

Of rather longer life was the Department of Economic Affairs (October 1964 to October 1969). This was responsible for the new regional economic planning system (which, at the time of writing, is still in existence but faces major uncertainties while decisions on local government reorganization and the publication of the Crowther Report on the Constitution are awaited).

In October 1969, the Labour Government created an 'overlord' for local government and regional planning with major responsibilities for local government reorganization and 'environmental pollution in all its forms'. The overlord – the Secretary of State for Local Government and Regional Planning – had federal powers in relation to the Ministry of Housing and Local Government and the Ministry of Transport, together with direct responsibility for the Regional Planning Councils and Boards (discussed in Chapter XII) which were transferred to him from the Department of Economic Affairs. At the same time, the Board of Trade's responsibilities in the field of regional economic development went to another super-Ministry: the Ministry of Technology. This had responsibility for industrial development certificates (but not office development certificates, which were transferred to the Ministry of Housing and Local Government), industrial estates in development areas, building grants and loans. The rationale here was that the Ministry which was responsible for dealing with the greater part of private and public industry was also responsible for executive decisions concerning the location of industry.

The Department of the Environment

This organization of central government functions had a life of only one year before the Conservative Government (elected June 1970) carried the process one stage further. The rationale underlying these most recent changes are set out in the October 1970 White Paper, *The Reorganization of Central Government*. So far as the subject-matter of this book is concerned, most of the relevant functions are now organized in a huge Department of the Environment under a Secretary of State (Mr Peter Walker). Except in Scotland and Wales, where the Scottish and Welsh Offices have major responsibilities, the new DOE is responsible for 'the whole range of functions which affect people's living environment'.

The White Paper described the new Department's functions as follows:

'It will cover the planning of land – where people live, work, move and enjoy themselves. It will be responsible for the construction industries, including the housing programme, and for the transport industries, including public programmes of support and development for the means of transport. There is a need to associate with these functions responsibility for other major environmental matters: the preservation of amenity, the protection of the coast and country-side, the preservation of historic towns and monuments, and the control of air, water and noise pollution: all of which must be pursued locally, regionally, nationally and in some cases internationally. And it will have the leading responsibility for regional policy: certain economic aspects, including industrial developments in the regions, will remain with the Department of Trade and Industry, but the Department of the Environment will have important executive powers for the development of regional infrastructure and the main-tenance of regional services. It will also have the particular responsi-bility of ensuring that people's rights are adequately protected wherever they are affected by the proposals of their neighbours or of public authorities. Local authorities are profoundly involved in these fields and the new Department will, therefore, carry responsi-bility at the centre for the structure and functioning of local govern-ment as well as for regional affairs.'[40]

The Secretary of State has final responsibility for all the functions of the Department (including all statutory powers). He is, however, concerned primarily with strategic issues of policy and priority, including public expenditure, which determine the operations of the Department as a whole. Currently, he also takes personal charge of the Department's co-ordinating work on environmental pollution.

The Department has three functional parts – Local Government and Development, Housing and Construction, and Transport Indus-tries, each with a separate Minister with the status (but not the legal position) of a Minister in charge of a separate department not represented in the Cabinet.

The new organisation is 'intended and expected to remain valid for a long time to come', but as with all functions and activities of central government a 'searching' examination is under way to determine 'whether they are necessary functions of central government and, if they are confirmed as necessary, whether they are rightly articulated in the department's organizational framework'. The primary purpose is 'to reduce and rationalize the functions of government'.

It follows that the structure of and allocations of functions within DOE are not fixed. At present (mid-1971) the broad three-fold division is:

Minister of Housing and Construction
Housing programmes and finance; housing improvement; building regulations; new towns; relations with the building and civil engineering industry; building research and development; Government accommodation at home and overseas; building for the armed forces, the Post Office, research establishments and the prison service; royal parks, palaces and ancient monuments.

Minister for Transport Industries
Ports; general policy on the nationalized transport industries; railways; inland waterways; Channel Tunnel; freight haulage; international aspects of inland transport; road and vehicle safety and licensing; sport and recreation.

A Parliamentary Under Secretary of State assists the Secretary of State in the co-ordination of work on environmental pollution, with special responsibilities in relation to clean air and noise.

Minister for Local Government and Development
Local government; regional, land use and transport planning; the countryside and conservation; roads; road passenger transport; water, sewerage and refuse disposal.

In Scotland somewhat similar changes were made as long ago as 1962, when town and country planning and environmental services were transferred from the Department of Health to a new Scottish Development Department which at the same time took over all the local government, electricity, roads and industry functions of the Scottish Home Department. The Scottish Development Department is not affected by the English reorganization.

In Wales, increasing responsibilities over a wide field have in recent years been transferred to the Welsh Office. So far as town and country planning is concerned they are unaffected by the new changes, though other important functions in relation to primary and secondary education, and child care, have been transferred to the Secretary of State for Wales.

In the following account the term 'Secretary of State' is used for the sake of simplicity, but it should be interpreted to refer to the Secretaries of State for the Environment, for Scotland and for Wales. Similarly, references to the Department of the Environment should be read as applying, *mutatis mutandis*, to the Scottish Development Department and the Welsh Office.

CENTRAL–LOCAL RELATIONSHIPS

The Secretary of State is charged with the duty of 'securing consistency and continuity in the framing of a national policy with respect to the use and development of land'. The powers are very wide and, in effect, give the Department the final say in all policy matters (subject, of course, to Parliamentary control). The extent of these powers is too wide to permit an adequate summary: they are discussed in detail at appropriate points in other chapters. For many matters the Secretary of State is required or empowered to make regulations; this delegated legislation covers a wide field. For example, one Order (the Use Classes Order) classifies industrial and commercial uses and permits 'changes of use' within each of the categories without the need for planning permission. Similarly, the advertisement regulations specify certain types of advertisement for which planning permission is 'deemed' to be given, and the General Development Order provides a detailed list of types of development which do not require planning permission. One function of the Department is thus (within the limits laid down by Parliament) to make legislation.

In a wide range of matters, approval is necessary for proposals made by a local authority. The Development Plan, for example, does not become operative until it has been approved by the Secretary of State. This approval can stipulate modifications in the plan; the Secretary of State has great discretionary powers here, since he is acting administratively and quasi-judicially. If a local planning authority fail to produce a plan (or a plan 'satisfactory to the Secretary of State'), he can act in default. Decisions of a local planning authority on applications for planning permission can, on appeal, be modified or revoked – even if the development proposed is contrary to the Development Plan. Proposals which the Secretary of State regards as being sufficiently important can be 'called in' for his decision.

In spite of all these powers it is not the function of the Secretary of State to decide detailed planning policies. This is the business of local planning authorities. The Secretary of State's function is to co-ordinate the work of individual local authorities and to ensure that their Development Plans and development control decisions are in harmony with broad planning policies. That this often involves rather closer relationships than might *prima facie* be supposed follows from the nature of the governmental and administrative processes. The line dividing policy from day-to-day administration is a fine one. Policy has to be translated into decisions on specific issues, and a series of decisions can amount to a change in policy. This is particularly important in the British planning system, where a large measure of administrative discretion is given to central and local government bodies. This is a distinctive feature of the planning system. The development plan is prepared by and administered by the same local body (unlike the position in the United States, where there is a traditional separation of functions). There is virtually no provision for external judicial review of local planning decisions: instead, there is the system of appeals to the Secretary of State. A foreign observer sees the position clearly:

'The absence of a written constitution makes the statute controlling in England. External review of the merits of local planning decisions is afforded by the Minister of Housing and Local Government. His ministry is a national agency exercising a supervisory power over local government and having no exact counterpart in the United States. Appeals are taken to the minister from local refusals of planning permission and from permissions with onerous conditions. English courts can review ministerial decisions, but their role in the determination of planning policy is peripheral.

'The area of discretion in English planning administration is enlarged further by the lack of separation of function which is traditional to American government. In America, the zoning ordinance is enacted by the local legislative body but is usually administered by the executive department and by nonelective boards created for this purpose. In England the local elected council which adopts the development plan also administers it. The failure to separate function in English planning has the healthy effect of forcing attention to the relationship between the individual decision and the general objectives to which, in a small way, it contributes. But this institutional framework blurs the distinction between policy making and policy applying and so enlarges the role of the administrator who has to decide a specific case.'[18]

It is this broad area of discretion which brings the Department in close contact with local planning authorities (though, as is explained later, it is not the only factor). The Department in effect operates both in a quasi-judicial capacity and as a developer of policy.

The Department's quasi-judicial role stems in part from the vagueness of planning policies. Even if these policies are precisely worded, their application can raise problems. Since a local authority has such a wide area of discretion, and since the courts have only very limited powers of action, the Department has to act as arbiter over what is fair and reasonable. This is not, however, simply a judicial process. A decision is not taken on the basis of legal rules as in a court of law: it involves the exercise of a wide discretion in the balance of public and private interest within the framework of planning policies. The procedure basically consists of the lodging of objections either to proposals in a draft development plan or to the decision of a local authority on a planning application. Such objections (or appeals, as the latter are called) are made to the Secretary of State, who then holds an inquiry in public. These inquiries are carried out by departmental inspectors of the Department but the final decision is the formal responsibility of the Secretary of State. There is no appeal against his decision except on a question of law.

The Department's role in policy formulation is not easy to summarize. Policies are usually couched in very general terms – preservation of amenity, restraining urban 'sprawl and so on – which give local authorities considerable leeway. Formal guidance (circulars, memoranda, bulletins, etc.) often does not provide a clear indication of the action which should be followed in any particular case. Proposals have to be considered 'on their merits' within the broad framework of a set of principles. These principles can – and do – change, at least in emphasis. Usually the change is gradual, perhaps even coming without a conscious step. And the motivating power may well be the local authorities themselves rather than the Department. All this makes it very difficult to present a clear-cut picture of central-local government relationships. The truth is that the position is not clear cut. What is clear is that there is little approaching a situation in which the central department determines policy while local governments carry the policy into effect as agents. The larger authorities 'have built up local administrations that can properly be regarded as citadels of local power'. Though central government may lay down national policies, 'it is in the twists and emphases which councils give to central policies, and the degree of co-operation or unwillingness which they show, that their own power lies. They do not have the paper guarantees of local sovereignty which states in a federal system possess, but they have some of the reality of power which comes from being on the spot, knowing the special qualities and demands of the local people, and being costly and difficult to replace if the central government finds them unsatisfactory.'[20] The general conception of local government in this country was succinctly set out in the *First Report of the Local Government Manpower Committee*:

'. . . local authorities are responsible bodies competent to discharge their own functions and . . . though they may be the statutory bodies through which Government policy is given effect and operate to a large extent with Government money, they exercise their responsibilities in their own right, not ordinarily as agents of Government Departments. It follows that the objective should be to leave as much as possible of the detailed management of a scheme or service to the local authority and to concentrate the Department's control at the key points where it can most effectively discharge its responsibilities for Government policy and financial administration.'

It is common to talk of central-local government relationships as constituting a 'partnership', and, though any such single term must oversimplify the situation, the description is apposite. Certainly there is no pressure (at least so far as town and country planning is concerned) for a take-over of functions by the Department. Their attitude was expressed in 1960 by the then Permanent Secretary, Dame Evelyn Sharp, in her evidence to the Royal Commission on Local Government in Greater London: 'I certainly could not accept, and I should be rather horrified if local authorities expressed a considered and deliberate view . . . that the main outlines of their plan ought to be a matter for central government'.[39] Indeed, it can be argued that the Department plays too passive a role!

The positive powers and functions of the Department should not, however, be minimized. Reference has already been made to the way in which it can override the decisions of a local authority on particular cases. It is worth examining this in more detail.

Planning Appeals

An unsuccessful planning applicant can appeal to the Secretary of State and a large number do in fact do so. Appeals* decided during 1970 numbered 5,786, of which 27 per cent were allowed (many subject to conditions) and 73 per cent dismissed. Here the Secretary of State has very wide powers. He may reverse the local authority's decision or subject it to conditions. He may quash or modify conditions which they have imposed. He may make those conditions more onerous, or he may even go to the extent of refusing planning permission altogether if he decides that the local authority should not have granted it.†

Though each planning appeal is considered and determined on its merits, the cumulative effect is an emergence of the Department's

---

* This discussion relates particularly to appeals under Section 23 of the Town and Country Planning Act, 1962. It does not deal specifically with advertisement appeals, appeals against enforcement notices, appeals to determine whether in doubtful cases planning permission is required or appeals against certificates of alternative development for the purposes of assessing compensation under Section 18 of the Land Compensation Act, 1961 – though the principles discussed are generally the same. Section 23 of the 1962 Act covers appeals:

(1) against a decision of a local planning authority to *refuse* planning permission for the development of land;

(2) against their decision to grant it *subject to conditions*: in this case the appeal is against one or more of the conditions;

(3) against their *failure* to issue a decision within the period prescribed – two months for ordinary applications and three months for applications affecting trunk roads.

See Ministry of Housing and Local Government *Planning Appeals: A Guide to Procedure 1969*, HMSO, 4th ed., 1969, p. 7.

† See Appendix for some illustrative appeal decisions.

Planning appeals in England and Wales, 1962–70*

| | In hand at beginning of year | Received | Withdrawn | Decided | | | | | Percentage of total decided by written representation | Outstanding at end of year |
| | | | | Allowed | | Dismissed | | Total | | |
				Number	Percentage	Number	Percentage			
1962	7,382	12,352	4,170	2,359	27·2	6,302	72·8	8,661	34·0	6,903
1964	6,797	14,345	4,429	2,001	22·9	6,725	77·1	8,726	39·0	7,987
1966	9,004	11,725	4,485	1,982	21·9	7,053	78·1	9,035	46·0	7,209
1968	6,545	10,250	2,976	1,778	25·1	5,303	74·9	7,081	53·6	6,738
1970	5,933	8,865	2,692	1,578	27·3	4,208	72·7	5,786	48·0	6,320

* Ministry of Housing and Local Government: *Handbook of Statistics* (annual). The figures relate only to appeals under Section 23 of the Town and Country Planning Act, 1962, i.e. against decisions, or failure to give decisions within the statutory period, of local planning authorities on application made to them for planning permission for development. See footnote on p. 54.

views on a wide range of planning matters. These have been made more explicit in 'statements of policy' published in the *Bulletin of Selected Planning Appeals* and in the *Development Control Policy Notes*. The effect of these on the policy of individual authorities may be difficult to assess, but clearly they are likely to have a very real influence. A local planning authority is unlikely to refuse planning consents for a particular type of development if it is convinced that the Department would uphold an appeal.

It is not, of course, every planning application that raises an issue of policy. Yet, until recently, all had to be dealt with by the Department's inspectorate. Nearly a half of appeals are settled by correspondence after an informal visit to the site and without a local inquiry. (This is termed *the written representations procedure*.) The Franks Committee on Administrative Tribunals and Inquiries argued that it was not satisfactory 'that a Government Department should be occupied with appeal work of this volume, particularly as many of the appeals relate to minor and purely local matters, in which little or no departmental policy entered'. An analysis of the subject-matter of appeals undertaken by the Department (and reported in the 1967 White Paper *Town and Country Planning*) confirmed this. About 60 per cent concerned small-scale development; many of these raised issues of purely local significance. They included such matters as minor residential development, small groups of shops, small caravan sites, betting shops, garages and minor changes of use. Rather more than a quarter related to single houses.

Another relevant point is that of all appeals made during the five years 1962 to 1967 97·5 per cent were decided as the inspector recommended.

In view of the delay which is inevitable in this appeals system (on average it has taken nine months to issue decisions) and the huge administrative burden it has placed on the Department, considerable thought has been given to possible alternatives. The solution adopted by the 1968 Planning Act is for the determination of certain classes of appeals by inspectors. The classes are determined by regulation and can thus be amended in the light of experience. This is a highly novel innovation and one on which caution is necessary. The 1970 regulations (SI 1970, No. 1454) provide for appeals broadly relating to such proposals as residential development of thirty houses or less (or, if the application does not specify a number, development for residential purposes on not more than one hectare of land); and certain developments of a non-residential character subject to limits of maximum floor area and site area. These classes are further limited in the detailed regulations (e.g. development affecting trunk and special roads, and hotels in London are excluded). Furthermore, the

Secretary of State can 'call in' appeals within these classes if he sees good grounds for so doing, for example in controversial cases. (Further details are to be found in the Statutory Instrument and in MHLG *Circular 76/70*.)

The first set of regulations, made in 1968 (and now repealed and replaced by the 1970 regulations), had the effect in 1969 of transferring 12 per cent of appeals to inspectors. It is anticipated that the new regulations will have the effect of increasing this proportion to 60 per cent.

The objectives of this innovation are to speed up the appeal procedure and to relieve the central government of detailed work which has taken up far too much of their effort, thereby prejudicing the work which central government should be doing on, for example, major issues of policy. In short, the intention is that the Department will be better able to fulfil its essential role.

'Call in' of Planning Applications

The power to 'call in' a planning application for decision by the Secretary of State is quite separate from that of determining an appeal against an adverse decision of a local planning authority. This power is not circumscribed: the Secretary of State may call in any application, and his decision is final. Though there is no general statement of policy as to which applications will normally be called in there are several categories which are particularly liable. In the first place, all applications for development involving a substantial departure from the provisions of a development plan which the local planning authority intend to grant must be sent to the Secretary of State together with a statement of the reasons for which they wish to grant the permission. This procedure enables the Secretary of State to decide whether the development is sufficiently important to warrant it being called in for his own determination. Secondly, mineral workings often raise problems of more than local importance and the national need for particular minerals has to be balanced against planning issues. Such matters cannot be adequately considered by local planning authorities and, in any case, involve technical considerations requiring expert opinion of a character more easily available to the Department. For these reasons, large numbers of applications for permission to work minerals have been called in. Furthermore, there is a general direction calling in all applications for the winning and working of ironstone in certain counties where there are large-scale ironstone workings. Thirdly, the power of call-in is generally used when the matter at stake is (as in the case of minerals) of more than local importance or interest. Examples of applications called in are those relating to the Brighton Marina, the Lee Valley development, the Bognor Regis Sewage outfall and the Samlesbury brewery proposal. About a hundred applications are called in each year.

When an application is called in, the Secretary of State must, if either the applicant or the local planning authority so desire, hold a hearing or public inquiry. The public inquiry is more usual, particularly in important cases.

The Secretary of State now has power under the Town and Country Planning Act, 1968, to refer development proposals of a far-reaching or novel character to an *ad hoc* Planning Inquiry Commission. This power has not yet been used (the Roskill Commission on the third London airport was set up under non-statutory powers, while the Greater London Development Plan Inquiry was established under the *general* powers to hold local inquiries conferred by Section 213 of the 1962 Town and Country Planning Act).

Further reference must also be made to the circulars, bulletins and handbooks published by the Department, and the studies on which some of them are based. Quite apart from straightforward statements of broad policies, these contain a great deal of technical guidance. It needs to be stressed that planning policies often raise technical issues which need a wider background of experience than is always to be found in a planning authority.

Then again, there are the controls operated by the Department over capital expenditure. These controls have tended to increase as economic and regional planning tools have gradually developed. For instance, 'in order that redevelopment plans could be based on more realistic assumptions of what can be afforded, local authorities in England and Wales were asked in September 1966 to submit their proposals for redevelopment schemes for the next five years, so that a programme of approved schemes could be drawn up'.[27]

It must be repeated, however, that local planning authorities are not agents of the Department. Though the Department can – and does – exercise many direct controls, it prefers (in accordance with British traditions) to wield its power in a gentlemanly fashion by way of exhortation, advice and informal contacts. This is particularly important at officer level. The chief planning officers of local authorities are not strangers to the Department's officials: on the contrary, relationships between them are close. And they are members of a small (but active) profession in which policy issues are constantly being discussed.*

* For a recent statement of central-local relationships see Chapter 3 of Richards, P. G., *The New Local Government System*, Allen & Unwin, 1968. A detailed account and valuable discussion of the role of the central department in relation to local planning authorities is given in Griffith, J. A. G., *Central Departments and Local Authorities*, Allen & Unwin, 1966, Chapter 5.

TRANSPORT

Transport is, of course, inseparable from town planning. The volume, nature and even mode of transport is governed by land use. Permitted densities and the type of development which is allowed affect the demand and nature of transport. Indeed, it is the closeness of the relationship between town planning and transport which led to the amalgamation of the two functions in the DOE.

This was preceded, in the Town and Country Planning Act of 1968, by an emphasis on structure plans which are intended to bring about a greater integration of transport and land use planning. Until the amalgamation, the Ministry of Transport was consulted by the Ministry of Housing and Local Government on the highway proposals in development plans, and agreement was reached before the plans were approved. Furthermore, the Planning Acts require local planning authorities to consult the central department responsible for transport before they grant permission for development which will affect trunk roads. After this consultation, the local planning authorities must comply with any direction given concerning the restriction of development. Under administrative arrangements made before the amalgamation, appeals made under the Planning Acts could be referred by the Ministry of Housing and Local Government to the Ministry of Transport where one of the issues on the appeal was the effect of the development on the use and safety of an actual or proposed highway.

All these consultations should be simpler now that the amalgamation has taken place.

Trunk Roads

Transport planning is, of course, far more than the control of applications and the design of plans. One major positive aspect is the designation of the lines of trunk roads. This is a central government responsibility. The DOE also has a major influence in determining road priorities by means of grants to local authorities for road construction and improvement. Indeed, in the relationship between local authorities and the central government 'the trend has been one of increasing centralized control of broad planning and strategy, with execution and management falling to the county boroughs and county councils'.[8]

In their evidence to the Royal Commission on Local Government in Greater London, the Ministry of Transport stated that 'the choice and order of priority of individual schemes on trunk roads is completely under the control of the Minister, and on classified roads priority is virtually determined by his control of grants – although in general he can only choose from among schemes which are put to him'. Both trunk roads and classified roads have been the subject of investigation by the Estimates Committee, to which the reader in search of a wealth of detail is referred.[9, 11] The subject of transport planning is discussed in a later chapter. Here attention is concentrated on providing a summary of the organization of the central department's road functions in so far as they relate to town and country planning.

It is important at the outset to make clear the distinction between trunk and other roads. Trunk roads form a national system of routes for through traffic. The 'highway authority' for these roads is the Secretary of State. It is his responsibility under the Highways Act of 1959 to keep under review the national system of routes for through traffic in Great Britain. (Responsibility for road administration in Scotland and Wales now rests with the respective Secretaries of State.) He can construct new trunk roads and designate existing roads as trunk roads. Motorways are 'special' trunk roads. Most new constructional work and improvement schemes are designed and supervised by local authorities acting as agents for the Department. All expenditure on trunk roads is met by the Department.

The programming of trunk road schemes is the responsibility of the central department:

'The road programme should be thought of as a continuous process extending over a number of years. Trunk road schemes take a long time to prepare up to contract letting stage, perhaps three or four years in the case of large schemes, and the detailed planning of schemes is normally commenced some four years in advance of the time it is expected that constructional work on these will start. A provisional selection of schemes for several years ahead is also made, so that a certain amount of preliminary work, such as making orders setting out the line of route, can be undertaken. Looking even further ahead, there is a special planning section in the Department with the task of working out in the light of the latest information about traffic trends, what the country's long-term road requirements are likely to be.'[11]

In short, so far as trunk roads are concerned, the Department is the policy-making body. It determines the programme, approves estimates and allocates money to individual authorities. The local authorities are merely the agents for carrying out the Department's policy.

For other roads a different system operates. The responsibility for these lies with local highway authorities. The Department's position is largely dependent upon its power to make grants. Up to 1967, specific grants for both improvement and maintenance were payable to local highway authorities for 'classified' roads. These grants were paid at rates of 75 per cent, 60 per cent and 50 per cent on Class I, II and III roads respectively.

Since April 1967, a new simplified system has operated. This was conceived within the general framework of a comprehensive review of central-local government financial relationships.[26] The purpose of the revised grant structure (introduced by the Local Government Act, 1966) is threefold.

(i) to concentrate specific Exchequer aid on roads which make an important contribution to the national highway system;
(ii) to strike a better balance of responsibility between central and local government, and to keep detailed control to the essential minimum;
(iii) to simplify the system of grants and classification to streamline highway administration.[32]

Under this system, highway works are divided into two categories: improvements and maintenance. Capital grants, at a rate of 75 per cent, are payable for improvements (not maintenance) on 'principal roads' only. (Principal roads are roughly equivalent to the previous Class I system.) All other grant aid (for improvements and maintenance) is given through the Rate Support Grant, which is a non-specific revenue grant for (nearly) all local government services. This grant takes into account both the mileage of highways and expenditure on improvement and maintenance.

INDUSTRIAL LOCATION CONTROL

Policies relating to industrial location control can be divided into two categories. Firstly, there are the negative controls operated via the Industrial Development Certificate (IDC) scheme, under which any industrial building or extension above a certain size requires the certification by the central government that it is consistent with the 'proper distribution of industry'. Secondly, there are the positive powers to attract industries to areas of high unemployment.

Until October 1969, the central department responsible for industrial location was the Board of Trade. At that date these responsibilities were transferred to a new Ministry of Technology together with those of the Department of Economic Affairs in relation to regional economic development. This left the Board of Trade with functions relating to external commercial policy and such matters as civil aviation, shipping, tourism, hotels and insurance. In October 1970, the Ministry of Technology and the Board of Trade were merged in a large Department of Trade and Industry (DTI). It is now the DTI which is responsible for industrial location and industrial aspects of regional policy.

Industrial Development Certificates

The control of industrial location is entirely a central government responsibility. Though certain local authorities have appointed indusrial development officers and many act in concert through industrial development associations, they have no statutory responsibility for industrial location policy. This may appear to be an overstatement, since an important part of a local authority's development plan will be concerned with industrial sites, and authorities in areas of unemployment will seek to attract new industry, while those in congested areas (particularly London) operate a policy of encouraging industrial dispersal. Nevertheless, the powers here are limited and in practice are much more concerned with siting than with general issues of location. The distinction is important. Though local authorities can erect factories in an attempt to encourage industrial growth and can buy up existing factories in order to reduce the level of employment, their real power lies in approving or rejecting planning applications for industrial development on particular sites. The question as to whether this industrial development should take place at all in the area is a matter for the DTI. In short, the Department is responsible for the *location* of industry, whereas local authorities are responsible for the *siting* of industrial developments. It follows that the DTI has an extremely important role to play: it is an executive as well as a policy-making body.

The general policy of the DTI is to encourage industrial expansion in areas of high unemployment and to restrict it in congested areas. This has been the interpretation of 'the proper distribution of industry' – a phrase which is nowhere defined in the legislation, though the Local Employment Act of 1960 does require the DTI (when considering whether an industrial development certificate should be granted) to have 'particular regard to the need for providing appropriate employment in development districts'.

No application for planning permission for the erection of an industrial building (normally exceeding 5,000 square feet – but less in some areas, particularly in southern England and the West Midlands) can be made unless it is accompanied by an industrial development certificate. This is a negative control and, furthermore, is limited in extent. There is no control over existing buildings. A firm which is refused permission for development in, say, the London area, may be able to purchase a vacated factory and thus create the very increase in employment which it was the Department's objective to prevent. This stems from the fact that the control is applied to building and not directly to employment. Under current powers the only alternative is the purchase by the local authority of the property – an extremely costly undertaking.

An IDC is generally made valid for the area of a local authority. The Department does not inquire whether the proposed site – if one has been chosen – is suitable. This is an issue of land use which falls within the scope of the local planning authority's functions. It thus follows that the granting of a certificate by the Department does not guarantee that the authorized development will, or can, take place.

Recent legislation has been directed towards a tightening up of the controls. Thus, the Control of Office and Industrial Development Act, 1965, extended the meaning of 'related development' to effect greater control over the creation of a substantial area of floor space by the accumulation of individual pieces of development, each of which is below the exemption limit. Similarly, the Industrial Development Act, 1966, extended the meaning of 'industrial building', thereby bringing under IDC control all buildings used or designed for use for scientific research. ('Scientific research' is defined as 'any activity in the fields of natural or applied science for the extension of knowledge'.) This Act also provided powers which ensure that planning permission is needed before space approved for 'ancillary purposes' such as storage can be converted to production use.

Development Areas
Policy relating to areas of high unemployment has changed considerably over the post-war years in response to changing conditions. The Special Areas of the pre-war legislation were converted into Development Areas by the Distribution of Industry Act of 1945. They were enlarged and added to, but the basic concept of large areas of persistent large-scale unemployment remained. By the end of the 'fifties the official view was that 'the steps which had been taken to rehabilitate these areas had achieved a large measure of success and many districts within the scheduled development areas – which contained nearly 20 per cent of the insured population – were no longer in any need of special assistance'.[10] On the other hand, the rate of economic and technical change had increased. Pockets of unemployment were occurring in small isolated places. A new and more flexible approach was needed. The first recognition of this was the 1958 Distribution of Industry (Industrial Finance) Act, which extended some of the central department's powers to non-development areas in which it was considered that high unemployment was likely to persist. The 1960 Act went much further: the former statutory schedule of development

areas gave way to a new concept of administratively determined districts. These were defined as localities in which, in the opinion of the Central Department, a high rate of unemployment exists, or is to be expected, and in either case is likely to persist, whether seasonally (e.g. in seaside resorts) or generally.

In the mid-'sixties, however, the concepts of 'growth areas' and more selective regional development policies gradually took shape. Increasingly it was felt that measures to relieve unemployment ought to be set within a framework of policy geared to facilitate growth in areas with the greatest economic potential. The change in focus can be clearly seen by comparing the definition of 'development districts' in the Local Employment Act, 1960, with that of 'development areas' in the Industrial Development Act, 1966:

Local Employment Act, 1960	*Industrial Development Act, 1966*
In this Act *development district* means any locality in Great Britain in which in the opinion of the Board . . . a high rate of unemployment exists, or is to be expected within such a period that it is expedient to exercise the said powers, and (in either case) is likely to persist, whether seasonally or generally.	The areas to be specified by the Board [as *development areas*] shall be those parts of Great Britain where, in the opinion of the Board, special measures are necessary to encourage the growth and proper distribution of industry; and in exercising their powers . . . the Board shall have regard to all the circumstances actual and expected, including the state of employment and unemployment, population changes and the objectives of regional policies.

In 1970 the development areas included the whole of Scotland (excluding the Edinburgh, Leith and Portobello Employment Exchange areas), the Northern Region, Wales (excluding parts of the south-east and north) and the westernmost parts of the South-Western Region (Cornwall and North Devon). The development areas cover a very extensive part of the land area of the country, and contain about a fifth of the employed population. In 1970 their average unemployment rate was 4·2 per cent, compared with a national average of 2·4 per cent.

Intermediate Areas .
Following the Hunt Report, which is discussed in Chapter XII, the Local Employment Act, 1970, introduced a new category of *inter-mediate areas*. These are areas in relation to which the responsible

Minister is 'of opinion that special measures are necessary to encourage the growth and proper distribution of industry, but that the economic problems of these localities are not so acute as to require the use of all the powers to provide assistance to industry which are available in relation to the development areas'. In mid-1970 these intermediate areas comprised parts of North-East Lancashire, North Humberside, the Yorkshire coalfield, parts of the Notts-Derby coalfield, Plymouth, the Leith Employment Exchange Area and parts of South-East Wales. They comprised about 5 per cent of the insured

Unemployment in Great Britain, 1970

Development Area:	Number (thousands)	Per cent
Northern	63·6	4·7
Merseyside	29·2	3·6
South-Western	6·6	4·9
Welsh	28·7	4·5
Scottish	75·4	3·9
All Development Areas	203·5	4·2
Intermediate Areas in*:		
England	36·3	3·7
Wales	7·7	2·8
Scotland	1·4	—
All Intermediate Areas	45·4	3·5
Other areas	322·8	1·9
Great Britain	551·5	2·4

* Average for the six months ended March 1970.

population of Great Britain and had an unemployment rate of 3·5 per cent, compared with 4·2 per cent in the development areas and 2·4 per cent nationally.

The positive powers of the DTI (as distinct from regulatory powers through the granting of industrial development certificates) can, in general, be used only in development and intermediate areas. Under these powers, the Department can buy or build factories for sale or renting; make grants to firms providing their own premises; and advance loans and give grants for 'general purposes'. There are further powers for other Government Departments to give grants for clearing derelict land* and for improving basic services.

* See Chapter VIII.

Further details and statistics are to be found in the Annual Reports on the Local Employment Acts. (Until 1970 these were presented by the Board of Trade; in 1970 by the Minister of Technology; and thereafter by the Secretary of State for Trade and Industry.)

OFFICE DEVELOPMENT CERTIFICATES

Pressures for the control of office development were resisted throughout the late 'fifties and early 'sixties on the ground that it would be impracticable. The 1963 White Paper, *London – Employment: Land*, argued the case well:

'The machinery for controlling the issue of industrial development certificates depends on knowledge of the firm which occupies the factory and on an assessment of the need for that firm to carry on its manufacture in a particular area. Many new factories are purpose-built and have heavy machinery installed; occupiers do not change often. New office blocks, on the other hand, are more often than not built for letting; this is, indeed, often the only way in which modern accommodation can be provided in units of a suitable size for small and medium-sized firms. Consequently, when the developer seeks planning permissions he may not know how many tenants he will have or who his tenants will be; and these tenants may change at frequent intervals. A Government Department trying to administer a control of this sort would, therefore, be without the basic information needed for the purpose. Even when a tenant was known it would be extremely difficult to judge the case put forward in support of an office in the central area by a commercial or professional firm. The Government do not believe that it would be practical to administer a system of control of office occupation either effectively or equitably.'[23]

Action along three lines was proposed and carried into effect. Firstly, planning controls over new office building were tightened. The issue here was a complicated legal one. In brief, the existing legislation allowed a 10 per cent increase in cubic capacity to owners rebuilding their premises. Since new buildings have lower ceilings and less circulation space, a 10 per cent increase in cubic capacity could involve as much as a 40 per cent increase in floor space. Attempts by local planning authorities to restrict this involved the risk of paying heavy compensation. The Town and Country Planning Act, 1963, removed any compensation liabilities which may arise when permission is refused for an increase in *floor space* of more than 10 per cent.

Secondly, an attempt was made to disperse more Government offices. It had been Government policy for many years to disperse Headquarters Departments and self-contained branches which could function away from London without loss of administrative efficiency. In 1962, of the total headquarters staff of 125,000, some 25,000 already worked outside London, and there were plans for moving a further 7,000. It was felt, however, that it was time for a thorough re-examination of the situation. A review was undertaken by Sir Gilbert Flemming. His (unpublished) report recommended the transfer of some 18,000 jobs from central London. A further examination of this issue was announced in the 1970 White Paper on *The Reorganization of Central Government*.

Thirdly, a new agency, the Location of Offices Bureau, was set up to encourage the decentralization of office employment from central London. The Bureau's main function is to provide an information and publicity service. Its operations are summarized in its annual reports.

The return of the Labour Government in 1964 was followed by the introduction of direct controls over office building through *Office Development Certificates*. The legislation (Control of Office and Industrial Development Act, 1965) applied the control only in the Metropolitan Region, but provided for its extension by Order to any other part of Great Britain. In August 1965, it was extended to the Birmingham Conurbation and in July 1966, to major parts of Southern England and the East and West Midlands.

The controls are very similar in form to the industrial development certificate control (though they are administered by the Department of the Environment). In the areas to which the Act applies an office development permit (like the industrial development certificate) must be obtained for development over 10,000 feet before planning permission can be given. In deciding whether to grant such a permit, the DOE 'shall have particular regard to the need for promoting the better distribution of employment in Great Britain'. The Department has complete discretion and there is no right of appeal or compensation if a permit is refused.

In considering an application for an ODP, the Department are guided by three principles: firstly, the activity for which new accommodation is sought must be one which cannot be carried on outside the area of the control; secondly, there must be no suitable alternative accommodation available; and, thirdly, the development must be essential in the public interest.

REFERENCES AND FURTHER READING

1 Board of Trade, *Control of Office and Industrial Development Act, 1965: Annual Reports by the Board of Trade*, House of Commons Papers, HMSO, annual.
2 Board of Trade, *Local Employment Acts: Annual Reports by the Board of Trade*, House of Commons Papers, HMSO, annual. (In 1970 presented by the Minister of Technology; thereafter by the Secretary of State for Trade and Industry.)
3 Brown, H. J. J., 'Digest of Planning Decisions', Part V of Heap, D., *Encyclopedia of the Law of Town and Country Planning*, Sweet and Maxwell, 1959. (In loose-leaf form with regular supplements.)
4 *Committee on Administrative Tribunals and Enquiries: Report* (Franks Report), Cmnd. 218, HMSO, 1957.
5 Cowan, P., et al., *The Office – A Facet of Urban Growth*, Heinemann, 1969.
6 Daniels, P. W., 'Office Decentralization from London – Policy and Practice', *Regional Studies*, Vol. 3, No. 2, September 1969, pp. 171–8.
7 Department of Economic Affairs and Board of Trade, *Investment Incentives*, Cmnd. 2874, HMSO, 1966.
8 Dunnett, Sir James, 'The Relationship between Central and Local Government in the Planning and Execution of Road Schemes', *Public Administration*, Vol. 40, Autumn 1962.
9 Estimates Committee, Session 1961–2 *Classified Roads*, H.C. Paper 227, HMSO, 1962.
10 Estimates Committee, Session 1962–3, *Administration of the Local Employment Act, 1960*, H.C. Paper 229, HMSO, 1963.
11 Estimates Committee, Session 1968–9, *Motorways and Trunk Roads*, H.C. Paper 102, HMSO, 1969.
12 Griffith, J. A. G., *Central Departments and Local Authorities*, Allen & Unwin, 1966, Chapter 5.
13 Hammond, E., *London to Durham: A Study of the Transfer of the Post Office Savings Certificate Division*, University of Durham, Rowntree Research Unit, 1968.
14 Hammond, E., 'Dispersal of Government Offices: A Survey', *Urban Studies*, Vol. 4, No. 3, November 1967, pp. 258–75.

15 Local Government Manpower Committee, *First Report*, 1950; *Second Report*, 1951, HMSO.

16 Location of Offices Bureau publications (obtainable from the Bureau, 27 Chancery Lane, London WC2):
Annual Reports.
Commuters to the London Office: A Survey, 1966.
White Collar Commuters: A Second Survey, 1967.
Offices in a Regional Centre: A Study of Office Location in Leeds, 1968.
Relocation of Office Staff: A Study of the Reactions of Office Staff Decentralised to Ashford, 1969.
Offices: A Bibliography, 1969.

17 McCrone, G., *Regional Policy in Britain*, Allen & Unwin, 1969.

18 Mandelker, D. R., *Green Belts and Urban Growth*, University of Wisconsin Press, 1962.

19 Marriott, O., *The Property Boom*, Hamish Hamilton, 1967.

20 Miller, B., 'Citadels of Local Power', *The Twentieth Century*, Vol. 162, October 1957.

21 MHLG, *Bulletin of Selected Appeal Decisions*, HMSO, 1947–63.

22 MHLG, *Planning Bulletins*, HMSO, 1962 and continuing.

23 MHLG, *London – Employment: Housing: Land*, Cmnd, 1952, HMSO, 1963.

24 MHLG, Circular 47/63, *Town and Country Planning Act, 1963*, HMSO, 1963.

25 MHLG, Circular 64/65, *Control of Office and Industrial Development Act, 1965*, HMSO, 1965.

26 MHLG, *Local Government Finance, England and Wales*, Cmnd. 2923, HMSO, 1966.

27 MHLG, *Report for 1965 and 1966*, Cmnd. 3282, HMSO, 1967.

28 MHLG, *Town and Country Planning*, Cmnd. 3333, HMSO, 1967.

29 MHLG, *Development Control Policy Notes*, HMSO, 1969 and continuing.

30 MHLG, *Planning Appeals: A Guide to Procedure 1969*, HMSO, 1969.

31 MHLG, *Report for 1967 and 1968*, Cmnd. 4009, HMSO, 1969.

32 Ministry of Transport, *Roads in England 1965–66*, H.C. Paper 232, HMSO, 1966.

33 Ministry of Transport, Roads Circular 1/68, *Traffic and Transport Plans*, HMSO, 1968.

34 Richards, P. G., *The New Local Government System*, Allen & Unwin, 1968.

35 *Royal Commission on Local Government in Greater London: Minutes of Evidence* and *Report*, Cmnd. 1164, HMSO, 1960.

36 Schon, D. A., *Beyond the Stable State*, Temple Smith, 1971.

37 Select Committee on Estimates, Session 1958–9, *Trunk Roads*, H.C. Paper 223, HMSO, 1959.
38 Self, P., *Town Planning in Greater London*, London School of Economics, Greater London Papers No. 7, 1962.
39 Sharp, E., *The Ministry of Housing and Local Government*, Allen & Unwin, 1969.
40 White Paper, *The Reorganisation of Central Government*, Cmnd. 4506, HMSO, 1970.
41 Wraith, R. E. and Lamb, G. B., *Public Inquiries as an Instrument of Government*, Allen & Unwin, 1971.

Chapter IV

THE LEGISLATIVE FRAMEWORK

The Town and Country Planning Act, 1968, and the equivalent Scottish Act of 1969 represent a landmark in the development of planning policy and administration. This new legislation is a major attempt to bring the planning system up to date, to shed the cumbersome and inflexible procedures of the established system, to redefine the respective roles of central and local government (with far less central concern with detailed planning matters) and to provide the framework for a far greater degree of citizen-participation in the planning process.

The changes in law are to be implemented by Ministerial Order. The intention (to quote from the Parliamentary Debates) is to bring the provisions of the Act into operation selectively 'as and when the administrative machine at both governmental and local authority level is able to cope with them'. In England and Wales the majority of the provisions of the Act are now operative but the new development plan system is being brought into operation by a series of commencement orders relating to particular areas. This is in line with the 1967 White Paper, which stated that the new system of 'structure', 'action area' and 'local' plans was to be introduced 'into those parts of the country where it can usefully be operated in advance of its general introduction when local government is reorganized'. But, even in areas where the new plans are being formulated, the existing system will continue in operation until the structure plans have been formally approved by the Minister. In short, the current development plans will continue in operation for some considerable time. It follows that it is necessary to discuss both systems.

In Scotland it has been announced (in July 1971) that there is no intention of making similar commencement orders but local authorities have been asked to begin preparations for transfer to the new system. The majority of the other provisions of the new legislation are, however, now operative.

This chapter only briefly touches on the role of citizen-participation in the new system: the main discussion is to be found in the final chapter, where a more appropriate framework can be provided.

DEVELOPMENT PLANS

Under the pre-war system of planning, an operative planning scheme was in effect a zoning plan. A developer could visit a local Town Hall and ask to see the planning scheme: he would be shown a written document and a series of coloured maps, each colour representing some particular use. From the published scheme the developer would find that particular pieces of land were zoned for industry, for open space, for residential development at not more than eight houses to the acre, and so on. The great advantage of this system to the developer was that there were no doubts as to what development would be permitted: it was all written down and had the force of law. But therein lay one of its gravest shortcomings: certainty for the developer meant inflexibility for the local authority. One way of circumventing this was for planning authorities to take advantage of the time-consuming and cumbersome procedure for preparing and obtaining approval to their schemes by remaining at the draft stage for as long as possible. Yet this had the opposite danger: the flexibility thereby attained could easily become mere expediency. The new system attempted to achieve a balance between these two extremes by the introduction of the flexible development plan. A development plan is essentially a statement of development proposals. It is intended to show, for example,

'which towns and villages are suitable for expansion and which can best be kept to their present size; the direction in which a city will expand; the area to be preserved as an agricultural Green Belt and the area to be allocated to industry and to housing'.[31]

The legislation, however, defined a development plan as 'a plan indicating the manner in which a local planning authority propose that land in their area should be used, whether by the carrying out thereon of development or otherwise, and the stages by which any such development should be carried out'. Furthermore, it was required that the development plan should 'define the sites of proposed roads, public and other buildings and works, airfields, parks, pleasure grounds, nature reserves and other open spaces, or allocate areas of land for use for agricultural, residential, industrial or other purposes'.

Unlike the pre-war 'operative scheme', the development plan does not of itself imply that permission will be granted for particular developments even if it appears that they are clearly in harmony with the plan. Development control is achieved by a system of planning permissions. The development plan merely sets out the intentions of the local planning authority. Though a developer is able to find out from the plan where particular uses would be likely to be permitted, his specific proposals still need to be considered by the local planning authority. When considering applications the authority are expressly directed to 'have regard to the provisions of the development plan', but the plan is not binding in any way, and, indeed, authorities are instructed to have regard not only to the development plan but also to 'any other material considerations'. Furthermore, in granting permission to develop, the authority can impose 'such conditions as they think fit'.

But though local planning authorities have considerable latitude in deciding whether to approve applications they have to be clear on the planning objectives for their areas, otherwise they have no adequate basis on which they can judge the merits and shortcomings of particular applications. This is the purpose of the development plan – on which great stress is laid in the legislation. A meaningful plan can be prepared only on the basis of an intensive study of existing conditions, trends and needs.

Some idea of the comprehensive approach required in the survey is given by the following list of matters on which the Ministry required the collection of information.

1 Existing land use; age and condition of buildings; quantities of building uses; residential density; land unsuitable for building purposes.
2 Ancient monuments and buildings of architectural or historic interest.
3 Rural community structure.
4 Population – natural change and migration.
5 Industry and employment.
6 Minerals.
7 Agriculture and forestry.
8 Communications – roads, railways, docks, harbours and canals; airports and airfields.
9 Proposed developments by Government Departments.
10 Public utilities – water supply and sewerage; electricity; gas; land drainage.
11 Social services.
12 National parks, conservation and amenity areas.
13 Holiday development.

This is merely a list of the main headings. The full list is a formidable one. An indication of the amount of detailed work involved can be given by considering one heading – the age and condition of buildings:

'The physical condition of buildings will be an important factor in determining the need for redevelopment. Maps should, therefore, be prepared for each area in respect of which a town plan is being prepared, distinguishing buildings as follows:

(*a*) Buildings which have suffered extensive war damage.
(*b*) Buildings already condemned or which would be scheduled for demolition under the Housing Acts if demolition were immediately practicable.
(*c*) Buildings of architectural or historic interest.
(*d*) Other buildings, classified by age as follows:

(i) Erected before 1875.
(ii) Erected between 1875 and 1914.
(iii) Erected since 1914.

This classification should give a first index to the areas to be considered for redevelopment. From the information so obtained, considered with other factors such as density, mixture of uses, layout, structural condition, and subjection to periodic flooding, other maps should be prepared to show:

(i) Areas requiring early development,
(ii) Areas becoming obsolete but which still contain some years of useful life,
(iii) Areas not likely to require redevelopment for many years.'

On the basis of this information and after all the necessary consultations with Government Departments, statutory undertakers and (in the case of counties) district councils, the local planning authority prepared a development plan. Strictly speaking this is a totally separate series of documents. The *Report of Survey* provides the background to and the basis of the plan, but it has no statutory effect. The legal documents consist of a *Written Statement* and a series of maps. The Written Statement is a short, formal (some would say excessively short and formal) document containing little more than a summary of the main proposals of the plan. It does not contain any argument for or against the proposals, or, indeed, the factual material on which these are based.

DESIGNATED LAND

An important part of the Written Statement is a list of sites 'designated for compulsory acquisition'. This can be a source of some confusion, since on the one hand it is not a complete list of sites that are to be compulsorily acquired during the period of the plan, and on the other hand, designation does not imply that the land will in fact be compulsorily acquired. What is achieved by designation is simply an extension of the powers of compulsory purchase, not only for local authorities but also for Government Departments and statutory undertakers. All these public authorities have specific powers of compulsory purchase for defined purposes, but if land is designated 'for the purpose of any of their functions' they become freed from the restrictions imposed by their existing powers. Normally, of course, the existing powers would be adequate, but designation provides a means whereby land can be acquired which otherwise could not have been acquired. This is particularly important in connection with the proposals of the Development Plan, since the local planning authority can designate any land which they decide needs to be developed comprehensively, and any land which needs to be compulsorily acquired 'in order to secure its use in the manner proposed by the plan'. In short, provided that the use is defined in the plan, land may be designated and thus compulsorily acquired.

These are extremely wide powers and they have been subject to considerable criticism. In the Committee Stage Debates on the Bill the Minister argued that 'it is in the interests of owners that they should know what land is likely to be required by the planning authority, by statutory undertakers or by Government Departments within a reasonable period', but in fact since these public authorities still retain their existing powers (and can thus compulsorily acquire land under these powers at any time whether or not the land in question is designated) and, since designated land might not in the event be acquired, this is little consolation either to the owners of designated land or to the owners of non-designated land. Nevertheless, development plans cannot be put into effect without some use of compulsory powers and the proposals of the plan itself contain the threat of compulsory acquisition (particularly in relation to public works). The designation of an area does confirm that it is likely to be compulsorily acquired within a certain period and to that extent gives the owners of land some knowledge of what is to happen.

Designation creates another difficulty: it puts a 'dead hand' on land, which may become unsaleable to anyone other than the authority for whom it is designated. As the Department has pointed out, 'this is one of the most serious difficulties associated within planning. Advance notice of intention may, temporarily, blight land needed in future for particular development: yet not to give notice may result in a waste of money'.[8]

Designated Land and the 1968 Act

The 1968 Act repealed the requirement that land to be compulsorily acquired under the powers of the Town and Country Planning Acts shall previously be designated in an approved development plan. As the White Paper concluded, 'experience has shown that it adds procedural complications without compensating benefits for anybody'. But though designation is no longer required, this is not the case with the powers of compulsory acquisition for planning purposes. The designation provisions have therefore been replaced by new provisions empowering local authorities to compulsorily acquire land needed in connection with development or for other planning purposes. These new powers are more extensive than those which they replace and they include the extension to all public authorities of the 'vesting procedure' previously available only to the (now defunct) Land Commission.*

Local authorities now have power to acquire compulsorily any land in their area if the Secretary of State is satisfied:

(*a*) that the land is required in order to secure or assist the treatment as a whole, by development, redevelopment or improvement or partly by one and partly by another method, of the land or of any area in which the land is situated; *or*

(*b*) that it is expedient in the public interest that the land should be held together with land so required; *or*

(*c*) that the land is required for development or redevelopment, or both, as a whole for the purpose of providing for the relocation of population or industry or the replacement of open space in the course of the redevelopment or improvement, or both, of another area as a whole; *or*

(*d*) that it is expedient to acquire the land immediately for a purpose which it is necessary to achieve in the interests of the proper planning of an area in which the land is situated.

COUNTY, TOWN AND PROGRAMME MAPS

Accompanying the Written Statement is a series of maps. For a county these include the County Maps and a related Programme Map (at a scale of 1 inch to the mile) covering the whole of the administrative county. For areas requiring more detailed planning there will be Town and Programme Maps at the larger scale of 6 inches to the mile.

In the case of a county borough there is, of course, no county map:

* See Chapter VI.

the principal maps are the Town Map and its related Programme Map.

The County and Town Maps indicate the developments which are expected in the twenty-year period of the plan (and possibly some important developments which are expected somewhat later) and the pattern of land use proposed at the end of the period. (In areas for which no notation is given – which may be extensive in counties – it is intended that the main existing uses should remain undisturbed.) A Programme Map shows the stages by which the proposed development is to be achieved. This usually distinguishes at least between the first five years and the remainder of the plan period. In this way private and public development is programmed in a co-ordinated way. Thus the development of housing estates is viewed in relation to the school-building programme and proposals for new roads. At the same time the various needs of an area can be seen as a whole and a set of priorities determined. During the period when the initial surveys were being undertaken, building resources were severely limited and a system of licensing was in operation. It was therefore necessary to relate the programme to the anticipated availability of resources. Furthermore, an estimate was required of the total cost of that part of the plan which was likely to be undertaken by the local authority. These financial estimates were necessarily very crude, but they did encourage a realistic approach to planning proposals.

A formidable amount of work was involved in the preparation of development plans. The 1947 Act required local planning authorities to submit plans to the Minister for approval within three years (by July 1, 1951), 'or within such extended period as the Minister may in any particular case allow', but not surprisingly most authorities could not meet the deadline. (Only twenty-two did, in fact, do so.)

The task of the DOE is to assess the general provisions of the plan, to weigh all objections to it, to hold a public local inquiry, to consider the report of the Inspector on the inquiry and finally to approve the plan with or without modification. Every plan has been modified in some degree before approval, sometimes very substantially. Local authorities often propose modifications in order to meet objections. About half the plans had been approved by 1955 and the bulk had been approved by 1959; but three were not approved until the early 'sixties: Denbighshire, part of Glamorgan and Manchester.

Development plans, unlike the old 'operative schemes', were not intended to be final statements – even of broad intentions. Local planning authorities were obliged to review them at least every five years, and additionally could propose amendments at any time.

The impossibility of coping with the preparation and approval of plans on the original time-scale greatly delayed the review procedure and many local authorities were still engaged on their first review in the mid-'sixties.

This was one of the major reasons for introducing the new structure plan system. However, since the new system is to be introduced gradually, provision has had to be made for the 'transition'. Existing development plans remain operative until superseded, but no further reviews or amendments are to be submitted to the Secretary of State (except with prior approval).

The reviews followed the same process as the initial plan: survey, draft written statement and maps, submission to the Department, local public inquiry, and approval with or without modification. Alterations or additions to development plans could be made at any time. Often these 'amendments' amounted to more detailed plans for particular areas. In counties, the Town Maps for the districts were commonly submitted in this way. Another type of detailed planning often submitted as a formal amendment was a Comprehensive Development Area plan.

COMPREHENSIVE DEVELOPMENT AREAS

In its consideration of the problems of post-war reconstruction the Uthwatt Committee examined the existing powers (under the Town and Country Planning Act, 1932, and the Housing Act, 1936) of local authorities to undertake redevelopment. These they found quite inadequate. In their view, 'the simplest and only effective method of achieving the desired results is to confer on the planning authority compulsory powers of purchase, much wider and more simple in operation than under existing legislation, over any land which may be required for planning or other public purposes'. In particular they recommended that there should be powers for the compulsory acquisition of the whole of war-damaged and of obsolete areas – later popularly termed 'blitz' and 'blight' areas. Only by such a means would it be possible to cut through the tangle of separate ownerships and make the whole of an area immediately available for comprehensive redevelopment. Some idea of the problems involved is provided by the well-known example of the 267-acre Duddeston and Nechells area in Birmingham.*

'Nearly 11 miles of existing streets, mostly narrow and badly planned. 6,800 individual dwellings, the density varying locally up to eighty to the acre.

* The quotation comes originally from a 1937 report of the City Engineer (Sir Herbert Manzoni). It is also to be found on page 6 of the Uthwatt Report.

5,400 of these dwellings classified as slums to be condemned.

15 major industrial premises or factories, several of them comparatively recent in date.

105 minor factories, storage buildings, workshops, industrial yards, laundries, etc.

778 shops, many of them hucksters' premises.

7 schools.

18 churches and chapels.

51 licensed premises.

Many miles of public service mains, water, gas and electricity, including over a mile of 42-inch trunk water main, nearly all land under carriage ways and consequently in the wrong places for good planning. Add to these a railway viaduct, a canal, a railway goods yard and a gas works and you have a beautiful problem in redevelopment.'

The procedure for dealing with areas such as this was lengthy and tortuous, and involved dealing with the separate problems under separate powers and persuading different Government Departments to give approvals without regard to their separate departmental priorities. Yet comprehensive redevelopment was obviously necessary if modern layouts and adequate provision for transport and amenities were to be made. (A trial layout for the area showed that a saving of twenty acres of land could be made on the street pattern alone.)

Many of the Uthwatt recommendations were incorporated in the Town and Country Planning Acts of 1944 and 1947. Local authorities were given powers to define 'comprehensive development areas' where it was desirable to develop or redevelop an area as a whole.* Such an area could include areas of war damage, areas of obsolete development or bad layout, land required for accommodating population displaced in connection with the redevelopment of the area or *any* land to be developed as a whole for *any* purpose defined in the development plan.

The principle underlying the comprehensive development area procedure was that 'because of the multiplicity of ownerships usually involved, the key to proper redevelopment of towns is public acquisition, to be followed either by the disposal of the land to private

* For further discussion see Chapter XI.

developers, under conditions ensuring that they will themselves carry out development in accordance with the plan for the area, or by direct development by the local authority'.

The comprehensive development area procedure is replaced in the 1968 Act by the 'action area' procedure discussed below.

THE CONTROL OF DEVELOPMENT

With certain exceptions, all development requires the prior approval of the local planning authority. The authority have considerable discretion in this matter. Though they must 'have regard to the provisions of the development plan' they may take 'any other material

Decisions on Planning Applications, 1969*

	Number	Percentage
Planning applications decided in 1969	402,714	100·0
Permissions granted	342,889	85·1
Refusals	59,825	14·9

* Ministry of Housing and Local Government, *Handbook of Statistics 1970*, HMSO, 1971. (Additionally there were 39,819 advertisement applications. Conditional permissions or permissions for a limited period are counted as 'permissions granted' except for caravan sites, where a distinction is made between consents given with and without a time limit.

In Scotland annual planning decisions averaged 21,703 over the period 1963–9, of which 93·8 per cent were granted and 6·2 per cent refused. (See SDD, *Report for 1970*, Cmnd. 4625, HMSO, 1971, p. 82.)

considerations' into account. Indeed they can approve a proposal which 'does not accord with the provisions of the plan'. If the proposal does not involve a substantial departure from the plan and does not 'injuriously affect the amenity of the adjoining land' their discretion is unlimited. In other cases they require prior approval of the Secretary of State.

The planning decisions of the authority can be one of three kinds: unconditional permission, permission 'subject to such conditions as they think fit', or refusal. The practical scope of these powers is discussed in a later section. Here it is necessary merely to stress that there is a right of appeal to the Secretary of State against conditional permissions and refusals. If the action of the authority is thought to be *ultra vires* there is also a right of appeal to the courts. Furthermore, planning applications which raise issues which are of major importance, or are of a particular technical nature, can be 'called in' for ministerial decision.

Development control necessarily involves some procedure for enforcement. This is provided by *enforcement notices* under which an owner who carries out development without permission or in breach of conditions can be compelled to 'undo' the development – even if this involves the demolition of a new building. A *stop notice* can also be used in conjunction with an enforcement notice to put a rapid stop to the carrying out or continuation of development which is in breach of planning control.

These are very strong powers and clearly it is important to establish the meaning of 'development', particularly since the term has a legal meaning far wider than in ordinary language.

THE DEFINITION OF DEVELOPMENT

In brief, development is 'the carrying out of building, engineering, mining or other operations in, on, over or under the land, or the making of any material change in the use of any buildings or other land'.* There are some legal niceties attendant upon this definition with which it is fortunately not necessary to deal in the present outline. Some account of the breadth of the definition is, nevertheless, needed. 'Building operations', for instance, include rebuilding operations, structural alterations of or additions to buildings and – somewhat curiously – 'other operations normally undertaken by a person carrying on business as a builder'; but maintenance and improvement works which affect only the interior of the building or which do not materially affect the external appearance of the building are specifically excluded. The demolition of a building does not *of itself* constitute development, though, of course, it may form part of a building operation, or lead to the making of a material change in the use of the land upon which it stood.

The second half of the definition introduces quite a different concept: development here means not a physical operation, but a change in the *use* of a piece of land or a structure. The change has to be 'material', i.e. substantial – a concept which it is clearly difficult to define; and which, indeed, is not defined in the Act. A change in *kind* (for example from a house to a shop) is material, but a change in *degree* is material only if the change is very substantial. For instance the fact that lodgers are taken privately in a family dwelling-house does not of itself constitute a material change so long as the main use of the house remains that of a private residence. On the other hand, the change from a private residence with lodgers to a declared guesthouse, boarding house or private hotel would be material. Difficulties arise with changes of use involving part of a building with secondary

* Town and Country Planning Act, 1962, Section 12. (This Act is a consolidating measure which repealed and re-enacted most of the provisions of the 1947 Act, together with much of the later legislation.)

uses and with the distinction between a material change of use and a mere interruption. Two changes of use are specifically declared in the legislation to be material. First, if a building previously used as a single dwelling-house is used as two or more dwelling-houses (thereby making decision under the Rent Restriction Acts on what constitutes a 'separate dwelling' relevant to planning decisions). Second, the deposit of refuse or waste material on land 'notwithstanding that the land is comprised in a site already used for that purpose, if either the superficial area of the deposit is thereby extended, or the height of the deposit is thereby extended and exceeds the level of the land adjoining the site'; in other words the deposit of refuse or waste material always constitutes development unless the deposit is made in a hole – and the shape of the hole is important because though a hole can be filled to the level of the adjoining land the superficial area must not be increased.

This is by no means the end of the matter, but enough has been recorded to show the breadth of the definition of development and the technical complexities to which it can give rise. Reference must, nevertheless, be made to one further issue. Experience has shown that complicated definitions are necessary if adequate development control is to be achieved, but the same tortuous technique can be used to exclude matters over which control is not necessary. Apart from certain matters which are specifically declared not to constitute development (e.g. internal alterations to buildings, works of road maintenance or improvement carried out by a local highway authority within the boundaries of a road), and others which though possibly constituting development are declared not to require planning permission, there is provision for the Secretary of State to make a *Development Order* specifying classes of 'permitted' development, and a *Use Classes Order* specifying groups of uses within which interchange is permissible.

The Use Classes Order
To deal first with the latter. The *Use Classes Order* prescribes classes of use within which change can take place without constituting development. Thus Class X is 'use as a wholesale warehouse or repository for any purpose', and Class XII is 'use as a residential or boarding school or residential college'. For some classes particular uses which would otherwise fall into a category are specifically excluded: for example, Class I is 'use as a shop for any purpose except as (i) a fried fish shop, (ii) a tripe shop, (iii) a shop for the sale of pet animals or birds, (iv) a cat's-meat shop, (v) a shop for the sale of motor vehicles'. As a result, to change a sweet shop into a book shop does not constitute development, but to change a shoe shop into

a 'noxious trade' such as a tripe shop does. These categories, it should be stressed, refer only to changes of use – not to any building work. Furthermore, the Order gives no freedom to change from one class to another; whether such a change constitutes development depends on whether the change is 'material'. It should also be noted that in granting permission for a particular use a local planning authority may impose conditions restricting that use and thus preventing the changes in use allowed by the Order. For instance, a local planning authority may decide that an office of a special character might be allowed in a residential area but at the same time may not wish the premises to be available for any type of office use. Conditions could be imposed on the planning permission which would overrule the general permission given for such a change in use by the Use Classes Order (Class II is 'use as an office for any purpose').

The General Development Order
The *General Development Order* gives the developer a little more freedom by listing classes of 'permitted development'. If a proposed development falls within these classes then no application for planning permission is necessary – the General Development Order itself constitutes the permission.* The Order includes certain developments by public authorities and nationalized industries, the erection of agricultural buildings (other than dwelling-houses), and permits the change of use from a fried fish shop, a tripe shop, etc. (as listed in Class I of the Use Classes Order), to any other type of shop – but not, of course, the other way round.

Permissions given under this Order are not unqualified. Apart from two 'standard conditions' relating to development which involves making or altering the means of access to a trunk or classified road or which 'creates an obstruction to the view of persons using any road by vehicular traffic at or near any bend, corner, junction or intersection so as to be likely to cause danger to such persons', particular conditions are laid down for each of the different classes of development listed. Thus, under Class I the enlargement, improvement or other alteration of a dwelling-house is permitted (including

* The distinction between the Use Classes Order and the General Development Order is that the former lists changes of use which do not constitute development, while the latter lists activities which, though constituting development, do not require *ad hoc* permission. The distinction was of importance during the time when development charges were imposed, since if there was no 'development' then no development charge was payable, whereas development was, by definition, eligible for a charge. (In fact, however, exemption from development charge was specifically made for many of these permitted developments.) These complexities are now mainly of historical interest and are not discussed further in this book.

the building of a garage) subject to limitations of size and elevation.*

This by no means complete account of 'development' is sufficient for present purposes. The cynic may perhaps be forgiven for commenting that the 'freedom' given by the Use Classes Order and the General Development Order is so hedged by restrictions, and frequently so difficult to comprehend (though he may note with relief that painting is not subject to control – unless it is 'for purposes of advertisement, announcement or direction') that it would be safer to assume that any operation constitutes 'development' and requires planning permission. The framers of the legislation have here been helpful. Application can be made to the local planning authority (either as part of an application for planning permission or as a separate application) for a 'determination' as to whether a proposed

---

* To give an illustration of the detailed way in which the law of planning is drawn up, the following is the full text of Class I of 'permitted development':

Class I: Development within the curtilage of a dwelling-house

Description of development

1. The enlargement, improvement or other alteration of a dwelling-house so long as the cubic content of the original dwelling-house (as ascertained by external measurement) is not exceeded by more than 1,750 cubic feet or one-tenth whichever is the greater, subject to a maximum of 4,000 cubic feet; provided that the erection of a garage, stable, loosebox, or coach-house within the curtilage of the dwelling-house shall be treated as the enlargement of the dwelling-house for the purposes of this permission.

2. The erection, construction or placing, and the maintenance, improvement or other alteration, within the curtilage of a dwelling-house, of any building or enclosure (other than a dwelling, garage, stable, loosebox or coach-house) required for a purpose incidental to the enjoyment of the dwelling-house as such, including the keeping of poultry, bees, pet animals, birds or other livestock for the domestic needs or personal enjoyment of the occupants of the dwelling-house.

Conditions

1. The height of such building shall not exceed the height of the original dwelling-house.
2. No part of such building shall project beyond the forwardmost part of the front of the original dwelling-house.
3. Standard conditions 1 and 2.

1. The height shall not exceed, in the case of a building with a ridged roof, 12 feet, or in any other case, 10 feet.
2. Standard conditions 1 and 2.

Standard Conditions 1 and 2 are:
1. This permission shall not authorize any development which involves the formation, laying out or material widening of a means of access to a trunk or classified road.
2. No development shall be carried out which creates an obstruction to the view of persons using any highway used by vehicular traffic at or near any bend, corner, junction or intersection so as to be likely to cause danger to such persons.

operation constitutes 'development' and, if so, as to whether planning permission is required. Should the local planning authority determine that the proposals do constitute or involve development, they have to inform the applicant of grounds on which they have reached this decision and also of his rights of appeal. Most planning decisions are administrative acts against which appeal lies only to the Secretary of State, but in the case of a determination of whether planning permission is required, the question is a mixed one of fact and law: thus not only is there the normal right of appeal against the local authority's decision to the Secretary of State, there is also a right of appeal against his decision to the High Court.

CONDITIONAL PERMISSIONS

A local planning authority can grant a planning permission subject to conditions. This can be a very useful way of permitting development which would otherwise be undesirable. Thus residential development in an area liable to subsidence can be permitted subject to the condition that the foundations are suitably reinforced, or a garage may be approved in a residential area on condition that 'no panel beating or paint spraying is carried out, and the hours of business are kept within reasonable limits'. The local planning authority's power to impose conditions is a very wide one. The legislation allows them to grant permission subject to 'such conditions as they think fit' – but this does not mean 'as they please'. The conditions must be appropriate from a planning point of view: 'the planning authority are not at liberty to use their powers for an ulterior object, however desirable that object may seem to them to be in the public interest. If they mistake or misuse their powers, however *bona fide*, the court can interfere by declaration and injunction'.* Three types of condition are specifically referred to in the legislation:

(1) Conditions can be imposed for regulating the development or use of *any* land under the control of the applicant, whether or not it is land to which the application relates, so long as there is a definite relationship between the object of the condition and the development permitted.
(2) A 'time condition' can be imposed on a permission. This is referred to in the legislation as 'permission granted for a limited period only'. Such a condition is particularly appropriate where the proposed development is undesirable on a long-term view, but there is no reason why a temporary permission should not be

* *Pyx Granite Co. Ltd.* v. *Ministry of Housing and Local Government*, 1 QB 554, p. 572. This famous case is widely reported in legal texts.

granted. This would occur where a local authority had definite plans for redevelopment in the near future.

(3) A condition can be imposed requiring operations to commence within a specified time. It should be borne in mind that planning permissions normally run with the land. This particular condition can be imposed where the planning proposals for the area will require substantial revision, but the degree of risk that the proposed development will conflict with these proposals is not sufficient to justify outright refusal.

Until the passing of the 1968 Act, there was no general time-limit within which development had to take place: unless a specific condition was imposed, planning permission development could take place at any time. The 1968 Act, however, made all planning permissions subject to a condition that development is begun within five years. If the work is not begun within this time-limit, the permission lapses. The Secretary of State or the local planning authority can vary the period, and there is no bar to the the renewal of permission after the period (whether it be five years or more or less) has elapsed.

The purpose of this new provision is to prevent the accumulation of unused permissions and to discourage the speculative land hoarder. (For this reason they apply to pre-1968 Act permissions as well as later ones.) Accumulated unused permissions could constitute a difficult problem for some local authorities: they created uncertainty and could make an authority reluctant to grant further permissions, which might result in, for example, too great a strain on public services. The new provision is directed towards the bringing forward of development for which permission has been granted and thus to enable new allocations of land for development to be made against a reasonable certain background of pending development.

The provision relates, however, only to the beginning of development and this apparently includes 'digging a trench or putting a peg in the ground'. But (if the permission is not a pre-1968 Act one) the trench-digger may be brought up against a further new provision: served with a *completion notice*. Such a notice states that the planning permission lapses after the expiration of a specified period (of not less than one year). Any work carried out after then becomes liable to enforcement proceedings.

ENFORCEMENT OF PLANNING CONTROL

If the machinery of planning control is to be effective some means of enforcement is essential. Under the pre-war system of interim development control there were no such means. A developer could go ahead without applying for planning permission, or could even ignore a refusal of permission. He took the risk of being compelled to 'undo' his development (e.g. demolish a newly built house) when, and if, the planning scheme was approved, but this was a risk which was often worth taking. And if the development was inexpensive and lucrative (e.g. a petrol station or a greyhound racing track) the risk was virtually no deterrent at all. This flaw in the pre-war system has been remedied. There is now machinery for dealing with development carried out without planning permission or in contravention of conditions laid down in a grant of permission.

Development undertaken without permission is not an offence in itself; but ignoring an 'enforcement' notice is – there is a maximum fine following conviction of £100 and a penalty of £20 for each day during which the requirements of the notice remain unfulfilled.

These are very drastic powers; but there is a number of safeguards. In the first place a local authority can serve an enforcement notice only 'if they consider it expedient to do so having regard to the provisions of the development plan and to any other material considerations'; in short, they must be satisfied that enforcement is necessary 'in the interests of good planning'. Secondly, in the case of building or other operations (but not of material changes of use) the notice must be served within four years of the development being carried out. (Prior to the 1968 Act this 'four year rule' applied to all development including change of use.) Thirdly – and this meets the case of development carried out in good faith, or ignorance – application can be made for retrospective permission. It is hardly likely that a local authority would grant permission for a development against which they had served an enforcement notice, but they could, of course, attach conditions; and for the owner there is the usual right of appeal. Fourthly, there is a right of appeal against an enforcement notice to the Secretary of State and to the courts. Appeal can be made on several grounds, e.g. that permission ought to be granted, that permission has been granted and that no permission is required.

The 1968 Act introduced a further enforcement device: the *stop notice*. This is an attempt to prevent delays in the other enforcement procedures (and advantage being taken of these delays) resulting in the local authority being faced with a *fait accompli*. Previously, when an appeal was lodged against an enforcement notice there was nothing to stop development continuing while the appeal was being 'determined'. The appeal could take several months, particularly in cases where a local inquiry was held. No liability was involved, since, until the enforcement order was made (if it was), no offence was being committed. The stop notice prohibits the continuation of development which is alleged (in the enforcement notice) to be in breach of planning control. Development carried out in contravention of a stop notice constitutes an offence. Local authorities must, however, use this new power with circumspection, since if the enforcement notice is quashed on appeal they are liable to pay compensation for loss due to the stop notice.

REVOCATION, MODIFICATION AND DISCONTINUANCE

The powers of development control possessed by local authorities go considerably further than the granting or withholding cf planning permission. They can interfere with existing uses and revoke a permission already given even if the development has actually been carried out.

A revocation or modification order is made when the development has not been undertaken (or before a change of use has taken place). The local authority must 'have regard to the development plan and to any other material considerations', and an order has to be confirmed by the Secretary of State. Compensation is payable on two grounds: first, for any expenditure or liabilities incurred after the permission has been granted (e.g. expenditure on the preparation of plans); and, second (following the 1954 Act), for the loss in the development value of the land. The logic in the latter is based on the curious situation caused by the abolition of development charges. The granting of planning permission increases the value of the land in question, but since no development charge is now levied the development value is thus given to the owner along with the planning permission. The revocation of that permission deprives the owner of a value which had been specifically given to him, hence compensation is payable. (Before the 1954 Act, logic demanded otherwise. The fact that revocation thereby deprived the owner of potential development value did not in itself warrant compensation, since if permission had been given the development value would be transferred to the State through the development charge.)

A revocation or modification order is not very often made. One case which attracted some attention was that of the Eton Fish and Chip Restaurant. This concerned an application for planning permission to use premises in Eton High Street as a fish and chip restaurant. The Eton Urban District Council granted permission (under delegated powers), but after a petition, mainly from local shopkeepers, decided to seek a revocation order on the ground that 'the existence of a fish and chip restaurant in the High Street would be detrimental to the amenities, would cause nuisance, offences and annoyance to occupiers of properties in the vicinity and to users of the public highway, and would adversely affect the general appearance of the High Street'. The order was confirmed by the Minister. In this particular case it would seem that planning permission had been given after inadequate consideration of publicity. The revocation was therefore a rectification of a 'mistake'.

Quite distinct from these powers is the much wider power to make a Discontinuance Order. This power is expressed in extremely wide language: an order can be made 'if it appears to a local planning authority that it is expedient in the interests of the proper planning of their area (including the interests of amenity)'. Again ministerial confirmation is required and compensation is payable – for depreciation, disturbance and expenses incurred in carrying out works in compliance with the order. Under this power, action can be taken against any development (or use) whether it was specifically permitted under the post-war planning Acts or established prior to the Acts. It would appear that an order will be confirmed only if the case is a strong one. In recently rejecting a discontinuance order on a scrap metal business in an 'attractive residential area', for instance, the Minister said: 'the fact that such a business is out of place in an attractive residential area must be weighed in the light of an important distinction between the withdrawal of existing use rights, as sought in the discontinuance order, and the refusal of new rights'. In this particular case the Minister did 'not feel justified in overriding the proper interests of the objector as long as his business is maintained on an inoffensive scale'. Other cases have established the principle that a stronger case is needed to justify action to bring about the discontinuance of a use than would be needed to warrant a refusal of permission in the first instance.

It needs to be stressed that British planning legislation does not assume – as does American planning – that existing non-conforming uses must disappear if planning policy is to be made effective. This may often be the avowed policy, but the Planning Acts explicitly permit the continuance of existing uses.

This problem of non-conforming uses is an extremely difficult one. As the Uthwatt Committee pointed out:

'The question whether the right to maintain, replace, extend and use an existing building is to subsist in perpetuity, notwithstanding that the building does not conform to the provisions of the scheme is fundamental in relation to the replanning of built-up areas. On the one hand, it would not be equitable, without compensation, at any time and for any reason to remove, or to prohibit the maintenance, replacement, extension or use of an existing building. On the other hand, an unqualified right, unless compensation is paid, to replace non-conforming buildings and to maintain existing uses

permanently is inconsistent with the present conception of planning.
'The problem is one of finding a proper balance between the two considerations.'

The Committee proposed that a 'life' should be placed on non-conforming uses and that at the expiration of that life the use should be brought to an end without compensation. This recommendation was not accepted and thus local planning authorities can extinguish a non-conforming use only by paying compensation: this can be a very expensive business.

CONTROL OF DEVELOPMENT UNDERTAKEN BY GOVERNMENT DEPARTMENTS, LOCAL AUTHORITIES AND STATUTORY UNDERTAKERS

Development by Government Departments does not require planning permission, but there are special arrangements for 'consultations'. The formal procedure is for the Government Department to submit to the local authority a 'Notice of Proposed Development'. 'Representations' can be made to the Department, and 'if the local planning authority has some substantial objection to the proposal which the developing department is unable to meet, the department will inform the Secretary of State, and the two departments will discuss with the authority whether anything can be done to meet the authority's point of view'.

Certain classes of development are excluded from the requirement for consultation, namely:

(a) secret development;
(b) minor operations and unimportant changes of use in which the local planning authority is unlikely to be interested because what is proposed will not materially affect the character of the neighbourhood;
(c) proposals for further buildings similar in type and demands on public services to those already existing on a site in their possession unless the buildings abut on a public highway or might be considered to affect amenity (either directly or in relation to eventual removal).

It is the Government Department which has the final say in any matters affecting their land. The legislation merely allows agreements to be made to ensure that, so far as is possible, their developments will be in harmony with the provisions of a development plan or the requirements of good planning.

Development undertaken by local authorities and statutory undertakers is subject to special planning procedures. ('Statutory undertakers' are defined as 'persons authorized by any enactment to carry
on any railway, light railway, road transport, water transport, canal,
inland navigation, dock, harbour, pier or lighthouse undertaking,
or any undertaking for the supply of electricity, gas, hydraulic
power or water'.) Where a development requires the authorization
of a Government Department (as do developments involving compulsory purchase orders, work requiring loan sanction, and developments
such as local authority housing on which Government grants are
paid) the authorization is usually accompanied by 'deemed planning
permission'. Much of the normal development of local authorities
and statutory undertakers (e.g. road works, laying of underground
mains and cables) is 'permitted development' under the General
Development Order. Local planning authorities are also 'deemed'
to have permission for any development in their area which accords
with the provisions of the development plan. The Secretary of State
has power, however, to require them to apply for his permission in any
particular case. Other local authorities (including those exercising
delegated powers) are normally required to obtain planning permission from the local planning authority. If a local planning
authority wishes to develop in the area of another planning authority
they must apply to the authority for planning permission in the same
way as would a private developer. Thus a county borough which
wishes to develop an overspill housing estate in the adjacent
county has to obtain planning permission from that county. In
all these cases there is the right of appeal to the Secretary of
State.

Statutory undertakers wishing to carry out development which is
neither 'permitted development' nor authorized by a Government
Department have to apply for planning permission to the local
planning authority in the normal way, but in the case of 'operational
land' appeals are considered jointly by the Secretary of State and the
'appropriate Minister'. ('Operational land' is land which, in respect
of its nature and situation, is not 'comparable with land in general'.
This is a rather imprecise definition, but land used for railway
sidings or a gas works is operational land whereas land used for
showrooms or offices is not.) Until recently statutory undertakers
could be 'controlled' only on the payment of compensation by the
local planning authority.

The privileged position of statutory undertakers has not escaped
criticism, and two highly controversial developments proposed in
1967 created a public outcry. The first was the proposal by the Southern Gas Board to erect a 128-feet-high gasholder in the historic

centre of Abingdon. The second was the proposal by the Gas Council for a terminal at Bacton in East Anglia to process North Sea Gas.

In the former case the Minister withdrew the Gas Board's right of 'permitted development' and planning permission for the gasholder was refused. Compensation of £250,000 was involved and this was met on a 50–50 basis between the local authorities concerned and the Gas Board.

In the Bacton case, permission for development was given after two exhaustive public inquiries, but subject to rigorous conditions.

These cases brought matters to a head. The original justification for the special position of statutory undertakers was that they are under an obligation to· provide services to the public and cannot, like a private firm in planning difficulties, go elsewhere. If a planning authority wished to restrict their activities, it was held that it was right for the extra costs to be reimbursed.

In the debates on the 1968 Town and Country Planning Bill the Minister said that the climate of opinion had now changed. It was still necessary for planning to pay sensible attention to the need to provide essential public services economically. But modern industrial undertakings had to be prepared to conduct their businesses in a way which minimized ugliness and to accept any reasonable cost involved in making their buildings, plant and operations acceptable to public opinion.

A working party of officials of statutory undertakers and Government Departments was set up to consider the planning implications of developments by statutory undertakers and to review the relevant planning legislation. The first fruits of their work were new provisions now incorporated in the 1968 Act. The Act provides that no land which is not already operational can become such unless certain planning requirements are met. The most important of these is that there shall be a specific planning permission for development for operational purposes. The Act also breaches the long-standing compensation principle. Compensation for refusal of planning permission is abolished in certain types of case.

At the time of writing the working party was reviewing other aspects of the planning control of statutory undertakers.

In the previous edition of this book this section ended with the comment that though statutory undertakers and Government Departments must consult with local planning authorities, they are either exempted from planning provisions or are effectively beyond their reach. This statement is no longer true, and it is likely that it will become even less so in the future.

CARAVANS

Caravan sites are subject to special provisions contained in Part I of the Caravan Sites and Control of Development Act, 1960, and the Caravan Sites Act, 1968.

Sir Arton Wilson's report, *Caravans as Homes*, highlighted the problems of residential caravanning. In 1959 about 60,000 caravans in England and Wales were being used as homes by some 150,000 people – mainly young married couples, often with small children. About 80 per cent of caravan dwellers hoped to move into normal dwellings. To quote the report, they live in carvans 'because they could not get other dwellings in the right places or on the right terms; or because caravans meet their needs for cheapness, convenience or mobility'. Some simply like caravan life.

The report estimated that about 38,000 of the 60,000 caravans were on sites for which permission, usually conditional or temporary, had been given; about 12,000 had 'existing use' rights; and about 10,000 were on sites which appeared to contravene planning control. With some notable exceptions, local authorities tended to regard caravans as a substandard form of accommodation and (less debatably) difficult to control. (It was the publicity given to a case in Egham which led to the setting up of the Arton Wilson Committee.) The caravan interests, on the other hand, argued the case for recognition of caravanning as an acceptable way of life and pressed for more positive approaches by the local authorities.

The 1960 Act gave local authorities new powers to control caravan sites, including a requirement that all caravan sites had to be licensed before they could start operating (thus closing loopholes in the planning and public health legislation). These controls over caravan sites operate in addition to the normal planning system: thus both planning permission and a licence has to be obtained. Most of the Act dealt with control, but local authorities were given wider powers to provide caravan sites.

The *Policy Note* on caravans states that: 'Planning policy recognizes the demand for sites. The main objectives of policy are, first, to enable the demand to be met in the right places, while preventing sites from springing up in the wrong places; and, second, to allow caravan sites, where permitted, to be established on a permanent or long-term basis, in order to facilitate the provision of proper services and equipment and to allow the occupants reasonable security of tenure.'[23]

In fact, of the 5,294 residential caravan planning applications decided in 1969, a quarter were refused and two-thirds were granted for a limited period only. Only 489 were granted without a time-limit.

Local authorities face strong pressure from their ratepayers 'to preserve local amenities and property values', to which caravans are seen as a threat. The DOE may be clear as to what 'planning policy recognizes' but the reality differs considerably from the official statement.

One group of caravanners is particularly unpopular: gypsies, or to give them their less romantic statutory description 'persons of nomadic life, whatever their race or origin' (but excluding 'members of an organized group of travelling showmen, or persons engaged in travelling circuses, travelling together as such'). The appalling conditions in which the majority of the 15,000 gypsies live in England and Wales were portrayed in the 1967 report of the Department's Sociological Research Section, *Gypsies and Other Travellers*.* As was stated in the foreword to this report, the basic problem is that no one wants gypsies around: 'all too often the settled community is concerned chiefly to persuade, or even force, the gypsy families to move on'. Under Part II of the Caravan Sites Act, 1968, local authorities in England and Wales (but not Scotland) have a duty to provide adequate sites for gypsies 'residing in or resorting to' their areas.

Holiday caravans are subject to the same planning and licensing controls as residential caravans. To ensure that a site is used only for holidays (and not for 'residential purposes'), planning permission can include a condition limiting the use of a site to the holiday season. Conditions may also be imposed to require the caravans to be removed at the end of each season or to require a number of pitches on a site to be reserved for touring caravans.

The *Policy Note* states that it is the aim 'to steer holiday caravan development to a limited number of areas, usually those in which caravans are already established, rather than allow them to be scattered more widely'.

In 1969, of the 1,657 planning applications for holiday caravan sites, 48 per cent were refused, 36 per cent granted for a limited period and 16 per cent granted without a time-limit.

PURCHASE NOTICES

A planning refusal does not of itself confer any right to compensation. On the other hand, revocations of planning permission or interference with existing uses do rank for compensation, since they involve a taking-away of an existing right. There are other circumstances in which planning controls so affect the value of the land to the owner that some means of reducing the hardship is clearly desirable. For example, the allocation of land in a development plan for a school

* See also the Scottish Report, *Scotland's Travelling People*, HMSO, 1971.

will probably reduce the value of houses on this land or even make them completely unsaleable. In such cases the affected owner can serve a notice on the local authority requiring them to purchase the property at an 'unblighted' price. Broadly, such a *purchase notice* can be served, if, as a result of a planning action, land becomes 'incapable of reasonable beneficial use'. In all cases ministerial confirmation is required. The cases in which a purchase notice can be served include:*

(i) refusal or conditional grant of planning permission;
(ii) revocation or modification of planning permission;
(iii) discontinuance of use;
(iv) 'planning blight'.

Normally, if an owner is refused permission to develop his land (or, if onerous conditions are laid down) there is nothing he can do about it – except, of course, to appeal to the Secretary of State. But, if the refusal or the conditions prevent him from obtaining 'reasonably beneficial use' of the land, he can serve a purchase notice. 'The question to be considered in every case is whether the land in its existing state and with its existing permissions (including operations and uses for which planning permission is not required) is incapable of reasonably beneficial use. In considering what capacity for use the land has, relevant factors are the physical state of the land, its size, shape and surroundings, and the general pattern of use in the area. A use of relatively low value may be reasonably beneficial if such a use is common for similar land in the neighbourhood.'[10]

A purchase notice is not intended to apply to a case in which an owner is simply prevented from realizing the full potential value of his land. This would imply the acceptance in principle of paying compensation for virtually all refusals and conditional permissions. It is only if the existing and permitted uses of the land are so seriously affected as to render the land incapable of reasonably beneficial use that the owner can take advantage of the purchase notice procedure.

Blight Notices

The redress by way of a purchase notice provided for owners affected by planning blight was introduced in 1959 (and extended in 1968, since when it has been termed a *blight notice*). The object is to deal with the problems presented to certain classes of owners by the fact that a development is planned to take place on their land at some future (probably uncertain) date. A development plan may, for instance, show the line of a proposed road, though not necessarily

* The 1968 Act makes corresponding provisions in relation to listed building consent. See pp. 169-70.

the year in which it is to be constructed. In the meantime, an owner who wishes to move and sell his property has to wrestle with the problem of 'blight'. These purchases notice provisions are restricted to owner-occupiers of houses and small businesses who can show that they have made reasonable attempts to sell their property but have found it impossible to do so except at a substantially depreciated price because of certain defined planning actions. These include land designated for compulsory purchase or allocated or defined by a development plan for any functions of a Government Department, local authority, statutory undertaker or the National Coal Board; and land on which the Secretary of State has given written notice of his intention to provide a trunk road or a 'special road' (i.e. a motorway).

The gradual introduction of the new type of development plan under the 1968 Act has involved new provisions in relation to planning blight. Briefly, the effect of these is that in those areas where a structure plan comes into force, blight caused by either the structure plan or the previous development plan is covered by the planning blight provisions until a local plan allocating land succeeds the old development plan. That local plan then becomes the relevant plan for the blight provision. Since local plans will provide a much more precise indication of the possibility of public acquisition of any land, the structure plan will no longer be relevant.

Structure plans, however, will lack this precise indication. Whether they will give rise to more or to less planning blight than the old development plan system remains to be seen. The Planning Advisory Group thought it unlikely that there would be any more and, 'in so far as they show less detail (e.g. town map primary school and minor open space allocations) it may be less'. On the other hand, in the debates on the Bill, it was officially stated that:

'When we are dealing with the structure plan for which there is no local plan in force, we have a new problem which is that, owing to the diagrammatic nature of the plans, no one will be able to say with certainty that this does or does not affect the claimant's property, but that nevertheless, because of that very uncertainty, a wider number of properties may be affected.'

But how far is it possible to go with compensation for planning blight?* Or, to put the matter in its broader context, how far ahead is it possible to plan in a democratic society? Some discussion of the problem is to be found in the final chapter; here it is sufficient

* See the debate on the Private Member's *Planning Blight and Worsenment Bill*, H.C. Debates, February 27, 1970. (The Bill, introduced by Mr Walter Clegg, failed to get a second reading.) Following the debate, the Ministry issued a circular (46/70) of guidance to local authorities which, *inter alia*, urged them to use their existing discretionary powers of purchase in appropriate cases.

to note that the 1968 Act effects a compromise. Compensation is payable for blight, except in cases where a planning proposal is not precisely defined and the local authority have a genuine doubt as to whether they will eventually need the land, yet are sure that they will not require it for at least fifteen years. In such cases a blight notice is met by a *counter-notice*, known in jargon as the 'fifteen-year counter-notice'.

It is at points such as this that even complex legislation reaches its limit and resort has to be had to ministerial exhortation and discretionary powers. Hardship cases should, according to official statements and ministerial circulars, be treated as sympathetically as possible. Unless there is little likelihood of a proposal being implemented in the foreseeable future (in which case this should be clearly and firmly stated 'so that prospective purchasers are not unnecessarily deterred'), hardship cases should be dealt with by 'discretionary purchase'. Loan sanction and any relevant Exchequer grant is normally given in such cases.

THE NEW DEVELOPMENT PLANS

The Report of the Planning Advisory Group

The system of development plans and development control set up under the Town and Country Planning Act of 1947 operated for two decades without significant change. During this time the system proved its value but it would be surprising if what was appropriate for the mid-'forties was equally relevant to the 'seventies. Furthermore, not only has the tempo of social and economic change increased but also the system has tended to develop its own rigidities. This is particularly the case with development plans. Unlike the 1932 Act 'schemes', they were intended to show only broad land-use allocations. But the definition of 'development plan' in the 1947 Act is a plan 'indicating the manner in which the local planning authority propose that land in their area should be used'. This, together with the way in which plans are mapped, has led inexorably towards greater detail and precision. 'The plans have thus acquired the appearance of certainty and stability which is misleading since the primary use zonings may themselves permit a wide variety of use within a particular allocation, and it is impossible to forecast every land requirement over many years ahead.'

Above all, 'it has proved extremely difficult to keep these plans not only up to date but forward looking and responsive to the demands of change. The result has been that they have tended to become out of date – in terms of technique in that they deal inadequately with transport and the interrelationship of traffic and land

D

use; in factual terms in that they fail to take account quickly enough of changes in population forecasts, traffic growth and other economic and social trends; and in terms of policy in that they do not reflect more recent developments in the field of regional and urban planning. Over the years the plans have become more and more out of touch with emergent planning problems and policies, and have in many cases become no more than local land-use maps.'

In short, the system has become out of tune with contemporary needs and forward thinking, and it is becoming bogged down in details and cumbersome procedures. The quality of planning is suffering and delays are beginning to bring the system into disrepute. As a result public acceptability, which is the basic foundation of the system, is beginning to crumble.

Certain changes could be – and were – made within the framework of the existing legislation, but these did not go far enough. [14, 15]

It was within this context of thinking that the Planning Advisory Group was set up in May 1964 to review the broad structure of the planning system and, in particular, development plans. Their report, *The Future of Development Plans*, published in 1965, proposed a basic change which would distinguish between the policy or strategic issues and the detailed tactical issues. Only the former would be submitted for ministerial approval: the latter would be for local decision within the framework of the approved policy.

For urban areas with populations over 50,000 a new type of *urban plan* was proposed which concentrated on the broad pattern of future development and redevelopment and dealt with the land-use/ transport relationships in an integrated way, but which excluded the detailed land-use allocations of the present town maps. Similarly for the counties a new form of *county plan* was proposed which dealt with the distribution of population and employment, the major communications network, the main policies for recreation and conservation, green belts, and the general development policy for towns and villages.

These were to provide a coherent framework of planning policy and would be submitted for ministerial approval. Each would identify *action areas* which would require comprehensive planning and on which action would be concentrated over the next ten years or so.

Local planning authorities would have power to prepare *local plans*, which would not be submitted for approval, but would conform with the policies laid down in the urban plan or county plan. These would serve as a guide to development control and a basis for the more positive aspects of environmental planning. The most significant of local plans would be those for the action areas. Ministerial approval of the action areas would be limited to the policy proposed, and the local planning authorities would prepare *action area plans*, which would provide the detailed basis for implementation.

These types of plans could not be produced by planning authorities acting in isolation: they needed to form part of a regional strategy and also of what was termed a sub-regional pattern. Here – assuming a continuation of the present structure of local government – the regional context would be provided by the Economic Planning Councils and Boards:

'These are likely to be primarily concerned with creating the conditions for economic growth in some regions and controlling the pace of growth in others, within the framework of national economic planning. As a part of this process they will have to be concerned with physical planning issues which are of regional significance, with the overall distribution of population and employment, green belt policy and any other limitations on growth in the conurbations. They must also encompass other physical factors of regional significance such as communications, water resources and major industrial projects; the economic implications of major development projects (motorways, docks, airports); and the impact of economic decisions on physical planning. It will consequently be necessary to associate local planning authorities with the regional planning process and to ensure that their development plans give effect to the intentions of the regional plan.'[16]

THE 1968 PLANNING ACT

Following a White Paper, *Town and Country Planning*, published in June 1967, legislative effect to the Planning Advisory Group's proposal was given by the Town and Country Planning Acts of 1968 (for England and Wales) and 1969 (for Scotland). These provide for structure plans and local plans; among the latter an important category is the action area plan.

Structure Plans

A *structure plan*, which has to be submitted to the Secretary of State for his approval, is primarily a written statement of policy, accompanied by diagrammatic illustrations for counties and major towns. Its range is considerably wider than the present development plans. It deals with broad land-use policies (but not with detailed land allocations) and with policies for the management of traffic and the improvement of 'the physical environment'. The legislation provides that the written statement *must*:

(*a*) formulate the local planning authority's policy and general proposals in respect of the development and other use of land in that area (including measures for the improvement of the physical environment and the management of traffic);

(b) state the relationship of those proposals to general proposals for the development and the other use of land in neighbouring areas which may be expected to affect that area; and

(c) contain such other matters as may be prescribed or as the Secretary of State may in any particular case direct.

The term 'plan' is perhaps misleading, since it might be expected to involve a map; but there is to be no map. Unlike the previous development plans (which required county and town maps, with related programme maps), the structure plan has to be accompanied only by 'diagrams, illustrations, and descriptive matter'.

The plan has to 'have regard to current policies with respect to the economic planning and development of the region as a whole' and 'to the resources likely to be available' for its implementation. High ideals must therefore be tempered by the facts of life.

Of particular note is the character of the survey which is to precede the plan. Differences in the content and scope of the surveys required under the earlier and the new legislation highlight the major change in planning philosophy. The earlier legislation is largely concerned with land use: 'a *development plan* means a plan indicating the manner in which a local planning authority propose that land in their area should be used'. The 'survey' required as a preliminary to this dealt predominantly with physical matters. Under the new legislation, emphasis is laid on major economic and social forces and on broad policies or 'strategies' for large areas. The 'survey' becomes a major part of the planning process. Unlike the earlier legislation, the Acts spell out the coverage of the survey. In the forefront are 'the principal physical and economic characteristics' of the area and, to the extent that they are relevant, of neighbouring areas as well. In formulating the structure plan, particular attention has to be paid 'to current policies with respect to the economic planning and development of the region as a whole' and to likely availability of resources. It is within this strategic framework that 'local plans' are to be drawn up.

The structure plan is essentially a statement of general policy designed to channel major forces in socially and economically desirable directions.

Another major change follows from this. Under the '1947 philosophy', a development plan had to be reviewed at least once every five years' and, for this purpose, fresh surveys had to be carried out. This proved totally impracticable for reasons already outlined. Under the new system the 'survey' is a continuing operation. Though some authorities already adopt this approach, the 1947 concept implied an assembly and interpretation of 'survey material' which was reviewed quinquennially and which led to an amendment of the development plan. The new concept sheds a mass of detail and focuses attention on the major trends: the continual review is designed to ensure that the strategy remains appropriate and adequate. The review relates essentially to the survey; when the review indicates that the structure plan is in need of alteration, the local planning authority will take the initiative of drawing up a new plan. Alternatively, the Secretary of State can direct an authority to submit proposals for an alteration to its structure plan if he regards it to be necessary in view of, for instance, major proposals in another area which will have an impact in the authority's area.

There is another significant difference in the wording of the requirement for a survey in the new Act. Whereas the earlier Acts required a local authority 'to carry out' a survey, the new legislation refers to the duty to *institute* a survey. This change was deliberately designed to facilitate the employment of consultants. As was stated in the Debates, 'the kind of surveys which we envisage would have to be made for some plans will require considerable expertise in fields where manpower is scarce. Some authorities will have been fortunate and have been able to recruit staff with those skills, but others will not. If there are outside consultants available who are able and willing to do the job, that will be satisfactory.'

Action Areas
Structure plans will 'indicate' *action areas* where major change by development, redevelopment or improvement may be expected. This, ideally, will involve more than simply picking out areas where the local authority think that action is needed. The intention is that the survey will identify and outline problems which require action; the written statement of the structure plan will discuss these problems, determine priorities and indicate areas where action is required not only on a comprehensive basis, but also at an early date. It will also discuss the nature of the required action, its extent and its feasibility in financial terms.

Action areas, it should be noted, are to be *indicated*, not *defined*. This deliberate wording was chosen for two reasons. First, if the boundaries of an action area were to be defined precisely and be subject (as part of the structure plan) to ministerial approval, this would involve the very thing which the new system is designed to avoid: detailed consideration by the Department and the embodiment of inflexible proposals in a statutory document. Second, it was thought likely that it would intensify the problems of planning blight.

If boundaries were drawn on a map they would most probably have to be redrawn when more detailed plans were prepared. Thus, some people who thought they would be affected would find that they had been misled, and others who thought they would not be affected would find that they were in fact within an action area. Objections would be made to a structure plan on the basis of individual interests rather than on the basis of the general nature of the proposals.

In short, the definition of an action area would be foreign to the essential concept underlying the structure plan – that it deals with general issues in broad terms; it is a policy document not a physical design plan. Fundamentally it is a matter of words and diagrams, not of maps.

Having given 'adequate publicity' to a structure plan (a matter which is discussed at length in Chapter XIII) it is submitted to the Secretary of State (who may approve it in whole or in part and with or without modifications and reservations; or reject it). Objections can be made, as with the old development plans, and a local inquiry may be held.

Local Plans

Essentially, a local plan is detailed elaboration of proposals sketched out as matters of broad policy in a structure plan. It will consist of a written statement, a map on an ordnance survey base, together with 'diagrams, illustrations and descriptive matter'. Regulations are to be made regarding the form and content of local plans.* The Acts provide for a great deal of flexibility – a matter which, in the Debates, the Ministers pleaded was essential to the underlying conception. It is envisaged that local plans will vary greatly. Where the proposed development is to be undertaken by a local authority, the local plan will be detailed. Thus those affected will know clearly what is proposed. But where the intention is that the development is to be undertaken privately, the local plan will simply provide broad guide-lines. To quote a ministerial statement:

'I think we are agreed that one of the defects of the present system is its negative nature and that planning authorities are not able to play the useful and constructive role in positive planning which we would like to see them play. We believe that some of the local plans of the kind that I have been indicating – that would give general broad indications for the developer – would take the form, as it were, of a brief for the developer and his architect. It might, for example, state the general objectives of the plan and the broad outlines of the

---

* See Appendix to this Chapter.

way in which the planning authority envisaged that they would be achieved. The proper groupings of usages within the area, the density and height of buildings on the site, provision for proper circulation of vehicles and foot passengers – matters of this kind will be indicated in the plan. It does not follow by any means that in such a case the planning authority would need to, or would want to, lay down at the plan-making stage the details of the buildings that it wants to see on the site to achieve the objectives of good design and satisfactory treatment of the environment. I think it will generally be considered advantageous to leave scope within the main framework for the imagination and initiative of private developers.'

The most radical feature of a local plan is that at no time does it require to be approved by the Secretary of State (though he has the power to direct that a local plan 'shall not have effect' unless he approves it: this is a reserve power intended to be used only in the exceptional case). The policy which it embodies has to be set out in an approved structure plan, but its elaboration and adoption are entirely a matter for the local authority. This revolutionary innovation goes to the very kernel of the philosophy underlying the new legislation – that the Department should be concerned only with important issues, and that local responsibility in local matters should become a reality.

There are four safeguards. First, this part of the Act applies only to selected authorities ('We propose to give these powers only to those local authorities which we believe will operate them responsibly'). Second, the local plans must be drawn up within the framework of the approved structure plan and must conform with the policy which is there set out. Third, the local authority are required to give 'adequate publicity' to their proposals *before* they are included in a local plan and to give 'adequate opportunity' for the making of representations on their proposals. In these and similar ways 'citizen-participation' is actually written into the legislation. Fourth (with one important difference), the normal statutory procedure will apply for the deposit of plans, the making of objections and the holding of a hearing or inquiry by an independent inspector. This will include the publication of the inspector's report.

The important difference from the traditional procedure is that the inspector will report to the local authority, not to the Secretary of State. This follows, of course, from the principle that the local plan is a local authority, not a central authority, matter.

It is clear that citizen-participation is more than a desirable adjunct to the new system – it is an essential feature. If citizen-participation fails, so will the system.

Citizen-participation is discussed, within a wider context, in the final chapter of this book.

Implementing the 1968 Planning Act
The new development plan system cannot be instituted quickly. Quite apart from the difficulties of changing over to a new style of plan, many local authorities are quite incompetent to handle the new system, either because of staffing or because of the irrelevance of their boundaries to the problems which beset them. To use the more diplomatic words of the White Paper, 'some local planning authorities lack the resources to make an immediate start on the new system, and some well-organized authorities administer areas which make it difficult for them to draw up a satisfactory structure plan of the new type'. But to await the reorganization of local government would have involved a very considerable delay (how long only time will show) and would have held back those authorities who are keen and able to make a start. Furthermore, a gradual introduction of the new system has the positive advantage of enabling experience to be gained before it becomes operative over the country as a whole. Thus the decision was taken to go ahead in advance of the establishment of an appropriate local government system.

This is being done in two ways. First, a 'forward structure plan programme' is being implemented under which the majority of planning authorities in England (outside London) together with a number of South Wales authorities are involved with the Department in discussions and preliminary work on structure plan preparation. Second, the substantive structure and local plan provisions are being brought into operation by a series of commencement orders relating to particular areas. The first of these, made in July 1971, related to the Teesside area, comprising Teeside County Borough and certain adjoining areas of the administrative counties of the North Riding of Yorkshire and Durham. Further commencement orders will be made following consultation with the local planning authorities concerned.

In the London area, the aim is to introduce the new system as soon as possible as part of the follow-up to the South-East Joint Planning Study, but this must await decisions on the regional strategy which are to be formulated in the light of consultation under way.

In Scotland, progress appears likely to be rather slower. A circular of July 1971 stated that it was intended to effect the transfer of the new system gradually, but local authorities were urged to begin revising the content of their development plans 'to accord with the needs of the new system'. Gentle pressure is being exerted to bring about co-operation between authorities which have not always worked together harmoniously:

'Pending local government reorganization, structure plans under the new system will frequently be appropriate for areas covering more than one local planning authority. In formulating their up-to-date policies for development planning, authorities will therefore have to consult much more widely with nearby authorities than has been usual in the past. Before some authorities can be formally transferred to the new system it may be necessary, in order to secure a satisfactory structure plan, to ask a group of authorities to act jointly'.[37]

This is an eloquent testimony to the inadequacy of the present local government structure. It is with good reason that the circular states that the Secretary of State does not propose to make any commencement order 'in the immediate future'.

PLANNING FOR TRAFFIC

Between 1950 and 1960 the number of vehicles on the roads of Great Britain doubled, to $9\frac{1}{2}$ million. By 1970 the number had increased to 15 million. The proportion of households with a car rose from less that a third in 1961 to over a half in 1970.

This enormous increase in traffic and the resultant urban thrombosis to which it has given rise is too striking and obvious to require detailed documentation. What is less apparent is the even greater rate of increase which may be anticipated in the future. There is a prospect of 27 million vehicles by 1980 and perhaps 40 million by 2010.

Coping with this flood of traffic presents extremely difficult problems. Road 'improvements' can easily destroy the town as a residential environment and, furthermore, be self-defeating. As American experience has shown: 'The greater the expenditures have been, the greater has become the need. With it all, no city can say, regardless of how much it has poured into providing conveniences for its motorists, that it does not have far more congestion and far greater inconvenience today than when it embarked on its costly venture.'[64]

One of the fundamental problems here is that of the location of traffic-generating uses. Until recently, attention was focused (as in the Barlow Report) on the heavy concentration of employment in central areas, the movement of population to outer areas and the resultant increase in commuting. The 'overspill' policy was the official answer to this. If jobs could be moved out along with population the traffic pressures on the central areas would be reduced and travel-to-work journeys reduced. It is coming to be realized that the situation is now much more complex than this. In London, for instance, the tide has turned and the working population of the inner areas is falling. At the same time an increasingly complex web of movements (largely made possible by the freedom provided by the motor car) is developing in Greater London and beyond.

Policy on this issue is currently in a stage of agonizing reappraisal. There is much talk of 'restructuring' major urban areas, but there is a noticeable note of doubt in the debates. Increasingly, emphasis is given to 'flexibility' – an admirable concept, but one which is difficult to reconcile with the fact that roads are far from flexible. They have to be planned ahead and, once built, become a major factor in the situation even if the assumptions on which they were planned are falsified.

The Buchanan Report

A major landmark in the development of thought in this field was the Buchanan Report.[56] This is a masterly survey which surmounts the administrative separatism which has until recently prevented the comprehensive co-ordination of the planning and location of buildings on the one hand and the planning and management of traffic on the other. With due acknowledgement of the necessarily crude nature of the methods and assumptions used, the Report proposes as a basic principle the canalization of larger traffic movements on to properly designed networks servicing areas within which environments suitable for a civilized urban life can be developed. The two main ideas here are for 'primary road networks' and 'environmental areas'.

'There must be areas of good environment – urban rooms – where people can live, work, shop, look about and move around on foot in reasonable freedom from the hazards of motor traffic, and there must be a complementary network of roads – urban corridors – for effecting the primary distribution of traffic to the environmental areas'.

This simple concept is not, of course, new, but the urgency of the need for its application on the scale required presents enormous problems. A striking result of the case studies included in the Report is the great scale of the networks and interchanges that are needed. The capital cost of the new primary distribution roads in the Newbury Scheme, for example, would be about £4½ million. But, as the accompanying report of the Steering Committee (the Crowther

Report) points out, 'This would be once-for-all expenditure. It is estimated that the motor vehicles registered in the Newbury area will pay in 1963 about £770,000 in licence duty and fuel duty. By 1983 it is estimated that the vehicles registered will be paying (assuming unchanged rates) at the rate of £1,560,000. This admittedly crude calculation serves to show "what a fund of future revenue there is available to finance a programme of urban redevelopment".'

But what of the alternatives? Buchanan stressed that the general lesson is unavoidable: 'If the scale of road works and reconstruction seems frightening then a lesser scale will suffice *provided there is less traffic.*' Crowther argues that the scope for deliberate limitations on the use of vehicles in towns would be almost impossible to enforce, even if a car-owning electorate were prepared to accept such limitations in principle. Not all would agree and, as traffic grows, the practical possibilities of the various forms of pricing assume an increased significance. Indeed, it is striking how far opinion on this has changed over the last few years. The White Paper, *Transport in London*, published in 1968, could say quite blandly (as could not have been said a decade earlier):

'The control of traffic must be regarded as a deliberate part of highway and transport planning. In many cases regulation is appropriate. But the price mechanism is often more flexible and more sensitive. It may in time prove possible and worthwhile to reflect in charging systems the costs which journeys on overcrowded roads impose on other road users. Meanwhile, parking charges and time-limits can provide effective control. There will have to be control of all street parking in inner London – with preference being given to short-term callers for whom the use of public transport may well be less convenient than for the regular commuter, and to residents. And there will also have to be control over the amount of privately available off-street parking space in new developments which attract a significant number of workers. (In the past, such space has often encouraged additional car commuting.) The GLC has recently announced new policies along these lines. Finally, there is need to control the ways in which publicly available off-street car parks can be used.'

To return to Buchanan, the great danger in his view lies in the temptation to seek a middle course between a massive investment in replanning and a curtailing of the use of vehicles 'by trying to cope with a steadily increasing volume of traffic by means of minor alterations resulting in the end in the worst of both worlds – poor traffic access and a grievously eroded environment'.

Improvement of public transport by itself is no answer to this, though it must be an essential part of an overall plan; indeed, the case studies show that it is quite impossible to dispense with public transport. The implication is that there must be a planned co-ordination between transport systems, particularly with regard to the work journeys in concentrated centres. On this, the Report recommended that 'transportation plans' should be included as part of the statutory development plans. This has now been accepted and passed into legislation by the 1968 Town and Country Planning Act (though its implementation will take many years). But of equal importance is the momentous Transport Act passed in the same year. Many of the provisions of this lie outside the scope of the present book, though they are by no means irrelevant to the issues selected for discussion. Attention here is focused on the integration of transport planning with 'town planning' and the establishment of new transport planning authorities in some of the conurbations.

TRAFFIC PLANNING MACHINERY

The 1967 White Paper *Public Transport and Traffic* opened on a lyrical note: 'one of the most precious achievements of modern civilization is mobility. It enriches social life and widens experience'. It continued by stressing the implications for planning and transport policy:

'To build mobility into the urban and rural life of this crowded island without destroying the other elements of good living must be one of the major purposes of transport policy. To achieve this, far-reaching changes in attitudes and administration will be necessary. The provision of transport – whether public or private – can no longer be considered in isolation from other developments. It must be built into the whole planning of our community life so that no factory is sited, no housing estate or "overspill" developed, no town re-planned without the implications for the movement of people and goods having been studied and incorporated from the outset.'

This, of course, is the rationale for the new type of development plans which will treat basic transport planning as a part of the general planning of the structure of each locality. But the important point is that 'basic transport planning' means far more than 'road planning', particularly since no conceivable road investment programme could support city structures designed on the basis that nearly all journeys were to be made by private car. (And it must not be forgotten that there will always be a significant proportion of households without cars. Even in the United States this is a fifth.)

In short, 'our major towns and cities can only be made to work effectively and to provide a decent environment for living by giving a new dynamic role to public transport as well as expanding facilities for private cars'.

Five 'principles of organization' flow from this:

1. Since local authorities are responsible for 'planning' they must be the authorities responsible for public transport.

2. All transport matters for which local authorities are to be responsible – the improvement of the local road network, investment in public transport, traffic management measures, the balance between public and private transport – must be focused in an integrated transport plan, which in its turn is related to the general planning for each area.

3. Investment in local public transport must be grant-aided by central government just as investment in the principal road network receives 75 per cent Exchequer grant.

4. The main network of public transport must be publicly owned.

5. The planning and operation of public transport can only be done intelligently over areas which make sense in transport terms. In some of the major urban areas the traffic situation is so bad and is deteriorating so rapidly that reorganization cannot await general legislation on local government.

Passenger Transport Authorities

The Transport Act, 1968, gives the Secretary of State power to set up Passenger Transport Authorities where he 'considers it expedient for the purpose of securing the provision of a properly integrated and efficient system of public transport to meet the needs of that area'. The first four areas are Greater Manchester, Merseyside, the West Midlands and Tyneside. (Elsewhere the problems are considered to be less acute and can await the reorganization of local government though voluntary co-ordinating machinery has been established.) In drawing the boundaries of the PTA areas, the main criterion has been the travel-to-work data from the 1966 Census. Account has, however, been taken of major expected developments: thus Redditch (a new town planned to take 33,000 people from Birmingham by the mid-'seventies, many of whom are expected to work in the conurbation) is included even though it currently has relatively insignificant passenger movements to and from the conurbation.

Each PTA consists of two bodies – the Authority which is concerned with policy, and an Executive which is responsible for the implementation of policy and for day-to-day management. A major first task of the Executive is to prepare a plan, for approval by the Authority, setting out 'proposals for the development of a system of public transport capable of serving the needs of the Area'. The Executive will also 'as an essential first step' take under control all the municipal bus undertakings in the Area.

Finally (in this selective summary account) the Executive will have to reach agreement with the Railways Board for the rail services which they require and will be responsible for providing any new systems of public transport which they (and, of course, the Authority) consider are needed in the Area. January 1972 has been set as the date for this provision to come into operation. All four PTAs will then have the duty of reviewing the local rail passenger services, deciding which are necessary for the passenger transport system of their Areas and reaching agreement with the Railways Board for their operation. The official announcement (made in July 1971) stated that, 'in this way the PTAs will be able to exert an effective influence over the local rail services and this will help them in the discharge of their statutory duty to secure the provision of an effective and efficient system of public transport for their Areas'.

The Finance of PTAs

The Executive have a duty at least to break even year by year. (The White Paper states the Government's belief that the new system 'will provide opportunities for a reduction in the costs of providing public transport'.) If the policies of the PTA result in a loss then the Authority must either change its policies or precept on the local authorities in the Area to make good that loss. This is a matter for the Authority to decide.

However, a new system of grants is being introduced to correct the imbalance which has existed in Government financial support for transport in urban areas (with Exchequer grants being available for major road improvements but not for expenditure on public transport). These amount to 75 per cent (the same rate as for major road improvement grants) of the approved cost of projects 'for the provision, improvement or development' of public passenger transport. Eligible projects include:

(a) major improvement or extension of railway lines – track, stations, signalling systems, re-equipment with stock special to the project and associated investment for railway services;
(b) provision of new fixed track rail and bus systems (e.g. tube railways, monorails, busways);
(c) construction or major improvement of:

   (i) bus stations and depots,
   (ii) terminals and vessels for local passenger ferry services,

(iii) interchanges, including car parks, for people transferring to and from public transport systems.

However, grants will be available only for projects which fit in with plans for the structure of the area, the land-use pattern, the road and rail network, the balance between public and private transport – in short, with the basic planning of the locality. Grants are also to be available for the acquisition of new buses (at a normal rate of 25 per cent), for bus fuel (at the rate of 8p a gallon), and for loss-making suburban railway services (initially at a rate of 90 per cent, but tapering off – on the assumption that the PTAs will reorganize the transport services on an overall viable basis). Before the end of 1975 it is proposed that these financial arrangements will be reviewed in consultation with the new metropolitan county councils which are expected to have taken over by then.

Transport Planning in London
London, characteristically, is different from the other major urban areas of the country. Its problems are so different in intensity and extent that special provisions have had to be made to deal with them. The position is too complex to allow adequate summary within the confines of this book, but some significant features can be indicated. (The 1968 White Paper, *Transport in London*, gives a much fuller picture.)

Basically, the objective is the same as in the provincial conurbations: to consolidate, as far as possible, transport and traffic planning under the single authority of the Greater London Council, which has the responsibility of preparing and implementing comprehensive transport plans. (Internally, the GLC have merged their department of highways and transportation with the planning department to form a new department of planning and tranportation.)

Under the provisions of the Transport (London) Act, 1969, the London Transport Board has been abolished and the underground railways and central (red) buses have been transferred to a new London Transport Executive. (The country (green) buses and the Green Line coaches have gone to the National Bus Company.) The Executive is the London equivalent to the provincial PTAs, and like them its members (but not their officers and employees) are appointed by the GLC. All of the London Transport Board's capital debt was written off before the transfer.

British Rail's commuter services (which stretch as far afield as Southend, Ashford, Reading and Bletchley, and are operationally interrelated with long-distance services) do not come directly under GLC control, but provision has been made to allow the Council to bring rail services into a common plan.

A full review of *The Future of London Transport* is to be found in a Report presented by the GLC Policy and Resources Committee to the Council in July 1971.[47]

Appendix

Since this Chapter was written, regulations relating to structure and local plans under Part I of the 1968 Town and Country Planning Act have been published, together with a lengthy memorandum (DOE Circular 44/71).

References and Further Reading

1 DOE, Circular 44/71 and Memorandum, *Town and Country Planning Act 1968, Part I: The Town and Country Planning (Structure and Local Plans) Regulations, 1971*, HMSO, 1971.
2 DOE, Circular 3/71, *Industrial Development – Exemption Limits for Industrial Development Certificates and Time Limits on Planning Permissions*, HMSO, 1971.
3 Heap, D., *Encyclopedia of the Law of Town and Country Planning*, Sweet & Maxwell, 1959 and periodic supplements.
4 Heap, D., *The New Town Planning Procedures*, Sweet & Maxwell, 1968.
5 Heap, D., *An Outline of Planning Law*, Sweet & Maxwell, 5th edition, 1969.
6 Karslake, H. H., *An Annotated Text of the Town and Country Planning Act, 1968*, Rating and Valuation Association, 1968.
7 Megarry, R. E., *Lectures on the Town and Country Planning Act, 1947*, Stevens, 1949.
8 MHLG, *Report for the Period 1950/51 to 1954*, Cmd. 9559, HMSO, 1955.
9 MHLG, *Caravans as Homes* (Arton Wilson Report), Cmnd. 872, HMSO, 1959.
10 MHLG, Circular 49/59, *Purchase Notices*, HMSO, 1959.
11 MHLG, Circular 42/60, *Caravan Sites and Controls of Development Act, 1960*, HMSO, 1960.
12 MHLG, *Caravan Parks*, HMSO, 1962.
13 MHLG, Circular 6/62, *Gypsies*, HMSO, 1962.
14 MHLG, Circular 58/65, *Development Plans*, HMSO, 1965.
15 MHLG, Circular 70/65, *The Town and Country Planning (Development Plans) Direction, 1965*, HMSO, 1956.
16 MHLG, *The Future of Development Plans: A Report by the Planning Advisory Group*, HMSO, 1965.
17 MHLG, *Gypsies and Other Travellers*, HMSO, 1967.
18 MHLG, *Town and Country Planning*, Cmnd. 3333, HMSO, 1967.
19 MHLG, Circular 5/68, *The Use of Conditions in Planning Permissions*, HMSO, 1968.
20 MHLG, Circular 49/68, *Caravan Sites Act 1968*, HMSO, 1968.
21 MHLG, Circular 15/69, *Town and Country Planning Act Part IV – Acquisition and Disposal of Land*, HMSO, 1969.
22 MHLG, Circular 26/69, *Purchase Notices*, HMSO, 1969.

23 MHLG, *Development Control Policy Notes*, HMSO, 1969–70.
  1. General Principles.
  2. Development in Residential Areas.
  3. Industrial and Commercial Development.
  4. Development in Rural Areas.
  5. Development in Town Centres.
  6. Road Safety and Traffic Requirements.
  7. Preservation of Historic Buildings and Areas.
  8. Caravan Sites.
  9. Petrol Filling Stations and Motels.
  10. Design.
  11. Amusements Centres.
24 MHLG, Circular 46/70, *Town and Country Planning Acts 1962 to 1968: Planning Blight*, HMSO, 1970.
25 MHLG, *Development Plans: A Manual on Form and Content*, HMSO, 1970.
26 MHLG, Circular 82/70, *Town and Country Planning Act 1968 – Part I: The New Development Plan System of Structure and Local Plans*, HMSO, 1970.
27 MHLG, *Handbook of Statistics* (Annual), HMSO.
28 MHLG, *Statistics of Decisions on Planning Applications* (Annual), HMSO.
29 Ministry of Local Government and Planning, Circular 58/51, *The Drafting of Planning Permissions*, HMSO, 1951.
30 Ministry of Local Government and Planning, *Town and Country Planning 1943–1951: Progress Report by the Minister of Local Government and Planning on the Work of the Ministry of Town and Country Planning*, Cmd. 8204, HMSO, 1951.
31 Ministry of Town and Country Planning, *Town and Country Planning Bill 1947: Explanatory Memorandum*, Cmd. 7006, HMSO, 1947.
32 Ministry of Town and Country Planning, Circular 40 (1948), *Survey for Development Plans*, HMSO, 1948.
33 Ministry of Town and Country Planning, Circular 100 (1950), *Development by Government Departments*, HMSO, 1950.
34 Parkes, W., 'Planning Control of Converted Dwellings', *Journal of Planning and Property Law*, 1968, pp. 6–11 and 160–1.
35 *Report of the Expert Committee on Compensation and Betterment* (Uthwatt Report), Cmd. 6386, HMSO, 1942.
36 SDD, Circular 49/71, *Publicity for Planning Proposals*, SDD, 1971.
37 SDD, Circular 52/71, *The New Development Plan System*, SDD, 1971:
38 SDD, *Scotland's Travelling People*, HMSO, 1971.
39 SDD, *Annual Reports*, HMSO.

PLANNING FOR TRAFFIC

40 Bayliss, B. T. and Edwards, S. L., *Transport for Industry* (*Summary Report*) Ministry of Transport, HMSO, 1968.

41 Buchanan, Colin and Partners, *The Conurbations*, British Road Federation, 1969.

42 Estimates Committee, Sub-Committee E, Session 1968–9. *Motorways and Trunk Roads* (H.C. Paper 475, HMSO, 1969).

43 Gray, P. G., *Private Motoring in Engand and Wales*, Government Social Survey, HMSO, 1969.

44 Greater London Council, *Kensington Environmental Management Study*, GLC, 1966.

45 Greater London Council, *Car Ownership in London*, GLC Research Report No. 10, 1970.

46 Greater London Council, *The Future of London Transport: A Paper for Discussion*, GLC, 1970.

47 Greater London Council, *The Future of London Transport: Report of the Policy and Resources Committee*, Council Minutes, July 6–7, 1971.

48 Herrmann, P. G., *Forecasts of Vehicle Ownership in Counties and County Boroughs in Great Britain*, Road Research Laboratory (Crowthorne, Berkshire), 1968.

49 *Journal of Transport Economics and Policy*, published three times a year (January, May and September) by London School of Economics.

50 Kirwan, R. M., 'Economics and Methodology in Urban Transport Planning', in Orr, S. C. and Cullingworth, J. B., *Regional and Urban Studies: A Social Science Approach*, Allen & Unwin, 1969.

51 Leeds City Council, Ministry of Transport and Ministry of Housing and Local Government, *Planning and Transport – The Leeds Approach*, HMSO, 1969.

52 Llewelyn-Davies, Weeks, Forestier-Walker and Bor, and Ove Arup and Partners, *Motorways in the Urban Environment*, British Road Federation, 1971.

53 London Transport Board, *Annual Reports*, HMSO.

54 Ministry of Transport, *Passenger Transport in Great Britain* (Annual Statistics), HMSO.

55 Ministry of Transport, *Roads in England* (Annual Report), HMSO.

56 Ministry of Transport, *Traffic in Towns* (Buchanan Report), HMSO, 1963. (Also published in shortened form by Penguin Books, 1964.)

57 Ministry of Transport, *Road Pricing: The Economics and Technical Possibilities* (Smeed Report), HMSO, 1964.

58 Ministry of Transport, *Transport Policy*, Cmnd. 3057, HMSO, 1966.
59 Ministry of Transport, *Public Transport and Traffic*, Cmnd. 3481, HMSO, 1967.
60 Ministry of Transport, *How Fast? A Paper for Discussion*, HMSO 1968.
61 Ministry of Transport, Roads Circular 1/68, *Traffic and Transport Plans*, HMSO, 1968.
62 Ministry of Transport, *Transport in London*, Cmnd. 3686, HMSO, 1968.
63 Ministry of Transport, *Roads for the Future: A New Inter-Urban Plan*, HMSO, 1969.
64 Political and Economic Planning, *Solving Traffic Problems – I: Lessons from America*, Planning Broadsheet No. 402, 1956.
65 Rhodes, G., *Administrators in Action: British Case Studies, Vol. II* ('The Wentworth By-Pass'), Allen & Unwin, 1965.
66 Tanner, J. C., 'Forecasts of Vehicle Ownership in Great Britain', *Roads and Road Construction*, November and December 1965.
67 Tanner, J. C., *Revised Forecasts of Vehicles and Traffic in Great Britain*, Road Research Laboratory (Crowthorne, Berkshire), 1967.
68 Tetlow, A. and Goss, A., *Homes, Towns and Traffic*, Faber, Revised Edition, 1968.
69 Thomas, J. M., *Some Characteristics of Motorists in Central London*, Greater London Papers, London School of Economics, 1968.
70 Thomas, R., *Journeys to Work*, Political and Economic Planning, 1968.
71 Thomson, J. M., 'An Evaluation of Two Proposals for Traffic Restraint in Central London', *Journal of the Royal Statistical Society*, Series A, Vol. 30, Part 3, 1967.
72 Working Party on the Introduction of a New Mode of Transport in Central London, *An Aid to Pedestrian Movement*, Westminster City Council, 1971.

Chapter V

THE LOCAL PLANNING MACHINE

THE ADMINISTRATIVE FRAMEWORK

For purposes of local government England and Wales is divided first into county boroughs and administrative counties. Administrative counties are further divided into three types of county districts – municipal (or 'non-county') boroughs, urban districts and rural districts. Rural districts are themselves divided into parishes, but as these have no planning function (except in relation to footpaths, which are discussed in Chapter IX), they can be ignored here.

County boroughs are 'all-purpose' authorities: they are responsible for all local government functions within their areas. A county borough is thus the education, health, housing, highway and planning authority inside its boundaries. In administrative counties functions are shared between the county and the districts. (The differences between the various types of district are unimportant for the present discussion.) All the major functions except housing are the responsibility of the county. Districts are responsible for housing, open spaces, sanitation, cemeteries and burial grounds, refuse collection and disposal, and so on. However, in certain services, of which town and country planning is one, there is a delegation of certain functions from counties to the larger districts.

To summarize the position so far as town and country planning is concerned: the planning authorities are county boroughs and administrative counties, but with some delegation within the latter to the larger districts. In London, planning powers are shared between the Greater London Council and the thirty-two Greater London Boroughs and the ancient City.

In England there are (in 1970) forty-five administrative counties and seventy-nine county boroughs outside Greater London, ranging in population from 30,000 (Rutland CC) and 33,000 (Canterbury CB) to 2,427,000 (Lancashire CC) and 1,084,000 (Birmingham CB). In

Greater London, the Greater London Council has a population of 7,612,000 with thirty-two Greater London Boroughs (all with populations between 143,000 and 323,000) and the City of London (4,780). In Wales, there are thirteen county councils, ranging in population from 18,600 (Radnor CC) to 748,000 (Glamorgan CC); and four county boroughs: Merthyr Tydfil (56,000), Newport (112,000), Swansea (171,000) and Cardiff (284,000). About a quarter of local authorities have populations of 100,000 or less. At the other extreme, there are seventeen authorities within the 500,000 to 1 million range, and six with populations exceeding a million.

In Scotland, the pattern of local government is different, though its weaknesses are even more pronounced than in England and Wales. There are five types of authority: the four counties of cities (Aberdeen, Dundee, Edinburgh and Glasgow), 22 large burghs, 176 small burghs, 33 counties and 196 districts of counties.

The counties of cities are all-purpose authorities. The large burghs have all functions except education and valuation. The small burghs are responsible for housing, minor roads, street lighting, cleansing and refuse collection, sewerage etc.

The county councils exercise all functions in the 'landward area' (i.e. outside burghs). Within large burghs they are responsible only for education and valuation. Within small burghs they are additionally responsible for health, social work, police, fire, planning, etc.

The district councils (unlike their English namesakes) have extremely limited functions. These relate to the maintenance of public ways and footpaths, and concurrent powers with the county council for community centres, places of entertainment, parks and recreation, allotments and rights of way.

Fifty-nine local authorities are planning authorities – the counties of cities, the county councils and the large burghs. These vary enormously in population, with a dozen having less than 200,000 and four with more than 250,000. They range from 12,000 to over 900,000.

The large variation in the size of local planning authorities has obvious implications both for the problems confronting them and the organization which they are able to adopt. The large authority is able to establish a separate planning department with a chief planning officer wholly concerned with planning. In the small authority there is neither the scope nor the resources for this; planning has to be combined with other functions, usually roads and engineering or architecture.

So far as the problems facing different sized authorities are concerned, the relationship is not so clear; indeed some small authorities, particularly in the older industrial areas, have acutely difficult planning problems. These have often to be tackled on an inadequate rate and grant income by a small staff. In the larger authorities there are at least the advantages which flow from large-scale organization – the opportunity to employ specialists in, for example, industrial and estate development, and landscaping, as well as research officers.

Rather clearer is the concentration of problems in different types of area: the huge problems of slum clearance, redevelopment and overspill in the conurbations, large-scale suburban development in the rural and semi-rural areas surrounding the big towns, preservation problems in historic towns, mineral workings in the countryside, the pressures for development in beauty spots and, in particular on the coast. In growing areas there is the problem of dealing with a spate of development applications and ensuring that plans are adequate to meet the needs. In static and declining areas the problem is not so much a matter of controlling development as of encouraging it. Some areas have plenty of room for new development (though they may have problems of inadequate water supply or sewage disposal), while others suffer from an acute shortage of space.

The list could be lengthened almost indefinitely, but the point is obvious. Though most authorities are faced with some difficult problems of redevelopment or development control, preservation, roads, transport and parking, housing and so on, these are unevenly distributed throughout the country. And often the sheer size of these problems bears little relationship to the staffing and financial resources of the planning authority which bears the responsibility for dealing with them. Generalization is therefore difficult.

PLANNING DEPARTMENTS

There is, however, one generalization which can be made: most counties have separate planning departments, whereas most urban authorities administer planning within an architect's or engineer's department. The reason for this is in part historical. Urban authorities have been responsible for town and country planning throughout its evolution: it developed gradually within the existing departmental structure. In the counties, on the other hand, planning did not become a general responsibility until the passing of the 1947 Act, when powers were transferred to them from the county districts. In recent years, however, an increasing number of the larger towns have established separate planning departments with a chief officer in charge, and professional pressures encouraging this are mounting. In some of the large authorities there may be *de facto* a separate department even though there is no separate designation. But the important point still stands: an adequately staffed planning machine cannot be achieved in a small authority.

It needs to be repeated, however, that the essential issue is one of size, not of status. The reports of the Local Government Commissions abound with references to the inadequacies of small planning authorities, whether they be counties or county boroughs. In most of the Welsh counties the size of the area is too small for the establishment of an adequate planning department:

'Few of the authorities employ a team of experts in the various branches of planning. For some of the smaller counties the planning department formed part of the County Architect's department, and even if the staff was adequate for normal day-to-day planning control it is difficult to see how serious consideration could be given to the wider aspects of planning.'[6]

The smaller county borough is in the same position. In Merthyr Tydfil (population 57,000), for example:

'. . . the Planning Department was associated with the Engineer's Department. Such a combination, whilst not ideal, can, it is true, be paralleled in many county boroughs and even a few counties, but in Merthyr the chief officer of the combined departments was also the Waterworks Engineer. What was even less satisfactory was that there was little differentiation of function at lower levels; those officers responsible for work in connection with planning also had extensive non-planning duties. The effective control of day-to-day planning was in the hands of a Chief Town Planning Assistant (salary £1,360–£1,535) and three unqualified assistants; two of the three assistants had extensive duties outside the field of planning and, in fact, no single officer was entirely free of extraneous duties. Thus much of the time of the staff of the Planning Department was actually occupied with other duties, for example, street-lighting schemes. No member of the department appeared to have qualifications specially in town planning, though the senior members had qualifications in municipal or civil engineering.'[6]

It is, of course, always tempting to dwell on the deficiencies of an administrative organization: these are easier to discuss, and in any case are usually comparatively well documented. The shortcomings of the present administrative structure of planning, however, justify this emphasis. The problem is particularly acute in the conurbations which, it should be remembered, at present accommodate over a third of the population. The following extract from the report of the Local Government Commission on Tyneside summarizes the structural deficiencies in one conurbation.

'We found that the Tyneside authorities were handicapped in two ways by the existing local government structure. In the first place, a number of authorities had not the strength in population or financial resources to enable them to deal effectively with some of their problems, particularly the big tasks of renewing and improving the whole urban environment, including housing. . . . There was a second handicap, as it seemed to us, under which the Tyneside authorities were labouring, irrespective of their individual strength; this was the interlocking nature of certain problems over the whole of the urban Tyneside, for instance, problems of town planning, including planning for industry; housing and overspill; communications; sewage disposal. The common factor among all these is the extent to which action taken – or action needed but not taken – in one area can have effects beyond the boundaries of that area and extending to other parts of the conurbation.'[5]

As this quotation clearly indicates, the size of a local planning authority can be important in terms of *area* as well as in terms of *population*. It is only in recent years that this distinction has been given the attention it deserves. The point is nicely made by Derek Senior in his *Memorandum of Dissent* to the *Report of the Royal Commission on Local Government in England*:

'The environmental-service authority must be in charge of a plannable unit, and the scale of such a unit is by definition fixed, within limits, in terms of the *area* served by its main centre. Its size in terms of population is whatever may be the number of people who live in the area from which that centre is more conveniently accessible than any other centre offering a comparable range of opportunities – provided only that this number is enough to sustain an authority with the minimum necessary staff. On the other hand, the scale of a unit responsible for the personal services is related to the *population* that throws up enough cases to keep the necessary professional and administrative staffs economically occupied. Its size in terms of area is whatever may be the acreage over which that population spreads itself – provided only that it forms a reasonable coherent arena of social activity and is not so extensive that its remotest inhabitants cannot easily reach its centre.'[19]

We shall return to this issue in the discussion, later in this chapter, on local government reorganization and again in the chapter on regional planning.

ADMINISTRATIVE ORGANIZATION

It follows from the previous discussion that the organisation of planning differs markedly between different areas. At one extreme are small authorities which cannot be said to have any planning organization at all; at the other extreme are the highly organized planning departments of some of the larger authorities. In this section some examples of the latter are given, based on information kindly provided by the Chief Planning Officers.

Liverpool

A separate City Planning Department was formed in Liverpool in 1963. The Department has a total establishment of 157 posts and is organized in four divisions, dealing with development control, policy and research, urban design and development, and administration.

The *Development Control Division* has fourteen planning officers and is responsible for the detailed examination of all proposals and applications for planning permission. These amount to approximately 2,000 a year and are increasing as a result of the large-scale redevelopment in the central area and increasing slum clearance in the outer areas.

The Division is also responsible for work in connection with the relocation of industry, shops, etc., affected by the Council's re-development and traffic schemes and for the implementation of the Council's planning policies and redevelopment schemes.

The *Policy and Research Division* is divided into two groups, one dealing with all aspects of research and the other with planning policy. The Research Group's work includes (*a*) socio-economic aspects as they affect planning policies, (*b*) planning standards, (*c*) traffic planning, including planning for vehicular and pedestrian movement and the co-ordination of various means of transport. The Group also services the other Divisions of the Department by providing information necessary for their work. There are seventeen officers in the Group. The Policy Section (eleven officers) is responsible for (*a*) the preparation of planning policies and the continuous review of the City's policy plan, (*b*) the preparation and review of district plans in the areas other than slum clearance areas, (*c*) the planning contribution to the City's capital works programme.

The *Urban Design and Redevelopment Division* is divided into two groups. In the Central Area Group the work involved covers the regular review of the present City Centre Plan policies and proposals and detailed design work connected with all urban design aspects of the renewal of central Liverpool. In the Outer Areas Group the work is involved with the renewal of the City's Inner Residential Area (existing population 200,000), planning for the clearance of 33,000 slums within the next seven years and the consequent comprehensive redevelopment with related social and community facilities. Planning Briefs and District Plans for the areas of major change (Inner Areas of the City) are prepared in this Division. There are sixteen officers in the Central Area Group and ten in the Outer Areas.

The *Administrative and Services Division* provides administrative, clerical and ancillary services throughout the Department. The Division has administrative and clerical units working in each of the Technical Divisions and they are responsible for the processing of development applications, correspondence, reports to Committees, staff records and the preparation of Annual Estimates.

The Department runs a Graduate Training Scheme whereby Graduates are sponsored on Planning and Traffic Engineering Courses at recognized schools and are paid a salary whilst studying. On completion of the course the Graduate is under agreement to remain with the Department for not less than two years.

Newcastle upon Tyne
The City Planning Department of Newcastle upon Tyne is organized in four main divisons. The *Policy and Redevelopment Division*, directed by the Principal Planner, has three sections. The Urban Structure Officer is responsible for all Structure Plan work and Development Plan up-dating and interpretation; planning research, sub-regional and regional planning, the development of computer techniques, and public participation at policy level. The Local Plans Officer is responsible for central area design work, the preparation of District Plans and some Action Areas, the preparation of models and other visual and design aids, and public participation at Local Plan level. The Implementation Officer is responsible for the implementation of all central area redevelopment proposals, the preparation of development briefs for public and private developers in major redevelopment areas, and negotiations with developers in respect of major redevelopment schemes.

The *Development Division* is headed by the Development Officer who exercises control through two Section Heads. The Assistant Development Officer supervises the work of the Design Officer, the Landscape Architect and the Revitalization Officer. He is responsible for the major programme of urban improvement by

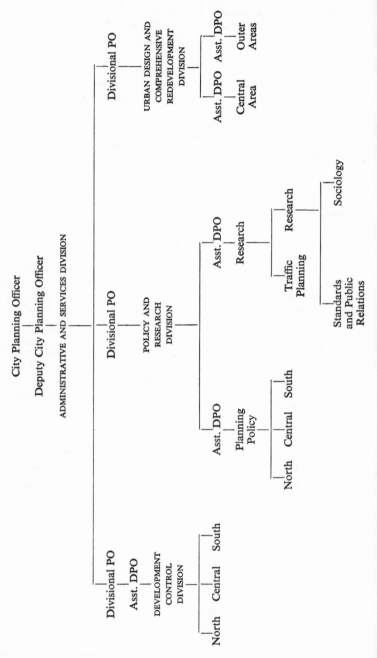

City of Liverpool Planning Department

City Planning Officer

Deputy City Planning Officer

means of Action Area plans, planning briefs, etc. He is also concerned with up-dating and monitoring the housing programme and securing planning objectives in the housing fields. In addition, he has specific responsibilities in relation to conservation areas.

The Deputy Development Control Officer is responsible for development control and enforcement.

The *Traffic Division*, under the control of the Traffic Engineer, and aided by two Senior Assistants, controls car parking provision and is concerned with the collection and analysis of traffic data for short and long term management and planning.

Finally, the *Administrative Division*, under the Chief Administrative Officer, provides central filing, typing, clerical and administrative services to the Department.

Lancashire County Planning Department

The organization of county planning departments is more complex because of the two-tier structure of local government in administrative counties. Delegation to 'second-tier' authorities is discussed later in the chapter. Here the organization in Lancashire is outlined.

The department is divided into a Headquarters Office in Preston, six Divisional Offices and two sub-offices, situated in Ormskirk, Manchester, Wigan, Bury, Rishton, St Annes, Lancaster and Ulverston. The Headquarters Office is divided into four sections, Architectural, Development, Research and Administrative, each under the leadership of a Section Head. The duties carried out by the various offices are as follows:

Architectural Section (Staff establishment – 42). Detailed layout of residential areas including site surveys in the case of overspill schemes; constructional drawings of roads, sewers and buildings; schemes for the redevelopment of town centres and for conservation areas; protection and preservation of buildings listed as being of architectural or historical importance; elevational control; engineering work on land reclamation schemes; the development of a number of the County's industrial estates. In addition architectural and engineering advice is available to Divisional Offices and Local Authorities.

Development Section (Staff establishment – 36). Preparation, implementation and periodical review of the Development Plan and Town Maps; definition and investigation of development areas; overspill and industrial location; investigation of mining problems in relation to development proposals; exploitation of minerals and mineral

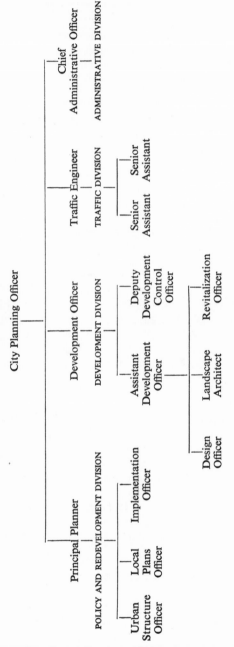

City of Newcastle upon Tyne Planning Department

Lancashire County Planning Department

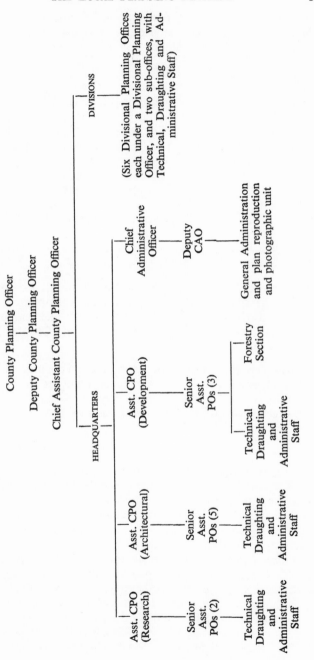

workings; protection and preservation of amenities and beauty spots; rural development; landscaping proposals for development and acquisition for tree planting and afforestation of derelict land.

Research Section (Staff establishment – 22). Collection, collation, analysis and interpretation of information relative to the basic problems of planning; organization of surveys; assistance in the industrial aspects of development control; participation in the preparation and review of the Development Plan and Town Maps; advice on matters relating to the movement of population, distribution and location of industry and the economic aspects of mineral workings; preparation of programmes for housing developments and the movement of overspill; liaison with Regional Bodies (North-West Economic Planning Council, North-West Sports Council. Standing Conference of Local Authorities in the North-West); advice on the provision and demand for recreation facilities in the County as a whole; and the administration of an Industrial Bureau for the guidance of industrial developers.

Administrative Section (Staff establishment – 36). Preparation of material for the Planning and Development Committee and its various Sub-Committees, budgetary control and administrative and clerical functions associated with Town and Country Planning Acts and other legislation.

Divisional Offices. Control of development, preparation of evidence for Appeals and Public Inquiries, preparation of certain Town Maps in consultation with Headquarters Office. The average establishment is for a technical staff of twelve and an administrative staff of six.

DELEGATION IN COUNTIES

The transfer of planning powers from districts to counties, which was effected by the 1947 Act, was generally agreed to be necessary – except by the districts. Larger authorities were needed to undertake the new and wider planning functions, to plan comprehensively over bigger areas and to hold the balance between any conflicting interests of urban and rural districts, to negotiate with other authorities on questions of regional importance such as the establishment of national parks and the planned provision for overspill from the congested conurbations. At the same time, the limited supply of qualified planning officers needed to be rationally distributed and concentrated in a smaller number of departments where their skills could be most effectively utilized. However, the opposition of the district councils to their loss of powers (in education and health as well as in town planning) led to the compromise of delegation. Delegation may be defined as an administrative device whereby some particular function of government is performed partly by one tier of authority and partly by another; it enables the 'upper-tier' authority to be responsible for general policy and finance, and the 'lower-tier' authority for the execution of policy within a given area. The lower-tier authority may be a separate local authority or it may be an organ of the upper-tier authority with or without members drawn from other authorities, though the latter might be more accurately termed decentralization (implying the discharge of responsibility by the upper-tier authority on an area basis).

Delegation should not, however, be regarded merely as a political expedient. It has very real advantages. In the first place there is the question of the sheer administrative load on upper-tier authorities. Now that so many functions have been transferred from districts to counties, the latter have become heavily burdened, whereas the districts have insufficient major functions to attract officers and councillors of the desired calibre. So long as the districts can support an adequate number of officials (which implies a certain minimum size) and can therefore cope successfully with delegated powers, delegation at one and the same time relieves the county of some of its administrative load and increases the general effectiveness of the district authority – thereby improving what the Royal Commission on Local Government in Greater London have termed 'the health of representative government'. The second advantage is intimately tied up with this. As the same Royal Commission stressed, there is no antithesis between healthy local government and efficient admini-stration.* The districts have the great asset of fuller acquaintance with local conditions and needs. They are more accessible to the local electorate. They are better placed for facilitating citizen participation in the planning process – a matter which, as is argued in the final chapter, is of considerable importance.

Delegation is thus in principle a positive device for capitalizing the respective advantages of county and district adminstration. It can work effectively, however, only if two requirements are met.

* It can be argued that the Royal Commission accepted this too whole-heartedly and, indeed, laid too much emphasis on their conception of 'healthy local government'. Their philosophy is summed up in the following extract: 'local government is with us an instance of democracy at work, and no amount of potential administrative efficiency could make up for the loss of active partici-pation in the work by capable, public-spirited people elected by, responsible to, and in touch with those who elect them' (*Report*, op. cit., p. 59). For further discussion in relation to housing and planning see J. B. Cullingworth, *Housing in Greater London*, London School of Economics, Greater London Papers No. 4, 1961.

E

First, the districts must constitute administrative units of adequate population and resources. For nearly a half this is not so. Some 700 districts in England and Wales have populations of less than 15,000; nearly 500 have less than 10,000; and over 200 have less than 5,000. But even if the districts are of the necessary minimum size there remains the question of the relationship between them and the county. A formal 'instrument of delegation' has to be translated into practice. Where relationships are good few problems may arise, but where relationships are strained and characterized by mistrust and suspicion, delegation may only exacerbate the problems it is designed to alleviate.

It follows that it is not easy to legislate for an effective system of delegation. Nevertheless, increased delegation (in other services as well as town and country planning) was one of the objectives of the Local Government Act of 1958. This Act was an attempt to modernize local government: it considerably altered the system of central government grants, it provided for the machinery for reorganizing local government structure, and it extended the powers and responsibilities of the larger district councils mainly by providing for greater delegation of certain functions from counties.*

Before 1958, the general situation was that delegated powers in relation to planning applications were exercised (in widely varying degrees) by county districts. The normal procedure was (and still is) for an application to be made to the district council, whether or not that district had any delegated powers. Where they had none the application was referred to the county (possibly with any 'observations' the district might wish to make). Some districts had limited powers for approving applications which were in conformity with the approved plan or which did not raise major policy issues. In such cases they would first receive advice from an area or divisional planning officer of the county. The crucial decision to be made here was, of course, on whether an application *was* in conformity with the development plan or whether it did raise *major* policy issues. Usually (but not in all areas) this decision was taken by the county. In some counties there was a system of area planning committees which might consist of equal numbers of representatives from the county and the district concerned. Some counties had both a scheme of delegation and a series of area committees. In short, there

---

* For a full discussion see G. Seward and G. H. Forster, *The Local Government Act 1958*, Charles Knight & Co., 1959. The legislation was preceded by three White Papers: *Areas and Status of Local Authorities in England and Wales*, Cmd. 9831, 1956; *Functions of County Councils and County District Councils in England and Wales*, Cmnd. 161, 1957; *and Local Government Finance (England and Wales)*, Cmnd. 209, 1957.

was a wide range of variations. These were, in practice, more marked than the formal published schemes suggested. It was because of this variation and because conditions differed so greatly between counties that the original intention of providing for automatic delegation of planning functions to the larger districts was abandoned.

The post-1958 delegation arrangements allowed districts with populations of 60,000 or more to claim a wide measure of delegated powers in relation to development control. In 'special circumstances' the Minister could require similar delegation to other districts. This was the only substantive change brought about by the scheme. For the rest there was ministerial exhortation:

'The Minister considers that it would now be right for county councils to review their arrangements for the exercise of planning powers, taking into account the views of their district councils, and, where appropriate, to revise those arrangements in order to give to district councils who so wish, and to whom adequate technical advice is available, an additional measure of delegation and freedom of action bearing in mind the size and characteristics of the county and the county districts, and the need for efficiency and economy in administration.'[10]

So far as town maps were concerned greater freedom of action might be given to districts 'in appropriate circumstances'. Where districts had the necessary staff they should, in the Minister's view, be given 'the fullest opportunity of co-operating with the planning authority'. Where this could not be done (for example where a town map affected more than one district) 'the fullest co-operation between the county and district councils should be maintained from the earliest stage of the preparation of any town map'.

This trend towards greater delegation was a feature of the early 'sixties. Enthusiasm (except on the part of the district councils) has definitely waned since then. In their evidence to the Royal Commission on Local Government, the Ministry of Housing and Local Government was highly critical.[16] In their experience, delegation did not lead to an improved speed or quality of development control. The advantages which flow from delegating some of the work load to district councils is offset by the shortage of qualified planning staff in most district offices, by the limited range of problems which arise within any one area, the difficulties caused by the natural inclination of district councils to take a 'narrow view', and the extra administrative complications that limited delegation usually entails. The Ministry thought that decentralization of planning control to area committees of the planning authority produced better results than delegation to another elected body. This view is supported by the report of the *Management Study on Development Control*. The management consultants who undertook this study concluded that, within the context of the current two-tier system in administrative counties, area committees provided the best method of reconciling the rights of individuals with speed of decision, low cost and the interests of the wider community.[12]

The Royal Commission's *Report* came out strongly against delegation but maintained that an essential corollary of their recommendations for a smaller number of local planning authorities was that there should be adequate decentralization and consultation.

Delegation has been a means of attempting to adjust planning machinery to an out-dated local government system. In recent years increasing attention has been focused on the alternative: changing the local government system to meet planning needs. This is a subject to which we now turn.

LOCAL GOVERNMENT REORGANIZATION IN
ENGLAND

Several references have already been made to the inadequacies of the present local government structure and the review which is now under way. A full discussion is inappropriate in the present context and, in any case, is likely to be overtaken by events.* There has been a remarkable change in attitudes over the last decade or so. The 1956 White Paper on *Areas and Status of Local Authorities in England and Wales*, and the review which followed it, had as a basic premise that

'a fundamental alteration of the existing structure could be justified only if it had shown itself to be incapable of meeting present day needs. That is not the situation. The present system has, over many years, stood up to the severest tests.'

Throughout the 'fifties, local government reorganization was conceived in terms of adjusting boundaries. The first major change came with the *Report of the Royal Commission on Local Government in Greater London* (the Herbert Report) and the 1964 London Government Act which followed it at speed which, in the light of previous experience, was staggering. Henceforth local government

---

* Reference may be made to Chapter VIII of P. G. Richards, *The New Local Government System*, Allen & Unwin, 1968, which outlines changes over the period 1945 to 1948; and to 'Local Government Boundaries Since 1888' in Volume III of the Report of the Royal Commission on Local Government in England, *Research Appendices*, HMSO, 1969, Cmnd. 4040–II.

reorganization was taken seriously. Change was in the air and debate centred on how radical the change should be. Piecemeal reorganization was brought to a halt and a Royal Commission on Local Government in England (the Redcliffe-Maud Commission) was set up and charged with the task of looking at the local government system (outside London) as a whole.

This was a major change in tactics. No longer could the hopelessly out-dated small authority successfully oppose reorganization. Rutland was no longer alone: the writing was on the wall for all. The evidence submitted to the Redcliffe-Maud Commission reflected a widespread agreement that the local government system needed radical overhaul. And when the Commission reported in June 1969, recommending the abolition of all the 79 county boroughs, 45 counties, 227 non-county boroughs, 449 urban districts and 410 rural districts, and their replacement by an entirely new system, the argument centred on alternative systems rather than on defence of the existing structure.

It is appropriate here to outline only the major recommendations of the Commission and those arguments which are relevant to town and country planning.

The Commission identified four 'basic faults' in the present pattern of working of local government:

1. Local government areas do not fit the pattern of life and work in modern England. The gap will widen as social, economic and technological changes quicken.
2. The fragmentation of England into 79 county boroughs and 45 counties, exercising independent authority and dividing town from country, has made the proper planning of development and transportation impossible. The result has often been an atmosphere of hostility between the county boroughs and the counties, and this has made it harder to decide difficult questions on their merits.
3. The division of responsibility within each county between the county council and a number of county district councils, together with the position of county boroughs as islands in the counties, means that services which should be in the hands of one authority are split up among several. This greatly complicates the work of meeting comprehensively the different needs of families and individuals.
4. Many local authorities are too small, in size and revenue, and in consequence too short of highly qualified manpower and technical equipment, to be able to do their work as well as it could and should be done.

Their proposed solution was the abolition of all existing authorities and the establishment of sixty-one new areas covering both town and country. In fifty-eight of these a unitary authority would be responsible for all services. In three 'metropolitan areas' (based on Birmingham, Manchester and Merseyside) responsibility for services would be divided between a metropolitan authority whose key functions would be planning, transportation and major development, and a number of metropolitan district authorities whose key functions would be education, the personal social services, health and housing.

These sixty-one new local authorities would form the operational level of local government but two other levels were thought to be needed. Underpinning and complementing the basic units, the Commission saw the need for smaller representative bodies 'to express the interest and sense of identity of the new local communities'. They therefore recommended 'local councils' which would succeed the present county boroughs, boroughs, districts and parishes. They would be concerned with local amenities and (in the case of the larger councils) would play a part in some of the main services for which the new 'unitary' authorities would have the major responsibility. The Commission referred, in particular, to housing, preservation (of buildings, trees, etc.), conservation, local development and highway improvement – all matters 'which may need action on the local scale as the wider one'.

At the other extreme, the Commission were convinced that higher level units were needed to set the strategic framework for the operational authorities. This need would increase with the growth of population, rising mobility, and the greater involvement of local government in economic questions. To meet this they proposed provincial councils (replacing the present economic planning councils) which would settle the broad economic, land use and investment framework for the planning and development policies of the operational units.

These were the main recommendations of the Majority Report. They rest on the argument that town and country are interdependent, that larger authorities are required, and that the interdependence of services is such that the main unit of local government should be all-purpose.

One member of the Commission, Derek Senior, could not accept the last of these three principles. In a weighty minority report (misleadingly termed *Memorandum of Dissent*), he makes a scathing, cogent criticism of this. He accepted the diagnosis but argued that the all-purpose authorities recommended in the Majority Report would fragment planning and development problems; in most

cases they would also be too remote for the democratic and responsive administration of the personal services and too unwieldy for the
efficient co-ordination of the whole range of local government
functions. In his view the Majority took too theoretical an approach
to the problem of local government organization in which the
requirements in population terms of administrative efficiency and
democratic control were analysed in abstraction from the facts of
social geography. He rejected the argument that the unitariness of
the all-purpose authority has inherent advantages which outweigh
all disadvantages. Indeed, the application of this line of thought
clearly involves authorities which are too small for planning and too
large for personal services. It also involves an ineffectual role for the
provincial authority, which cannot be given development powers
without destroying the unitary principle. Similarly the local councils
cannot be given decision-making powers:

'In short, by calling in the provincial and "local" councils to reduce
the deficiencies inherent in their unitary authorities, my colleagues
would at best compromise what is most valuable in the concepts of
the provincial and "local" councils and at worst turn their one-tier
system into a three-tier one with units inappropriate in scale and
composition for most purposes at every level.'[19]

It is worth devoting further space to Senior's argument since it
highlights fundamental issues in the current debate on the reorganization of local government to cope efficiently with the problems
of town and country planning.
   A basic argument is that 'if one wants the interests of a region as
a whole to prevail through the democratic process, one must create
a structure which enables these interests to find effective expression
in action'. The first requirement, therefore, is to define areas of
community interest – not in terms of the small community to which
people feel they 'belong', but 'the *objective* community of interest
which binds together the people who participate in a self-contained
complex of social and economic activities based on a single centre'.
The objective must be to identify areas of interdependence over
which effective action can be taken. Indeed, a major reason for the
establishment of the Royal Commission was the inadequacy of the
present structure to take effective action. Senior gives a striking
example from North and Central Lancashire. A 'new city' is currently
under consideration for the Leyland-Chorley area:

'We have been plainly warned that social damage of a serious kind
would surely result if this project were to be carried out otherwise

than in the context of an operative overall plan for the whole region. When its feasibility was established, the Minister of Housing and Local Government appointed a joint team of planning and economic consultants to assess its predictable impact on the Blackburn and Burnley districts, where higher unemployment, poorer housing conditions, lower rateable values and a less salubrious climate have led to emigration and declining standards. Their conclusion was that the Leyland-Chorley development, though vital to the future prosperity of the region as a whole, could do grave and lasting local damage, especially to the Burnley district, unless an overall plan for the whole area from the Pennines to the coast resulted in a great improvement in east-west transport and communications *before* the building of the new city was far advanced. Then – and only then – the people of the Calder Valley towns who found jobs in the new city's factories and offices could conveniently commute from their present homes, and enterprises ancillary to these new industries could be economically sited in those towns. Otherwise the new city would go on draining the life out of the Calder Valley for many years before its benefits could begin to be felt there. With luck, if the Reorganization Act provides for the establishment of a regional planning *and development* authority for the whole of this area, it may be just in time.

'Meanwhile the Minister has announced that the Lancashire County Council, in concert with the local authorities concerned, is to make a project study of an improved road link between the Calder Valley and the M6; that he himself, in consultation with the local authorities, proposes to employ consultants to prepare pilot schemes of urban renewal in North East Lancashire; and that he will invite the Lancashire County Council together with the Blackburn and Burnley County Borough Councils, in consultation with the Regional Economic Planning Council and Board, to prepare a plan to form the basis of future development, to make the best use of a new Calder Valley road, and to reserve suitable sites for industrial development. Later the Government will discuss with the North East Lancashire local authorities the best way of meeting their needs in the light of the programme for the development of the new city. *All this elaborate ad-hockery and central government intervention would be unnecessary if there were already a single planning and development authority for the whole city region.* If my colleagues have their way, it may yet be all in vain.'[19]

Senior's alternative proposals are for a two-level structure comprising thirty-five regional authorities, responsible for the planning-transportation-development complex of functions (including water supply, sewerage, refuse disposal and other technical services), for capital investment programming and for police, fire and education; and 148 district authorities responsible for the health service, the personal social services, housing management, consumer protection and all other functions involving personal contact with the citizen. Additionally he proposes, at 'grass-roots' level, common councils representing existing parishes and towns or parts of towns small enough to have a real feeling of community, and at the other extreme five provincial councils.

Apart from Senior's fundamentally different set of proposals, two other 'notes of reservation' accompany the Majority Report. Sir Francis Hill and Mr R. C. Wallis outline proposals which would have the effect of increasing the number of unitary authorities from 58 to 63. Mr J. L. Longland, on the other hand, proposed a reduction to 50.

Proposals of the Royal Commission on Local Government for England (outside London)

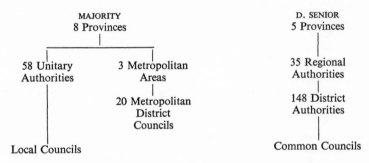

The Royal Commission on Local Government was charged with the task of renewing the structure of local government in relation to existing functions and within the context of the current division of responsibility between local and central government. There is, therefore, little discussion of local-central relationships, though the points are made that 'provincial councils will give the national government new opportunities for decentralizing power and developing new methods of collaboration between central and local government', and that 'the new metropolitan and unitary authorities will be strong enough for Parliament and central government to trust them with increased responsibility and substantially relax the present detailed supervision'.

Senior, on the other hand, devotes a whole chapter to the issue, with the justification that the setting up of the Crowther Commission on the Constitution radically changes the framework of thinking on local government reorganization. We return to this issue in the chapter on regional planning.

WALES

Wales was excluded from the terms of reference of the Redcliffe-Maud Commission on the ground that consideration of the specific problems of the Principality had already reached an advanced stage as a result of the work of the Local Government Commission for Wales (set up under the Local Government Act, 1958) and the further study which had been made of their 1962 Report.[6] Furthermore, the need for early action in Wales was considered to be particularly urgent in view of the very large number of small and inadequate authorities. To quote the 1967 White Paper[25] (which outlined 'for public discussion' the Government's reorganization proposals): 'it was apparent that local government in the Principality could be reorganized on lines that would secure its early strengthening'. (Nevertheless, by the time of writing, no reorganization had commenced!)

The problem of Wales, and particularly of central Wales, is that the counties have very small scattered populations and extremely small resources. The Local Government Commission proposed a reduction in the number of counties from thirteen to seven, the demotion of Merthyr Tydfil from a county borough to a non-county borough, and boundary extensions to Cardiff, Newport and Swansea. These proposals were very strongly opposed particularly by those counties which were, in the process of amalgamation, to be divided.

LONDON

While, over most of the country, reorganization is being considered, in London it has been effected. The London Government Act, 1963, came into operation in 1965. In brief, the Act established a Greater London Council covering an area of about 620 square miles and a population of nearly eight million; and 32 new London Boroughs (plus the unmolested ancient City of London). These replaced the London County Council, 28 Metropolitan Boroughs, the County Council of Middlesex, and the County Boroughs of Croydon, East Ham and West Ham. Considerable parts of Essex, Hertfordshire, Kent and Surrey were transferred to the new Greater London area.

In this area the London Boroughs are the main local authorities but the Greater London Council has important functions in relation to strategic planning and services which need to be planned and administered over a wider area – overall planning, main highways, traffic control, overspill housing and the fire and ambulance services.

The GLC has the responsibility of preparing the strategic Development Plan (now technically a 'structure plan') for the whole of the Greater London area. (This was published in 1969.) It lays down the policies relating to population, housing, employment, transport and, indeed, all major issues which come within the compass of strategic planning. Within this 'strategic framework' the London Borough Councils will each produce their own local development plans.

Originally it was intended that these would also be structure plans, but in November 1970 it was announced that amending legislation would be introduced to eliminate this requirement. The change has been necessitated by the length of time required to process the Greater London Development Plan. As the Minister for Local Government and Development stated in the House of Commons (10 November 1970): 'the processing thereafter of a further 33 Borough structure plans will be so time-consuming that there is every prospect that the strategic plan itself will have required further modification in the light of changing circumstances before the last structure plan has been approved and local plans adopted'.

The Boroughs will therefore be required only to prepare local plans within the framework of the GLC structure plan.

The position in London is unique. The relationship between the GLC and the London Borough Councils is not the same as that between a county and a county district. The Boroughs are large authorities with major responsibilities in their areas: indeed, they are *the* local authorities for their areas. The GLC is the local planning authority for Greater London *as a whole*: the Boroughs are the planning authorities for their areas – though there is a complex web of inter-relationships. In certain areas, such as Covent Garden, and in relation to certain types of development of strategic importance such as transport terminals, university development, major places of public assembly, the GLC itself is the local planning authority. Planning applications for other developments of 'strategic significance' have to be referred by the Borough Councils concerned to the GLC, and there is a wide range of provisions for consultations.

A convenient summary of the situation in relation to the development plan and the 'partnership' of the GLC and the Boroughs is to be found in the *Statement* of the Greater London Development Plan. This underlines the fact that the GLDP is intended to form the 'context' for the Borough Plans which will follow it; but in practice a hard and fast division of functions is neither possible nor desirable. Indeed, it is possible (to say the least) that, when the Borough Plans are prepared within the 'context', issues will emerge that require a revision of this context. The GLDP is therefore essentially a conceptual plan at this stage. It states a set of principles for the future development of Greater London which will have to undergo a 'process of validation' over a number of years.

The *Statement* couches the issues very much in technical terms, but in reality the crucial problems are policy and political ones. The policies and politics of the individual Boroughs are not necessarily consonant with those of the GLC. It is not without good reason that the Redcliffe-Maud Commission (majority) stressed the advantages of the all-purpose authority – 'local government in its simplest, most understandable and potentially most efficient form'. But in some areas (a few, according to the majority; everywhere, according to Senior) there are overriding benefits to be obtained from a two-tier structure. Nowhere is this clearer than in London. There has then to be a 'partnership' or what the GLC inelegantly refer to as an 'iterative process'. But it would be naïve to assume that this makes life easy: on the contrary, it underlines the fact that planning has far more to do with politics than with technical issues.

LOCAL GOVERNMENT REORGANIZATION IN SCOTLAND

A separate Royal Commission on Local Government in Scotland (the Wheatley Commission) reported in 1969 and proposed a two-tier structure of seven regional and thirty-seven district authorities.[22] It was recommended that the regional authorities should be responsible for the major services involving heavy expenditure which need administration over a wide area (e.g. strategic planning, transportation and roads, industrial development, house-building and management, education, social work, police and fire services). District authorities would, in the main, be responsible for the planning and development of the local environment: local planning, environmental health, housing improvement, clean air, building control, amenity and recreational facilities.

LEGISLATION FOR REORGANIZATION

It is virtually impossible to keep abreast of proposals for local government reorganization. Any account given here would almost inevitably be rapidly made out of date. White Papers on *Reform of Local Government in England* (February 1970) and *Local Government Reorganization in Glamorgan and Monmouthshire* (March 1970) have already been overtaken by changes proposed by the Conservative Government elected in June 1970. At the date of writing, three more documents have been published: White Papers on *Local Government in England: Government Proposals for Reorganization* and *Reform of Local Government in Scotland*, together with a 'consultative document' on *The Reform of Local Government in Wales*. Legislation is promised for England and Wales in the 1971–2 Parliamentary session and for Scotland in 1972–3.

In view of this it seems appropriate (somewhat despairingly) to postpone further discussion until a later edition of this book, when, hopefully, proposals for reorganization will have been translated into legislation.

REFERENCES AND FURTHER READING

1 Cullingworth, J. B., *Housing in Greater London*, London School of Economics, Greater London Papers No. 4, 1961.
2 Cullingworth, J. B., *Report to the Minister of Housing and Local Government on Proposals for the Transfer of GLC Housing to the London Boroughs*, MHLG, 1970, 2 vols.
3 DOE, Circular 8/71, *Local Government Reorganization in England: Proposed New Areas*, HMSO, 1971.
4 Greater London Council, *Greater London Development Plan: Statement*, GLC, 1969.
5 Local Government Commission for England, *Report No. 5: Report and Proposals for the Tyneside Special Review Area*, HMSO, 1963.
6 Local Government Commission for Wales, *Report and Proposals for Wales*, HMSO, 1963.
7 MHLG, *Areas and Status of Local Authorities in England and Wales*, Cmd. 9831, HMSO, 1956.
8 MHLG, *Functions of County Councils and County District Councils in England and Wales*, Cmnd. 161, HMSO, 1957.
9 MHLG, *Local Government Finance (England and Wales)*, Cmnd. 209, HMSO, 1957.
10 MHLG, Circular 58/59, *Delegation of Planning Functions*, HMSO, 1959.
11 MHLG, *London Government: Government Proposals for Reorganization*, Cmnd. 1562, HMSO, 1961.
12 MHLG, *Management Study on Development Control*, HMSO, 1967.
13 MHLG, Circular 21/70, *Reform of Local Government in England: Areas and Boundaries*, HMSO, 1970.
14 Richards, P. G., *Delegation in Local Government*, Allen & Unwin, 1956.
15 Richards, P. G., *The New Local Government System*, Allen & Unwin, 1968.
16 Royal Commission on Local Government in England, *Written Evidence of the Ministry of Housing and Local Government*, HMSO, 1967.

17 Royal Commission of Local Government in England, *Local Government Reform* (Summary of the Report and D. Senior's 'Alternative Conclusions and Recommendations'), Cmnd. 4039, HMSO, 1969.

18 Royal Commission on Local Government in England, *Vol. I. Report* (Redcliffe-Maud Report), Cmnd. 4040, HMSO, 1969.

19 Royal Commission on Local Government in England, *Vol. 2. Memorandum of Dissent by Mr D. Senior*, Cmnd. 4040—I, HMSO, 1969.

20 Royal Commission on Local Government in England, *Vol. 3. Research Appendices*, Cmnd. 4040—II, HMSO, 1969.

21 Royal Commission of Local Government in Greater London, *Report* (Herbert Report), Cmnd. 1164, HMSO, 1960.

22 Royal Commission on Local Government in Scotland, *Report and Appendices* (Wheatley Report), Cmnd, 4150, HMSO, 1969.

23 Secretary of State for the Environment, *Local Government in England: Government Proposals for Reorganisation*, Cmnd. 4584, HMSO, 1971.

24 Secretary of State for Scotland, *Reform of Local Government in Scotland*, Cmnd. 4583, HMSO, 1971.

25 Secretary of State for Wales, *Local Government in Wales*, Cmnd. 3340, HMSO, 1967.

26 Seward, G. and Forster, G. H., *The Local Government Act, 1958*, Charles Knight & Co., 1959.

27 Town Planning Institute, 'Planning Administration: The Establishment of Separate Planning Departments – A Statement of Policy by the Town Planning Institute', *Journal of the Town Planning Institute*, Vol. 49, No. 3, March 1963.

28 Welsh Office, *The Reform of Local Government in Wales*, Consultative Document, HMSO, 1971.

Chapter VI

PLANNING AND LAND VALUES

'It is clear that under a system of well-conceived planning the resolution of competing claims and the allocation of land for the various requirements must proceed on the basis of selecting the most suitable land for the particular purpose, irrespective of the existing values which may attach to the individual parcels of land.'[14] It was the task of the Uthwatt Committee, from whose report this quotation is taken, to devise a scheme which would make this possible. Effective planning necessarily controls, limits, or even completely destroys, the market value of particular pieces of land. Is the owner therefore to be compensated for this loss in value? If so, how is the compensation to be calculated? and is any 'balancing' payment to be extracted from owners whose land appreciates in value as a result of planning measures? This problem of compensation and 'betterment' arises fundamentally 'from the existing legal position with regard to the use of land, which attempts largely to preserve, in a highly developed economy, the purely individualistic approach to land ownership'. This 'individualistic approach', however, has been increasingly modified during the past hundred years. The rights of ownership were restricted in the interests of public health: owners had (by law) to ensure, for example, that their properties were in good sanitary condition, that new buildings conformed to certain building standards, that streets were of a minimum width, and so on. It was accepted that these restrictions were necessary in the interests of the community – *salus populi est suprema lex* – and that private owners should be compelled to comply with them even at cost to themselves. 'All these restrictions, whether carrying a right to compensation or not, are imposed in the public interest, and the essence of the compensation problem as regards the imposition of restrictions appears to be this – at what point does the public interest become such that a private individual ought to be called on to comply, at his own cost, with a restriction or requirement designed to secure that public interest? The history of the imposition of obligations without compensation has been to push that point progressively further on and to add to the list of requirements considered to be essential to the well-being of the community.'* But clearly there is a point beyond which restrictions cannot reasonably be imposed on the grounds of 'good neighbourliness' without payment of compensation – and 'general consideration of regional or national policy require so great a restriction on the landowner's use of his land as to amount to a taking away from him of a proprietary interest in the land'.

This, however, is not the end of the matter. Planning sets out to achieve a selection of the most suitable pieces of land for particular uses. Some land will therefore be zoned for a use which is profitable for the owner, whereas other land will be zoned for a use having a low – or even nil – private value. It is this difficulty of 'development value' which raises the compensation problem in its most acute form. The development value which may legitimately – or hopefully – be expected by owners is in fact spread over a far larger area than is likely to be developed. This *potential* development value is therefore speculative, but until the individual owners are proved to be wrong in their assessments (and how can this be done?) all owners of land having a potential value can make a case for compensation on the assumption that their particular pieces of land would in fact be chosen for development if planning restrictions were not imposed. Yet this *'floating value'* might never have settled on their land, and obviously the aggregate of the values claimed by the individual owners is likely to be greatly in excess of a total valuation of all the pieces of land. As Haar has nicely put it, the situation is akin to that of a sweepstake: a single ticket fetches much more than its mathematically calculated value, for the simple reason that the grand prize may fall on any one holder.[3]

Furthermore, the public control of land use necessarily involves the shifting of land values from certain pieces of land to other pieces: the value of some land is decreased, while that of other land is increased. Planning controls do not destroy land values: in the words of the Uthwatt Committee, 'neither the total demand for development nor its average annual rate is materially affected, if at all, by

* *Uthwatt Report*, [14], p. 20. In a footnote there is reference to a dictum of Wright, J. (1 K.B. 458): 'A mere negative prohibition, though it involves interference with an owner's enjoyment of property, does not, I think, merely because it is obeyed, carry with it at common law any right to compensation. A subject cannot at common law claim compensation merely because he obeys a lawful order of the State'. However, full acceptance of this common law rule would necessarily result in hardship and inconsistent treatment between individuals (e.g. between the owners of land zoned for agriculture and land zoned for building).

planning ordinances'. Nevertheless, the owner of the land on which development is prohibited will claim compensation for the full potential development of his land, irrespective of the fact that that value may shift to another site.

In theory, it is logical to balance the compensation paid to aggrieved owners by collecting a betterment charge on owners who benefit from planning controls. But previous experience with the collection of betterment had not been encouraging. The principle had been first established in an Act of 1662 which authorized the levying of a capital sum or an annual rent in respect of the 'melioration' of properties following street widenings in London. There were similar provisions in Acts providing for the rebuilding of London after the Great Fire. The principle was revived and extended in the Planning Acts of 1909 and 1932. These allowed a local authority to claim, first 50 per cent, and then (in the later Act) 75 per cent, of the amount by which any property increased in value as the result of the operation of a planning scheme. In fact, these provisions were largely ineffective since it proved extremely difficult to determine with any certainty which properties had increased in value as a result of a scheme (or of works carried out under a scheme) or, where there was a reasonable degree of certainty, how much of the increase in value was directly attributable to the scheme and how much to other factors. The Uthwatt Committee noted that there were only three cases in which betterment had actually been paid under the Planning Acts, and all these were before the 1932 Act introduced a provision for the deferment of payment until the increased value had actually been realized either by sale or lease or by change of use. In short, it had not proved possible to devise an equitable and workable system.

The Uthwatt Committee concluded that the solution to these problems lay in changing the system of land ownership under which land had a development value dependent upon the prospects of its profitable use. They maintained that no new code for the assessment of compensation or the collection of betterment would be adequate if this individualistic system remained. The system itself had inherent 'contradictions provoking a conflict between private and public interest and hindering the proper operation of the planning machinery'. A new system was needed which would avoid these con- tradictions and which so unified existing rights in land as to 'enable shifts of value to operate within the same ownership'. The logic of this line of reasoning led to a consideration of land nationalization. But this the Committee rejected on the grounds that it would arouse keen political controversy, would involve probably insuperable financial problems, and would necessitate the establishment of a complicated national administrative machinery. In their view the solution to the

problem lay in the nationalization not of land itself but of all development rights in undeveloped land.

THE 1947 ACT

Essentially, this is precisely what the 1947 Town and Country Planning
Act did. Effectively, development rights and their associated values
were nationalized. No development was to take place without permission from the local planning authority. If permission were refused,
no compensation would be paid (except in a limited range of special
cases). If permission were granted, any resulting increase in land value
was to be subject to a development charge. The view was taken that
'owners who lose development value as a result of the passing of the
Bill are not on that account entitled to compensation'. This cut through
the insoluble problem posed in previous attempts to collect betterment values created by public action. Betterment had been conceived
as 'any increase in the value of land (including the buildings thereon)
arising from central or local government action, whether positive,
e.g. by the execution of public works or improvements, or negative,
e.g. by the imposition of restrictions on the other land'. The 1947 Act
went further: all betterment was created by the community, and it
was unreal and undesirable (as well as virtually impossible) to distinguish between values created, e.g. by particular planning schemes,
and those due to other factors such as the general activities of the
community or the general level of prosperity.

If rigorous logic had been followed, no payment at all would have
been made for the transfer of development values to the State, but this
– as the Uthwatt Committee had pointed out – would have resulted in
considerable hardship in individual cases. A £300 million fund was
established for making 'payments' to owners who could successfully
claim that their land had some development value on the 'appointed
day' – the day on which the provisions of the Bill which prevented
landowners from realizing development values came into force. Considerable discussion took place during the passage of the Bill through
Parliament on the sum fixed for compensation and it was strongly
opposed on the ground that it was too small. The truth of the matter
was that in the absence of relevant reliable information any global sum
had to be determined in a somewhat arbitrary way; but in any case it
was not intended that everybody should be paid the full value of their
claims. Landowners would submit claims to a centralized agency – the
Central Land Board – for 'loss of development value', i.e. the difference between the 'unrestricted value' (the market value without the
restrictions introduced by the Act) and the 'existing use value' (the
value subject to these restrictions). When all the claims had been

received and examined, the £300 million would be divided between claimants at whatever proportion of their 1948 value that total would allow. (In the event the estimate of £300 million was not as far out as critics feared. The total of all claims eventually amounted to £380 million.)

The original intention was to have a flexible rate of development charge. In some cases 100 per cent would be levied, but in others a lower rate would be more appropriate in order to encourage development 'on account of economic conditions in the country generally, or in particular areas where unemployment is above the average', or where it was important to secure 'a particular piece of development now, instead of in, say twenty years'.* However, when the Regulations came to be made, the Government maintained that the policy which had been set out during the passage of the Bill through the House was unworkable. The only explanation given for this was that 'the whole conception is that the value of land is divided into two parts – the value restricted to its existing use and the development value. The market value is the sum of the two. If, by the action of the State, the development value is no longer in the possession of the owner of the land, then all he has left is the existing use value. Moreover, the fund of £300 million is being provided for the purpose of compensating the owner of land for this reduced value . . . therefore the owner of land can have no possible claim to any part of the development value and it is logical and right that the State should, where development takes place, make a charge which represents the amount of the development value.' The whole idea of variable development charges (particularly for the depressed areas) was rejected, and a flat-rate 100 per cent levy introduced.

These provisions – of which only the barest summary has been given here – were very complex, and, together with the inevitable uncertainty as to when compensation would be paid and how much it should be, resulted in a general feeling of uncertainty and discontent which did not augur well for the scheme. The principles, however, were clear. To recapitulate, all development rights and values were vested in the State: no development could take place without permission from the local planning authority and then only on payment of a betterment charge to the Central Land Board. The nationalization of development rights was effected by the 'promised' payment of compensation. As a result landowners only 'owned' the existing-use rights of their land and it thus followed, first, that if permission to develop was refused no compensation was payable, and, secondly, that the price paid by public authorities for the compulsory acquisition

* *H.L. Debates*, Vol. 432, Col. 983, January 29, 1947. See also *H.C. Debates*, Vol. 451, Cols. 294–5, May 26, 1948.

of land would be equal to the existing-use value, i.e. its value excluding any allowance for future development.

THE 1947 SCHEME IN OPERATION

The scheme did not work as smoothly as was expected. In their first annual report the Central Land Board 'noted with concern some weeks after the Act came into operation that despite the liability for development charge land was still being widely offered and, still worse, taken at prices including the full development value'. This remained a problem throughout the lifetime of the scheme – though the magnitude of the problem still remains a matter of some controversy. It is certainly true that conditions were such that developers were prepared to pay more than existing-use prices for land; but the conditions were rather extraordinary. As the Board pointed out in their second report:

'The evidence available to the Board of prices paid for land for development suggests that sales at or near existing use value are more the exception than the rule. To a large extent this is due to the severe restriction on building. Building licences are difficult to get and the developer who has been fortunate enough to obtain one is often willing to pay a much inflated price for a piece of land upon which to build. In other words, a "scarcity value" attaches at present to the possession of a licence. The theory that the development charge would leave the developer unwilling or unable to pay more than existing use value for his land is not at present working out in practice, especially since a would-be house-owner who pays building value to the seller of the land, as well as a development charge to the Board, is still paying less in the total cost of his house than he would have to pay for an existing house with vacant possession.'

It was to prevent such problems that the Central Land Board had been given powers of compulsory purchase at the 'correct' price. These powers were used – not as a general means of facilitating the supply of land at existing-use prices, but selectively 'as a warning to owners of land in general'. Furthermore, they were used only where an owner had actually offered his land for sale at a price above existing-use value. Thus, purchase by the Board would have done nothing to facilitate an increase in the total supply of land for development even if they had been much more numerous. But, in fact, their very rarity served only to make the procedure arbitrary in the extreme and, indeed, may have added to the reluctance of owners to offer land for development at all.

The Conservative Government which took office in 1951 was intent on raising the level of construction activity and particularly the rate of private house-building. Though, within the limits of building activity set by the Labour Government, it is unlikely that the development charge procedure seriously affected the supply of land it is probable that the Conservative Government's plans for private building would have been jeopardized by it. This was one factor which led the new Government to consider repealing development charges.

The basic difficulty was that purchasers of land were compelled to pay a premium above the existing-use value in order to persuade an owner to sell: a development charge of 100 per cent therefore constituted a permanent addition to the cost of development. Moreover, the basis of the development charge was uncertain:

'Since it is assessed on the difference between the value of the land without permission to develop and its value for the development permitted, the amount of the charge is inevitably a matter of judgment and valuation – and therefore for negotiation, in the same way as the price of land is a matter for negotiation. In some cases quite small adjustments in the two values during the process of such negotiation will have a very large effect on the amount of development charge finally assessed. This is inherent in the nature of the charge, but the effect is to destroy confidence in its validity. Those who view development charge as a tax on development – and they are in the great majority – look for some definite relation between the amount assessed and the cost of the land or of the development; and their failure to find any makes them very critical of the method of assessment'.[19]

Further problems began to loom ahead as the final date for payments from the £300 million fund (July 1, 1953) drew near. First, the payment of this sum of money over a short period would have a considerable inflationary effect. Secondly, all claimants on the fund would receive payment whether or not they had actually suffered any loss as a result of the 1947 Act. (Some would have already recovered the development value of the land by selling at a high price; others may never have wished to develop their land, and, indeed, might even have bought it for the express purpose of preventing its development.) But the main difficulty was that if compensation were paid out on this 'once for all' basis, 'it would be exceedingly difficult for any future Government ever to make radical changes in the financial provisions, however badly they were working. For all the holders of claims on the fund would have been compensated for loss of development value – those who will be allowed to develop their land as well as those who will not.'

Some amendment of the 1947 Act scheme was clearly necessary, but though there might have been agreement on this, there was no equal agreement on what the amendments should be. There was a real fear that an 'amendment' which satisfied developers would seriously weaken or even wreck the planning machine: the scheme was part of a complex of planning controls which might easily be upset and result in a return to the very problems which the 1947 Act was designed to solve. Various proposals were currently being canvassed, but the most popular was a reduction in the rate of development charge. The intention was to provide an incentive to owners to sell their land at a price which took account of the developer's liability to pay the (reduced) charge. The Government took the view that this was not possible: 'vendors of land, like vendors of any other commodity, will always get the best price that they can, and the development charge, however small, would in effect be passed on, in whole or in part, to the ultimate user of the land'. Furthermore, the Government's objective was not merely one of easing the market in land: they were particularly concerned to encourage more private development, and even a low rate of development charge would act as a brake. On the (implicit) assumption that market prices for land would rise, the time would inevitably come when the charge would begin to greatly exceed the corresponding claim on the £300 million fund. Finally, it was felt that once the rate of development charge was reduced there would be no clear principle as to the level at which it should continue to be levied – 'the process of reduction, once begun, would be difficult to stop'. In short, the Government held that the financial provisions of the 1947 Act were inherently unsatisfactory and could not be sufficiently improved by a mere modification: what was needed was a complete abolition of development charges.

THE 1954 SCHEME

The abolition of development charges was made on the ground that they had proved 'too unreliable an instrument to act as the lynch-pin of a permanent settlement'. But, at the same time, if the main part of the planning system was to remain, some limit to the liability to compensation for planning restrictions was essential. Otherwise effective planning controls would become prohibitively expensive: the cost of compensation for restrictions, if paid at the market value, would be crippling. The solution arrived at was to compensate only 'for loss of development value which accrued in the past up to the point where the 1947 axe fell – but not for loss of development value accruing in the future'.

There were some clear advantages in this scheme: not only was the State's liability for compensation limited, but it was to be paid only if and when the owner of land suffered from planning restrictions. The compensation would be the 'admitted claim' on the £300 million fund (plus one-seventh for accrued interest on the amount of the claim). But not all admitted claims were to be met, even where loss of development value was caused by refusal of planning permission or by conditions attached to a permission. The 1932 Act had clearly established the principle that compensation should not be paid for restrictions imposed in the interest of 'good neighbourliness' and this principle was extended. No compensation was payable for refusal to allow a change in the use of a building; or for restrictions regarding density, layout, construction, design and so on; or for refusal to permit development which would place an undue burden on the community (e.g. in the provision of services). Some of these matters clearly fall within the 'good neighbour' concept,* while others are based on the principle that compensation is not to be paid merely because maximum exploitation has been prevented so long as development of a reasonably remunerative character is allowed.

The 1954 scheme† did not put anything in place of the development charge: the collection of betterment was now left to the blunt instruments of general taxation. Hence the attempt to 'hold the scales evenly between those who were allowed to develop their land and those who were not' was abandoned, but the use of 1947 development values as a 'permanent basis for compensation' safeguarded the public purse. On the other hand this meted out only a very rough justice to owners. The official view – at this date – was that this was not so:

'It may be suggested that to limit compensation in the way proposed will work unfairly in certain cases. Land which in 1947 had little development value, and therefore no claim or only a small claim on the fund, may at some future date acquire considerable development value. Values will tend to follow the development plans, and land which acquires a high development value will normally be land on which development will be permitted; but there will be exceptions and it may be thought that to limit compensation in these cases will

* The Act did, however, extend this principle drastically: a matter which evoked some opposition. For a fuller discussion see, for example, F. V. Corfield, *Compensation and the Town and Country Planning Act, 1959*, Solicitors' Law Stationery Society, 1959, p. 53 *et seq.*

† There were two Acts. The Town and Country Planning Act, 1953, abolished development charges, while the Town and Country Planning Act, 1954, limited compensation for the loss of development values to those sites for which a claim had been approved, and then only under defined circumstances when an application to develop was actually refused.

inflict hardship on owners who are refused permission to develop or whose land is bought compulsorily. It is important, however, to remember that all transactions in land since 1947 have taken place in the full knowledge that the 1947 development value was the most that anyone would hope to receive by way of compensation from the £300 million fund. Purchasers in future will be able to safeguard themselves by ensuring that permission to develop is forthcoming before they pay more than current existing-use value or, where a claim on the fund passes with the land, current existing-use value plus 1947 development value.'[19]

But this ignored the fact that the new scheme established a dual market in land. Compensation both for planning restrictions (in cases where a claim had been admitted) and for compulsory purchase by public authorities was to be paid on the basis of existing use plus any admitted 1947 development value, but private sales would be at current market prices. The difference between these two values might be very substantial, particularly where development of a far more valuable character than had been anticipated in 1947 took place. Furthermore, with the passage of time land values generally would increase, especially if inflation continued. Whatever theoretical justification there might be for the dual market it would appear increasingly unjust. Again, there is a real distinction between the hardships inflicted by a refusal of planning permission (i.e. the loss of the development value of land) and that caused by the loss of the land itself (i.e. compulsory purchase). In the first case the owner retains the existing use value of his land and is worse off only in comparison with owners who have been fortunate in owning land on which development is permitted and who can therefore realize a capital gain. But in the second case compulsory acquisition at less than market price involves an actual loss since the owner is not only deprived of his property, he is also compensated at a price which might be less than he paid for it and would almost certainly be insufficient to purchase a similar parcel of land in the open market.

Finally, though it must be generally accepted that individuals cannot be protected from foolish actions based on an inadequate knowledge of the law, the situation following the 1954 Act was so complex and – because of the inevitable unpredictability of the necessity for compulsory purchase – so risky that it appeared likely (in retrospect at least) that public opinion would demand a further change. There was an omen of this even while the legislation was passing through Parliament. A certain Mr Pilgrim had bought, in 1950, a vacant plot of land adjoining his house. To pay for this he raised a mortgage of

£500 on his house. Some years later the Romford Borough Council compulsorily acquired the land at the existing-use value of £65. (No claim had ever been made on the £300 million fund for loss of development value.) Mr Pilgrim committed suicide. Naturally the case attracted a lot of attention and as a result a new provision was introduced in the 1954 Bill to alleviate the position of persons, usually small owners, who suffered loss on compulsory acquisition because there was no established claim on the £300 million fund. This provision permitted the payment of an *ex gratia* supplement in cases of this kind.

To recapitulate, the effect of the complicated network of legislation which was now (1954) in force was basically to create two values for land according to whether it was sold in the open market or acquired by a public authority. In the former case there were no restrictions and thus land changed hands at the full market price. But in the latter case the public authority would pay only the existing (1947) use value plus any agreed claim for loss of 1947 development value. This was a most unsatisfactory outcome. As land prices increased, due partly to planning controls, the gap between existing use and market values widened – particularly in suburban areas near green belt land. The greater the amount of planning control, the greater did the gap become. Thus, owners who were forced to sell their land to public authorities considered themselves to be very badly treated in comparison with those who were able to sell at the enhanced prices resulting in part from planning restrictions on other sites. The inherent uncertainties of future public acquisitions – no plan can be so definite and inflexible as to determine which sites will (or might) be needed in the future for public purposes – made this distinction appear arbitrary and unjust. The abolition of the development charge served to increase the inequity.

The contradictions and anomalies in the 1954 scheme were obvious. It was only a matter of time before public opinion demanded further amending legislation.

THE 1959 ACT: THE RETURN TO MARKET VALUE

Opposition to this state of affairs increased with the growth of private pressures for development following the abolition of building licences. Eventually the Government was forced to take action. The resulting legislation (the Town and Country Planning Act, 1959) restored 'fair market price' as the basis of compensation for compulsory acquisition. This, in the Government's view, was the only practicable way of rectifying the injustices of the dual market for land. An owner now obtained (in theory at least) the same price for his land irrespective of whether he sold it to a private individual or to a public authority.*

These provisions thus removed a source of grievance, but they did nothing towards solving the fundamental problems of compensation and betterment, and the result proved extremely costly to public authorities. If this had been a reflection of basic principles of justice there could have been little cause for complaint, but in fact an examination of the position shows clearly that this was not the case.

In the first place, the 1959 Act (like previous legislation) accepted the principle that development rights should be vested in the State. This followed from the fact that no compensation was payable for the loss of development value in cases where planning permission was refused. But if development rights belong to the State, surely so should the associated development values? Consider, for example, the case of two owners of agricultural land on the periphery of a town, both of whom applied for planning permission to develop for housing purposes – the first being given permission and the second refused on the ground that the site in question was to form part of a green belt. The former benefited from the full market value of his site in residential use, whereas the latter could benefit only from its existing value. No question of compensation arose since the development rights already belonged to the State, but the first owner had these given back to him without payment. There was an obvious injustice here which could have eventually led to a demand that the 'penalized' owner should be compensated.

Secondly, as has already been stressed, the comprehensive nature of our present system of planning control has had a marked effect on values. The use for which planning permission has been, or will be, given is a very important factor in the determination of value. Furthermore, the value of a given site is increased not only by the development permitted on that site, but also by the development not permitted on other sites. In the example given above, for instance, the value of the site for which planning permission for housing development was given might be increased by virtue of the fact that it was refused on the second site.

---

* There were several qualifications, *inter alia*:

No account was taken of any increase in the value of the site which was brought about by the development scheme for which the land was being acquired.

If the development scheme increased the value of contiguous land belonging to the same owner, this increase was set off against the compensation payable on the land to be acquired. (No account was taken of any decrease in the value of land attributable to the threat of compulsory acquisition.)

THE LAND COMMISSION, 1967-71

Mounting criticism of the inadequacy of the 1959 Act led to a number of proposals for a tax on betterment, by way either of a capital gains tax or of a betterment levy. The Labour Government which was returned to power in 1964 introduced both. The 1967 Finance Act introduced a capital gains tax and the 1967 Land Commission Act introduced a new betterment levy. Broadly, the distinguishing principle was that capital gains tax was charged on increases in the current use value of land only, while betterment levy was charged on increases in development value. The Land Commission was abolished by the Conservative Government in 1971, but a summary account of its powers and operations is appropriate.

The rationale underlying the Land Commission Act was set out in a 1965 White Paper:

'In the Government's view it is wrong that planning decisions about land use should so often result in the realizing of unearned increments by the owners of the land to which they apply, and that desirable development should be frustrated by owners withholding their land in the hope of higher prices. The two main objectives of the Government's land policy are, therefore:

    (i) to secure that the right land is available at the right time for the implementation of national, regional and local plans;
    (ii) to secure that a substantial part of the development value created by the community returns to the community and that the burden of the cost of land for essential purposes is reduced.'[18]

To enable these two objectives to be achieved a Land Commission was established (with headquarters located at Newcastle upon Tyne – in line with the dispersal of offices policy). The Commission could buy land either by agreement or compulsorily, and it was given very wide powers for this purpose. The second objective was met by the introduction of a betterment levy on development value. This was necessary not only to secure that a substantial part of the development 'returned to the community', but also to prevent a two-price system as existed under the 1954 Act. The levy was deducted from the price paid by the Commission on its own purchases and was paid by owners when they sold land privately. A landowner thus theoretically received the same net amount for his land whether he sold it privately, to the Land Commission, or to another public authority.

Compulsory Purchase
Though the Commission could buy by agreement they had to have

effective powers of compulsory purchase if they were 'to ensure that the right land is made available at the right time'. There were two reasons for this. First, though the levy was at a rate (initially 40 per cent) thought to be adequate to leave enough of the development value to provide 'a reasonable incentive', some owners of land might still be unwilling to sell. Secondly, though the net price obtained by the owner of land should have been the same irrespective of whether the body to whom he sold it was private or public, some owners might have been unwilling to sell to the Land Commission.

The Act provided two sets of compulsory powers. One was the normal powers available to local authorities, with the usual machinery for appeals and a public inquiry. Under these powers the Commission has to disclose the purpose for which they required the land. These powers could be used for purchasing land scheduled for development in a development plan, or for land permitted for development.

Of particular importance was the provision whereby land could be acquired by means of a *vesting declaration*. The advantages of a vesting declaration were that the Commission obtained a good title to the land (without investigation of the title) and could dispose of it for development as soon as the declaration took effect. By this means the delays of the normal conveyancing procedure were to be avoided. (Local authorities now have the same powers under the Town and Country Planning Act, 1968.)

The second set of compulsory powers were not to become operative until the 'second appointed day' and were to be brought into effect only if it appeared 'that it is necessary in the public interest to enable the Commission to obtain authority for the compulsory acquisition of land by a simplified procedure'. They were intended to provide a rapid procedure under which objectors would have no right to state their case at a public inquiry, and the Commission need not disclose the purpose for which the land was required. The purpose here was to deal quickly and effectively with landowners who were holding up development. In fact they did not become operative during the lifetime of the Land Commission.

Management and Disposal of Land
It was intended that the Commission would often be acquiring land in advance of need. They were, therefore, given wide powers of managing and disposing of land; but they could also develop land themselves. Land could be sold or leased to public or private bodies for any purpose – even if the purpose was different from the one for which the land was purchased. Land which was sold could be made subject to restrictions and future development value could be reserved to the Commission. Such land disposals were known as 'crownhold'.

Normally, the Commission had to dispose of land at the best price they could obtain, but there was one important exception. This was the 'concessionary crownhold disposition' which could be made for land which was to be developed *for housing purposes*. Here the Commission could dispose of land at less than the market price. All such housing land was subject to crownhold restrictions or covenants. In the case of owner-occupiers the Commission had the right of pre-emption on terms which ensured that the amount of the concession (and future increases in development value) accrued to them. Concessionary crownholds were also applicable to 'bodies which can effectively supervise the assignment of such houses', such as housing associations.

The Betterment Levy
The levy differed from the development charge of the 1947 Act in two important ways. First, it did not take all the development value. The Act did not specify what the rate was to be, but it was made clear that the initial rate of 40 per cent would be increased to 45 per cent and then to 50 per cent 'at reasonably short intervals'. (In fact, it never was.)

The second difference from the development charge was that though the levy would normally be paid by the seller, if 'when the land comes to be developed, it still has some development value on which levy has not been taken in previous sales, that residual value will be subject to levy at the time of development'. Thus (ignoring a few complications and qualifications), if a piece of land was worth £500 in its existing use but was sold for £3,500 with planning permission, the levy was applied to the difference, i.e. £3,000 – the levy, at the initial rate was £1,200. If, however, the land were sold (at existing use value plus a 'hope' value that planning permission might be obtained) at £1,000, while the full development value was £3,500, the levy would be paid by both seller and purchaser: £200 by the former and £1,000 by the latter.

Certain bodies were exempt from the levy – for instance, local authorities, newtown development corporations, the Housing Corporation and housing societies.

The proceeds of the levy were expected to amount to £80 million in a full year. In fact, however, the amount levied did not approach this figure. In 1968–9 it amounted to £15 million and in 1969–70 £31 million.

Land for Development
The Commission's first task was to assess the availability of, and demand for, land for house-building, particularly in the areas of greatest pressure. In their first annual report, they pointed to the difficulties in some areas particularly in the South East and the West

Midlands where the available land was limited to only a few years' supply. Most of this land could not, in fact, be made available for early development. Most of it was in small parcels; some was not suitable for development at all because of physical difficulties; and, of the remainder, a great deal was already in the hands of builders. Thus there was little that could be acquired and developed immediately by those other builders who had an urgent need for land. All this highlighted the need for more land to be allocated by planning authorities for development.

The Land Commission had to work within the framework of the planning system. Though a Crown body, they did not operate as such and thus were subject to the same planning control as private developers. The intention was that the Commission would work harmoniously with local planning authorities and form an important addition to the planning machinery. As the Commission pointed out, though Britain has perhaps the most sophisticated planning system of any country, it is one designed to control land use rather than to promote the development of land. The Commission's role was to ensure that land allocated for development was in fact developed – by channelling it to those who would develop it. They could use their powers of compulsory acquisition to amalgamate land which was in separate ownerships and acquire land whose owners could not be traced. They could purchase land from owners who refused to sell for development or from builders who wished to retain it for future development.

In their first report, the Commission gently referred to the importance of their role in acting 'as a spur to those local planning authorities whose plans have not kept up with the demand for various kinds of development'. Though they stated their hope that planning authorities would allocate sufficient land, they warned that in some cases they might have to take the initiative and, if local authorities refused planning permission, go to appeal. In their second report their line was much stronger. They pointed out that, in the pressure areas, they had had only modest success in achieving a steady flow of land on to the market. This was largely because these are areas in which planning policies are aimed at containing urban growth and preserving open country.

In 1969–70 the Commission purchased 1,000 acres by agreement and a further 240 acres by the use of its compulsory powers. But the use of these compulsory powers was on the increase, and a further 2,500 acres were subject to compulsory purchase at March 1970.

The Dissolution of the Land Commission
The Land Commission was abolished in 1971. Altogether, during its

brief existence, it actually purchased 2,800 acres (though, in November 1970, a further 9,000 acres were in the pipeline). So far as betterment levy was concerned £72 million was assessed of which (at November 1970) £46 million had been collected.

It is not easy to appraise the success which the Commission had. It was only beginning to get into its stride in 1970 when a new Government was returned which was pledged to its abolition on the grounds that it had 'no place in a free society'. The official statement (in the House of Commons on July 22, 1970) that it had failed 'to make a worthwhile contribution to the release of land in the areas of acute land shortage' can hardly be taken as an objective assessment. This, however, is not the place to embark on the assessment which is required. It must suffice to say that the problem of land availability (and the related issue of high land prices) remains. A DOE Circular of December 1970 (*Circular* 10/70) urged local authorities to ensure that 'a wholly adequate supply of land is made available as soon as possible and that such a supply continues to keep well abreast of demand'. It also uttered the mild warning that 'the Secretary of State will take whatever measures are open to him to facilitate the provision of additional land for housing purposes'.

The demise of the Land Commission, like that of the Central Land Board some fifteen years earlier, is eloquent testimony to the political nature of planning. Planners may talk in technical terms, but the essential issues are political.

REFERENCES AND FURTHER READING

1 Ashworth, W., *The Genesis of Modern British Town Planning*, Routledge, 1954.
2 Corfield, F. V., *Compensation and the Town and Country Planning Act, 1959*, Solicitors' Law Stationery Society, 1959.
3 Haar, C. M., *Land Planning Law in a Free Society*, Harvard University Press, 1951.
4 Hall, P. (Ed.), *Land Values*, Sweet & Maxwell, 1965.
5 Harris, B. and Nutley, W. G., *Betterment Levy and the Land Commission*, Butterworth, 1967 (with a supplementary 'Service Volume').
6 Heap, D., *Encyclopaedia of Betterment Levy and Land Commission Law and Practice*, Sweet & Maxwell, 1967 (in loose-leaf form with regular supplements).
7 Heap, D., *Introducing the Land Commission Act*, Sweet & Maxwell, 1967.
8 Land Commission, *Annual Reports*, HMSO.
9 Land Commission, *Statements and Memoranda; Extra-Statutory Concessions* (reproduced in Heap, D., *Encyclopaedia of Betterment Levy and Land Commission Law and Practice*, Sweet & Maxwell).
10 MHLG, *Betterment Levy: An Explanatory Memorandum on Part III of the Land Commission Act, 1967*, HMSO, 1967.
11 MHLG, *Modifications in Betterment Levy*, Cmnd. 4001, HMSO, 1969.
12 Ministry of Local Government and Planning, *Town and Country Planning 1943-1951 Progress Report*, HMSO, Cmd. 8204, 1951.
13 Parker, H. R., *Paying for Urban Development*, Fabian Society, 1959.
14 *Report of the Expert Committee on Compensation and Betterment* (Uthwatt Report), Cmd. 6386, HMSO, 1942.
15 Seward, G. and Stewart Smith, W. R., *The Land Commission Act, 1967*, Knight, 1967.
16 Turvey, R., *The Economics of Real Property*, Allen & Unwin, 1957.

F

17 Wells, Sir Henry, 'Land for Housing', *Housing Review*, Vol. 17, No. 6, November-December 1968, pp. 174–7.
18 White Paper, *The Land Commission*, Cmnd. 2771, HMSO, 1965.
19 White Paper, *Town and Country Planning Act, 1947; Amendment of Financial Provisions*, Cmd. 8699, HMSO, 1952.

Chapter VII

AMENITY

THE CONCEPT OF AMENITY

'Amenity' is one of the key concepts in British town and country planning; 'it underlines all modern planning administration and is necessarily one of the Ministry's main preoccupations'. Yet it appears only four times* in the 1947 Act (and the consolidated 1962 Act), and nowhere in the legislation is it defined. The Act merely states that 'if it appears to a local planning authority that it is expedient in the interests of amenity', they may take certain action – in relation, for example, to unsightly neglected waste land or to the preservation of trees. It is also one of the factors that may need to be taken into account in controlling advertisements and in determining whether a discontinuance order should be made. It is a term widely used in planning refusals and appeals; indeed the phrase 'injurious to the interests of amenity' has become part of the stock-in-trade jargon of the planning world. But like the proverbial elephant, amenity is easier to recognize than to define – with the important difference that, though all would be agreed that an elephant is such, there is considerable scope for disagreement on the degree and importance of amenities: which amenities should be preserved, in what way they should be preserved, and how much expense (public or private) is justified. The problem is relatively straightforward in so far as trees are concerned, as is apparent from the excellent book *Trees in Town and City* produced by the Ministry in 1958. It is much more acute in connection with electricity pylons – yet the Central Electricity Generating Board is specifically charged not only with maintaining an efficient and co-ordinated supply of electricity but also with the preservation of amenity. Here the question is not merely one of sensitivity but also of the enormous cost of preserving amenities: the cost of undergrounding the largest lines is about £1 million a mile as compared with £75,000 overhead. Apart from the apparently insoluble problems of cost, there is the problem of determining how much control the public will accept. Poor architecture, ill-conceived schemes, 'mock-Tudor' frontages may upset the planning

* Town and Country Planning Act, 1962, Sections 28, 29, 34 and 36.

officer, but how much regulation of this type of 'amenity-injury' will be publicly acceptable? And how far can negative controls succeed in raising public standards? Here emphasis has been laid on design bulletins, design awards and such ventures as those of the Civic Trust – a body whose object is 'to promote beauty and fight ugliness in town, village and countryside'. Nevertheless, local authorities have power not only to prevent developments which would clash with amenity (e.g. the siting of a repair garage in a residential area) but also to reject badly designed developments which are not intrinsically harmful. Indeed 'outline planning permission' for a proposal is often given on the condition that detailed plans and appearance meet the approval of the authority.

Thus, though amenity may be an elusive quality, it is one which has constantly to be borne in mind and decided upon by planning practitioners. But amenity is more than good design. As Lord Holford has put it:

'. . . amenity is not a single quality, it is a whole catalogue of values. It includes the beauty that an artist sees and an architect designs for; it is the pleasant and familiar scene that history has evolved; in certain circumstances it is even utility – the right thing in the right place – shelter, warmth, light, clean air, domestic service . . . and comfort stations.'[18]

This extensive concept of amenity underlines its important role in British town and country planning. Its all-embracing yet vague character makes it at one and the same time crucial and vulnerable. To particularize, the Department has stated:

'The following are cases in which the claim of amenity is fairly clear, though the decision on each must turn on the balance of conflicting interests: the disturbance of a residential area caused by noise from a saw mill or a repair garage, by the smell or flies from pig sties, by dust or smoke from industry, or by the general bustle created by the establishment of a business; the spoiling of a stretch of country by ugly houses or perhaps by any houses at all; the erection anywhere of a badly designed or badly sited building, unsightly in itself or unneighbourly; the alteration or destruction of a particularly charming or interesting building; any development likely to concentrate traffic in places where there is not enough room to take it comfortably; failure to provide enough shops, schools and open space to serve the neighbourhood; the felling of trees even though mature, with no provision for replanting; advertisement hoardings in unsuitable places. Anything ugly, dirty, noisy, crowded, destructive, intrusive or uncomfortable may "injure the interests of amenity" and, therefore, be of concern to the planning authority.'[39]

This goes far towards encompassing a major part of 'planning': and another passage in the same report goes even further: 'The new towns are themselves essays in amenity, and in the replanning of damaged and blighted areas of existing towns, and in the framing of development plans for country and town alike, the fundamental requirements are those of amenity – pleasant and convenient living conditions, a decent amount of open space and proper facilities for recreation.' There is a striking similarity between these official pronouncements and the arguments put forward a half-century earlier by those who campaigned for the introduction of town planning.

In recent years, however, there has been a marked sharpening of interest in amenity, caused partly by the rapid rate of development, and an awareness of the inadequacy of the planning system automatically to preserve and enhance amenity. The Transport Act of 1968, for instance, enables the use of a road by vehicles to be prohibited on amenity grounds for certain periods of the day. Perhaps the most striking provision is to be found in the 1968 Countryside Act which requires every Minister, Government Department and public body to have regard to the desirability of conserving the natural beauty and amenity of the countryside in all their functions relating to land. Lawyers may rightly point out that this does not constitute, of itself, an effective restriction on any statutory power or discretion, but it is an important statement of policy and one which the statutory and voluntary guardians of amenity will seize upon whenever it is infringed. There is more to planning than law.

The preservation and development of amenity thus form a basic objective of planning policy. From this point of view, amenity can hardly be discussed separately. Nevertheless, there are certain matters where planning controls are specifically, and almost exclusively, concerned with amenity. The control of advertisements is a prime example of this.

CONTROL OF ADVERTISEMENTS

The need to control advertisements has been long recognized. Indeed, the first Advertisements Regulation Act of 1907 antedated by two years the first Town Planning Act. But even when amended and extended (in 1925 and 1932) the control was quite inadequate. Not only were the powers permissive, they were also limited. For instance, under the 1932 Act the right of appeal (on the ground that an advertisement did not injure the amenities of the area) was to the magistrates court – hardly an appropriate body for such a purpose. The 1947 Act set out to remedy the deficiencies. There are, however, particular difficulties in establishing a legal code for the control of advertisements. Advertisements may range in size from a small window-notice to a massive hoarding; they range in purpose from a bus-stop sign to a demand to buy a certain make of detergent; they could be situated alongside a cathedral, in a busy shopping street or in a particularly beautiful rural setting; they might be pleasant or obnoxious to look at; they might be temporary or permanent; and so on. The task of devising a code which would take all the relevant factors into account and, at the same time, achieve a balance between the conflicting interests of legitimate advertising or notification and 'amenity' presents real problems. Advertisers themselves frequently complain that decisions in apparently similar cases have not been consistent with each other. The official Departmental view is that no case is exactly like another and hard and fast rules cannot be applied: each case has to be considered on its individual merits in the light of the tests of amenity and – the other factor taken into account – public safety.

The control of advertisements is exercised by Regulations. The Secretary of State has very wide powers of making regulations 'for restricting or regulating the display of advertisements so far as appears to the Secretary of State to be expedient in the interests of amenity or public safety'. The question of 'public safety' is rather simpler than that of amenity – though there is still ample scope for disagreement: the relevant issue is whether an advertisement is likely to cause danger to road users (and also to 'persons using railways, inland waterways, coastal waters and airfields'). Examples are advertisements which obstruct the line of sight at a corner or bend, or obstruct the view of a traffic sign or signal, and illuminated advertisements which are likely to dazzle or confuse road users or are likely to be mistaken for traffic lights.

The definition of an advertisement is not quite as complicated as that of 'development', but it is very wide: 'advertisement means any word, letter, model, sign, placard, board, notice, device or representation, whether illuminated or not, in the nature of and employed wholly or partly for the purpose of advertisement, announcement or direction. . . .' Five classes of advertisement are 'excepted' from all control – those on enclosed land, within a building, on or in a vehicle, incorporated in and forming part of the fabric of a building, and displayed on an article for sale. As one might expect, there are some interesting refinements of these categories, which can be ignored for the present purposes (though we might note, in passing, that a vehicle must be kept moving, or to use the more exact legal language, must be nor-mally employed as a moving vehicle on any highway or railway – and the same applies to vessels). With these exceptions, no advertisement may be displayed without 'consent'. However, certain categories of advertisement can be displayed without 'express consent'; so long as the local authority takes no action they are 'deemed' to have received consent. These include bus-stop signs and timetables, hotel and inn signs, profession or trade plates, 'To Let' signs, election notices, statutory advertisements and traffic signs.

Except in relation to advertisements to which the 'deemed consent' procedure applies, a local authority can serve a *discontinuance order* when they are satisfied that removal is necessary 'to remedy a sub-stantial injury to the amenity of the locality or a danger to members of the public'. There is the normal right of appeal to the Secretary of State.

This is not, however, all there is to advertisement control. In some areas, e.g. national parks or near a cathedral, it may be desirable to virtually prohibit all advertisements of the poster type and to seriously restrict other advertisements including those normally displayed by the ordinary trader. Accordingly, local planning authorities have power to define 'Areas of Special Control' where 'special protection on grounds of amenity' is thought desirable. (Over a third of England and Wales is now subject to this 'special control'.) Within an Area of Special Control the general rule is that no advertisement may be dis-played; such advertisements as are given express consent are con-sidered as exceptions to this general rule.

This has proved a very difficult field in which to obtain unanimity, but the effectiveness of the controls and agreements is very apparent to the European (and, still more, the American) visitor.

CONSERVATION

Britain has a remarkable wealth of historic buildings, but changing economic and social conditions often turn this legacy into a liability. The cost of maintenance, the financial attraction of redevelopment, the need for urban renewal, the roads programme and similar factors often threaten buildings which are of architectural or historic interest. This is a field in which voluntary organizations have been particularly active – as witness the work of the National Trust, the Ancient Monuments Society, the Society for the Protection of Ancient Buildings, the Victorian Society and others. As is so often the case, voluntary effort preceded State action. The Society for the Protection of Ancient Buildings was founded in 1877. The National Trust (or to use its full name, the National Trust for Places of Historic Interest or

Natural Beauty) was founded in 1895. Though the first State action came in 1882 with the Ancient Monuments Act, this was important chiefly because it acknowledged the interest of the State in the preservation of ancient monuments. Such preservation as was achieved under this Act (and under similar Acts passed in the following thirty years) resulted from the goodwill and co-operation of private owners. It was not until 1913 that powers were provided to compulsorily prevent the damage or destruction of monuments. Strictly speaking, the Ancient Monuments Acts are outside the legal realm of town and country planning, but their objectives and scope demand that they be considered within the same context. The term 'ancient monument' is defined very widely and could include almost any building or structure made or occupied by man at any time: the DOE is responsible for the care and preservation of prehistoric settlements, Roman walls, Norman castles and Gothic abbeys. It is advised by three Ancient Monuments Boards for England, Scotland and Wales, who recommend monuments whose preservation is of national importance. Such monuments are 'scheduled': obligations are thereby imposed on owners and occupiers. The owner of a scheduled monument must give the Department three months' notice if he wishes to repair, alter, demolish or, indeed, do any work affecting it.

There are over 12,000 protected monuments in Britain. In cases where a monument is in danger of destruction or damage, an *Interim Preservation Notice* (lasting for a maximum period of twenty-one months) or a more permanent *Preservation Order* can be made, which prohibits any work without the written consent of the Secretary of State. The Department can become the 'guardian' of a monument whereby it becomes permanently responsible for preservation, maintenance and management, or it can acquire monuments. In total, over 700 monuments are in the charge of the Department.

Under the Historic Buildings and Ancient Monuments Act, 1953, the DOE has power to make grants for the preservation of 'buildings of outstanding historic or architectural interest' – and of their contents and adjoining land. It can also purchase such buildings or accept them as gifts. Three Historic Buildings Councils (for England, Scotland and Wales) were set up as advisory bodies. The 1953 Act was passed primarily to deal with the problem of preserving houses or buildings which were inhabited or 'capable of occupation' – these were not covered by the earlier legislation.

LISTED BUILDINGS

Under planning legislation, the DOE maintains lists of buildings of 'special architectural or historic interest'. There are two objectives here. First, 'listing' is intended to provide guidance to local planning authorities in carrying out their planning functions. For example, in planning redevelopment, local authorities will take into account listed buildings in the area. Buildings in a slum clearance area may be preserved with the aid not only of grants from the Historic Building Council but also with house improvement grants available under the Housing Acts. Secondly, and more directly effective, when a building is listed no demolition or alteration which would materially alter it can be undertaken by the owner without the approval of the local authority. This is technically termed *listed building consent*.

Applications for listed building consent have to be advertised and any representation must be taken into account by the local authority before they reach their decision. Where demolition is involved, the local authority has to notify the appropriate local amenity society, and a number of other bodies, namely the Ancient Monuments Society, the Council for British Archaeology, the Georgian Group, the Society for the Protection of Ancient Buildings, the Victorian Society, as well as the Royal Commission on Historical Monuments. Again, any representations have to be taken into account when the application is being considered.

If, after all this, the local authority are 'disposed to grant consent' for the demolition (and, in certain cases, the alteration) of a listed building, they have to refer the application to the Secretary of State so that he can decide whether to 'call in' the proposal and deal with it himself.

All these provisions apply to listed buildings (of which there were, at the end of 1968, 115,000), but the Secretary of State has power to list a building at any time, and local authorities can serve a *building preservation notice* on an unlisted building; this has the effect of protecting the building for six months, thus giving time for considering whether or not it should be listed.

With a listed building the presumption is in favour of preservation. Indeed 'listing' is in essence a collective preservation order. It is an offence to demolish or to alter or extend a listed building unless listed building consent has been obtained. This is different from the general position in relation to planning permission where an offence arises only after the enforcement procedure has been invoked. Fines for illegal works to listed buildings are related to the financial benefit expected by the offender.

The legislation also provides a deterrent against deliberate neglect of historic buildings. This was one way in which astute owners could circumvent the earlier statutory provisions: a building could be neglected to such an extent that demolition was unavoidable, thus giving the owner the possibility of reaping the development value of the site. In such cases the local authority can now compulsorily acquire the building at a low price, technically known as 'minimum compensation'. If the Secretary of State approves, the compensation is assessed on the assumption that neither planning permission nor listed building consent would be given for any works to the building except those for restoring it to, and maintaining it in, a proper state of repair; in short, all development value is excluded.

The strength of these powers (and others not detailed here) reflect the concern which is felt at the loss of historic buildings. They are not, however, all of this penal nature. Indeed, ministerial guidance has emphasized the need for a positive and comprehensive approach. Grants are available under the Local Authorities (Historic Buildings) Act, 1962, the Historic Buildings and Ancient Monuments Act, 1953, and under the Housing Acts. Local authorities can also purchase properties by agreement, possibly with grant-aid from the DOE under the 1953 Act. Furthermore, an owner of a building who is refused 'listed building consent' can, in certain circumstances, serve a notice on the local authority requiring them to purchase the property. This is known as a *listed building purchase notice*. The issue to be decided here is whether the land has become 'incapable of reasonably beneficial use'. It is not sufficient to show that it is of less use to the owner in its present state than if developed.*

More important is the emphasis on areas, as distinct from individual buildings, of architectural or historic interest. This was introduced by the Civic Amenities Act, 1967 (promoted as a private member's Bill by Duncan Sandys, President of the Civic Trust, and passed with Government backing). This gave statutory recognition for the first time to the area concept and made it a *duty* of local planning authorities 'to determine which parts of their areas are areas of special architectural or historic interest, the character of which it is desirable to preserve or enhance' and to designate such areas as *conservation areas*. When a conservation area has been designated, the Act requires special attention to be paid in all planning decisions to the preservation or enhancement of its character and appearance.

Given a framework of this kind, there is considerable scope for voluntary action in 'preserving or enhancing' the character of an area. Great impetus to the formation and effectiveness of local civic and amenity societies has been given by the Civic Trust. When the Trust was founded in 1957 there were only 200 such societies in Great Britain; by April 1969 there were 670 registered with the Trust.

The Trust now publishes a large number of pamphlets and provides assistance and advice to local societies. Its regular *Progress in Creating Conservation Areas* provides not only a complete list of conservation

* For further discussion on *purchase notices* see pp. 94–7 above.

areas, but also detailed reports and maps on individual schemes. (In June 1971 the number of conservation areas in Great Britain had reached 1,385.)

Mention should be made of the Historic Buildings Bureau and the Preservation Policy Group. The former is a small Government agency, set up in 1954, which has the function of bringing together buyers and sellers of those historic buildings which qualify for inclusion in the statutory lists and need special help to find a market. The Preservation Policy Group was set up in 1966 'to co-ordinate the special studies of historic towns and consider the results, to consider what changes are desirable in current legal, financial and administrative arrangements for preservation, including the planning and development aspects, and to make recommendations'. The Group assisted in framing proposals which are now incorporated in the 1968 Town and Country Planning Act (and which are summarized above). The four studies – of Bath, Chester, Chichester and York – have now been published.

In May 1970, the Preservation Policy Group reported and made recommendations, *inter alia* for greater financial aid to be provided for historic buildings, for legislation to provide for a new type of General Conservation Scheme on which Exchequer grants would be paid to meet 50 per cent of the deficiency, and for pilot studies of this nature to be carried out in Bath, Chester, Chichester and York in advance of the legislation.[36]

These recommendations are still under discussion, but major increases in the total grants for historic buildings were announced in June 1971. These are to increase from £575,000 in 1969/70 to £1 million in 1971/72.

ECCLESIASTICAL BUILDINGS

Ecclesiastical buildings are exempt from the provisions of the Ancient Monuments Act and the Planning Acts. This exemption dates back to 1912 when Archbishop Davidson successfully argued that the Church had its own system of law for protecting churches. Until very recently a corollary of this was that churches of outstanding architectural or historic interest were not eligible for grants on the recommendation of the Historic Buildings Councils. The Redundant Churches and other Religious Buildings Act, 1969, however, provides for grants (initially up to £200,000) for the preservation of selected buildings which are no longer used as places of worship. Exchequer aid is to be channelled through the Redundant Churches Fund set up by the Church of England under the Pastoral Measure, 1968. An equal contribution to the Fund is to be made by the Church Commissioners.

These measures apply only to Church of England buildings. However, redundant places of worship of other denominations can now be transferred to the Secretary of State if he wishes to acquire them for preservation under the Historic Buildings and Ancient Monuments Act, 1953.

PRESERVATION OF TREES AND WOODLANDS

'Trees are an indispensable raw material, but they are no less necessary as an adornment of town and country, and they are also a great joy in themselves. "Trees", said R. L. Stevenson, "are the most civil society." It is this aspect of trees which has led to the introduction into most recent Planning Acts of special provisions by which trees may be preserved, though without prejudice to good forestry and good farming.'[39]

Trees are clearly – so far as town and country planning is concerned – a matter of amenity. Indeed, the powers which local authorities have with regard to trees can be exercised only if it is 'expedient in the interests of amenity'. Where the local authority are satisfied that it is 'expedient', they can make a tree preservation order – applicable to trees, groups of trees, or woodlands. Such an order can prohibit the cutting down, topping or lopping of trees except with the consent of the local planning authority. Mere preservation, however, leads eventually to decay and thus defeats its object. To prevent this, a local authority can make replanting obligatory when they give permission for trees to be felled. The aim is to avoid any clash between good forestry and the claims of amenity. But the timber of woodlands always has a claim to be treated as a commercial crop, and though the making of a Tree Preservation Order does not necessarily involve the owner in any financial loss (isolated trees or groups of trees are usually planted expressly as an amenity), there are occasions when it does. Yet though woodlands are primarily a timber crop from which the owner is entitled to benefit, two principles have been laid down which qualify this. First, 'the national interest demands that woodlands should be managed in accordance with the principles of good forestry', and secondly, where they are of amenity value, the owner has 'a public duty to act with reasonable regard for amenity aspects'. It follows that a refusal to permit felling or the imposition of conditions on operations which are either contrary to the principles of good forestry or destructive of amenity ought not to carry any compensation rights. But where there is a clash between these two principles compensation is payable. Thus in a case where the 'principles of good forestry' dictate that felling should take place, but this would result in too great a sacrifice of amenity, the owner can claim compensation for the loss which he suffers. Normally a compromise is reached whereby the felling is deferred or phased. An early case reported in the *Progress Report* of the Ministry of Town and Country Planning[39] is illustrative:

'In the Conway Valley a large estate had changed hands and, as often happens in such cases, an application was made for a licence to fell the trees, which are a particularly beautiful feature of the landscape, visible from many directions and from a considerable distance. The local planning authority were consulted and made a tree preservation order which was confirmed. A subsequent application to the local planning authority for permission to fell some 750 trees, stated to be mature, was refused on the grounds that any felling would be injurious to amenity. In granting permission, on appeal, for the felling of 174 specified trees, the Minister observed that felling likely to cause serious injury to the woodland character of the area could not be justified unless the future welfare of the woodlands or other urgent public need made such a course unavoidable. He was satisfied, however, that felling to the extent specified in his decision would not only be harmless to amenity but would also benefit the woods since it would help the growth of young trees. "Merely to forbid the felling of any trees however old and rotten they may become, is to doom the wood to death. This would be to betray our trusteeship for future generations both of trees and of mankind." '

The commercial felling of timber is subject to licence from the Forestry Commission and special arrangements exist for consultation between the Commission, the DOE and the local planning authority.

Planning powers go considerably further than simply enabling local authorities to preserve trees. The National Parks and Access to the Countryside Act, 1949, enabled planning approvals to be given subject to the condition that trees are planted, and local authorities themselves have power to plant trees on any land in their area. With the increasing vulnerability of trees and woodlands to urban development and the needs of modern farming, wider powers and more Exchequer aid have been provided by the Civic Amenities Act, 1967, the Countryside Act, 1968, and the Town and Country Planning Act, 1968. Local Planning authorities are now *required* to ensure that conditions (preferably reinforced by tree preservation orders) are imposed for the protection of existing trees and for the planting of new ones. This, together with the Department's continuous emphasis on the importance of trees, has led to a substantial increase in the number of tree preservation orders being made. In 1964, 662 orders were submitted to the Ministry for confirmation; in 1967 there were 737, and in 1970, 1,621.

Prior to the Civic Amenities Act, tree preservation orders had to be confirmed by the Minister. The Act introduced 'provisional tree preservation orders' which take immediate effect. Following the Town and Country Planning Act, 1968, ministerial confirmation is needed only where there is an objection to the order.

The Countryside Act widened the compensation provisions to cover cases where an owner is required to replant in the interests, not of commercial forestry, but of amenity. It also empowered the Forestry Commission to plant and manage trees in the interests of amenity and to acquire land for this purpose. Previously, the Commission's powers were limited to growing trees for timber. Also noteworthy is the provision of an Exchequer grant for local authorities (and, in certain circumstances, individuals and societies) who plant trees for amenity purposes anywhere in the countryside and acquire land for the purpose. These new provisions reflect the increasing importance attached to the amenity value of trees.

The planting of trees on highways has a forty-year history. The 1925 Roads Improvement Act gave local authorities powers to acquire land on the side of highways 'for the purposes of planting and amenity'. Lack of technical expertise led to some unhappy results and the Road Beautifying Association was established in 1928 to rectify this. Though a voluntary body, this Association did notable work, for example on the Kingston and Dorking by-passes, the Dorking-Leatherhead road, the Denham-Rickmansworth section of the North Orbital Road, the Basingstoke and Romney by-passes, the Woodbridge and Colchester by-pass and the Market Harborough by-pass. Following the 1937 Trunk Roads Act, the Association was officially appointed as adviser on trunk road planting to the Ministry of Transport. This work is now carried out directly by the DOE with advice from an expert Advisory Committee on the Landscape Treatment of Trunk Roads, but the Association's services are still retained by a number of local authorities, and, among its recent achievements is the tree belt screening for the Esso refinery extension at Fawley on Southampton Water. The DOE has a 'countryside planting programme', and in 1967-8 over half a million trees and shrubs were planted near trunk roads and motorways.[40]

Like so many aspects of amenity, trees are the particular concern of voluntary bodies. The Men of Trees is one such body – founded in 1923 by Richard St Barbe Baker. Several branches exist in this country and there are many overseas. But the need for action on the part of public authorities is becoming increasingly recognized. In 1956, local authorities who were undertaking slum clearance or redevelopment were exhorted (in MHLG *Circular* 36/56) not to fail 'to seize this unique opportunity to introduce more trees into their areas', and a handsome book published by the Department in 1958 (*Trees in Town and City*) maintained that 'hardly a street could not be improved, if someone would give thought to planting the right trees in the right places'. One of the Department's series of Design Bulletins (*Landscaping for Flats*) dealt with planting in the wider context of landscaping: 'No single factor has a greater effect on the appearance of a housing estate than the presence – or absence – of trees'. The problem is only in part one of costs; it is much more one of sensitivity and thoughtfulness. To a large extent, the basic issues are the same as those involved in good design: a subject to which we now turn.

PLANNING AND GOOD DESIGN

Good design is an elusive quality which cannot easily be defined. As Lord Holford has said, 'Design cannot be taught by correspondence; words are inadequate, and being inadequate may then become misleading, or even dangerous. For the competent designer a handbook on design is unnecessary, and for the incompetent it is almost useless as a medium of instruction.'[21] Yet local authorities have to pass judgment on the design merits of thousands of planning proposals each year, and pressure is mounting from governmental, official and professional bodies for higher design standards to be imposed. The principles of good design and their execution lie outside the scope of this book; here reference can be made only to the powers and practices of local authorities, and some of the particular problems which arise. It needs to be stressed, however, that good design is not basically a matter of cost, but of the combined skills and sensitivity of the architect, the client and the builder.

Planning authorities have a clear legal power to grant planning permission subject to conditions relating to design and appearance. Planning permission is frequently given for a proposed development on the basis of an 'outline application', and subject to the condition that the detailed plans meet with their approval: if the detailed plans are unsatisfactory they can be rejected. There is a difficult problem here which basically stems from the fact that it is not the function of the planning authority to provide developers with good designs, and the amendment of a poor design may produce a compromise result almost as unsatisfactory as the original. Furthermore, the impossibility of laying down generally applicable principles (except that of employing a 'good' architect!) makes the task of the local planning authority a difficult one. A well-staffed and organized authority will spend considerable time with developers discussing sketch-plans – but not all authorities are well staffed or organized and the importance which is placed on this aspect of planning control varies greatly between authorities. Some have prepared notes for the guidance of developers, and there are various publications of the DOE and of voluntary bodies which have the same objective. Major developments are often referred to the Royal Fine Art Commissions for their opinion.

Yet some local authorities are still apparently under the impression that the Department will allow appeals against planning refusals based solely on design grounds. This is not so – as the various ministers have emphatically declared, and as can be deduced from the published decisions on planning appeals. Perhaps the best statement of policy on this question is to be found in the June 1969 *Bulletin of Selected Planning Appeals*:

'One of the objects of planning is to prevent bad design and to encourage good. But unfortunately it is not possible to lay down rules defining what is good and what is bad; and much may in any event turn on the site. Moreover, opinions, even expert opinions, can often differ.

'It is therefore difficult to offer useful advice to intending developers other than the obvious advice that they should take trouble to ensure that the designs submitted are good. If they are in doubt how to ensure this, the authority may be able to help them if they ask for advice before starting on plans.

'Two questions can arise on design. The first is whether the design is bad in itself: fussy or ill proportioned, or downright ugly. The second is whether, even if the design is not bad in itself, it would be on the particular site: right out of scale with close neighbours (which does not mean that it need be similar to neighbouring designs), an urban design in a rural setting, or a jarring design or the wrong materials in a harmonious scene.

'It is obviously desirable that in operating control over designs authorities should be guided by the advice of a qualified architect; and if a district council have not got this, the county council may be able to assist them. Authorities should always be prepared to arrange for this architectural adviser to discuss proposals with developers, whether at the outset on a request for advice or when plans have been submitted about which they are doubtful.

'Planning control should not be used to stifle initiative and experiment in design; a design is not bad because it is new and different – it may be very good. Designs should be rejected only if the objection is clear and definite and can be explained. It is not enough to say that a design will "injure the amenities" or "conflict with adjoining development"; it must be explained why it will do so.

'In general, planning control of design should be exercised with

great restraint. But where a design is plainly shoddy or badly proportioned or out of place, the authority should not hesitate to ask for
something better.'

But the written word cannot have the required impact – on either
the developer or the local planning authority; hence the superiority
of the well-illustrated *Design Bulletins* and *Housing Manuals* issued
by the Department. Also important – though probably of limited
impact – are the Design Awards made by the DOE on the recommendations of regional panels of judges appointed jointly by the Secretary
of State and the Royal Institute of British Architects.

Normally, planning permission and appeals excite little public
interest even when the proposals are of particular importance. In part
this may be because of the inadequate publicity given to development
proposals, and the restrictions to which 'third parties' are subject – a
matter which is discussed in the final chapter. To a very limited extent,
the Royal Fine Art Commission and the Royal Fine Art Commission
for Scotland are able to fill this gap. Appointed under Royal Warrant,
their functions are to advise Government Departments and other
public bodies when requested to do so and when the Commissions
think that their advice would be useful. They can also offer advice if
they think that a project may affect amenities of public or national
importance. In practice this means that anyone can raise a question of
'public amenity or artistic importance' with them: it is for the Commissions to decide whether the question is of sufficient importance to
warrant their attention. Any advice, however, has to be given to a
public body.

The Commissions can call witnesses before them and inspect sites.
Their outspoken reports have referred to a very wide range of developments, from the colour of telephone kiosks to the siting of power
stations in National Parks. The work of the Commissions is not fully
reported and, indeed, a totally misleading impression can be gained
from their periodic reports,[43] which concentrate on the more important developments referred to them on which they are not satisfied
with the final outcome. Thus the 1957 (English) Report, for example,
refers to their misgivings on high buildings adjacent to the Royal
Parks; their objections to the Park Lane carriageway in Hyde Park;
their regret that planning permission had been given for the development of a site in Lincolns Inn Fields; their concern over the unimagi-
native designs for barrack blocks and other Army buildings, and the
damage to amenities caused by the use of rural land by Service
Departments; their alarm at the outcrop of ribbon development, the
very low standard of speculative housing and the need for more architectural advice to local planning authorities. Increasingly, the work of

the Commission is concerned with broad issues of 'public amenity or artistic importance'.

In recent years, they have devoted a major part of their time to the problems arising from 'the all-pervading demands of traffic in towns, over-dense building on urban sites and the lack of co-ordinated planning – even of public services'.

It is difficult to assess what impact the Commissions have: certainly it is by no means as great as the Commissions would wish. They can only advise, and, if their advice is rejected, report accordingly. Where an authority 'is not prepared to accept the Commission's general recommendations, whether on account of undertakings already given or for other reasons', they are faced with the difficult choice between withdrawing their interest entirely and trying to improve in detail a scheme of which it fundamentally disapproves. 'In many cases the Commission feels that its duty to the public requires the second course, but by adopting it, it runs the risk of being made partially responsible in the eyes of the public for the final result.'[43]

There are other amenity and preservation societies which act as watch-dogs, such as the Councils for the Protection of Rural England and Wales, the Georgian Group, the Victorian Society, and so on. Of particular note is the Civic Trust founded in 1957 on the initiative of Mr Duncan Sandys to promote high standards of architecture and civic planning and to encourage a wider interest in the appearance of towns and villages.

All these bodies do useful work, but their impact is limited. The fundamental problem, as repeatedly stressed by such bodies as the Council for the Protection of Rural England and the Royal Institute of British Architects, is to educate public opinion – and the lay members of local planning committees. Though more adequate planning powers would assist, there is no substitute for this. The Secretary of State has power to provide by order that appeals against decisions of local planning authorities on matters of design and appearance should be referred to an independent tribunal and to himself. This power has never been used: but, even if it were, it would not affect poor designs which are passed by local authorities and on which there is consequently no appeal.

Of more significance are the sixty-eight architectural advisory panels originally set up in the 1920s. These panels, which considered 14,000 planning applications in 1967, give advice to local planning authorities and district councils exercising delegated powers. In the words of the panels' Central Committee, the lay members of local authorities should not only 'strive to raise general standards of design, they should do this without frustrating creative work: they are, however, unlikely to succeed without competent advice and assistance from the architectural profession. The panels can assist all authorities regardless of size but they are of particular value to those authorities who do not themselves employ qualified architects.'[7] Over 600 architects serve on these panels. They undoubtedly contribute to the improvement of standards of design but, of course, they can operate only where they are welcomed.

HIGH BUILDINGS

For centuries towns have been developed with low buildings, and intrusions into the skylines were reserved for religious, military, and cultural buildings.[19] The first competitors were the chimneys, the mills and the factories of the Industrial Revolution – the symbols of new power. But a general movement upwards was held back by constructional and technical limitations, as well as by the shock of dismay at what Pevsner has called the unredeemable horror of the fourteen-storey Queen Anne's Mansions, built in 1878. (The horror has now been 'redeemed' by demolition.) The advent of steel and reinforced concrete frames, the lift and new methods of fire-fighting* opened up enormous possibilities for high buildings, thus giving scope for architectural freedom and for intensive and profitable development of expensive sites. The increasing profitability of high-density redevelopment, together with the smallness of many redevelopment sites, have led to a situation where, to quote the sixteenth report of the Royal Fine Art Commission, 'the dominating consideration in the instructions given to the architect is all too often simply the desire for the largest area of lettable floor space consistent with planning procedure on small and restricted sites; . . . this is no way to produce fine urban architecture'. In the Commission's view the drabness and mediocrity of many of the buildings recently constructed in city centres spring from the restricted site and opportunities available to the architect. This is essentially a problem of the assembly of land, techniques of comprehensive development and the adequacy of planning powers. Even if individual high buildings are of architectural merit there still remains the problem of their siting. The Royal Fine Art Commission have repeatedly complained of the siting of high buildings on the fringes of city parks (where there is the particular temptation of easy 'angles of light' and the fine view afforded to the occupiers) and the intrusion of giant blocks of flats or offices in small town squares. The problem has

---

* Before the fire-fighting methods devised for New York skyscrapers, the traditional maximum length of the fireman's ladder was only 100 feet. Buildings above this height were generally prohibited for fire-safety reasons. The tower of London University (210 feet) was reluctantly approved by the London County Council only on condition that the upper floors were not occupied! See A. Ling.[19]

attracted most attention in Greater London* where two types of control are exercised. The first is 'Plot Ratio Control',† by which the amount of floor space is determined in relation to the area of the site. A single-storey building covering the whole of a site would have a plot ratio of 1:1, as would a two-storey building covering a half of the site, or a three-storey building covering a third of the site. The system makes for flexibility and effectively prohibits the canyon building of Manhattan. It can be used in conjunction with planning standards relating to daylighting, car-parking, etc., none of which it supersedes.

Aesthetic control cannot be operated in a similar fashion and the situation in London is now further complicated by the division of responsibility between the GLC and the London Boroughs. Proposals for buildings over 150 feet in the central area, and 125 feet elsewhere in Greater London, have to be referred to the GLC for direction. The GLC have produced (as part of the Greater London Development Plan) a report which sets out the basis for a threefold classification of land in London, together with a map which shows in broad terms the areas to which the three categories might apply.[16] This non-statutory map is a guide for the London Boroughs; the definition of areas is a matter for local development plans.

The three categories are:

(i) Areas in which high buildings are inappropriate.
(ii) Areas which are particularly sensitive to the impact of high buildings.
(iii) Areas in which a more flexible or positive approach is possible.

The GLC policy (to be applied within their area of competence) is set out on page 181.

Height is, of course, relative. The GLC study defines a high building 'as one which significantly exceeds the height of its surroundings, and includes all types of structures including masts, pylons, cooling towers, chimneys, etc.'.

---

* But see T. Sharp's report on Cambridge,[48] where he recommends the prohibition of tower blocks everywhere in the City and a maximum permitted height of five storeys; and the paper by the Royal Fine Art Commission for Scotland on tall buildings in Edinburgh.[44]

† See *A Plan to Combat Congestion in Central London*, London County Council, 1957. Plot ratio control was introduced in 1948, replacing the control by means of height zoning, angular limits, and a system of percentage of site covered by buildings at different levels of the building. It has the advantage of allowing a greater flexibility in design, and of allowing an advance estimate to be made of the floor area which can be permitted on any given site. The system was originally outlined in Ministry of Town and Country Planning, *The Redevelopment of Central Areas*, 1947, where it is referred to as the Floor Space Index.

GLC policy on high buildings

	Category (i) Areas in which High Buildings are inappropriate	Category (ii) Areas which are particularly sensitive to the impact of High Buildings	Category (iii) Areas in which a more flexible or positive approach is possible
General Indication of Areas	(a) Within or with a visual relationship to famous areas of Special Character (e.g. Whitehall, Trafalgar Square, the Tower of London, Hampton Court). (b) Within or with a visual relationship to other areas of high environmental quality or unified design (e.g. Blackheath and Greenwich Park, the central Royal Parks). (c) Situations in which high buildings would spoil traditional or famous views (e.g. Houses of Parliament, St Paul's Cathedral, Buckingham Palace). (d) Major high points and ridges (e.g. Sydenham Hill, Harrow-on-the-Hill, Shooter's Hill).	(a) Areas of visual significance such as other high points and ridges not covered in category (i) (e.g. Hainault, Alexandra Palace ridges). (b) Areas of rural character (e.g. Barnes Common, Epping Forest, parts of the Green Belt). (c) Certain Thames-side areas. (d) Other areas of Metropolitan Importance. (e) Areas of Architectural or Historic Interest.	Areas not covered by the other categories.
General Policy	Normally proposals for high buildings within these areas would be refused. Exceptions would be rare.	The indication of these areas has been related to the policy for Areas of Metropolitan Importance. It may be necessary to consider some areas as potential ones in which high buildings would be inappropriate. It must be open to the Council and other local planning authorities to add others as experience and knowledge are gained.	Decisions within this category must be related to the character of the area and its density. Depending upon experience and future pressure this category may need refinement.
		That a development conforming with the general height of surrounding buildings would have serious disadvantages and that the freedom of layout resulting from a high building would enable major public improvements and amenities to be achieved. That the proposal would not harm the essential character of the surrounding area. That the high building would identify and emphasize a point of civic or visual significance both locally and in relation to the urban scene over the whole areas from which it will be visible.	That the building would preferably identify and emphasize a point of visual significance.
Criteria to be used in judging proposals	Not applicable.		

Applicable to both Category (ii) and Category (iii)

That the proposed building, from wherever it is seen, would not mar the skyline nor intrude to the detriment of any famous or pleasant view.
That the proposal would be very carefully related to its surroundings, both existing and proposed, and especially to any other high buildings or prominent features in the vicinity.
That the site is sufficiently large and comprehensive to secure a complete and well-designed setting of lower buildings and/or landscaped open space.
That the amenities and development possibilities of surrounding sites and buildings would not be impaired.
That in view of the inevitable prominence of a high building it should be of outstanding architectural quality.
That due account is taken of the effects of wind turbulence in the siting of any high building and that every effort has been made to contain or eliminate such turbulence.

The new policy is an attempt to overcome the inadequacies of earlier approaches (which were detailed in previous editions of this book). Whether the Royal Fine Art Commission will have further criticism to make remains to be seen.

This discussion highlights some of the problems inherent in the British planning system, and indeed, in any attempt to control development in a society where there is a predominantly individualistic pattern of land ownership. There is a definite limit to the area over which controls can be effectively, usefully and equitably operated – and this is particularly so in relation to amenity and aesthetics. To the economist, probably the most striking aspect of this summary of the problem in relation to high buildings is the complete absence of any reference to economics. Critics of the Greater London Council seem to assume not only that the Council has extraordinary legal powers and financial resources (e.g., to make high buildings materialize at will) but also that it can largely ignore the economics of high buildings on particular sites.

The limit to controls is not, however, only economic: there is the further question of how far it is justifiable to exercise controls in the interests of amenity and aesthetics.* Sometimes there is a clear public responsibility: there would be no doubt as to what decision ought to be taken on an application to erect a 300-feet-high slab block in Parliament Square; but a large number of cases are by no means as simple as this, and on many issues the final judgment must be a subjective one. This raises the further question of how much society is prepared to pay for amenity and beauty – the same question which arises with power stations and pylons in national parks. No piece of administrative machinery will ever abolish these fundamental issues.

To conclude on an optimistic note, however, there is abundant evidence to support the view of the Preservation Policy Group, expressed in its 1970 Report,[36] that 'there has been a revolution over the past five years in the way old buildings are regarded, and in the importance now attached by public opinion, to preservation and conservation'. The same heightened public concern can be seen in relation to all the issues discussed in this chapter.

---

* For a passionate argument against high building see Sharp, T., *Town and Townscape*, John Murray, 1968.

REFERENCES AND FURTHER READING

1 Advertising Association, *Advertising Outdoors*, 1962.
2 Advertising Association, *How Advertising Disciplines Itself*, 1962.
3 Advertising Industry Consultative Committee, *Code of Standards for Advertising on Business Premises*, 1960.
4 Ancient Monuments Boards for England, Wales and Scotland, *Annual Reports* (published in one volume), HMSO.
5 Cambridgeshire and Isle of Ely County Council, *A Guide to Historic Buildings Law*, second edition, 1970.
6 Carter, E., *The Future of London*, Penguin Books, 1962.
7 Central Committee for the Architectural Advisory Panels, *The Architectural Advisory Panels*, 1969.
8 Central Electricity Generating Board, *Electricity and the Environment*, CEGB, 1970.
9 Civic Trust, *Magdalen Street, Norwich*, 1959.
10 Civic Trust, *Conservation Areas: Preserving the Architectural and Historic Scene*, 1967.
11 Civic Trust, *Street Improvement Schemes*, 1967.
12 Civic Trust, *The Civic Society Movement*, 1967.
13 Countryside Commission, Annual Reports, HMSO.
14 Crowe, S., *The Landscape of Roads*, Architectural Press, 1960.
15 Fedden, R., *The Continuing Purpose: A History of the National Trust, Its Aims and Work*, Longmans, 1968.
16 Greater London Development Plan, *Statement* and *Report of Studies* (Chapter 8: 'The Metropolitan Scene'), GLC, 1969.
17 Historic Buildings Councils for England, Wales and Scotland, *Annual Reports*, (published separately), HMSO.
18 Holford, Sir William, *Preserving Amenities*, Central Electricity Generating Board, 1959.
19 Ling, A., 'Skyscrapers and their Siting in Cities', *Town Planning Review*, Vol. 34, No. 1, April 1963.
20 London County Council, *A Plan to Combat Congestion in Central London*, LCC, 1957.
21 MHLG, *Design in Town and Village*, HMSO, 1953.
22 MHLG, *Trees in Town and City*, HMSO, 1958.
23 MHLG, *Bulletin of Selected Planning Appeals*, No. 1–13, HMSO, 1947–58; *Selected Planning Appeals* (*Second Series*), No. 1–5, 1959–63, HMSO.

24 MHLG, *New Houses in the Country*, HMSO, 1960.
25 MHLG, Circular 51/63, *Development near Buildings of Special Architectural or Historical Interest*, HMSO, 1963.
26 MHLG, *Landscaping of Flats*, Design Bulletin No. 5, HMSO, 1963.
27 MHLG, Circular 53/67, *Civic Amenities Act, 1967 – Parts I and II*, HMSO, 1967.
28 MHLG, *Historic Towns: Preservation and Change*, HMSO, 1967.
29 MHLG, *Bath: A Study in Conservation*, HMSO, 1968.
30 MHLG, *Chester: A Study in Conservation*, HMSO, 1968.
31 MHLG, *Chichester: A Study in Conservation*, HMSO, 1968.
32 MHLG, *York: A Study in Conservation*, HMSO, 1968.
33 MHLG, Circular 61/68, *Town and Country Planning Act, 1968 – Part V: Historic Buildings and Conservation*, HMSO, 1968.
34 MHLG, *Preservation of Historic Buildings and Areas*, Development Control Policy Note No. 7, HMSO, 1969.
35 MHLG, Circular 1/69, *Town and Country Planning (Tree Preservation Order) Regulations 1969*, HMSO, 1969.
36 MHLG, *Preservation Policy Group: Report to the Ministry of Housing and Local Government, May, 1970*, HMSO, 1970.
37 MHLG, circular 96/69, *Control of Advertisement Regulations*, HMSO, 1969.
38 Ministry of Town and Country Planning, *The Redevelopment of Central Areas*, HMSO, 1947.
39 Ministry of Town and Country Planning, *Town and Country Planning Progress Report 1943–1951*, Cmd. 8204, HMSO, 1951. (Chapter X, 'Amenity'.)
40 Ministry of Transport, *Roads in England: Report by the Ministry of Transport for the Year Ended 31st March, 1968*, H.C. Paper No. 1, November, 1968.
41 Nottinghamshire County Planning Department, *Newark: Action for Conservation*, Notts. C.C., 1968.
42 Royal Commission on Historical Monuments, *Monuments Threatened or Destroyed*, HMSO, 1963.
43 Royal Fine Art Commission, *Periodic Reports (Twentieth Report*, Cmnd. 3905, HMSO, 1969.)
44 Royal Fine Art Commission, Scotland, *Periodic Reports, (Report for 1964 to 1966*, Cmnd, 3364, HMSO, 1967).
45 Ryan, P., *The National Trust*, Dent, 1969.
46 Scottish Development Department, Memorandum 74/70, *Town and Country Planning (Scotland) Act, 1969 – Part V* (issued with Circular 73/70, *Historic Buildings and Conservation*), SDD, 1970.

47 Scottish Development Department, *Scotland's Historic Buildings: A Guide to the Legislation which Protects them*, SDD, 1970.
48 Sharp, T., 'Dreaming Spires and Teeming Towers', *Town Planning Review*, Vol. 33, No. 4, January, 1963.
49 Sharp, T., *Town and Townscape*, John Murray, 1968.
50 Ward, P. (ed.), *Conservation and Development in Historic Towns and Cities*, Oriel Press, 1968.
51 Worskett, R., *The Character of Towns: An Approach to Conservation*, Architectural Press, 1969.

Chapter VIII

PROTECTION OF THE ENVIRONMENT

THE CONTROL OF POLLUTION

Concern about pollution is not new: it was as early as 1273 that action in Britain was taken to protect the environment from polluted air: a royal proclamation of that year prohibited the use of coal in London. (It was not effective, despite the dire penalties: it is recorded that a man was sent to the scaffold in 1306 for burning coal instead of charcoal.)

What is new (apart from the abolition of capital punishment) is, first, the huge scale of the pollution problem and, secondly, the increasing determination to tackle it. 1970 – European Conservation Year – saw the publication of the White Paper from which the title of this chapter is taken, and the establishment of a Royal Commission on Environmental Pollution. Previously there had been numerous inquiries on specific problems of pollution – from the Beaver Committee on air pollution, to the Pippard Committee on 'the effects of heated and other effluents and discharges on the condition of the tidal reaches of the River Thames'; from the Browne Committee on refuse storage and collection, to the Wilson Committee on the problem of noise; from the Key Committee on 'the experimental disposal of house refuse in wet and dry pits', to the Jeger Committee on sewage disposal. By contrast the remit of the Royal Commission is boundless: 'to advise on matters, both national and international, concerning the pollution of the environment; on the adequacy of research in this field; and the future possibilities of danger to the environment'. At the same time, governmental machinery for dealing with pollution has been reorganized. Until October 1960, responsibilities for the control of environmental pollution were distributed among ten different ministers: in this month, the Secretary of State for Local Government was given the responsibility for co-ordinating Government action in this field. This has now passed to the new mammoth ministry significantly called the Department of the Environment.

Only a few issues can be touched on here: fuller treatment is to be found in the literature listed at the end of the chapter. The selection of issues must be arbitrary: like 'town and country planning' and 'amenity', 'environmental pollution' admits of no simple delimitation. The issues selected are derelict land, minerals, air pollution and noise.

DERELICT LAND

Derelict land – defined as 'land so damaged by industrial or other development that it is likely to remain out of use unless subjected to special treatment' – is commonly thought of as a legacy of the Industrial Revolution. Certainly there is an appalling legacy: in 1969 there were (in England alone) 96,000 acres of derelict land. What is not usually realized is the scale of continuing dereliction. Some 6,000 acres are used each year for surface mineral working of which some 4,000 are for sand and gravel extractions. Additionally, 500 acres are used for the tipping of colliery spoil and a further 500 acres become derelict from other causes. The Department's 1963 brochure, *New Life for Dead Lands: Derelict Areas Reclaimed*, put the total (for England and Wales) at about 150,000 acres. Of this, some 60,000 acres consisted of spoil heaps, 60,000 acres of excavations and 'holes in the ground', and 30,000 acres of other types of dereliction.

Unfortunately, the statistics are inadequate to allow an adequate picture to be drawn of the rate at which land is being currently consumed. Thus, a railway closure, or the closure of a coal mine with large heaps of spoil means that land ceases to be in use and so technically becomes derelict. In recent years there has been a gross annual increase of from 3,000 to 6,000 acres of derelict land, offset in part by nearly 2,000 acres a year of reclamation by local authorities. This does not, of course, signify that land is being currently consumed on this scale. The statistics reflect the bringing into account of pre-planning control activities, often at the point of time when the user of the land ceases operation.

Nevertheless, there can be little doubt that the problem is being contained rather than solved. This is borne out by the figures in the Table which have been obtained from the Department of the Environment. These relate to England only. The recent apparent increase in dereliction was brought about partly by reappraisal and resurvey by local authorities, as well as by railway and colliery closures. Plans are in hand for a more widely based survey which will include land in active use and land subject to restoration conditions (both excluded from the current figures).

Much derelict land (particularly waste tips and abandoned industrial land) is concentrated in relatively small parts of the older industrial areas of the North, the Midlands and South Wales. It is this 'random incidence' (to use a phrase of the Hunt Committee) which hinders a more rapid rate of reclamation. Quite small local authorities with small resources of money, staff or expertise may find themselves faced with large problems. Even larger authorities may be faced with a formidable problem. The Hunt Committee called for a national programme and the establishment of a derelict land reclamation agency.

Derelict Land and Reclamation, England, 1964-1967

	Total derelict land	Land reclaimed/landscaped
	(acres)	(acres)
1964	84,900	2,076
1965	90,986	2,061
1966	92;876	1,641
1967	92,643	1,639
1968	93,920	2,113
1969	95,722	2,504

Reclamation of Derelict Land

Great advances in reclamation techniques have been made since the 'thirties. Slow and costly 'pick and shovel' methods have now given way to modern earth-moving machines which can move mountains of material at relatively low cost. Techniques of 'making soil' have been refined and it is now possible to make grass and trees grow in the most uncongenial conditions. Furthermore, rising land values and the need for sites for open space, playing fields and all types of urban development have added an impetus to reclamation, particularly in or near urban areas. But local authorities have no statutory duty to reclaim derelict land or to improve its appearance. Their powers are purely permissive and, as is so often the case, much depends on the energy of individual local authorities. Some have paid scant attention to the problems, whereas others have appointed staff to deal with them and have worked to a planned programme. The Department have maintained that probably two-thirds of existing derelict land could either be reclaimed or improved in appearance by landscaping – 'what is wanted is a determination by the local authority concerned to deal with all the land that might be treated within a given time'.*

There are various powers available to local authorities quite apart from their normal powers to provide housing, open space and schools under which they can acquire derelict land and reclaim it during the normal course of development. Derelict land can also be acquired under the wider powers provided by the Planning Acts; these enable

---

* *New Life for Dead Lands*, p. 3. The remaining third 'has perhaps less claim for immediate attention because it is remote from urban or village communities and has not become a source of nuisance or concern to the public'.

local authorities to undertake any work for which powers are not already available. Finally, the National Parks and Access to the Countryside Act gives specific powers for the acquisition of derelict land and the restoration and improvement of such land whether or not it is owned by the local authority. There is, thus, no shortage of powers. The question of finance is, however, different. Costs of reclamation vary widely, but the average is around £1,300 per acre in England and rather more in Wales. It would cost around £100 million to reclaim the 70,000 acres in England and Wales which are thought to justify treatment.

Government grants towards the cost of acquisition and reclamation of derelict land are available under several Acts. Under the Industrial Development Act, 1966, the rate is 85 per cent in development areas, provided that the clearance of the land 'is expedient with a view to contributing to the development of industry'. The Local Government Act of the same year provided a 50 per cent grant for other areas. Following the report of the Hunt Committee, the Local Employment Act, 1970, provided for 75 per cent grants in intermediate areas and also in 'derelict land clearance areas'. The latter are areas where the 'economic situation in the locality is such' that it is 'particularly appropriate with a view to contributing to the development of industry in the locality' that grants should be paid.

This complicated system is a result of an attempt to give differential assistance according to the local employment needs of different areas. The underlying rationale is (in the words of the Hunt Committee) that an unfavourable environment depresses economic opportunity: dereliction 'deters the modern industry which is needed for the re-vitalization of these areas and helps to stimulate outward migration'. There is, thus, a clear ulterior motive. The same is not the case with the grants (this time at the rate of 75 per cent) in national parks and areas of outstanding natural beauty. Here the objective is the 'enhancement of natural beauty' or at least the restoration of beauty.

Additional to these two specific grant schemes, there is Exchequer assistance through the resources element of the rate support grant. Here the object is straightforward assistance to local government finance. (The 'resources element' – similar to the earlier rate deficiency grant – is payable to any authority with rate resources lower than the national average in proportion to their population.)

Considerable progress with reclamation has been made by a number of authorities. Lancashire County Council, for example, has an annual programme of tree planting on derelict land: between 1951 and 1968 more than 1½ million trees were planted on 85 sites covering 850 acres. A programme of reclamation on colliery waste sites is also under way; examples of these with illustrations (which are far more eloquent than words) are given in the Ministry's brochure *New Life for Dead Lands*. More exciting is the use of flashes or wet gravel pits for sailing – for instance, Pennington Flash in Lancashire and the disused gravel workings at Horbury in the West Riding. Where land can be made attractive for housing, the increased site values can quickly recoup the cost of reclamation – as in the Wallbrook housing scheme at Coseley in Staffordshire.

The problem remains, however, of keeping pace with new dereliction. It has been reported that in Lancashire there had been an 'addition of 4,000 acres to Lancashire's derelict acreage in ten years . . . over 14,000 Lancashire acres were in current use for mineral extraction and tipping; . . . these activities accounted for two acres in every five taken each year for development of all kinds; . . . in the present administrative and financial circumstances the County Council could not hope to keep pace with the spread of dereliction'. At first sight this seems incomprehensible; surely the planning machine is adequately geared to control these operations, at least to the extent of ensuring that any dereliction is cleared up when the operations are finished? Here it is necessary to examine the scope and character of planning controls over mineral workings.

CONTROL OF MINERAL WORKING*

The reconciliation between economic and amenity interests in mineral working is an obvious matter for planning authorities. It would, however, be misleading to give the impression that the function of planning authorities is simply to fight a continual battle for the preservation of amenity. Planning is concerned with competing pressures on land and with the resolution of conflicting demands. Amenity is only one of the factors to be taken into account. Thus it is a general policy to ensure that mineral working is carried on 'with proper regard for the appearance and other amenities of the area', and that when the working is finished the land should (wherever practicable) not be left derelict but be 'restored or otherwise treated with a view of bringing it back to some form of beneficial use'. At the extreme – where mineral working would involve 'too great injury to the comfort and living conditions of the people in the area or to amenities generally' – mineral working can be limited or even prevented. Here a balance has to be struck between the economic need for minerals and the interests of amenity, and it is

* Provisions relating to the control of mineral workings are scattered about several Acts and numerous regulations and circulars. A useful comprehensive summary is given in the Ministry's memorandum *The Control of Mineral Working* (revised edition 1960) though this is now outdated by the Town and Country Planning Act, 1968. (Unless otherwise indicated, quotations are taken from this source.)

relevant (and indeed essential) to consider whether economic needs can be satisfactorily met from other sources with less damage to amenity.

There is, however, the equally important matter of safeguarding mineral deposits. Planning authorities have the positive function of ensuring that mineral deposits are not unnecessarily sterilized by surface development but are kept available for exploitation.

These are the broad policy matters with which planning authorities are concerned. The necessary powers are provided in the Planning Acts. Briefly these are for the making of the essential survey of resources and potentialities, the allocation of land in development plans, and the control (by means of planning permission) of mineral workings.

The survey required for the development plan is not, of course, simply a geological one. The planning authority has to assess the amount of land required for mineral working, and this requires an assessment of the future demand likely to be made on production in their area.

Mineral undertakers have long-standing powers to obtain rights over land containing mineral deposits. These were extended by regulations made under the Town and Country Planning Act of 1947. With the range of powers available, mineral workings cannot, without good cause, be prevented by private landowners.

Powers to control mineral workings stem from the definition of 'development', which includes 'the carrying out of . . . mining . . . operations in, on, over or under land'. Further, the tipping of waste constitutes development (i.e. a material change of use) if, generally speaking, the area or height is extended. Special provisions apply to the National Coal Board's operations, which can be ignored for the moment. Apart from this, all mineral workings, ancillary buildings, depositing of waste, and the construction of means of access to sites, require planning permission. Because of the national need for minerals, planning authorities have been strongly advised by the DOE to pay attention to economic considerations: 'A fundamental concern of planning policy must be to ensure a free flow of mineral products at economic cost'. The long-term planning that is required for mineral exploitation means that planning permissions have generally been given for a working with a long life – commonly not less than fifteen years, and on occasion, up to sixty years. Before reaching a decision on an application, it is often necessary for the planning authority to consult a number of interested parties: the Ministry of Agriculture, the Forestry Commission, the statutory water undertakers, a river or conservancy board, and perhaps the Countryside Commission, the Nature Conservancy and the Inspector of Ancient Monuments. The representations of these bodies can lead to the making of conditions or the reinforcement of conditions which the planning authority wishes to impose in the interest of amenity. Conditions can be imposed, for example, requiring a phased programme of work in order to minimize the disturbance to agriculture, or a planned programme of working and restoration can be required. Conditions relating to restoration are among the most important. A mineral undertaker cannot, however, be required to put the land to any specific use after extraction has been completed, but, *where practicable*, he can be required to leave it in a condition comparable to that in which he found it. Unfortunately, restoration is not always 'practicable'. 'The extent to which reclamation is possible will depend first on the physical nature of the quarry. About one-third of the land used for quarrying represents the wet working of gravel; about one-third deep quarries working into a hillside or deep holes in the ground or a combination of both; one-sixth shallow quarries; and the remaining sixth, workings in which a thin seam is extracted from beneath thick overburden. Wet gravel pits and other excavations which become waterlogged can be reclaimed only when suitable extraneous filling material is available at an economic cost; they sometimes have value for fishing, yachting or other recreational purposes, possibly after some landscape treatment has been carried out. Other deep holes can generally be put to use only when filling material is available. Waste material – including any overburden – can sometimes be used to reclaim part of the quarry or to raise the general level sufficiently for use to be made of the whole. (But the cost of such operations can often make this impracticable.) Shallow quarries and some hillside quarries where the floor is not much below the level of the adjoining land can often be brought back to use readily without the necessity of filling. Quarries working thin seams beneath thick overburden can also be readily reclaimed, the most numerous of this class being ironstone quarries.'

The Ironstone Restoration Fund

Of particular interest in this connection is the Ironstone Restoration Fund. This was established under the Mineral Workings Act, 1951, to assist in the financing of reclamation in the Midlands ironstone field where working was by opencast methods. Generally, ironstone operators and landowners make a contribution to the Fund for each ton of ironstone extracted by opencast working. The Exchequer makes a further contribution. Payments are made from the Fund for old derelict workings and for new workings where the cost of restoration exceeds a certain sum per acre. By the end of March, 1968, the Fund had paid (or would pay) £255,000 for the restoration of land left derelict before 1950; £1,250,000 for the restoration of subsequent workings in accordance with the conditions attached to planning permissions; £130,000 for approved works not required by conditions but deemed necessary for amenity or agricultural purposes; £438,000 for work authorized by the Ministry of Agriculture to bring restored land into a good state of cultivation and fertility; and £28,000 for the afforestation of worked ironstone land. Because of rising costs new legislation is currently before Parliament which will ensure that the Fund remains solvent.

The principle underlying this scheme – that land exploitation carries with it a duty to shoulder at least part of the costs of restoration – would at first sight seem capable of extension. A similar principle – that exploitation involves costs to others which should be borne at least in part by the exploiters – is accepted in the Cheshire brine pumping subsidence scheme. The Brine Pumping (Compensation for Subsidence) Act, 1891, provided for payments to certain owners of property damaged by subsidence, from the proceeds of a levy on each ton of white salt produced within the Northwich area. The Cheshire Brine Pumping (Compensation for Subsidence) Act, 1952, brought the scheme in line with modern operating conditions and considerably extended the area over which it operated. The procedure is, thus, basically the same as with ironstone restoration – a levy on all operators related to their production. For a nationalized industry the principle can be extended further, as in the Coal Mining (Subsidence) Acts of 1950 and 1957. These place on the National Coal Board the responsibility for making good any damage caused by subsidence resulting from coal mining – or the working of coal and other minerals simultaneously. Under the 1950 Act, grants were paid by the Treasury to the Board in respect of additional expenditure which the Act imposed on them, but this arrangement was not repeated in the 1957 Act. Thus, the Board carries the whole financial responsibility for subsidence damage.

Restoration can be a difficult and expensive operation. It follows that (as with subsidence) there is a case for 'pooling' in order that, for example, the costs of achieving some socially desirable restoration does not involve prohibitive expense for a particular operator. Some costs can, however, legitimately be placed squarely on individual operators. This is the case with improving the appearance of mineral workings by tree and shrub planting. Planning permission for mineral operations can be made conditional on adequate screening being provided.

Coal

Planning control over the operations of the National Coal Board is subject to special provisions. Briefly, the continued working of mines

G

begun before July 1, 1948, is 'permitted development', and, therefore, does not require specific planning approval. The same applies to the continuance of waste tipping. Furthermore, there is a general permission for any development in connection with coal industry activities (as defined in section 63 of the Coal Industry Nationalization Act, 1946) and carried out in the immediate vicinity of a pithead.* However, certain restrictions can be imposed (on the erection of buildings) in the interest of amenity. Mining operations on new sites require planning permission in the ordinary way.

Only 4 per cent of coal output in Britain comes from opencast workings – a very much lower proportion than in other countries. One of the reasons for the low proportion is that, despite its profitability, opencast working arouses considerable opposition – from farmers, local authorities, local inhabitants, amenity organizations and even miners. Clearly the visual impact of opencast working is far greater than that of deep mining, yet the loss of amenity is temporary and full restoration is practicable and usual; indeed, there can be a resultant improvement in amenity.

Opencast coal working began during the war under emergency legislation. It continued under this legislation until 1958 and, though usually constituting 'development', was therefore outside the scope of planning control. The Opencast Coal Act, 1958, laid down a special method of control operated by the then Minister of Power (now the Secretary of State for Trade and Industry). Notices must be served on the local authorities concerned and, if they raise objections, a public local inquiry must be held. The Secretary of State for Trade and Industry can direct that planning permission for the operations concerned 'be deemed to be granted'. His direction may include conditions of the sort commonly applied to planning permissions, and must include conditions to secure the restoration of the site. Where the land is in agricultural use it is normally obligatory for the conditions to provide for the restoration of the land so that it is fit for agricultural use.

Recent Developments

The problem of reconciling economic needs with those of amenity admits of no simple solution in a small highly industrialized country; and the indications are that the problem will become more, rather than

---

* This constitutes 'permitted development' under the General Development Order (see chapter IV, p. 83, et seq.). However, under the same Order, a Directive can be made withdrawing a particular development from this class. In one reported case this power was used to limit mining in order to reduce serious subsidence dangers. See Ministry of Housing and Local Government, *Selected Planning Appeals*, Bulletin No. XL, 1952 (XI/19) and Bulletin No. XII, 1957 (XII/37 and 38).

less, acute. This is partly because of the increasing need for minerals and partly because of the increasing claims of a population which is steadily growing. Planning controls have achieved a considerable improvement both in resolving conflicts in the light of the relative importance of the claims and in the restoration of mineral workings. The techniques now available for reclamation, screening and landscaping hold considerable promise for the success of an accelerated programme. What is needed is a positive planning approach. Relatively few local authorities have embarked on extensive programmes of reclamation or improvement. As with so many aspects of positive planning (as distinct from regulatory controls) the weak link is often the capability of local authorities. Unfortunately, the areas with the largest problems are often the least able to afford the relatively small expense involved or – more important – the necessary staff. This problem has been alleviated in Scotland and Wales by the setting up of Derelict Land Units to stimulate and assist local authorities. In England, a 'central group' for derelict land reclamation has been established, with local authority participation, in the Department of the Environment.

The Mines and Quarries (Tips) Act, 1969, gave local authorities new powers to ensure that disused waste tips do not constitute a danger to the public and provided for Exchequer grants. Unfortunately, the Act cannot be used to achieve landscaping for amenity purposes unless this is an incidental result of essential remedial measures.

More encouraging are the stringent conditions imposed by the Secretary of State in granting planning permission for certain developments such as that of Cleveland Potash Limited in the North Riding of Yorkshire and by the Rio Tinto Zinc Corporation in Snowdonia and the Lake District. But the increasing economic pressures for mineral exploitation will present some nice political problems for the future in assessing what price can be paid for the preservation of the environment.

CLEAN AIR

Those who pollute the air are no longer sent to the gallows, but, though gentler methods are now preferred, it was not until the disastrous London smog of 1952 (resulting in 4,000 deaths) that really effective action was taken. The Beaver Report of 1954 described the effects of air pollution on health, and made comprehensive recommendations on the prevention of pollution by smoke from industry and domestic chimneys, grit and dust, sulphur dioxide, motor vehicle exhausts and smoke from railway locomotives. Particularly telling was the Committee's estimate of the economic cost of pollution: £50 million a year through inefficiently burning fuel; £150 million in lost efficiency in agriculture, industry and transport caused by reduced plant growth and hours of daylight and increased illness; and £150 million from corrosion (due largely to sulphur dioxide) – all in 1954 prices. (More recent estimates suggest that the cost of corrosion amounts to £600 million a year.)

In recent years there has been a growing emphasis on reducing air pollution as a part of a more general policy of environmental improvement. The Hunt Committee for instance, in discussing problems of economic growth, argued that 'tackling air pollution, like clearing derelict land, is a necessary part of the environmental rehabilitation which the older industrial areas need'.

Domestic Smoke

The Clean Air Acts of 1956 and 1968 prohibit the emission of dark smoke, provide for the control of the emission of grit and dust from furnaces and establish a system for the approval by local authorities of chimney heights. However, the principal source of air pollution is domestic smoke and it is here that powers are the most extensive. Local authorities are empowered to establish *smoke control areas* (subject to approval by the Secretary of State) in which the emission of smoke from chimneys constitutes an offence. This involves the conversion of grates to enable smokeless fuels to be burned. Grants are given (normally) equal to seven-tenths of the approved expenditure on the cost of installing smokeless appliances. (Central government re-imburse local authorities four-sevenths of their expenditure except where a local authority house is concerned, in which case the proportion is 40 per cent.) The provisions here are flexible. Grant can be made not only on conversion of open grates but also, as an alternative, an equivalent amount can be given towards the cost of installing central heating or electric space heaters.

A *Memorandum* on the 1956 Act[17] stressed the need for detailed surveys of proposed smoke control areas, and the importance of consultation with local fuel producers and distributors, before orders were made defining the areas. Caution was urged:

'The establishment of smoke control areas will necessarily be gradual; it will need to be undertaken in stages, over a period of years in the larger towns. Progress will be governed by the supply of smokeless fuels, the rate at which appliances can be converted or replaced, and the rate at which local authorities are able to formulate and carry through their smoke control plans. Above all, progress – and indeed the whole success of the operation – will depend upon public support;

upon people's understanding of the problems involved, and their readiness to co-operate in smoke control measures.'

The heart of the problem lies in the appropriately-termed 'black areas'. These are areas, listed by the central departments, which in the words of the Beaver Committee 'experience a high frequency of fog in which urban and industrial density produce large amounts of pollution'. By the end of 1970, about 56 per cent of the premises in the 'black areas' of England had been included in local programmes, but progress is very uneven over the country. In Greater London nearly 70 per cent of premises are covered by smoke control orders. (As a result there has been a 50 per cent increase in winter sunshine over London.) But there are still twenty-one local authorities in the 'black areas' of England which have not yet made any smoke control orders. One particularly tricky problem here is that of persuading mine workers to give up their concessionary coal in favour of smokeless fuels or cash. Both the Hunt Committee and the Royal Commission have deplored the inadequate action on the part of some northern authorities. The latter, in their first report, quote from a publication of the Warren Spring Laboratory:

'The question posed by this position is whether with existing knowledge the North can be made as free from smoke as the South. . . . By the vigorous application of the domestic provisions of the Clean Air Act, and the changing social framework, the great housing estates of outer London have been made as free from smoke as any urban areas in the South, and the inner core of Central London is within striking distance of achieving the same state of cleanliness in spite of its very high population density. This is not something that can only be achieved in the South because the data for Sheffield, a great industrial town in the North, show the same spectacular progress.'

The 1968 Clean Air Act empowers the Secretary of State to direct a local authority to draw up and carry out a clean air programme for their area. These powers have not, as yet, been used.

In spite of set-backs in periods when local authorities are urged to restrain expenditure, public expenditure on the conversion of open grates to smokeless heating arrangements increased from £2·2 million in 1964–5 to £5·1 million in 1969–70.

Industrial Emissions
There are two systems of control of industrial emissions to the atmosphere in Britain. Most industrial processes are controlled by local authorities under the Clean Air and Public Health Acts. There are,

however, certain processes which, because of their nature or the specialized and complex methods necessary to minimize emissions, are controlled by an expert and centralized Inspectorate responsible directly to the Secretary of State for the Environment. This Alkali Inspectorate, as it is termed, originally came into being under the Alkali Act of 1863, now replaced by the Alkali Etc. Works Regulation Act of 1906 and the Alkali Etc. Works Order of 1966. A new Order, introduced in 1971, considerably extends the Department's control over manufacturing operations which were previously regulated by local authorities. These new measures affect grit and dust emissions from mineral industry processes, discharges from processes used in the petro-chemical industry and emissions from the smelting of aluminium.

For several years, because of complaints about dust, the Inspectorate had been called in by local authorities to advise on the control of grit and dust emissions from processes involving the crushing, grinding, drying, heating and handling of metallurgical slags, pulverized fuel ash, limestone, chalk, igneous rocks, gypsum, china clay, ball clay and china stone. These processes have now been 'scheduled' and brought under the direct control of the Alkali Inspectorate.

The new Order also covers petroleum works and the primary smelting of aluminium. Until recently, primary aluminium smelters have operated only in Scotland (and were scheduled under the Scottish Alkali Acts). With the development of smelters in England and Wales the Alkali Inspectorate has been involved from the outset in specifying the best practicable means of controlling emissions from these.

The 1971 Order also brings under the control of the Inspectorate processes involving the use of di-isocynates and the manufacture and purification of acrylates. (Di-isocynates are used, for example, in the manufacture of expanded plastics; acrylates are used, *inter alia*, for surface coatings for plastic production fibres and textiles.)

As is apparent, this is a highly technical field which involves specialist knowledge not to be expected among local authority staffs: hence the centralization of responsibility in the Alkali Inspectorate.

Pollution by Vehicles
More in the public eye is air pollution by motor vehicle exhausts. The United States Government is requiring stringent standards – despite strong opposition from manufacturers. The White Paper, however, states that 'in Europe, due to the differences in climatic conditions, air pollution from petrol-engined vehicles presents a different and less acute problem, and the development of a completely pollution-free car might not be the most sensible use of resources'. The matter is

being 'kept under review'; and the Royal Commission, in its first report, have warned against complacency. This is a field in which more research is called for: even though diesel fumes 'can be very offensive ... there is no firm evidence that the present level of these pollutants is a hazard to health'. But the same can be said about slum housing. It is to be expected that levels of public tolerability will rise, though the cost will have to be borne by a car-owning electorate.

NOISE

'Quiet costs money ... a machine manufacturer will try to make a quieter product only if he is forced to, either by legislation or because customers want quiet machines and will choose a rival product for its lower noise level.'[7]

This, in one sense, is the crux of the problem of noise. More – and more powerful – cars, aircraft, transistor radios and the like must receive strong public opprobrium before manufacturers – and users – will be concerned with their noise level. Similarly, legislative measures and their implementation require public support before effective action can be taken.

There is abundant evidence that this is growing: from the figures collected by the Association of Public Health Inspectors showing that the number of complaints of noise nuisance received by local authorities is increasing at the rate of about 10 per cent a year,[36] to the Cabinet decision to locate a third London airport at Foulness.

Transport is the main noise menace. The Road Research Laboratory have estimated that between 25 and 45 per cent of the urban population live in roads with traffic noise levels likely to be judged undesirable for residential areas; if noise levels are not reduced, the projected increase in vehicles will raise the proportion by 1980 to between one-third and two-thirds. The White Paper maintained that new regulations which came into effect in April 1970, have halted the trend towards increasing noise. It cannot be said that this is apparent: in any case (in the words of the Royal Commission) this will not do much to satisfy the public demand for *less* noise.

Aircraft noise is particularly obnoxious, and a battery of new powers have been introduced in recent legislation, such as the Airports Authority Act, 1965, and the Civil Aviation Act, 1968. This is a field in which international co-operation is particularly important, and the first fruits of the International Conference on Aircraft Noise (convened by the British Government) came with the 1970 Air Navigation (Noise Certification) Order. Subsonic jet aircraft will no longer be allowed to land or take off in the United Kingdom unless

they have a certificate from the Government of the country of registration that they comply with certain defined noise standards. This
anticipates an international noise certification scheme in the formulation of which Britain is playing a leading part. So far as commercial
supersonic flights are concerned, the White Paper states that it is the
Government's view that those which could cause a boom to be heard
on the ground should be banned.

As is evident from the tone of the previous paragraph (based on
Government announcements) this is an area in which Government is
prone to make impressive proclamations which suggest that significant
progress is being made. It is here that bodies such as the Royal
Commission on Environmental Pollution and the recently established
Noise Advisory Council have an important role to play. On aircraft
noise, the former ends a review of aircraft noise abatement by noting
that 'if the volume of air transport continues to expand at a rate of
15 per cent per annum, the nuisance from aircraft will not easily be
remedied, particularly if supersonic is added to subsonic flights'.
Similarly, stimulating comments may be expected from the Secretary
of State's Noise Advisory Council which has as its terms of reference,
'to keep under review the progress made generally in preventing and
abating the generation of noise, to make recommendations to Ministers with responsibility in this field and to advise on such matters as
they may refer to the Council'.

But action depends not only on political but also on technical
know-how. Here, investment in research is crucial and it is encouraging to note that this is increasing. Whether an annual expenditure of
£1¼ million a year on aircraft noise research projects is sufficient is
another question.

OTHER ENVIRONMENTAL POLLUTANTS

Many other pollutants and aspects of pollution would need to be discussed in a comprehensive account, including domestic and industrial
waste, pesticides and fertilizers, water resources, litter, car cemeteries,
pollution of the sea and radioactive waste disposal. A brief discussion
is to be found in the White Paper, *The Protection of the Environment*
and in the *First Report of the Royal Commission on Environmental
Pollution*. Further references are given on the following pages.

References and Further Reading

1 Arguile, R. T., 'Some Notes on Open cast Coal Mining', *Journal of the Town Planning Institute*, Vol. XLVIII, June 1962, pp. 170–1.
2 Arvill, R., *Man and Environment: Crisis and the Strategy of Choice*, Penguin Books, revised edition, 1969.
3 Barber E. G., *Win Back the Acres*, Central Electricity Generating Board, 1963.
4 Barr, J., *Derelict Britain*, Penguin Books, 1969.
5 Civic Trust, *Derelict Land*, 1964.
6 Committee on Air Pollution (Beaver Committee), *Interim Report*, Cmd. 9011, HMSO, 1953; *Report*, Cmd. 9322, HMSO, 1954.
7 Committee on the Problem of Noise, *Noise: Final Report* (Wilson Report), Cmd. 2056, HMSO, 1963.
8 Crowe, S., *Tomorrow's Landscape*, Architectural Press, 1956.
9 DOE, Circular 42/71, *The Dangerous Litter Act, 1971*, HMSO, 1971.
10 Fraser Darling, F., *Wilderness and Plenty*, BBC, 1970.
11 Goldman, M. I., *Controlling Pollution: The Economics of a Cleaner America*, Prentice-Hall, 1967.
12 Hunt Report, *The Intermediate Areas*, Cmnd. 3998, HMSO, 1969, especially pp. 135–141.
13 Hilton, K. J., *The Lower Swansea Valley Project*, Longmans, 1967.
14 MHLG, *Standing Technical Committee on Synthetic Detergents: Progress Reports*, HMSO, periodic.
15 MHLG, *Prevention of River Pollution* (Hobday Report), HMSO, 1949.
16 MHLG, Clean Air Act 1956: *Memorandum on Miscellaneous Provisions*, HMSO, 1956.
17 MHLG, Clean Air Act 1956: *Memorandum on Smoke Control Areas*, HMSO, 1956.
18 MHLG, Circular 30/60, *Local Employment Act, 1960: Rehabilitation of Derelict, Neglected or Unsightly Land*, HMSO, 1960.
19 MHLG, *The Control of Mineral Working*, HMSO, revised edition, 1960.
20 MHLG, *Smoke Control (England and Wales): Summary of Programmes Submitted by Local Authorities for the establishment of Smoke Control Areas*, Cmnd. 113, HMSO, 1960.

21 MHLG, *Pollution of the Tidal Thames* (Pippard Report), HMSO, 1961.
22 MHLG, *Pollution of Waste by Tipped Refuse* (Key Report), HMSO, 1961.
23 MHLG, *Smoke Control (England and Wales), 1962–1966: Summary of Programmes submitted by local authorities for the establishment of Smoke Control Areas*, Cmnd, 1890, HMSO, 1962.
24 MHLG, *New Life for Dead Lands: Derelict Areas Reclaimed*, HMSO, 1963.
25 MHLG, Circular 17/67, *Rehabilitation of Derelict Neglected or Unsightly Land: Industrial Development Act, 1966 and Local Government Act, 1966*, HMSO, 1967.
26 MHLG, *Refuse Storage and Collection* (Browne Report), HMSO, 1967.
27 Circular 16/70, *Mines and Quarries (Tips) Act 1969: Grants to Local Authorities*, HMSO, 1970.
28 MHLG, Circular 17/70, *Derelict Land*, HMSO, 1970.
29 MHLG, *Report of the Working Party on Sewage Disposal: 'Taken for Granted'*, HMSO, 1970.
30 Natural Environment Research Council, *Annual Reports*, HMSO.
31 National Coal Board, *Annual Reports*, HMSO.
32 National Society for Clean Air, *Clean Air Year Book*, NSCA, annual.
33 Nicholson, M., *The Environmental Revolution*, Hodder & Stoughton, 1970.
34 North West Economic Planning Council, *Derelict Land in the North West*, NWEPC, 1969.
35 Oxenham, J., *Reclaiming Derelict Land*, Faber, 1966.
36 Road Research Laboratory, *A Review of Road Noise*, 1970.
37 Royal Commission on Environmental Pollution, *First Report*, Cmnd. 4585, HMSO, 1970.
38 Scottish Development Department, *Report of the Committee on the Drainage of Trade Premises* (Hill Watson Report), Cmnd. 9117, HMSO.
39 Taylor, R., *Noise*, Penguin Books, 1970.
40 Warren Springs Laboratory, *Annual Reports*, HMSO.
41 Water Resources Board, *Annual Reports*, HMSO.
42 White Paper, *The Protection of the Environment: The Fight Against Pollution*, Cmnd. 4373, HMSO, 1970.

Chapter IX

PLANNING FOR LEISURE

The subject – and the problem – of planning for leisure is a large one. It encompasses national parks, access to the countryside, nature reserves, camping, caravanning, rambling and youth hostelling, waterways, parks and many other aspects of recreation. It involves difficult questions of amenity – if only because too many people can easily destroy the amenities they seek. Some aspects of preservation have been discussed in Chapter VII; here we shall be concerned with some of the major issues not merely of preserving and safeguarding amenities but of catering in a positive way for the increasing demand for leisure from a population which itself may experience an increase of a quarter by the turn of the century.

NATIONAL PARKS AND ACCESS TO THE COUNTRYSIDE

The demand for public access to the countryside has a long history, stretching from the early nineteenth-century fight against enclosures, James Bryce's abortive 1884 Access to Mountains Bill, and the attenuated Access to Mountains Act of 1939, to the promise offered by the National Parks and Access to the Countryside Act of 1949 – an Act which, among other things, poetically provides powers for 'preserving and enhancing natural beauty'. Many battles have been fought by voluntary bodies such as the Commons, Open Spaces and Footpaths Preservation Society and the Council for the Protection of Rural England (whose annual reports clearly indicate that their continued activity is still all too necessary), but they worked largely in a legislative vacuum until the Second World War. By the end of the 'twenties the campaign for public access to the countryside became concentrated on the need for national parks such as had been established in Europe and North America, but though an official National Park Committee reported (in 1931) in favour of a national policy, no Government action was taken. The mood engendered by the Second World War

augured a better reception for the Scott Committee's emphatic statement that 'the establishment of National Parks in Britain is long
overdue'. The Scott Committee had very wide terms of reference and
for the first time an overall view was taken of questions of public
rights of way and rights of access to the open country, and the establishment of national parks and nature reserves within the context of
a national policy for the preservation and planning of the countryside.
Government acceptance of the necessity for establishing national
parks was announced in the series of debates on post-war reconstruction which took place during 1941 and 1943, and the White Paper on
The Control of Land Use referred to the establishment of national
parks as part of a comprehensive programme of post-war reconstruction and land use planning. Not only was the principle accepted but,
probably of equal importance, there was now a central government
department with clear responsibility for such matters as national
parks. There followed a series of reports on national parks, nature
conservation, footpaths, and access to the countryside.

THE DOWER AND HOBHOUSE REPORTS

The Dower Report was a personal report to the Minister of Town and
Country Planning by John Dower, published 'for information and as
a basis for discussion'. A national park was defined as 'an extensive
area of beautiful and relatively wild country, in which, for the nation's
benefit and by appropriate national decision and action:

(*a*) the characteristic landscape beauty is strictly preserved;
(*b*) access and facilities for public open-air enjoyment are amply
    provided;
(*c*) wild life and buildings and places of architectural and historic
    interest are suitably protected; while
(*d*) established farming is effectively maintained'.

This conception of a national park was accepted by the Hobhouse
Committee who also agreed with Dower's proposal for a special
National Parks Commission – 'a body of high standing, expert
qualification, substantial independence and permanent constitution,
which will uphold, and be regarded by the public as upholding, the
landscape, agricultural and recreational values whose dominance is
the essential purpose of National Parks'. This Commission would
select the areas for national parks and would employ in each park
administrative and technical staff, headed by an Assistant Commissioner. These local executive bodies would act on behalf of the
Commission and the local planning authority for each park. Management was to be under the control of an *ad hoc* Park Committee

consisting of a chairman and fourteen members appointed by the Commission, together with fourteen members appointed by the local authorities in whose areas the park was situated. The whole cost of administering the parks was to be borne by the Exchequer.

This administrative organization was devised in accordance with the conception of *national* parks as envisaged in both the Dower and Hobhouse Reports. Since the legislation departed substantially from these recommendations, it is worth outlining the reasoning to be found in these Reports. National parks were to be administered for the benefit of the nation: this apparent tautology had the implication that planning in park areas should not be carried out by the ordinary local government bodies with the Commission acting as an adviser and supplier of grants. Such a system would 'tend to separate and oppose, rather than to unite and fuse, the national and local points of view and requirements; it would multiply delays by inserting an additional rung in the planning ladder; and by dividing responsibility, it would encourage inefficient administration and patchy compromise plans. . . . If National Parks are provided *for* the nation they should clearly be provided by the nation. . . . Their distinct costs should be met from national funds.'

To appreciate the force of this line of reasoning it is necessary to realize that national parks were not envisaged as rural museums. The new administration was viewed not merely as a machine for operating controls but also as a means of implementing 'a progressive policy of management, designed to develop the latent resources of the national parks for healthy enjoyment and open-air recreation to the advantage of the whole nation'. Among the management functions listed in the two reports were the acquisition of land for specific purposes (the Hobhouse Committee envisaged a tenth of the area of national parks coming into the Commission's hands during the first ten years of the operations); the removal or improvement of disfigurements or 'inappropriate' development (e.g. the surface restoration of abandoned mineral workings); the prevention of litter and of damage to crops, walls, trees, etc., the collection and disposal of rubbish, and the carrying out of repair works; skilled management to foster natural rejuvenation of trees, and a programme of steady and discriminating tree planting; assisting local highway authorities in the provision of parking places, viewpoints and other subsidiary roadworks needed for the benefit of visitors; the provision (often through voluntary bodies) of holiday accommodation – quiet hostels for elderly people, holiday camps or guest-houses for families, camps and hostels for younger people, camping and caravanning sites; the establishment of National Park Centres for field studies; the development of facilities for fishing, riding, small-boat sailing; and so on.

THE NATIONAL PARKS AND ACCESS TO
THE COUNTRYSIDE ACT, 1949

The Government, however, took the view that the newly constituted planning authorities (under the 1947 Act) should be given the responsibility for national parks: these authorities were only just beginning to function and it was unreasonable at this stage to suggest that they were incapable of meeting this responsibility. A National Parks Commission was to be established but its functions were to be mainly advisory. As might be expected, criticism was centred on this issue. It was suggested that county councils would be concerned primarily with local interests and would not be keen to incur expenditure for the benefit of visitors. One speaker commented that the proposed Commission bore about the same relationship to that recommended by the Dower and Hobhouse Reports as a baby's comforter bore to a real feeding-bottle: 'it may be superficial resemblance, attract and soothe the innocent, but it stops short and there is nothing behind it.'*

The Government, however, were not to be shaken. Probably they felt that they had already taken sufficient powers away from local government and that it was politically inadvisable to create another *ad hoc* executive body. Be that as it may, the new functions were laid on the shoulders of local authorities. The National Parks Commission had a predominantly advisory role. (The past tense is used since the National Parks Commission was replaced by the Countryside Commission in 1968.) It had a general duty to advise the Minister on matters affecting the natural beauty of the countryside – primarily but not exclusively in national parks and other 'areas of outstanding natural beauty'. Its main executive function was to select, after consultation with the local authorities concerned, the areas where it considered that national parks should be established. It also had a general responsibility for considering what action was required in the parks in order that these objects might be fulfilled, but could only make recommendations to planning authorities and 'representations' to the Government.

Having decided that executive functions should be the responsibility of local authorities, the problem immediately arose as to what should be done in cases where a park lay in the area of more than one local authority. The Act provided that in such cases a joint planning board

---

* W. S. Morrison in the Second Reading Debates, *H.C. Debates*, Vol. 463, col. 1491. Argument by analogy always carried the risk that the opposite party will turn it to its own advantage. So it was in this case: the Minister replied that a comforter is not used to comfort the baby – 'it is used to preserve the amenities of the neighbourhood; so is the National Parks Commission!' (*op. cit.*, col. 1657).

National Parks in England and Wales

	Date designation confirmed	Area (sq. miles)	Local authority areas	Administrative arrangement
Peak District	1951	542	Derbyshire CC Staffordshire CC Cheshire CC West Riding CC Sheffield CBC	Joint Board
Lake District	1951	866	Cumberland CC Lancashire CC Westmorland CC	Joint Board
Snowdonia	1951	845	Caernarvonshire CC Denbighshire CC Merioneth CC	Joint Advisory Committee*
Dartmoor	1951	365	Devon CC	Committee of the County Council
Pembrokeshire Coast	1952	225	Pembrokeshire CC	Committee of the County Council
North York Moors	1952	553	North Riding CC	Committee of the County Council
Yorkshire Dales	1954	680	North Riding CC West Riding CC	Joint Advisory Committee*
Exmoor	1954	265	Devon CC Somerset CC	Joint Advisory Committee*
Northumberland	1956	398	Northumberland CC	Committee of the County Council
Brecon Beacons	1957	519	Breconshire CC Carmarthenshire CC Monmouthshire CC	Joint Advisory Committee*
		5,258		

* There are separate Park Planning Committees in each of the constituent counties.

was to be the normal organization, though exceptionally a joint advisory committee might be established as an alternative. In fact, due to the strenuous opposition of local authorities (who were particularly anxious about the financial implications) only two joint Boards were set up. Four parks have Joint Advisory Committees as well as separate Park Planning Committees in each of the constituent local authorities. The remaining four parks lie wholly within the area of one local authority and are administered by a single local authority committee.

Whatever the form of administration, one-third of the members are nominated by the Commission. The intention is to ensure that there is always a number of people serving on the planning authority who are known for their interest in the national parks movement as distinct from purely local problems.

A full account of the work of the National Parks Commission (and its successor, the Countryside Commission) is given in their annual reports. Here only a few significant points can be raised.

A problem which has particularly exercised the attention of the Commission and the Park Authorities is that of development by Government Departments and statutory undertakers. Fears that this would prove a major problem were voiced during the debates on the Bill. Indeed, it was pointed out that 'the demands of these bodies would be more difficult to resist than those of private developers since the Government would in effect be not only the judge but also the defendant. The catalogue of what Lord Strang, former Chairman of the Commission, has called 'alien intrusions' is a formidable one, and includes new defence installations in the North Yorkshire moors and on the Pembrokeshire Coast; masts for the GPO, the Air Ministry, the Ministry of Aviation, for defence or for communications or for air navigation: masts for the police and other services and for transport undertakings; a nuclear electricity generating station and a pumped storage installation in Snowdonia with the accompanying network of transmission lines on pylons for the supergrid; overhead distribution lines in every part of the country; two oil refineries and an oil terminal on Milford Haven astride the eastern boundary of the Pembrokeshire Coast Park; recurrent and increasing demands for water in almost every national park, culminating in the great controversy aroused by the claims of the Manchester Corporation upon Ullswater and Bannisdale. The problem is an intractable one. By their very nature national parks are ideally suitable for military training; they contain valuable mineral deposits; some of them can provide unrivalled water resources; the development programme of the Central Electricity Generating Board (to meet a demand for electricity which is doubling every ten years) involves a wide and high-powered transmission network and thus more and bigger pylons which cannot be hidden in the landscape and which cannot be obviated – except at enormous cost – by placing cables underground. These are all symptoms of the enormous pressures on land exerted by an increasingly affluent society in a densely populated country.

It would, however, be misleading to give the impression that the Commission have had no success. Much more effort is now being expended to make 'inevitable' developments as unharmful as possible. Statutory undertakers such as the Central Electricity Generating Board are now legally required to plan their operations with regard to amenity and to employ landscape architects; and public companies can be obliged or persuaded to do likewise. The nuclear power station in Snowdonia and the development by the petroleum companies at Milford Haven can be instanced.

This conflict between utility and beauty arises in a less spectacular but more intense form in connection with the livelihood and living conditions of the people who inhabit the parks. National parks in this country are not vast reserves of the kind found in Africa or America. They are areas of designated land in which ordinary rural life, rural industry and afforestation continue normally. The people living in these areas rightly demand modern amenities such as electricity and telephones, good-quality housing and – obviously – employment. These 'amenities' may clash with those sought by visitors, but the inhabitants cannot be expected to forgo these 'alien intrusions'. Nor should they be expected to shoulder the financial burdens involved in placing cables underground, in using expensive materials in new buildings for the sake of pleasant appearance, or in repairing damage caused by visitors.

The biggest conflict, however, is that between the twin purposes of the Act: to preserve amenities and to promote the enjoyment of the public. The Pembrokeshire Coast Park Planning Committee has stressed that there is a conflict between the desire to extend the enjoyment of a thing of beauty and the danger that if this opportunity is offered too widely and without proper care the result will be the destruction of the beautiful thing itself. The same concern is increasingly being expressed throughout the parks. The Lake District Planning Board has warned that tourism in the Lake District is, by sheer weight of numbers, killing what it seeks to enjoy. Similar fears have been expressed by voluntary bodies. Thus, the Friends of the Lake District argue that the park 'is gradually being destroyed by too many people' and the Ramblers' Association maintain that 'there is a grave danger that the more popular national parks will be overwhelmed by the sheer number of vehicles crowding into them'.

There is no easy solution to this; but clearly there comes a time when restrictions have to be imposed. Developments to foster public enjoyment – such as road improvements and caravan sites – have to be curtailed in order to prevent too many people frustrating their own purposes. The situation can be met in part by the scheduling and public acquisition of certain areas in each park as a reserve, to be kept free of all developments. An expansion of facilities for parking, camping, accommodation and the like is, nevertheless, necessary. Both these require a more positive approach than has been evidenced since the passing of the 1949 Act. A change in policy was heralded by the 1966 White Paper, *Leisure in the Countryside*. This is discussed, together with the 1968 Countryside Act, later in this chapter.

AREAS OF OUTSTANDING NATURAL BEAUTY

Both the Dower and the Hobhouse Reports proposed that, in addition to national parks, certain areas of outstanding landscape beauty should be subject to special protection. These areas did not (at that time) require the positive management which it was assumed would characterize national parks, but 'their contribution to the wider enjoyment of the countryside is so important that special measures should be taken to preserve their natural beauty and interest'. The Hobhouse Committee proposed that these 'Conservation Areas' should be the responsibility of local planning authorities, but would receive expert assistance and financial aid from the National Parks Commission. Advisory Committees (with a majority of local authority members) would be set up to ensure that they would be comprehensively treated as a single unit. A total of fifty-two Conservation Areas, covering 9,835 acres was recommended – including, for example, the Breckland and much of central Wales, long stretches of the coast, the Cotswolds, most of the Downland, the Chilterns and Bodmin Moor.

The 1949 Act did not contain any special provisions for the care of Conservation Areas, the power under the Planning Acts being considered adequate for the purpose. It did, however, give the National Parks Commission power to designate *Areas of Outstanding Natural Beauty* and provided for Exchequer grants on the same basis as for national parks. So far, twenty-seven Areas have been designated and the Commission are having discussions with local authorities concerning a further eight.

Generally, Areas of Outstanding Natural Beauty are smaller than National Parks. They are the responsibility of local planning authorities who have powers for the 'preservation and enhancement of natural beauty' similar to those of park planning authorities. Unfortunately, despite the Exchequer grant-aid which is available for 'improvement' schemes, local planning authorities are often reluctant to make use of their powers. This is partly due to their unwillingness to incur the necessary expenditure and partly to the fact that they simply do not think in terms of catering for the holiday-maker. Some authorities, however, have followed more enlightened policies. Recent examples quoted in the annual reports of the National Parks Commission and the Countryside Commission include reclamation of a

Areas of Outstanding Natural Beauty

	Date designation confirmed	Area (square miles)
Gower	1956	73
Quantock Hills	1957	38
Lleyn	1957	60
Surrey Hills	1958	160
Northumberland Coast	1958	50
Cannock Chase	1958	26
Dorset	1959	400
Shropshire Hills	1959	300
Malvern Hills	1959	40
Cornwall	1959	360
North Devon	1960	66
South Devon	1960	128
East Hampshire	1962	151
East Devon	1963	103
Isle of Wight	1963	73
Forest of Bowland	1964	310
Chichester Harbour	1964	29
Solway Coast	1964	41
Chilterns	1965	309
Sussex Downs	1966	379
Cotswolds	1966	582
Anglesey	1967	83
South Hampshire Coast	1967	30
Norfolk Coast	1968	174
Kent Downs	1968	326
Suffolk Coast and Heaths	1970	151
Dedham Vale	1970	22
		4,464

former RAF camp in Cannock Chase, a discontinuance order on a scrap-dump near Old Sodbury, the purchase of land for public access at Durlston Head, Swanage (which is on the route of the South-West Peninsula Coastal Footpath), and increased public access in the Surrey Hills. Nevertheless, there is a good reason to lament with the Commission that progress has been very slow.

THE COASTLINE

About a third of the coastline of England and Wales is included in National Parks and Areas of Outstanding Natural Beauty. Additionally, development plans indicate 'Areas of High Landscape Value' and 'Areas of Scientific Interest' – national nature reserves or sites of special scientific interest notified to local planning authorities by the Nature Conservancy. Then there are coastal areas owned or protected by the National Trust. Nevertheless, the pressures on the coastline are proving increasingly difficult to cope with. Growing numbers of people are attracted to the coast for holidays, for recreation and for retirement. Furthermore, there are economic pressures for major industrial development in certain parts, particularly on some of the estuaries: Milford Haven and Southampton Water are cases in point.

The problem is a difficult one which cannot be satisfactorily met simply by restrictive measures: it requires a positive policy of planning for leisure. A welcome move in the right direction was started in 1963 with MHLG Circular 56/63, *Coastal Preservation and Development*, to local planning authorities with coastal boundaries. This argued that because the coast is of exceptional value and subject to heavy pressures for development it merits special study and control. Authorities with coastal boundaries were, therefore, asked to make a study of their coastal areas in consultation with the National Parks Commission and, for scientific advice, the Nature Conservancy. The circular was followed in 1965 by a letter expressing the deep concern of the Planning Ministers about the worsening situation and the inadequacy of the measures being taken to prevent the spread of development on the coast. Meantime, local planning authorities were exhorted to speed up plans and policies. MHLG Circular 7/66, *The Coast*, asked for clear statements 'of each planning authority's policy for their coastal area in standard cartographic form'. Nine regional conferences on coastal preservation and development were held in 1966 and 1967 and resulted in a series of detailed reports.

These formed the base of a major coastal study on which a number of major reports have been published by the Countryside Commission. Their final reports *The Planning of the Coastline* and *The Coastal Heritage* were published in 1970. The former attempts to clarify the problems and to identify the principles which should guide planning action. The latter amplifies the arguments for stringent protection of the finest coastal scenery. It proposes that these should be designated as *Heritage Coasts*, for each of which there would be a delegation of planning and management functions from the local planning authority to a special committee whose members would include nationally supported representatives. Each Heritage Coast would have a suitably trained Conservation Officer with a staff, including wardens. The salary of a Conservation Officer and the administrative costs of management within each Heritage Coast should be eligible for a special 90 per cent Exchequer grant.

These recommendations, which bear a striking resemblance to those of the Dower and Hobhouse Reports on national parks are currently 'under consideration'. Whether the outcome will bear a similar resemblance remains to be seen.

PUBLIC RIGHTS OF WAY

The origin of a large number of footpaths is obscure. As a result, innumerable disputes have arisen over public rights of way. Before the 1949 Act these disputes could be settled only by a case-by-case procedure, often with the evidence of 'oldest inhabitants' playing a leading role. The unsatisfactory nature of the situation was underlined by the Scott, Dower and Hobhouse Reports, as well as by the Special Committee on Footpaths and Access to the Countryside. All were agreed that a complete survey of rights of way was essential, together with the introduction of a simple procedure for resolving the legal status of rights of way which were in dispute. The National Parks Act provided for both.

Responsibility for making the survey of paths rests with county councils. Obviously footpaths are far more important in the countryside than in urban areas and for this reason county boroughs are not obliged to undertake a survey, but they can do so if they feel that one is needed (twenty-nine have in fact adopted the survey provisions of the Act). Urban areas within administrative counties can be excluded from a survey if the Minister agrees. Maps are prepared in three stages: draft, provisional and definitive. A *draft map* shows the paths over which the council, as a result of its survey, decides that there are reasonable grounds for believing that a public right of way exists. When this is published, 'representations' can be made for certain paths to be excluded or new ones added. There is a right of appeal to the Minister. This procedure provides an opportunity not only for objections from landowners, but also for organizations and individuals concerned with the preservation of rights of way to present their case for paths which are not included in the map. After all objections and appeals have been settled, a *provisional map* is published incorporating all the changes which have been decided. At this stage landowners can contest a path by appealing to Quarter Sessions for a declaration as to the existence or non-existence of rights of way. Subject to certain rights of appeal to the High Court, these declarations are final. When all the disputed cases have been dealt with by Quarter Sessions, a *definitive map* is published: this provides conclusive evidence of the existence of all rights of way shown on it – though there is provision for revision.

The preparation of this 'Doomsday Book of Footpaths' has proved a laborious and lengthy process. Much of the work has fallen on parish councils who naturally have a much more intimate and detailed knowledge of local history and local conditions than a district or county council. The Act actually specifies that parish councils are to

be consulted – the only reference in the whole field of planning legislation to these bodies. Parish councils, however, have negligible
financial resources and have to rely entirely on the assistance of
volunteers. Indeed, the Ministry have stated that a great deal of the
survey work can be carried out by volunteers, and some county
councils have made formal requests for assistance to voluntary bodies.
To meet this demand several of these bodies have formed a Central
Rights of Way Committee. This Committee gives advice and assistance to surveying authorities on all footpath questions, and promotes
and co-ordinates the organization of voluntary effort.

Under the Act, the normal completion date for the preparation of
draft maps was to be December 1952; in fact, it was not until June
1960 that all draft maps had been published, and at the end of 1960
definitive maps had been published for only fourteen whole counties
and parts of three other counties. The reason lies in the fact that so
much of the burden is placed on voluntary bodies – a matter on which
there has been considerable controversy. But though slow, the work is
proceeding, and (to lapse into the official language of the Ministry's
Annual Reports) 'once done, the job will be done for all time, and is
very well worth doing'!

A Footpaths Committee, under the Chairmanship of Sir Arthur
Gosling, was appointed in 1967 'to consider how far the present system
of footpaths, bridleways and other comparable rights of way in
England and Wales and the arrangements for the recording, closure,
diversion, creation and maintenance of such routes are suitable for
present and potential needs in the countryside and to make recommendations'.

Its report was published in 1968, and the majority of the recommendations have been implemented in the Countryside Act, 1968,
and the Town and Country Planning Act, 1968. These include placing
a duty on landowners to maintain stiles and gates, and requiring highway authorities to make a contribution towards the cost, providing
for pedal cyclists to use bridleways, and placing a duty on highway
authorities to signpost footpaths and bridleways where they leave a
metalled road. A special review must be made of roads used as public
paths so that public rights over them will be clear.

LONG-DISTANCE FOOTPATHS

Though work on the footpaths survey has been disappointingly slow,
considerable progress has been made with what are officially termed
'long-distance routes'. These hikers' highways now extend over
1,400 miles and include the 250-mile long Pennine Way and the
168-mile Offa's Dyke Path. The designation of these routes has been

equally laborious, but they have had the attention and backing of the National Parks Commission – which has official responsibility for their establishment. The Commission are the initiating body: they make the proposals, discuss them with the local authorities concerned and present a report to the Secretary of State. This shows the route together with existing public rights of way, and may contain proposals for the improvement of paths and the provision of new ones; ferries;

Long-distance footpaths

	Date approved	Length (miles)
Pennine Way	1951	250
Pembrokeshire Coast Path	1953	167
Offa's Dyke Path	1955	168
South Downs Way	1963	80
South West Peninsula Coast Path:		
North Cornwall	1952	135
South Cornwall	1954	133
South Devon	1959	93
Somerset and North Devon	1961	82
Dorset	1963	72
Cleveland Way	1965	93
North Downs Way	1969	141
		1,414

and accommodation, meals and refreshments. However, though eligible for Exchequer grant, the implementation of approved proposals rests with district councils. The Commission can negotiate, persuade and offer assistance, but they can go no further. Furthermore, since the completion of the statutory survey of rights of way by local authorities has (in the words of the Commission) been so woefully slow, the legal status of footpaths is often uncertain. This – and particularly the slow progress made with the creation of new rights of way – has held back the completion of approved long-distance routes.

Only on four footpaths are rights of way complete – the Pennine Way, the Cleveland Way, the Pembrokeshire Coast Path and Offa's Dyke Path.

ACCESS TO OPEN COUNTRY

The question of footpaths is only one aspect of the much wider issue of public access to the open countryside. The Hobhouse Committee wanted the public to have an automatic right of access over all uncultivated land – whether mountain, moor, heath, down, cliff, beach or shore, and including suitable stretches of inland water. This the Government did not feel able to accept. It was argued that legislative intervention was quite unnecessary over wide areas since *de facto* access was already granted. What was required was machinery for providing access where it was needed: and, in equity, the onus of establishing the need (and the claim that it should be met) should be placed on those who sought additional facilities – rather than the onus of establishing that there ought not to be access being placed on landowners. This approach had an additional practical and administrative advantage: to grant a general right of access would involve dealing with a large number of objections, whereas if local authorities simply decided to which areas new access provisions should apply, the number of objections would be far more manageable. Accordingly, the Act empowers local planning authorities to provide rights of access either by making agreements with owners, or failing that, by making 'access orders'. Agreements and orders are subject to ministerial confirmation, and compensation for any consequent depreciation in the value of land is payable. The effect of an access agreement or order is to give the public the right to go on access land 'for the purpose of open-air recreation' – which does not include playing organized games – without being treated as trespassers. The public must, however, comply with any particular restrictions laid down in the agreement and with certain generally applicable restrictions designed to prevent damage to and interference with farming. In some cases it was envisaged that public acquisition might be desirable, and either the local planning authority or the Secretary of State can purchase 'open country', if necessary by compulsion.

When the Bill was passing through Parliament fears were expressed by the open-air societies that if local authorities were left to provide access only as and when they thought it necessary, they would hesitate to act in fear of the many opposing interests that would undoubtedly be aroused. It was argued that a general requirement was necessary compelling local planning authorities to survey the open country in their areas and to take the action necessary to secure additional access: this would not only ensure that local planning authorities made use of their new powers, but would also be likely to make landowners more prepared to enter agreements since they would know from the result of the general survey the probable total extent of the access requirements. An amendment was introduced which required local planning authorities to make a general survey (by December 16, 1951) and to report (normally within one year of the completion of the survey) what action has been taken. Rights of Access Maps are required and these must be made public. Anyone who feels that the authority have not done enough can make representations to the

Secretary of State, who can direct the authority to make additional access orders or, in default, make them himself.

Little information is available on the operation of these provisions, but it was not until 1960 (nine years later) that all authorities completed the survey. The 1957 Report of the MHLG noted that fifty county councils and one park planning board had decided that no action was needed under the Act to secure increased facilities for access. Only seven had submitted maps showing the extent of open country in their areas and the action which had been taken to secure public access. Figures published by the Countryside Commission reveal that 73,957 acres of land in National Parks and Areas of Outstanding Natural Beauty were, in 1970, subject to access agreements or have been acquired by local planning authorities.

The 1968 Countryside Act contains important new provisions relating to access. The definition of 'open country' is widened to include woodlands, rivers or canals and land immediately adjacent to these waterways. This is part of the more purposive approach to recreational planning which is further discussed later in this chapter.

FORESTRY

Forestry is relevant in several ways to the subject matter of this book. In the first place it makes major claims on land: the forest area of Great Britain amounts to 4·5 million acres. Forestry Commission land totals nearly three million acres, of which 1·8 million acres are under plantation. The Commission plant some thirty to forty thousand acres each year. However, an adequate discussion of the land needs for forestry and of forestry policy would take us too far afield.* Here attention is concentrated on two issues: access to forestry land and the conflict between amenity and forestry.

'It is almost a truism that in these small islands it is necessary to reconcile the claims of amenity and economic utilization; if they are kept in watertight compartments there will not be enough land to go round.' So stated the Forestry Commissioners in their 1943 report on *Post-War Forest Policy*. It is in recognition of this fact that the Forestry Commissioners have evolved a positive policy for providing access facilities in State Forests. The policy was first worked out in the New Forest and Dean Forest, the only two of the many Royal Forests which have survived substantially intact from Norman times. Today there are seven Forest Parks of which two are in England and Wales. Additionally there is New Forest, in Hampshire, which though not a

* See the *Annual Reports* of the Forestry Commissioners and the Report by them on *Post-War Forest Policy*, Cmd. 6447, 1943.

Forest Park, can be regarded as such, since it provides equivalent access and recreational facilities.

Some of the land within the boundaries of Forest Parks is too rocky, peaty or exposed for economic afforestation: this 'unplantable' land may form as much as three-quarters of mountainous areas. The object of the Forest Parks is to make this land available to the public for recreation and, at the same time, to provide cheap and convenient camping sites. Each of the parks contains properly equipped camping sites which were used by nearly 850,000 people in 1969.

Both within and outside the Forest Parks it is the Commission's policy 'to open their plantations to the public wherever this can be done without undue risk of damage, for example through fire, and without prejudicing the legitimate interests of lessors, sporting tenants and neighbours'.

Nevertheless, as the Council for Wales and Monmouthshire have stressed in their *Report on the Welsh Holiday Industry*, it is important to recognize that this is not a statutory duty of the Forestry Commission. Nor is it part 'of a comprehensive conscious policy for the visitor based on carefully long-term objectives accompanied by appropriate powers and finance. . . . The Commission must continue to give overwhelming weight to its statutory duty of caring for the trees, and anything it does for the visitor will be an afterthought.' The Council have recommended that the Forestry Commission be charged with direct responsibility (though subordinate to its present function) to plan and develop its properties in order to provide for the community at large the opportunities for enjoying natural surroundings.

It is unfortunate that the Forest Park achievements and the positive policies of the Forestry Commission in relation to access and recreation appear to attract less public attention than their afforestation programme. Much of this must inevitably take place in national parks and areas of outstanding natural beauty – which, it must be remembered, cover over 9,700 of the 58,000 square miles of England and Wales. Afforestation is a necessary economic activity which, together with agriculture, must remain the dominating form of activity over large parts of the national parks. Quite apart from national needs these activities are, in any case, necessary if the inhabitants of these areas are to have employment. Nevertheless, a conflict of interests can occur, particularly when afforestation leads to a complete change in the character of wild and remote areas. The Forestry Commission always consults with the Countryside Commission who make proposals concerning the type and extent of planting. Critics of the Forestry Commission accuse them of blanketing whole hillsides with one species: unfortunately this 'may sometimes be inevitable, but normally scientific forestry and an eye to landscape dictate a much more varied tree cover'. In fact, the Forestry Commission makes a strenuous effort to strike a balance between amenity and utility: witness is borne to this fact by the cases outlined in the annual reports of the Countryside Commission. In the face of a strong amenity case they may even withdraw a proposal completely. Where agreement cannot be reached, the matter is referred for adjudication to the responsible Ministers.

Forest Parks in Great Britain

Forest Park	Situation	Area (acres)
Dean	Gloucestershire and Monmouth	35,000
Snowdonia	Snowdonia National Park	23,700
Border	Mainly Northumberland	126,000[a]
Glen Trool	Galloway	130,127
Queen Elizabeth (Ben Lomond, Loch Ard and the Trossachs)	Perthshire – Stirlingshire	50,000
Argyll	Argyll	63,000
Glen More	Inverness-shire	12,500
New Forest[b]	Hampshire	67,000

[a] Neighbouring woodlands owned by the Forestry Commission (including some within the Northumberland National Park) bring the total area in this region up to 178,000 acres – the largest expanse of forest in the British Isles.

[b] Though not a Forest Park, the New Forest provides similar access and recreational facilities. It is administered under special Acts of Parliament.

More difficult are private afforestation proposals. The Countryside Commission have strongly argued the case for some form of control, but the Government have preferred to encourage a voluntary scheme. (Agriculture and forestry do not constitute 'development' and therefore do not require planning permission.) Such an agreement has been worked out between Timber Growers' Organization, the County Landowners' Association, the Forestry Commission and the Countryside Commission. This provides for private proposals to be informally submitted to Park Planning Authorities for comment and discussion. A survey – which must of necessity take a considerable time – is to be undertaken in each national park, with a view to dividing land in the parks as far as possible into three categories:

(a) areas where there is a strong presumption that afforestation would be acceptable;

(b) areas where, although there is a presumption against afforestation, proposals might be acceptable; and

(c) areas where there is a strong presumption against afforestation.

The scheme is, of course, purely voluntary and there is no power for enforcement. With increasing pressure for more afforestation in certain areas – particularly in Northumberland and in the Yorkshire Dales – the case for bringing large-scale afforestation in national parks under planning control is becoming stronger.

NATURE CONSERVATION

The concept of wild life 'sanctuaries' or nature reserves is one of long standing, and, indeed, antedates the modern idea of national parks. In other countries some national parks are in fact primarily sanctuaries for the preservation of big game and other wild life, as well as for the protection of outstanding physiological features and areas of outstanding geological interest. British national parks are somewhat different in concept: the emphasis is on the preservation of amenity and providing facilities for public access and enjoyment. The concept of nature conservation, on the other hand, is primarily a scientific one concerned particularly with research on problems underlying the management of natural sites and of vegetation and animal populations. Nevertheless, as the Huxley Report on *Conservation of Nature in England and Wales* pointed out, there is no fundamental conflict between these two sets of interests: 'Their special requirements may differ, and the case for each may be presented with too limited a vision: but since both have the same fundamental idea of conserving the rich variety of our countryside and sea-coasts and of increasing the general enjoyment and understanding of nature, their ultimate objectives are not divergent, still less antagonistic'. However, to ensure that recreational, economic and scientific interests are all fairly met presents some difficulties. Several reports dealing with the various problems were published shortly after the war. The outcome was the establishment of the Nature Conservancy, constituted by a Royal Charter in March 1949 and given additional powers by the National Parks and Access to the Countryside Act. (The Conservancy is now a component body of the Natural Environment Research Council.) The Conservancy's main duties are to give scientific advice, to establish and manage nature reserves and to organize and develop research. It is the question of nature reserves which has particular relevance to the subject of this book. The Conservancy have powers to acquire land or to enter into agreements with owners in order that nature reserves may be established. In agreement cases the owner remains in full possession and has responsibility for management, but he agrees to manage in accordance with the advice of the Conservancy so as to preserve the scientific interest of the particular area. Local planning authorities can also – in consultation with the Conservancy – set up

Local Nature Reserves. The 'declaration' of a Reserve does not of itself confer any public right of access whatsoever. Furthermore, the powers to make access agreements or orders in 'open country' are clearly not applicable to Reserves: to make such an order over a Nature Reserve would be a contradiction in terms. This does not mean, however, that access to Reserves is generally prohibited. It is the policy of the Conservancy to allow as much access as is compatible with proper scientific management. About a half of the land in National Nature Reserves is generally open to the public without any restriction; the remainder is open only by permit.

THE EMERGENCE OF POSITIVE PLANNING FOR LEISURE

During the 'sixties there developed an increasing awareness on the part of Government that a much more positive approach was needed to the provision of facilities for leisure, recreation and sport. This can be seen in a wide range of fields (stretching beyond the confines of this book) – from the 'arts' to waterways, from sports provision to tourism, and from urban parks to caravanning.

Reports, White Papers and legislation now constitute an impressive library. Several new agencies have been established: some, such as the Sports Council, with wide advisory responsibilities; some, such as the British Tourist Authority and the three Tourist Boards (for England, Scotland and Wales), with responsibilities for the provision of amenities and facilities; others, such as the Lee Valley Regional Park Authority, with specific regional development and management responsibilities. A number of existing bodies have been given new responsibilities: the Waterways Board for example and, of particular importance, the National Parks Commission which has now become the Countryside Commission.

Much of all this is, as yet, only full of promise. It is too early to assess the impact. But clearly there has been a major move towards a positive approach on a significant scale.

All that can be attempted here is a rapid summary of a selected number of recent legislative changes.

COUNTRY PARKS

Hitherto, national recreational policy has been largely concerned with national parks, 'areas of outstanding natural beauty', and the coast. Studies undertaken by the Greater London Council in connection with the Greater London Development Plan underline the need for a positive policy in relation to metropolitan, regional and country parks. One such park is being developed in the Lee Valley under special legislation. The Lee Valley Regional Park Authority was established in January 1967 with members appointed by fifteen local authorities and with powers to precept on the GLC and the County Councils of Essex and Hertfordshire. This particular area (amounting to nearly 10,000 acres) is largely derelict and has been for many years. (It is now a quarter of a century since Abercrombie's *Greater London Plan* envisaged the valley as 'an opportunity for a great piece of regenerative planning'.) It has been graphically described (by the Civic Trust) as 'London's kitchen garden, its well, its privy and its workshop . . . London's back door'. The Lee Valley Regional Park Master Plan proposes a very wide range of facilities for recreation and education including twelve major multi-purpose recreation centres as well as four major centres for youth activity, water sports, motor sports and industrial archaeology. These are to be linked by river, canal, parkland and a park road (with tolls), footpaths and bridleways.

The Lee Valley project is an ambitious scheme. It is an exercise in 'regeneration' as well as in recreational planning. It is perhaps unique. But the concept of a major 'out-of-door' recreational facility has attracted considerable discussion in recent years and is now embodied as part of contemporary wisdom in the 1968 Countryside Act. As the 1966 White Paper, *Leisure in the Countryside*, explained, 'country parks' can achieve several desirable objectives at one and the same time. Country parks 'would make it easier for town-dwellers to enjoy their leisure in the open, without travelling too far and adding to congestion on the roads; they would ease the pressure on the more remote and solitary places; and they would reduce the risk of damage to the countryside – aesthetic as well as physical – which often comes about when people simply settle down for an hour or a day where it suits them, somewhere "in the country" – to the inconvenience and indeed expense of the countryman who lives and works there'.

The Countryside Act defines a country park as 'a park or pleasure ground for the purpose of providing or improving opportunities for the enjoyment of the countryside by the public'. This is a rather broad (not to say vague) definition – a matter of some importance, since the Act also provides for Exchequer aid (of 75 per cent) of 'approved expenditure' on country parks: for land acquisition; for landscaping, car parks, lavatories and roads; litter removal; warden services; and major items of renewal and repair.

The Countryside Commission have 'amplified' the statutory definition. Their provisional definition is 'an area of land or land and water normally not less than 25 acres in extent designed to offer to the public, with or without charge, opportunity for varied recreational activities in the countryside'. They have also 'suggested' that to be recognized by the Commission (a necessary step en route to Exchequer aid) a country park must be:

(a) readily accessible for motor vehicles and pedestrians;
(b) provided with an adequate range of facilities, including, as a minimum, parking facilities, lavatories and a supervisory service;
(c) operated as a single unit and managed by a statutory body or private agency or a combination of both.

By September 1970, eighteen country parks had been approved and 103 were at an advanced stage of planning.

Picnic places
The Countryside Act also provides new powers for local authorities in relation to picnic sites. The White Paper explained that these sites 'will be places in the countryside and on the coast where a country park would not be justified, but something better than a lay-by is needed by the family who want to stop for a few hours, perhaps to picnic, perhaps to explore footpaths, or simply to sit and enjoy the view and the fresh air'. Accordingly, local authorities are empowered to provide and manage picnic sites. An Exchequer grant is now available for the development of picnic sites. By September 1970, twenty-three picnic sites had been approved and sixty-three were under consideration or awaiting submission of details.

THE COUNTRYSIDE COMMISSION

The Countryside Commission replaced the National Parks Commission in 1968. The change of name signifies an extension of function. Responsibilities in relation to National Parks and Areas of Outstanding Natural Beauty remain; but to these are added the duty 'to review, encourage, assist, concert or promote the provision and improvement of facilities for the enjoyment of the countryside generally, and to conserve and enhance the natural beauty and amenity of the countryside, and to secure public access for the purpose of open air recreation'.

The Commission have an important specific duty to undertake and commission research. To assist in this and to bring together the many bodies concerned (in varying degrees) with recreation a Countryside Recreation Research Advisory Group (CRRAG) has been set up and is chaired and serviced by the Commission. The members include representatives of the British Tourist Authority, the British Waterways Board, the Nature Conservancy, the Sports Council, the Forestry Commission and the Water Resources Board.

The Group maintains a comprehensive central record of research studies in the field of countryside recreation and conservation. A *Research Register* is published periodically and a modest research programme is under way.

A particularly interesting power given to the Commission under the Countryside Act is that to initiate and assist experimental projects involving some new element of countryside planning, and designed to illustrate their appropriateness to the area in which they are carried out or to similar areas.

Their *Third Report* refers to several experimental projects under way, including an experimental centre for education and recreation at Morwellham Quay in the Tamar Valley (created by the Dartington Amenity Research Trust); a fully automatic coin-operated rising-step barrier at a popular car park adjoining a picnic site overlooking the Solent (carried out with the co-operation of Hampshire County Council); and a traffic control scheme in the Goyt Valley.

RIVERS AND CANALS

Leisure in the Countryside promised that the Government would seek to evolve, in conjunction with the river authorities, public bodies and others concerned, comprehensive plans for developing the use for recreation of the country's waterways, natural or artificial. A major problem of canals, highlighted in the British Waterways Board's report on *The Facts About The Waterways*, is that the minimum cost of keeping non-commercial routes open is at least £600,000 a year. To keep them open for pleasure cruising would add a further £340,000.

Following extensive discussions with the various interested parties and the publication, in 1967, of a White Paper, *British Waterways: Recreation and Amenity*, the 1968 Transport Act provided a 'new charter for the waterways'. The Board's waterways are classified into:

(i) Commercial Waterways: to be principally available for the commercial carriage of freight;
(ii) Cruising Waterways: to be principally available for cruising, fishing and other recreational purposes; and
(iii) the remainder.

The effect of the new arrangements is that over 1,400 miles of waterways will remain open for pleasure cruising. The Board's annual deficits (on all operations) are borne by the Exchequer. It was originally proposed that the financial position in relation to cruising waterways would be reviewed after five years. However, the Government were persuaded that such a formal review would create uncertainty and discourage private commercial investment and development (e.g.

in the building of marinas or the provision of cruising craft for hire). Instead, an Inland Waterways Amenity Advisory Council has been established, one of whose functions will be to consider proposals for the closure of individual waterways 'if this becomes necessary in the national interest'. The Council's functions are, however, not narrowly circumscribed; they include:

(a) to advise the Board and the Secretary of State on any proposals to add to or reduce the Cruising Waterways;
(b) to consider any matter affecting the use or development for amenity or recreational purposes, including fishing, of the Cruising Waterways, and any matter with respect to the provision of services of facilities for those purposes on the Cruising Water-ways or the Commercial Waterways and, where they think it desirable, to make recommendations on such matters to the Board or to the Minister after consulting the Board; and
(c) to be consulted by the Secretary of State on certain proposed Orders to be made by him.

Much of the Board's 'amenity' work is undertaken in co-operation with other bodies. Of particular interest is the Birmingham city centre redevelopment scheme, at the junction of the Birmingham Canal and the Birmingham and Fazeley Canal, where old industrial buildings are being replaced by multi-storey housing set in landscaped gardens. Included in the layout is a new canalside public house, a restaurant and a canalside walk. Some typical old canal cottages are being restored. Most of this work is being carried out by Birmingham Corporation, but the Board are to improve their land and installations facing the site, to dredge the canal adjoining the development, and to provide overnight and permanent moorings and facilities for canal cruisers. Other examples of co-operative schemes are given in the Board's Annual Reports.

TOURISM

Tourism is Britain's top dollar earner and the fourth largest source of foreign currency: in short, it is a very important economic activity. It is also one which is increasing in importance: the annual number of overseas visitors, for instance, doubled during the 'sixties.

Until recently, Government support for this activity has been meagre – unlike the position in many other countries.

The growing hotel shortage, the inadequacy of the semi-private British Travel Association and the increasing awareness of the econo-mic importance of the industry have, however, at last resulted in

H

significant Government action and assistance. The Development of Tourism Act, 1969, established a new statutory tourist organization and provides for grants and loans to hotels. (It also contains enabling powers for the registration of hotels and other tourist accommodation and for requiring them to display room charges, but these powers are not yet in operation.)

The statutory organization consists of four bodies: the British Tourist Authority, and Tourist Boards for England, Scotland and Wales. Despite the self-denying emphasis which official statements have placed on catering for currency-producing overseas visitors, the Authority and the Boards have a wide-ranging function 'to encourage the provision and improvement of tourist amenities and facilities in Great Britain'.

It is, of course, far too early to attempt an assessment of this new legislation. Much will depend on the character and strength of the BTA and the Tourist Boards. It does, however, constitute a force of considerable potential in positive planning for leisure.

In previous editions of this book the discussion of positive planning for leisure dealt mainly with American material and experience; there was little that could be recounted of policies and achievements in Britain. The current position is one of great promise on a wide range of fronts. Perhaps a later edition will be able to recount significant achievements.

RESOURCES FOR RECREATIONAL PLANNING

This account of planning for leisure, incomplete though it is, demonstrates the increasing attention which the issue is receiving. A fuller treatment would include a discussion of the Sports Council and the Regional Sports Councils, physical education, the provision made by the new towns, the development of 'arts centres', financial aid to the live theatre, museums and libraries, and recreational gardening (the term coined by the Thorpe Committee on Allotments as the appropriate description of the modern function of allotments). It would also discuss recent surveys of leisure activity and the increasing attention given by local planning authorities to recreational planning – particularly in the Greater London Development Plan. An earlier edition of this book included a summary of the latter and of the Government Social Survey Report *Planning for Leisure*, but it is becoming increasingly difficult to present a comprehensive picture within the confines of one chapter of a book devoted to a much broader field. This is heartening. Matters have changed very significantly since the first edition, written in 1963, referred to 'the much neglected subject of planning for leisure – a crucial problem which unfortunately attracts little political controversy and correspondingly little action'. Nevertheless, the mounting pressures on our limited land resources, coupled with the meagre financial provision made for investment in recreational facilities, gives no ground for complacency. The Countryside Act of 1968 was full of promise but, for this to be realized, a considerable increase in expenditure is required. In 1969–70, Exchequer provision for the Countryside Commission totalled only £720,700, while the net rate-borne expenditure of national park authorities was only £452,433. The Commission, in their *Third Report*, lament that they 'have again been prevented by financial stringency from performing our statutory duties in ways best calculated to serve the functions conferred on us by the Countryside Act'. Perhaps a significant increase in investment will follow the report of the recently announced 'major review of national parks'. This review, announced in May 1971, is being undertaken by Lord Sandford, joint Parliamentary Under-Secretary of State at the DOE (with special responsibility for the countryside). A report is to be published and, in the words of the Secretary of State for the Environment, 'thereafter, action must be taken'.

REFERENCES AND FURTHER READING

1 Arvill, R., *Man and Environment*, Penguin Books, Revised Edition, 1969.
2 Bonham-Carter, V., *The Survival of the English Countryside*, Hodder & Stoughton, 1971.
3 British Waterways Board, *Annual Reports*, HMSO.
4 British Waterways Board, *The Future of the Waterways*, HMSO, 1964.
5 British Waterways Board, *The Facts About the Waterways*, HMSO, 1966.
6 British Waterways Board, *Leisure and the Waterways*, HMSO, 1967.
7 Burton, T. L., *Recreation Research and Planning*, Allen & Unwin, 1971.
8 Burton, T. L., *Experiments in Recreational Research*, Allen & Unwin, 1971.
9 Burton, T. L. and Wibberley, G. P., *Outdoor Recreation in the British Countryside*, Wye College, University of London, Studies in Rural Land Use, Report No. 5, 1965.
10 Campbell, I., *A Practical Guide to the Law of Footpaths*, Commons, Open Spaces and Footpaths Preservation Society, 1969.
11 Council for the Protection of Rural England, *Annual Reports*, CPRE.
12 Council for Wales and Monmouthshire, *Report on the Welsh Holiday Industry*, Cmnd., 1950, HMSO, 1963.
13 Countryside Commission, *Regional Coastal Reports* (HMSO, 1967–8):
    1 *The Coasts of Kent and Sussex.*
    2 *The Coasts of Hampshire and the Isle of Wight.*
    3 *The Coasts of South-West England.*
    4. *The Coasts of South Wales and the Severn Estuary.*
    5 *The Coasts of North Wales.*
    6. *The Coasts of North-West England.*
    7. *The Coasts of North-East England.*
    8. *The Coasts of Yorkshire and Lincolnshire.*
    9. *The Coast of East Anglia.*
14 Countryside Commission, *The Coasts of England and Wales: Measurements of Use, Protection and Development*, HMSO, 1968.

15 Countryside Commission, *Coastal Recreation and Holidays*, HMSO, 1969.

16 Countryside Commission, *Picnic Sites*, HMSO, 1969.

17 Countryside Commission, *Nature Conservation at the Coast*, HMSO, 1970.

18 Countryside Commission, *The Planning of the Coastline*, HMSO, 1970.

19 Countryside Commission, *The Coastal Heritage*, HMSO, 1970.

20 Countryside Commission, *Annual Reports*, HMSO (*Third Report 1969–70*, H.C. Paper, 181, December 1970).

21 Countryside Commission, *Research Register No. 3*, published by the Commission, September 1970.

22 DOE, *National Parks and Access to the Countryside Act, 1949 and the Countryside Act, 1968; Explanatory Memorandum on Grants*, HMSO, 1971.

23 Douglass, R. W., *Forest Recreation*, Pergamon Press, 1969.

24 Dower, M., *Fourth Wave – The Challenge of Leisure* (A Civic Trust Survey), reprinted from *The Architects Journal*, January 20, 1965, Civic Trust.

25 Forestry Commission, *Forestry in the Landscape*, HMSO, 1966.

26 Forestry Commission, *Forestry in the British Scene*, HMSO, 1968.

27 Greater London Council, *Surveys of the Use of Open Space*, GLC, 1968.

28 Greater London Council, *Greater London Development Plan: Report of Studies* (Chapter 5), GLC, 1969.

29 Johnson, W. A., *Public Parks on Private Land in England and Wales*, Johns Hopkins, 1971.

30 Lee Valley Regional Park Authority, *Lee Valley Regional Park*, 1969 (published by the Authority, Myddleton House, Bulls Cross, Enfield, Middlesex).

31 MHLG, *Leisure in the Countryside*, Cmnd, 2928, HMSO, 1966.

32 MHLG, Circular 44/68, *Countryside Act*, 1968, HMSO, 1968.

33 MHLG, *Report of the Footpaths Committee* (Gosling Report), HMSO, 1968.

34 MHLG, *Departmental Committee of Inquiry into Allotments: Report* (Thorpe Report), Cmnd. 4166, HMSO, 1969.

35 Ministry of Town and Country Planning, *National Parks in England and Wales* (Dower Report), Cmd. 6628, HMSO, 1945.

36 Ministry of Town and Country Planning, *Conservation of Nature in England and Wales* (Huxley Report), Cmd. 7122, HMSO, 1947.

37 Ministry of Town and Country Planning, *Report of the National Parks Committee (England and Wales)* (Hobhouse Report). Cmd, 7121, HMSO, 1947.

38 Ministry of Town and Country Planning, *Footpaths and Access to the Countryside: Report of the Special Committee (England and Wales)*, Cmd. 7207, HMSO, 1947.

39 Ministry of Transport and Civil Aviation, *Report of the Committee of Inquiry into Inland Waterways*, Cmnd. 486, HMSO, 1958.

40 Ministry of Transport, *Transport Policy*, Cmnd. 3057, HMSO, 1966 (Chapter VIII: 'Inland Waterways').

41 Ministry of Transport, *British Waterways: Recreation and Amenity* Cmnd. 3401, HMSO, 1967.

42 Ministry of Works and Planning, *Report of the Committee on Land Utilisation in Rural Areas* (Scott Report), Cmd. 6378, HMSO, 1942.

43 Mutch, W. E. S., *Public Recreation in National Forests: A Factual Study*, Forestry Commission, HMSO, 1968.

44 National Parks Commission, *Annual Reports*, H.C. Papers, HMSO.
   The National Parks Commission has now been replaced by the Countryside Commission.
   See *Nineteenth Report of the National Parks Commission and First Report of the Countryside Commission for the Year Ended September 30th, 1968*, H.C. Paper 33, HMSO, 1968.

45 Nature Conservancy, *The Nature Conservancy Handbook, 1968*, HMSO, 1968.

46 Nature Conservancy, *The Nature Conservancy: Progress 1964–1968*, HMSO, 1968.

47 Outdoor Recreation Resources Review Commission, *Outdoor Recreation for America*, US Government Printing Office, 1962.

48 *Royal Commission on Common Land: Report*, Cmnd. 462, HMSO, 1958.

49 Sillitoe, K. K., *Planning for Leisure: An Enquiry into the Present Pattern of Participation in Outdoor and Physical Recreation and the Frequency and Manner of Use of Public Open Spaces, Among People Living in the Urban Areas of England and Wales*, Government Social Survey, HMSO, 1969.

50 Sports Council, *Planning for Sport: Report of a Working Party on Scales of Provision*, Central Council for Physical Recreation, 1968.

51 Sports Council, *The Sports Council: A Review 1966–69* (with bibliography), Central Council for Physical Recreation, 1969.

52 Stamp, D., *Nature Conservation in Britain*, Collins, 1969.

53 Town Planning Institute, *Planning for the Changing Countryside*, 1968.

54 Wolfenden Committee, *Sport and the Community*, Central Council for Physical Recreation, 1960.

Chapter X

NEW AND EXPANDING TOWNS

THE CASE FOR NEW TOWNS

In the context of post-war planning the arguments in favour of new towns were simple and overwhelming. The large cities – above all London – had grown too large: improved housing conditions had been obtained at unwarranted social and economic cost. Yet the need for more houses had not abated: on the contrary, it had been increased by the cessation of building during the war, by population growth and (at the time only dimly understood) household growth, and by the recognition and acceptance of the need for major reconstruction and thinning out of congested urban areas. Further large-scale peripheral expansion could not be countenanced: the only alternative was long-distance dispersal. Some of this could go to expanded small towns, but the scale of the problem was too great to be dealt with solely by this means. Further, it was obvious that the local government machinery was not suited to undertake building on the scale required, even if local housing situations made it politically viable that local authorities could contemplate a major building programme for non-local people. The basic solution, therefore, was the building of new towns by new *ad hoc* agencies.

The main alternatives were private enterprise and government-sponsored corporations. Private enterprise was rejected by the Reith Committee. They stated:

'While it is desirable to provide every opportunity for private development, we have come to the conclusion that in an undertaking of so far-reaching and special a character as the creation of a new town, ordinary commercial enterprise would be inappropriate. Apart from the risks involved, both in matters of finance and in execution, such a policy would of necessity result in the creation of a private monopoly.'

Three essential features of early post-war new town policy were thus:

(i) Their basic function was to relieve the housing pressures of London and other big cities.

(ii) This was to be achieved by 'the antithesis of the dormitory suburb' – by 'self-contained and balanced communities for work and living'.

(iii) New town development was to be carried out by government-sponsored corporations.

But a fourth feature needs stressing: new towns were only part of a wider policy for the distribution of population and employment. Other parts of this policy were green belts, industrial location control and expanded towns. No proper assessment of the achievements of the British new towns can be made without a parallel assessment of these other parts of the wider policy.

TWENTY-EIGHT NEW TOWNS

The Earlier Post-War New Towns

The new towns policy was thus conceived largely as a means of dealing with urban congestion. The eight London new towns have had this as their prime objective. The policy has, however, been applied to other problems.* Even in the London ring of new towns, there is one – Basildon – where a primary object has been rural slum clearance. (The area was one of extensive unplanned and largely unserviced shack development.)

Of the six original provincial new towns, five were in areas of regional decline – Peterlee, Aycliffe, East Kilbride, Glenrothes and Cwmbran. *Corby* was a special case, with the predominant objective of providing housing for the growing work-force of the Stewarts and Lloyds' steel works. Yet, in a real sense, all of these six new towns were special cases. *Peterlee*, the miners' town (built on the top of a coal field) aimed at concentrating, in one urban area, development which would otherwise have been scattered throughout a number of small mining villages, none of which could provide town facilities and amenities. *Aycliffe*, adjacent to a major trading estate, developed from a war-time Royal Ordnance Factory. It aimed at capitalizing on this investment, but (because of intense local opposition in an

---

* A sketch of each of the new towns is given in *Town and Country Planning 1943–51, Progress Report*, Cmd. 8204, HMSO, 1951, p. 125 ff.; L. Rodwin, *The British New Towns Policy*, Harvard University Press, 1956, chapter 7; and F. J. Osborn and A. Whittick, *The New Towns: The Answer to Megalopolis*, Leonard Hill, Revised Edition, 1969.

area where the local MP happened to be Hugh Dalton, the Chancellor of the Exchequer) was restricted initially to a target population of a mere 10,000. *Cwmbran*, five miles from the centre of the 100,000 population bounty borough of Newport, but attractively placed for industry, had 8,000 existing jobs and a growing problem of journeys to work. Here the objective, as in Corby, was to serve industrial growth, but in a location which was agreed to be far from ideal, yet (to use the laconic words of an official report) one to which 'there was no alternative available which would not be open to still worse objections'.* (The cynics were more pointed: if England and Scotland had new towns then Wales had to have one: a badly located new town was better than none at all.) *East Kilbride*, four miles 'over the hill' from the edge of Glasgow was proposed in the Abercrombie-Matthew Clyde Valley Regional Plan: its twin aims were to take overspill from Glasgow and to act as a growth point in a favourable area of Central Scotland. *Glenrothes*, again the product of a regional plan (the Mears Plan for Central and South-East Scotland), was conceived as a major plank in the policy of developing the East Fife coalfield to offset the decline of the Lanarkshire coalfields, but the disastrous failure of the Rothes Colliery led to a change in aim: Glenrothes became a centre for regional development loosely linked with Glasgow overspill.

Cumbernauld

Cumbernauld stands on its own – in several senses. It was the only new town designated in the 'fifties. Like East Kilbride it was proposed in the Clyde Valley Regional Plan, it is close to Glasgow and has a high level of commuting. Architecturally it is unique, and for this reason (rather than its location on the top of an exposed hill in central Scotland) it has proved most popular with architects: the seal of professional approval was provided when the town became the first winner of the R.S. Reynolds Memorial Award for Community Architecture. It also claims to be the safest town in Britain: road accidents are only 22 per cent of the national average, allegedly because of the advanced road design and segregation of traffic and pedestrians – what Zweig has termed 'traffic architecture'.[29]

The New Towns of 1961–6

Cumbernauld was the one new town designated during the ten years of 1951 to 1960. Between 1961 and 1966, seven more were designated: five in England and two in Scotland.

* *Town and Country Planning 1943–51*, Progress Report, Cmd. 8204, HMSO, 1951, p. 128. The quotation continues: 'by careful planning and firm control it would be possible to make and keep the New Town a separate community'.

The New Towns 1970

London Ring	Location (distance in km.)	Original	Population 1970	Ultimate
Basildon (1949)	London 48	25,000	83,000	134,000
Bracknell (1949)	London 45	5,000	37,300	60,000
Crawley (1947)	London 48	9,000	67,800	79,000
Harlow (1947)	London 40	4,500	76,500	90,000
Hatfield (1948)	London 33	8,500	26,300	29,000
Hemel Hempstead (1947)	London 47	21,000	70,000	80,000
Stevenage (1946)	London 50	7,000	66,300	105,000
Welwyn Gdn City (1948)	London 35	18,500	43,600	50,000
Total: London Ring		**98,500**	**470,800**	**627,000**
English Provinces:				
Aycliffe (1947)	Durham 19	100	24,000	45,000
Corby (1950)	Leicester 37	15,700	50,500	80,000
Milton Keynes (1967)	London 80	44,000	50,000	250,000
Northampton (1968)	London 106	131,000	130,600	260,000
Peterborough (1967)	London 133	83,000	88,400	188,000
Peterlee (1948)	Durham 16	200	24,000	30,000
Redditch (1964)	Birmingham 22	32,000	39,800	90,000
Runcorn (1964)	Liverpool 22	30,000	36,400	90,000
Skelmersdale (1961)	Liverpool 21	10,000	27,300	80,000
Telford (1963)*	Birmingham 48	70,000	78,000	250,000
Warrington (1968)	Manchester 24	122,000	133,000	209,000
Washington (1964)	Newcastle 10	30,000	26,000	80,000
Total: English Provinces		**558,000**	**708,000**	**1,652,000**
Wales				
Cwmbran (1949)	Cardiff 29	12,000	46,400	55,000
Newtown (1967)	Aberystwyth 43	5,000	5,500	13,000
Total: Wales		**17,000**	**51,900**	**68,000**
Scotland				
Cumbernauld (1955)	Glasgow 24	3,000	32,400	100,000
East Kilbride (1947)	Glasgow 14	2,400	66,300	100,000
Glenrothes (1948)	Edinburgh 50	1,000	30,000	75,000
Irvine (1966)	Glasgow 42	35,000	42,000	120,000
Livingston (1962)	Edinburgh 24	2,000	14,000	100,000
Total: Scotland		**43,400**	**184,700**	**495,000**
Total: Great Britain		**717,000**	**1,415,000**	**2,842,000**

* Designated as Dawley in 1963 with ultimate population of 90,000; designated area extended in 1968 and renamed Telford.

The dates in brackets indicate year of designation.

The table excludes the Central Lancashire new town, designated in 1971.

Four of the English towns are intended for overspill from two conurbations: *Skelmersdale* and *Runcorn* for Merseyside, and *Redditch* and *Dawley* for the West Midlands. They are, therefore, essentially the same in concept as the London new towns, though Dawley differs in three ways. First, whereas the other three towns have clear locational advantages, Dawley is relatively inaccessible and outside the main line of development in the Midlands. Secondly, its terrain is, to put it mildly, inhospitable. Or, to use the more romantic words of Arnold Whittick, the site is 'rich in relics of the iron industry and can justly claim to be the cradle of the industrial revolution'.[28] Be that as it may, it is an expensive town to develop. Thirdly, its designated areas was more than doubled in 1968 when its name was changed to *Telford* and its target population increased from 90,000 to 220,000. This brings it into the 'new city' class of the later 'sixties.

The fifth English new town of the 1961-6 period is *Washington* – some ten kilometres from Newcastle upon Tyne. This was the first provincial English new town to be explicitly proposed as part of a comprehensive regional programme.* Also of significance is the fact that it was the first new town intentionally sited as an extension of a conurbation. Other new towns (East Kilbride for example) may well eventually become extensions of conurbations but this was far from the intention. Washington is the prime example of a marked change in planning policy. Previously, new towns were conceived as a means of preventing urban growth: Washington is conceived as a means of accommodating it.

The two Scottish new towns of this period were both conceived as growth points in a comprehensive regional programme for Central Scotland, though starting from very different bases: *Livingston*, some 24 kilometres from Edinburgh had a base population of 2,000, while *Irvine*, on the Ayrshire coast had 35,000.

Newtown (Montgomeryshire) is a rather strange case of the use of the new town machinery for promoting regional development. It is situated in the largest area of rural depopulation in the country (England and Wales). Consultants reported that the case for a 'new town *Newtown*' was a weak one, if conceived solely in terms of a focal point for economic and social development in mid-Wales.† They concluded that designation could be justified only if overspill reception from the West Midlands were incorporated into the plan. Nevertheless, optimists strongly support the view of the previous Secretary of State for Wales that the new town will stem and,

* See *The North-East: A Programme for Regional Development and Growth*, Cmnd. 2206, HMSO, 1963.

† *A New Town for Mid-Wales – Consultants' Proposals*, HMSO, 1966.

ultimately, reverse the exodus of population from mid-Wales. Whether this can be achieved with an expansion of the scale envisaged – from 5,500 to 13,000 – remains to be seen.

The New Towns of 1967–71

Apart from Newtown, five new towns were designated between 1967 and 1971. One of the most striking features of these latest new towns (like the enlargement of Dawley into Telford which was determined during the same period) is their huge size. In comparison with the Reith Committee's 'optimum' of 30,000–50,000, Milton Keynes' 250,000 and Central Lancs' 500,000 are massive. But size is not the only striking feature. Another is the fact that four of them are based on substantial existing towns. At the date of designation, *Peterborough* had 83,000 population, *Northampton* 131,000, *Warrington* 122,000 and *Central Lancashire* 250,000. Of course, town building has been going on for a long time in Britain and all the best sites have already been taken by what are now old towns. The time was bound to come when the only place left for new towns were the sites of existing towns.

In this situation, and given the scale of expansion, traditional terms such as 'new towns' and 'expanding towns' become inappropriate. Like the term 'overspill' they are now out of date. As with so many other aspects of town and country planning, new concepts are being embodied in old terms. Just as 'overspill' is being misleadingly applied to the accommodating of a major population increase, so the term 'new towns' is being used for major regional developments based on old towns.

Of course, few of the earlier new towns were built on virgin sites (and those that were – Aycliffe and Peterlee – have had the most difficult time). Basildon had a scattered population of 25,000, while Hemel Hempstead was a substantial township of 21,000. But none of these earlier towns was in the same population class as the latest. Indeed, the original population of all the thirteen new towns designated between 1946 and 1951 was only fractionally greater (at 130,000) than that of the single 'new new' town of Warrington (at 122,000).

It would, however, be a mistake to infer that these relatively mammoth new towns were designated because the supply of alternative locations had run out. The reasoning has a number of strands. First, older towns are in need of rejuvenation and a share in the limited capital investment programme. It is not self-evident that economic sense or social justice is achieved by another round of traditional type new towns. Related to this is the old economic argument that nothing succeeds like success. Or, to be more accurate and precise, a major development with a population base of 80,000–130,000 or more has a flying start over one which has a mere 5,000–10,000. A wide range of facilities is already available, and (hopefully) can be expanded at the margin. There are numerous other advantages such as the much more varied housing market. On the other hand, the disadvantages are yet to be assessed.

It is also noteworthy that every one of these five newest towns are on excellent communications routes for both road and rail – four of them on the electrified rail line to Euston. This is 'linear planning' on a grand scale.

But perhaps too much should not be made of common features. The newest new towns are as varied as the older ones – and there is always (or at least hopefully always) Newtown as an exception to the general rule. Probably the only strictly valid common denominator is that they are all intended to assist in the accommodation of population increase. Three – Milton Keynes, Peterborough and Northampton are linked with London overspill, while Warrington and Central Lancashire are linked with Merseyside and South-East Lancashire overspill, though the links are somewhat tenuous.

THE SELECTION OF SITES

The selection of sites for 'new' towns is very difficult in a small country such as Britain. The requirements are numerous: an adequate water supply (but avoiding the sterilization of a material part of the catchment areas for the water supplies of the region); good drainage; a reasonably flat site – not too hilly (which would be expensive) nor too flat (which would detract from the interest and potentialities of the site); near main roads and a through railway line (but not too close since this might involve extra costs for bridging, underpasses, relief roads and so on); a reasonable distance from existing large urban developments; not forgetting the avoidance of areas of 'outstanding natural beauty', of great historical interest, of mining subsidence or large surface workings, and of first-class agricultural land. Clearly these ideal requirements can rarely be met: the problem then becomes one of balancing costs and benefits.

Of the ten sites proposed in Abercrombie's Greater London Plan only two – Stevenage and Harlow – were actually designated. Four were rejected on the grounds that they were too close to existing towns and therefore unlikely to survive as separate entities: Redbourn (near Hemel Hempstead, St Albans and Harpenden); Stapleford (near Hertford); Margaretting (near Chelmsford); and

Holmwood (near Dorking – and in a particularly beautiful piece of countryside). Ongar was rejected partly because of its inadequate rail service (and the high cost of making it adequate) – a difficulty which applied also to Redbourn. White Waltham was situated in an area of valuable agricultural land and, furthermore, would have put a nearby airfield out of use. Crowhurst was considered unattractive to industry and too near Crawley, which had been proposed to take the place of Holmwood.

In the provinces the problem of the risk of subsidence has been acute. A proposed town at Mobberley in Cheshire, though near to Manchester, was seriously considered but rejected because of liability to subsidence due to salt mining. In South Wales attempts to find a suitable site for a new town which could serve workers on the trading estate at Treforest, near Pontypridd, proved abortive.

There is, additionally, the political context within which decisions on new sites are made: this may exacerbate the physical problems or, alternatively, reduce the importance which is attached to them.*

DESIGNATION

Once a site has been chosen the first formal step is *designation*. This is accomplished by means of a draft order, following which there are consultations with interested parties – particularly the local authorities concerned. If any objections cannot be settled administratively, a public inquiry must be held. 'The inquiry is not a judicial or quasi-judicial one; it is a step in the administrative process by means of which objections are publicly stated and the Minister is made aware of the extent to which his proposals are opposed. . . . Before any case comes to inquiry, the proposed site and possible alternatives have been exhaustively investigated, so that it is unlikely that the inquiry will disclose any major factor of which the Minister is not aware.'[3] Unfortunately, though such an attitude may be realistic, it is not one likely to be welcomed by local opponents: at the very least there is a clear need for an enlightened public relations policy. This was notably lacking in the early days of the new towns programme and considerable opposition – and litigation – resulted.

Objections to earlier new towns generally resulted at most in the exclusion of certain areas of agricultural land from the designated area: 317 acres at Crawley, 394 at Harlow, 763 at Bracknell, 1,050 at Corby and 2,020 at Hemel Hempstead. The designated area, can however, be extended at a later date, in which case – unless there are no objections – a further public inquiry is held. Bracknell, for

* See, for example, Rodwin's comments on Cwmbran and Aycliffe, *op. cit.*, pp. 122–4.

instance, had its designated area increased by over 1,500 acres in 1961 and 1962.

THE NEW TOWN DEVELOPMENT CORPORATIONS

The New Towns Act of 1946* provides for the setting up of development corporations to plan and create new towns wherever the Minister is satisfied 'that it is expedient in the national interest' to do so. The corporations have powers 'to acquire, hold, manage and dispose of land and other property, to carry out building and other operations, to provide water, electricity, gas, sewerage and other services, to carry on any business or undertaking in or for the purposes of the new town, and generally to do anything necessary or expedient for the purposes of the new town or for the purposes incidental thereto'.

This followed the recommendations of the Reith Committee[14] that a new and separate agency (with no other responsibilities) should be created for each new town. The justification for this was that the creation of a new town was not simply a matter of erecting buildings: it also involved 'the development of a balanced community enjoying a full social, industrial and commercial life'.

The corporations are not, however, the sole agency in new town development. Despite the apparently all-embracing character of their powers, they are not local authorities: education and local health services, for example, remain the responsibility of the normal local government machinery. Water, sewage disposal, gas and electricity, and hospitals are likewise the responsibility of the normal local or public authority. Nevertheless, where the necessary provision is beyond the technical or financial resources of the local authority, the development corporations can assist by undertaking the work themselves or by making a financial contribution: this applies particularly to water, sewerage and sewage disposal facilities. This provides a useful degree of flexibility, though it has often been a source of friction between the development corporations and local authorities. Much time and effort has had to be spent on determining the allocation of expenditure between these two types of authority. The problem is aggravated by their very different characters:

'. . . relations between the New Town Corporation and the Urban District (or Borough) Council are likely to require careful handling, even granted that there is goodwill on both sides, and unfortunately

---

* The New Towns Act of 1946 and later legislation has now been consolidated in the New Towns Act, 1965, and the New Towns (Scotland) Act, 1968.

goodwill has been the exception rather than the rule. The Councillors are aware that the members of the Corporation devote less of their time to the business of the New Town than do the Councillors; that the members are paid but the Councillors are not; that the members are for the most part "strangers from London", while the Councillors are all local residents; and that the members are nominated by a Minister while the Councillors are elected by the ratepayers. The Councillors would be more than human if they did not on occasion feel some measure of both envy and resentment.'6

FINANCE

Development corporations also differ from a local authority in that they are wholly financed from the Exchequer. Advances are made by Government Departments out of issues made to them for this purpose from the Consolidated Fund. The New Towns Act of 1946 authorized issues up to £50 million to cover the needs of the first few years, but this total has been successively increased by later Acts. (The present total, authorized by the New Towns Act of 1969, is £1,100 million.) Exchequer advances are payable over sixty years, with interest at the rate prevailing at the date on which the advance is made. There is no concealed subsidy in the form of a concessionary rate of interest: the loans are made at a rate which reflects the current rate for Government credit. The Reith Committee had recommended that all finance should be found by the State by way of loan, but in fact the administration of these loans has proved to be very different from the Reith conception. The Reith Committee argued that it was 'most important that the financial autonomy and responsibility of the corporation shall be assured, and that development shall not be delayed or restricted by discussions of policy arising over applications for public advances'. This posited a degree of freedom for the corporations which it would be difficult to reconcile with public accountability. The balance is not easy to achieve, particularly where expenditure is proposed on risky ventures or developments for which there is no financial return. Since it is public money which is being invested, the Treasury have to ensure that each proposal is reasonable. But the Act goes further: it specifically requires that before approval is given to any proposal, the Secretary of State must be satisfied that 'having regard to all the circumstances' a reasonable financial return can be expected. This gives the central departments a very large degree of control over the operations of the development corporations. In fact, new towns policy – both generally and in relation to individual towns – is framed by the Department of the Environment, not by the development corporations. Since it is the central government which is providing the capital it is difficult to see how this can be otherwise.

The position may well be different in the newer 'partnership' towns where the local authorities will be playing a major, not a subordinated, role. How this will work out in practice remains to be seen.

ASSESSING NEW TOWN ACHIEVEMENTS

Twenty-eight new towns with a current population of over $1\frac{1}{2}$ million: rising to 3 million or more by the turn of the century; ranging in original size from less than 100 to 250,000 and in ultimate size from a possible 13,000 (Newtown) to 500,000 (Central Lancs); differing in density, character, location and economic potential; and with various, and sometimes changing objectives – what criteria can be used for assessing their achievements? And is the assessment to be in terms of the adequacy of provision (however that is interpreted) or in terms of alternatives forgone? If the former, what is more significant: reduction in commuting, architectural merit, range of amenities, 'balance', impact on conurbation housing problems, financial profit and loss, reduction in road accidents, satisfaction of residents. . .? If the latter (alternatives forgone), would it have been a better economic investment (or a better social policy) to facilitate a larger amount of development on the periphery of the conurbations or, at the other extreme, to plan major developments in central Wales, the Borders or the Highlands?

No apology is needed for not embarking on even a superficial assessment here. Space permits only a brief account of progress in relation to employment and housing.

Unfortunately, even a summary of physical achievements is difficult to provide since there is no comprehensive statistical return of the progress of development in the new towns. More generally (to the bewilderment and astonishment of foreign visitors) incredibly little attempt has been made to learn from the experience gained in the new towns: Government has taken an attitude which can only be described as nonchalant. Further, few serious academic studies have been undertaken.

The Reith Committee recommended the establishment of a Central Advisory Commission – both for 'harmonizing policy and practice' and for 'pooling information and experience'. This recommendation was never implemented, and such research, monitoring and statistical work which has been done within Government has, at least until recently, been on an extremely limited scale. Furthermore, it has only been in recent years that any attempt has been made to undertake a comprehensive review of the new towns programme – and even this has been in terms mainly of regional planning policies and national public expenditure.

The figures in the following account are taken from the summaries provided annually in *Town and Country Planning* – the Journal of the Town and Country Planning Association.

EMPLOYMENT

The basic conception underlying the new towns was that they should be 'balanced' communities within which the majority of the inhabitants would both live and work. It follows that (to the extent to which this objective is attained) the rate of development will be determined by the growth of local employment. Industrial location in new towns is subject to the same DTI control as exists over the country generally. The need to steer industry away from the high employment area of the south to the areas of unemployment in the north proved difficult in the early years to reconcile with the need to stimulate industrial development in the London new towns, but once they became established these towns rapidly achieved boom conditions – to such an extent, in fact, that it became difficult to build houses at an adequate rate. Less favoured new towns – particularly Peterlee – have found the attraction of industry to be a longer term difficulty. Generally speaking, however, the new towns have been able to offer sites and an environment which have proved most attractive to industrialists.

Development corporations are free to either build factories themselves and let them to firms, or lease sites on which the firms can build their own factories. (In a few exceptional cases the central government have agreed to the freehold disposal of sites.) It is generally felt that a balance of the two is desirable: letting produces a greater profit to the corporation, but the leasing of sites is thought to provide a welcome degree of stability and insurance against the effect of an economic crisis.

By the end of 1970, over 45 million square feet of factory space had been built in the new towns, of which 24 million were in the London ring, 11¼ million in Scotland and 10¼ million in the other new towns of England and Wales. Together with factories existing at the dates of designation the total amounted to nearly 70 million square feet in some 2,400 firms employing over a third of a million people. Aycliffe is excluded from these figures: adjacent to this new town is a DTI industrial estate employing nearly 9,500 people.

These statistics refer in the main to manufacturing industry: they exclude service industries which account for between 20 and 40 per cent of total employment. Service employment increases in response to local demands as the new towns grow: though provision can be – and is – made for them, they cannot be stimulated in the same way as can manufacturing industry. By December 31, 1970, some 2,300 shops (comprising 5·8 million square feet) had been completed since the dates of designation.

Office employment, of course, can be encouraged, particularly as the large school populations enter the juvenile labour market. At the end of 1970, some 3¾ million square feet of new office had been completed and a further 1¾ million square feet under construction. Several Government Departments have offices in the new towns – the Stationery Office at Basildon, the Meteorological Office at Bracknell, the General Post Office at Hemel Hempstead, as well as the usual local offices of the Department of Health and Social Security and the Inland Revenue.

HOUSING

Nearly two-thirds of the capital expenditure incurred by development corporations has been for housing. The corporations have built 178,000 houses and have been the main provider in all the new towns. They are not, however, the only house-building agency: local authorities have provided over 23,000 houses for renting, and private builders a similar number for owner-occupation. Increasing emphasis is being placed on owner-occupation, partly because of the rising demand for this form of tenure and partly because of the need to attract more private capital into the new towns. In 1967 the Minister advised development corporations that in new towns started since 1961 the aim should be to achieve 50 per cent owner-occupation by the end of the planned build-up period. In the older new towns the aim is to achieve this proportion in new building.

The overwhelming demand in all the new towns has been for houses with gardens. Development has, therefore, been at low densities. This has led to the criticism that they lack 'urban character' – an aesthetic view which seems at variance with the principle of providing the type of dwellings which people want. In fact, great ingenuity and skill has been shown by the development corporations in planning a wide variety of architectural types, a range of interesting layouts and a generally high standard of landscaping. Of course, by no means all the schemes have been successful (though opinions will differ on which these are), but the general standard of new town housing is undoubtedly superior to the generality of post-war housing.

Unlike local authorities, development corporations have no pool of low-cost pre-war housing nor can they meet any deficiencies on their housing accounts from rate subventions. Their rents thus

Housing in the New Towns to December, 1970

Name	Total completed at December 31, 1970 (est.) from date of designation		
	DCs & NTC	LA	Others
London Ring			
Basildon	17,660	2,680	1,210
Bracknell	8,501	360	316
Crawley	12,527	1,931	3,701
Harlow	20,695	927	1,033
Hatfield	4,218	1,607	283
Hemel Hempstead	12,126	2,744	2,731
Stevenage	16,833	961	1,075
Welwyn Gdn City	6,254	1,244	425
Total: London Ring	98,814	12,454	10,774
Others in England and Wales			
Aycliffe	6,103	30	91
Corby	7,243	1,822	983
Cwmbran	7,525	1,790	844
Milton Keynes	36	1,265	870
Newtown	59	6	93
Northampton	27	1,256	2,634
Peterborough	—	600	1,050
Peterlee	6,652	74	179
Redditch	2,091	353	140
Runcorn	1,797	234	418
Skelmersdale	4,730	410	361
Telford	1,222	475	675
Warrington	—	773	2,091
Washington	1,710	743	462
Total: Others in England and Wales	39,195	9,831	10,891
Total: England and Wales	138,009	22,285	21,665
Scotland			
Cumbernauld	8,645	115	61
East Kilbride	17,973	114	296
Glenrothes	7,897	297	276
Irvine	480	766	915
Livingston	4,507	—	39
Total: Scotland	39,617	1,292	1,587
Total: Great Britain	177,773	23,577	23,252

reflect the high costs and interest rates of the post-war period. There are, however, significant differences between different new towns, and between older and newer (Parker Morris standard) houses within individual towns.

Curiously, there is no published collation of rents for new towns in England and Wales. For Scotland, however, there is an annual return of *Rents of Houses Owned by Public Authorities*. The 1970 return gave an average annual standard rent (i.e. ignoring rebates) of £133. Though not high by comparison with English rents this was approaching twice the average local authority rent in Scotland (£74).

THE COMMISSION FOR THE NEW TOWNS

The New Towns Act of 1946 envisaged that the new towns would eventually be transferred from the development corporations to local authorities. This was in line with Howard's principle that there should be local control and that profits (particularly those resulting from increases in land values) should accrue to the benefit of the towns themselves. It did, however, depart from the Reith Committee's majority view that it was unwise for the functions of (virtually monopoly) land ownership and local government to be combined in a single body.

In fact, as the time for the transfer approached it became clear – to the Conservative Government, if not to the Opposition – that ownership and management should remain in the hands of a body which was independent of the local authority. The New Towns Act of 1959 set up an *ad hoc* public body for this purpose – the New Towns Commission. This Commission will take over all the assets and liabilities of each of the development corporations. To date, Crawley, Hemel Hempstead, Hatfield and Welwyn Garden City have been transferred. The previous Labour Government was committed to some transfer of assets to local authorities, but the extent and terms of this were not decided before the election of 1970. No announcement on this issue has yet been made by the present Government.

The Commission are charged with the duty 'to maintain and enhance the value of the land held by them and the return obtained by them from it' while at the same time having 'regard to the purpose for which the town was developed and to the convenience and welfare of the persons residing, working, or carrying on business there'. They have powers to make contributions towards the cost of providing amenities for the town or of providing water supplies, sewerage or sewage disposal services. They can purchase land by agreement (but not compulsorily) either in or near the towns, and promote or assist business activity. Local committees must be set up in each town to manage residential property.

The Commission were established in October 1961, and the assets and liabilities of four new towns have so far been transferred to them. Apart from the local committee (who have full delegated powers for housing management), a local Executive has been set up in each of the towns. These, in fact, consist almost entirely of officers transferred from the development corporations, and deal with the bulk of the Commission's executive functions. Only a small headquarters staff is maintained in London.

Although the new towns for which the Commission are now responsible have reached the stage at which large-scale planned immigration is being reduced, they have a high rate of natural growth. House building will, therefore, continue at a high level for some time. Special attention is being given to the needs of second-generation families (the newly wed children of present tenants) and of old people, of which there is a considerable number wishing to move into the new towns in order to live near to their married children.

Responsibility for providing subsidized rented dwellings is being transferred to the local authorities in these new towns. The Commission's role is increasingly limited to building houses for sale and to making land available for building by the local authority, private builders, housing associations and self-build groups. However, as an exception to the general rule, the DOE have permitted the Commission to provide subsidized dwellings for elderly people moving into the towns. For a discussion of the movement of elderly people to new and expanding towns, see *The Needs of New Communities*[2], pp. 17-20.

EXPANDING TOWNS

The New Towns Act was the first instalment of the 'overspill' plan: the second was to be an Act to facilitate town expansion by local authorities. This, however, was deferred until the immediate postwar housing shortage had been met. It was contrary to the political facts of life to expect local authorities to build houses for families from other areas while they still had severe housing problems of their own. It was, therefore, not until 1952 that the Town Development Act was passed.

The essential difference between the New Towns Act and the Town Development Act is apparent from their full titles. The New Towns Act is 'an Act to provide for the creation of new towns by means of development corporations'; the Town Development Act is 'an Act to encourage town development in county districts for the relief of congestion or overpopulation elsewhere'. The former set up special agencies to deal with a problem which was by implication, beyond the competence of local authorities. The latter did precisely the opposite: it provided 'encouragement' to local authorities to meet the overspill problem themselves 'by agreement and co-operation'.* As Mr Macmillan (then Minister of Housing) stressed, 'the purpose of the Bill is that large cities wishing to provide for their surplus population shall do so by orderly and friendly arrangements with neighbouring authorities . . . it is our purpose that all these arrangements should be reached by friendly negotiation and not imposed by arbitrary power'. Such financial help was to be provided as would be necessary to get the job going. At the present time this consists of a housing subsidy and a 50 per cent grant towards the cost of main sewerage, sewage-works and water-works required for the development. The Act also empowers an exporting authority to make contributions to the 'receiving authority'. In practice, although it is of doubtful equity, exporting authorities wishing to participate in a scheme must make an annual contribution for each family rehoused from their areas.

County Councils have power under the Local Government Act of 1948 to make contributions towards expenses incurred by county districts and, in practice, those which welcome overspill within their administrative area do render substantial financial assistance.

Actual development can be undertaken by the receiving authority itself; or by the exporting authority acting either as an agent for the receiving authority or on its own account; or by the county council in whose area the receiving authority is situated.

Tenants can be selected either from the housing list of the exporting authority or by means of an industrial selection scheme. In the latter case only families who secure employment in the receiving area are eligible for rehousing there.

Town development is very widely defined, as:

'Development in a county district (or partly in one such district and partly in another) which will have the effect, and is undertaken primarily for the purpose of providing accommodation for residential purposes (with or without accommodation for the carrying on of industrial or other activities, and with all appropriate public services, facilities for public worship, recreation and amenity, and other requirements) the provision whereof will relieve congestion or overpopulation elsewhere'.

* This and the following quotations are from the Second Reading debates in the House of Commons, *H.C. Debates*, vol. 496, col. 725, *et seq.*

This description of the Act serves to show how flexible its provisions are.* Since town development is undertaken by Local authorities with widely different problems and varying size and wealth, this flexibility is essential.

A town expansion scheme can operate successfully only if all the local authorities concerned – the 'exporting' authority, the 'reception' authority and the county council – are able and willing to co-operate, and if the Department of Trade and Industry are likewise able and willing to assist in persuading industry to move into the expanding town. There are big difficulties – technical, administrative, financial, social and political – to be overcome. These constitute a severe strain on the local government machine. However, given a fortuitous combination of circumstances, experience has shown that town expansion schemes can operate to the great benefit of small towns.

Haverhill is a case in point: situated in the south-east corner of West Suffolk, this 4,000 population town saw in the Town Development Act a means of arresting its economic decline and obtaining modern urban facilities which it so clearly lacked. Blessed with a local government machine of a calibre hardly to be expected in a small town, a co-operative and forward-looking County Council, and considerable technical and financial assistance from both this County Council and the exporting authority (the Greater London Council), the town has already provided over 2,100 houses and 600,000 square feet of factory space.

Schemes operated in conjunction with the Greater London Council have the advantage of very favourable financial and technical aid which an authority of this size and wealth can provide. Nevertheless, their contribution to the solution of the London overspill problem has not been impressive. In an attempt to increase the provision, the former London County Council proposed to undertake the building of a new town in Hook, Hampshire. This was strongly opposed by the Hampshire County Council, who proposed alternative areas for expansion. These alternative proposals (at Basingstoke and Andover) were accepted and, since the Hampshire County Council is an active participant in the schemes, hold out a promise of development at a faster speed than is usual with town expansion. They are also on a larger than normal scale: Basingstoke, in particular,

---

* However, the Act did not provide for the expansion of a county borough, even though this might in some cases have been preferable to expanding a very small town from, say, a population of 5,000 to one of 10,000. The exclusion of county boroughs also resulted in the peculiar situation that the Municipal Boroughs of Swindon (population 80,000) and Luton (120,000) could take advantage of the Act, whereas Northampton (100,000) could not. This limitation was removed by section 34 of the Housing Act, 1961.

is envisaged as expanding from 26,000 to 75,000–80,000. By the end of 1970, over 5,000 dwellings had been completed.

Town Development Schemes 1970

ENGLAND AND WALES (June, 1970)

'Exporting' area	No. of schemes	Dwellings provided by local authorities for town development purposes		Factories completed at 30.6.70 (sq. ft.)
		Total to be built	Completed at 30.6.70	
Greater London	31	89,453	41,445	21,848,734
Birmingham	15	21,222	7,485	3,428,511
Bristol	4	2,278	2,278	—
Liverpool	4	18,526	4,970	2,588,365
Manchester	4	8,514	1,361	538,942
Newcastle upon Tyne	2	10,517	1,513	1,426,856
Salford	1	4,518	4,518	—
Walsall	2	444	444	—
Wolverhampton	4	4,527	4,327	67,526
Total: England and Wales	67	159,999	68,341	29,898,934

SCOTLAND (September, 1970)*

	No. of 'Receiving' Areas	Houses to be built by public authorities for Glasgow overspill	
		Total to be built	Completed at 30.9.70
	42	18,205	9,780
Total: Great Britain	109	178,204	78,121

* The Scottish figures relate to areas which have 'overspill agreements' with Glasgow. Only ten of these are 'town development schemes'.

PROVINCIAL SCHEMES

In the schemes for provincial conurbations progress has been very slow. Several factors are responsible for this. The exporting authorities have not been so well organized as the Greater London Council to make the Town Development Act work. They have not been so convinced of the necessity of attempting to make it work, or at least, they have maintained that the scale of their problems requires direct central government action by way of new towns rather than the small-scale assistance to their problems likely to be achieved by 'fiddling around with the Town Development Act'. Then there is the problem of attracting industry to provincial town expansion schemes. For the small number of towns which have welcomed the idea of expansion this has proved the crucial problem.

More frequently, however, there is considerable local opposition to expansion. Apart from the technical and financial difficulties and the strong force of inertia, receiving authorities are generally small, vulnerable and highly disinclined to take risks. There is a fear that expansion will do more harm than good, that it will change the social as well as the physical character of the town – and that it may have unwelcome political consequences. The public inquiry into the proposals for an expansion scheme for Westhoughton was opened with the recorded voice of Vera Lynn singing 'Land of Hope and Glory' as 500 objectors slowly marched in procession to the town hall. Before the inquiry opened, prayers were said in local churches against the scheme; 9,000 out of the 11,000 people on the electoral roll had signed a petition; 1,400 objections had been lodged; and two local coach proprietors laid on free day-trips to Bolton, where the inquiry was held.

Though an extreme case, this does illustrate the difficulties facing town expansion proposals. It would be tedious to describe the situation in each of the major congested areas, since the story is so much the same in each. Birmingham experience may be taken as illustrative. The City has had negotiations with over 100 authorities all over the country, from Exmouth and Barnstaple in the south to Nantwich and Winsford in the north, and from Merioneth and Holyhead in the west to Cromer and Wisbech in the east. Many of the agreements which have been made are unlikely to provide any significant number of houses since the reception authorities are unwilling to build until families are willing to move, and the majority of families are not prepared to move to areas having a restricted range of jobs. Most of the local authorities who have approached Birmingham have done so in the hope that they may secure additional industry, but the City Council, of course, has no powers to direct indsutry to expansion areas and its attempts to persuade industry to move have met with only limited success. The potential town expansion areas are typically small and isolated and are, therefore, unattractive to industrialists and their workers.

Until recently the official pronouncements on the Town Development Act have been aimed at encouraging local authorities to overcome the inherent difficulties of town expansion policies, rather than providing an objective assessment of the adequacy of the policies. But a revealing comment is to be found in the evidence presented to the Royal Commission on Local Government in Greater London by the Ministry of Housing and Local Government:

'Five or six years' experience of the Town Development Act has shown that these schemes are most difficult to bring to fruition. Small authorities are naturally nervous about the financial and social consequences of embarking on a scheme of which the residual risk falls and is bound to fall on themselves. In addition, there are many ways in which the areas may fail to fulfil the tests of a "good" overspill area – for instance, it may be off the main communication routes or be surrounded by first-class agricultural land, or if it is a "good" overspill area, the town may not wish to expand. Generally speaking those towns are most anxious to expand under the Act which have not the attractions to industry and private enterprise which would make expansion natural.'

This is a striking indictment of the framework within which town development has had to operate. It is now accepted that though the Town Development Act provides an opportunity for dealing with the problems of those small towns which are prepared to accept the challenge which it offers (and the difficulties to which it gives rise), it is a weak makeshift. The crux of the matter is that the present structure of local government is quite inadequate to handle problems of overspill and regional restructuring.

SCOTTISH SCHEMES

Scottish provisions for town development were enacted in the Housing and Town Development (Scotland) Act, 1957. Currently there are ten officially designated 'town development schemes' of which the latest is at Erskine (Renfrew) where 3,000 houses for Glasgow overspill are to be built by the Scottish Special Housing Association (SSHA). Glasgow is the only local authority in Scotland recognized under the Act as an 'exporting authority'. To date it has concluded 'overspill agreements' with 42 local authorities for a total of 18,205 houses. Some of these, however, are very small in scale (e.g. for 75 houses in Alloa and Kelso) and some in remote areas where no houses have, in fact, been provided – or likely to be provided (e.g. 50 houses in Sutherland County and 300 in Wick).

The SSHA plays an important role in Scottish housing. Originally established in 1937 to supplement the housing efforts of local authorities in the 'Distressed Areas' its functions have been gradually widened. It now concentrates on the provision of houses for incoming workers in areas of economic expansion.

Perhaps even more clearly than in the case of England, the problems of overspill and town development in Scotland are entwined with those of regional planning and development. Further discussion of these wider problems is to be found in Chapter XII.

REFERENCES AND FURTHER READING

1 Best, R. H., *Land for New Towns*, Town and Country Planning Association, 1964.
2 Central Housing Advisory Committee, *The Needs of New Communities: A Report on Social Provision in New and Expanding Communities*, HMSO, 1967.
3 Commission for the New Towns, *Reports* (annual), HMSO.
4 Cullingworth, J. B., 'Some Administrative Problems of Overspill'. *Public Administration*, Vol. 37, No. 4, Winter 1959.
5 Cullingworth J. B. and Karn, V. A., *The Ownership and Management of Housing in the New Towns*, HMSO, 1968.
6 Duff, A. C., *Britain's New Towns*, Pall Mall Press, 1961.
7 Heraud, B. J., 'The New Towns and London's Housing Problem'. *Urban Studies*, Vol. 3, No. 1, 1966, pp. 8–21.
8 Heraud, B. J., 'Social Class and the New Towns', *Urban Studies*, Vol. 5, No. 1, February 1968, pp. 33–58.
9 Karn, V. A., *Housing Surveys of Crawley, Stevenage, Aycliffe and East Kilbride*, University of Birmingham, Centre for Urban and Regional Studies, Occasional Papers 8–11, 1970. (Distributed by Research Publications Services Ltd.)
10 London County Council, *The Planning of a New Town*, LCC, 1961.
11 Long, J. R., *The Wythall Inquiry*, Estates Gazette, 1962.
12 MHLG, *Handbook of Statistics*, HMSO, annual.
13 Ministry of Local Government and Planning, *Town and Country Planning 1943–1951: Progress Report by the Minister of Local Government and Planning on the Work of the Ministry of Town and Country Planning*, Cmd. 8204, HMSO, 1951.
14 Ministry of Town and Country Planning, *New Towns Committee: Interim Report*, Cmd. 6759, 1946; *Second Interim Report*, Cmd. 6794, 1946; *Final Report*, Cmd. 6876, 1946 (Reith Reports).
15 New Town Development Corporations, *Annual Reports*, HMSO.
16 Nicholson, J. H., *New Communities in Britain*, National Council of Social Service, 1961.
17 Ogilvy, A. A., 'The Self-contained New Town', *Town Planning Review*, Vol. 39, No. 1, April 1968.
18 Orlans, H., *Stevenage*, Routledge & Kegan Paul, 1954.

19 Osborn, F. J. and Whittick, A., *The New Towns: The Answer to Megalopolis*, Leonard Hill, Revised Edition, 1969.
20 Rodwin, L., *The British New Towns Policy*, Harvard University Press, 1956.
21 Royal Commission on Local Government in England, *Written Evidence of the Ministry of Housing and Local Government*, HMSO, 1967.
22 Ruddy, S., *Industrial Selection Schemes: An Administrative Study*, University of Birmingham, Centre for Urban and Regional Studies, Occasional Paper 5, 1969. (Distributed by Research Publications Services Ltd.)
23 Schaffer, F., *The New Town Story*, MacGibbon & Kee, 1970.
24 Sharp, E., *The Ministry of Housing and Local Government*, Allen & Unwin, 1969.
25 Thomas, R., *London's New Towns: A Study of Self Contained and Balanced Communities*, PEP Broadsheet 510, 1969.
26 Thomas, R., *Aycliffe to Cumbernauld: A Study of Seven New Towns in their Regions*, PEP Broadsheet 516, 1969.
27 *Town and Country Planning:* The first issue of each calendar year is devoted to new towns and includes the most comprehensive set of statistics available. This issue also contains a statistical summary of Town Development schemes.
28 *Town and Country Planning:* Special Issue, January–February 1968, 'New Towns Come of Age'.
29 Zweig, F., *The Cumbernauld Study*, Urban Research Bureau and Wates Ltd, 1970.

CONSULTANTS' REPORTS

(all published by HMSO unless otherwise indicated)

Ipswich: A Study in Town Development, 1965. Obtainable only from DOE.
Northampton, Bedford and North Bucks Study: An Assessment of Inter-related Growth, 1965.
Peterborough: An Expansion Study, 1965. Obtainable only from DOE.
Worcester Expansion Study, 1965. Obtainable only from DOE.
A New City: A Study of Urban Development in an area including Newbury, Swindon and Didcot, 1966.
A New Town for Mid-Wales – Consultants' Proposals, 1966.
Dawley: Wellington: Oakengates – Consultants' Proposals for Development, 1966.

Expansion of Ipswich Designation Proposals: Consultants' Study of the Town and its Sub-Region, 1966.

Expansion of Northampton – Consultant's Proposals for Designation, 1966.

Expansion of Peterborough – Consultant's Proposals for Designation, 1966.

Expansion of Warrington – Consultant's Proposals for Designation, 1966.

South Hampshire Study: Report on the Feasibility of Major Urban Growth, 3 vols., 1966.

Ashford Study: Consultants' Proposals for Designation, 1967.

Central Lancashire: Study for a City – Consultants' Proposals for Designation, 1967.

Central Lancashire New Town Proposal: Impact on North East Lancashire, 1968.

Expansion of Ipswich: Comparative Costs – A Supplementery Report, 1968.

Llantrisant – Prospects for Urban Growth, 1969.

Chapter XI

URBAN RENEWAL

Until the late 'fifties, policy was directed towards providing additional houses, extra school places, more open spaces and so on. Re-development – the substitution of new social capital for old – took second place. The need to plan 'comprehensively' and to improve and preserve as well as to redevelop became more and more obvious as the inadequacies of small-scale clearance and redevelopment became apparent. It increasingly became realized that the improvement of urban living conditions required more than the substitution of new for old buildings, or the clearance of a few industrial eyesores, or the building of by-passes. It requires an approach which is aimed at improving the whole physical fabric of urban life – not merely replacing the threadbare patches. Urban renewal is a convenient shorthand description of this approach. It implies not only redevelopment but also rehabilitation and conservation. It embraces a policy for the improvement of obsolescent structures which cannot yet be demolished, the clean air campaign, a programme for providing twentieth-century amenities in nineteenth-century towns, and an acceptance of the motor car as a major feature of contemporary life.

The field is very large and only a selection of some of the more important issues can be discussed. In this chapter attention is concentrated on comprehensive redevelopment, slum clearance, and improvement areas.

COMPREHENSIVE REDEVELOPMENT

Redevelopment involves far more than the simple replacement of old buildings by new ones. It has to provide a solution to the problems arising from obsolete road and street patterns and the need to separate traffic and pedestrians. It has to cope with the problems resulting from the increasing land needs of most urban uses – for the movement, parking and garaging of cars, for housing at densities which are acceptable on modern standards, for open space, for educational provision and so on. These needs cannot be satisfactorily met within the physical limitations imposed by out-of-date street patterns and the equally important limitations often created by a multiplicity of ownerships.

Comprehensive Development Areas

Post-war planning legislation acknowledged the necessity for dealing with these problems on a comprehensive basis: indeed the securing of 'comprehensive redevelopment' was one of the major objectives of the 1944 and 1947 Acts. These empowered local authorities to define as an 'area of comprehensive development':

'Any area which in the opinion of the local planning authority should be developed or redeveloped as a whole, for any one or more of the following purposes, that is to say for the purpose of dealing satisfactorily with extensive war damage or conditions of bad layout or obsolete development, or for the purpose of providing for the relocation of population or industry or the replacement of open space in the course of development or redevelopment of any other area or for any other purpose specified in the plan.'

This is a very wide provision which permits the use of comprehensive development area procedures for schemes varying from a small housing project to the 1,300 acre 'new town' for Stepney and Poplar in the East End of London. Though a CDA plan is drawn up by the local planning authority they need not undertake the actual development themselves: much of the office development in, for instance, the City of London and on the South Bank of the Thames has been carried out by private developers within the framework of CDA plans. A large proportion of the central redevelopment in Coventry, on the other hand, has been carried out by the City Council themselves. Indeed, the machinery was devised within a political context which assumed that local authorities would play the major role in redevelopment:

'Most of the well-known redevelopment schemes since the war have been carried out under the Town and Country Planning Acts of 1944 and 1947. These Acts came into being at a time when it seemed likely that central area redevelopment would for the most part be undertaken comprehensively by local authorities. They were based largely on the premise that land would be acquired by local authorities at existing use values, and it was contemplated that they would be applied mainly to areas of blitz and blight, where values were unlikely to be high. At that time the private developer had not the opportunity to tackle redevelopment on a large scale. Consequently, central area redevelopments have so far been carried out in circumstances which have necessitated or favoured public ownership and action. The procedure under these Acts was designed to meet that particular set of circumstances, and has owed some of its success to the fact that the local authority concerned has been able to reinforce its planning powers with the wider, more detailed and more adaptable powers attaching to ownership.'[14]

Conditions, of course, changed radically in the late 'fifties and 'sixties. Controls over private building were abolished, thus releasing a big backlog of demand for commercial development. At the same time, the changed compensation provisions and the increase in land values combined to discourage local authorities from undertaking development themselves. As another writer has put it, 'the draughtsmen of this Act were thinking more of war damaged areas and slum conditions than of pulsating town centres with high commercial values. . . . The procedure of the Act is not geared for rapid operation.'[15]

Increasingly in the 'sixties the extensive proposals put forward by private developers could not be considered in relation to a 'comprehensive' plan, for the simple reason that the plans had not been prepared. Nor could they be prepared at speed when major planning implications were involved. The procedure for designating 'comprehensive development areas' was elaborate and cumbersome. The amount of survey work, map-drawing and detailed planning required made the whole process lengthy. The basic problem with the CDA procedure was that it 'does not and was not intended to provide a suitable medium for the working out of policies for the town centre as a whole'.[2]

This did not give rise to insurmountable problems when local authorities were the main instigators of redevelopment. Attention was concentrated on particular areas, and private interests were not unduly affected since private land-values had been stabilized. But when private proposals for redevelopment began to be put forward for numerous different areas concurrently, there was simply not enough time to give the necessary consideration to all the relevant long-term issues involved. Private interests could not be made to wait indefinitely since 'time is money', and, in any case, local authorities are statutorily required to give a decision within two months of the date of a planning application.

The Town Centre Map

There was mounting criticism of this situation and an attempt to meet it was made in a series of *Planning Bulletins* issued by the

I

Ministry of Housing and Local Government. Local authorities were advised to prepare a non-statutory Town Centre Map, showing in broad outline their proposals for the future development of the town centre. The Town Centre Map enables particular proposals to be seen in the context of the town centre as a whole. It aims at assisting in the process of 'Survey – Analysis – Plan' which should underlie any important planning decision or proposals. It is intended 'to provide the public with a clear picture of what is proposed for the town centre and to enable persons interested to express their views on these proposals before the stage of formal submission to the Minister is reached.'[2]

The case for this new planning instrument was outlined in the Planning Bulletin, *Town Centres – Approach to Renewal*:

'What is needed is a means by which the local authority, in conjunction with the local planning authority, can make a broad and relatively quick assessment of the problems and possibilities of the town centre, and which can be developed into a sound basis for more detailed decisions. The aim should be to systematize and simplify the work and discussion which goes into planning for renewal. For this purpose what is wanted is not a plan suitable for statutory submission to the Minister but a map which reflects the process of survey, analysis and policy formation which are behind any planning decision or formal proposal for amendment of the development plan. If such a map is prepared and is used as the basis of planning in the central area and is available for public examination and discussion, the Minister will take full account of it in any matter which comes to him for decision.

'The purpose of introducing such a map is to aid and simplify the job of planning for renewal. It is not intended as an elaborate or highly technical document. It should be a simple statement of major objectives.'

The preparation of such a map, of course, entails a great deal of survey work, though it is stressed that there is no need for policy discussions to be held back until the detailed surveys are complete – 'ideas can be hammered out while the field work proceeds: the one will influence the other'. These surveys should take into account the regional factors affecting the future of the town and particularly of its centre. Important factors here are the competition of other centres (existing and planned); the amount of car-ownership (existing and predicted); the use and potentialities of private and public transport; the limitations of access to the centre imposed by the existing road system; and so on. Within the town centre attention has to be paid to:

Land use – density and amount of floor space.

Property values – with particular attention to the comparative costs of acquisition in different parts of the town centre, and sites where values could be significantly increased by redevelopment or improvement.

Town character – distinguishing features and buildings worth preserving, needing improvement, and ripe for development.

Pedestrian movement – main pedestrian flows and meeting places within the centre, with reference to congestion, adequacy of pavements, safety and conflict with vehicular traffic.

Vehicular movement – volume and direction of flow at different times, origin and destination; service access; public transport.

Parking – amount, location, duration and trends, related as far as possible to particular parts and functions of the town centre.

The analysis of this survey material needs to be 'directed to the formulation or reappraisal of planning policies and objectives in the town centre'. A recommended 'sequence of survey analysis' would be to determine the prospects for change; the prospects for retaining and improving the features of buildings which bring prosperity and give character to the town centre; the need for change; the opportunities for planned change; the likely rate of implementation; and a broad programme of priority between the various needs revealed by the analysis.

The Town Centre Map itself should reflect the broad land-use framework, illustrating a co-ordinated policy of renewal and presenting a guide for public and private redevelopment activities; and a firm road and traffic pattern designed to remove unnecessary traffic from the central area and to facilitate the segregation of vehicles and pedestrians within it.

The concept underlying this 'planning instrument' is that of a partnership between local authorities and private enterprise. The local authority is envisaged as having the role of initiator and overall planner: this should not 'pass by default to individual developers who, however competent their proposals, cannot perform the local authority's functions or absolve them of responsibility for the result'. The local authority's position is considerably strengthened by their powers to achieve land assembly, without which many of the opportunities for other than patch-work redevelopment cannot be implemented. The strength of private enterprise lies in its knowledge of the market, its ability to exploit commercial opportunities and its access to capital.

Action Areas

The situation is now to be considerably affected by the 1968 Planning Act. Under the new system, an area requiring comprehensive treatment at an early date will be designated as an *action area*. This will be subject to ministerial approval (with the usual provisions for objections and a public inquiry, but supplemented by those for public participation).* Should compulsory acquisition be necessary this will follow the normal procedure, again necessitating ministerial approval. In short, there is no longer any need for a formal CDA submission. The powers of compulsory acquisition, however, remain, as do the planning grants for this purpose.

Planning Grants

Specific planning grants (except for comprehensive redevelopment of areas of extensive war damage) were abolished in 1959 as part of the reform of local government finance. Between 1959 and 1968 these grants were 'absorbed' (along with many other specific grants) in the *general grant* introduced by the Local Government Act, 1958. The objective was to give local authorities 'a great increase of responsibility in determining the money to be spent on the various services in accordance with local needs'. A further reform, introduced by the Local Government Act, 1966, increased the relative importance of general grants, but brought back the specific planning grants† – for comprehensive development of 'areas of bad layout or obsolete development', the provision of public open space and the reclamation of derelict land.

Grants are therefore now available for the comprehensive redevelopment of areas of extensive war damage (popularly known as 'blitz') and areas of bad layout or obsolete development ('blight'). These 'blitz and blight' grants amount to 50 per cent of the notional loan charges calculated on the annual loss arising in any particular year. The loss is calculated by taking the capital cost of acquisition, clearing and preliminary development, and subtracting from this the value realized from time to time on disposal of the land by sale, lease or appropriation for other local authority services for new uses after it has been cleared and serviced.

Estimates published in the Ministry's *Handbook of Statistics* forecast total grants of £4·0 million in 1969–70, £4·9 million in 1970–1, £4·2 million in 1971–72, and £4·3 million in 1972–73.

* See Ch. IV, p. 101.

† For a general discussion of the changes in local government finance, see Sharp, E., *The Ministry of Housing and Local Government*, Allen & Unwin, 1969, Chapter VII.

INADEQUATE HOUSING

Obsolete and obsolescent housing forms the major part of the physical problem of urban renewal – though the fact that so much of this housing is concentrated in the inner areas of large towns provides a real opportunity for dealing with the concurrent problems of obsolete road patterns and inadequate facilities.

The size of the qualitative housing problem is difficult to measure. Over 6 million – about a third – of houses in Britain date from before the First World War, and of these probably 2 million are over 100 years old. Age, of course, is by no means an infallible guide to conditions, but many of these old houses are slums, lack essential amenities or are in a bad state of disrepair. They are socially, if not physically, obsolete, and would be demolished as 'slums' or included in 'clearance areas' or 'comprehensive development areas' on account of their 'bad layout' or 'obsolete development' (to use the statutory phrases) were this economically possible.

Over a third of a million houses were demolished in the slum clearance programme which began in 1930. By 1938 demolitions were running at the rate of 90,000 a year. Had it not been for the war, over a million of these old houses would have been demolished by 1951. The virtual cessation of house-building during the Second World War involved an accumulation of quantitative need which could not be quickly satisfied: slum clearance had to be postponed. The limited house-building programme was almost entirely devoted to providing new houses until 1954. Even repairs were not to be undertaken if they necessitated 'substantial calls' on building resources. In effect, therefore, not only was there a postponement of slum clearance, but also an enforced neglect of existing houses for over fourteen years.

Standards

The size of the slum problem is of course essentially related to the standards adopted. A 'slum' is more easily recognized than defined. The quality of housing has a number of different dimensions. The Denington Committee drew attention to five:

(i) the structure and condition of housing (stability, damp, natural lighting, etc.);
(ii) the equipment and services built into housing (WC, water supply, drainage, artificial lighting, etc.);
(iii) the quality of the surrounding environment (air pollution, noise, open space, traffic conditions, etc.);

(iv) the space available to individual households (persons per room, bedroom requirements, etc.);
(v) the privacy available in dwellings occupied by more than one household (sharing accommodation and facilities, sound insulation, etc.).

The assessment and quantification of these is no easy matter and there is considerable scope for area variation and personal judgment. This is particularly clear when an overall assessment is required of the need for slum clearance or improvement.

Statutory definitions relate predominantly to structure, physical condition and plumbing. In England and Wales the legislation lists a number of matters which have to be taken into consideration, but a house is deemed 'unfit for human habitation' only 'if it is so far defective in one or more of the said matters that it is not reasonably suitable for occupation in that condition'. There is thus considerable scope for judgment.

The 'said matters' are:

repair
stability
freedom from damp
internal arrangement
natural lighting
ventilation
water supply
drainage and sanitary conveniences
facilities for the preparation and cooking of food and for the disposal of waste water.

Following the Scottish Housing Advisory Committee's 1967 Report on *Scotland's Older Houses*, the Scottish legislation attempted a greater degree of objectivity. Dispensing with the concept of 'unfitness' it introduced a *tolerable standard*.

A house is held to meet this if it:

(a) is structurally stable;
(b) is substantially free from rising or penetrating damp;
(c) has satisfactory provision for natural and artificial lighting, for ventilation and for heating;
(d) has an adequate piped supply of wholesome water available within the house;
(e) has a sink provided with a satisfactory supply of both hot and cold water within the house;

(*f*) has a water closet –
  (i) available for the exclusive use of the occupants of the house within the house or, where the house forms part of a building, within that building, and
  (ii) readily accessible from, and suitably located, within the house or building, as the case may be;
(*g*) has an effective system for the drainage and disposal of foul and surface water;
(*h*) has satisfactory facilities for the cooking of food within the house;
(*i*) has satisfactory access to all external doors and outbuildings.

Despite the greater clarity and objectivity of the Scottish standard it is apparent that the subjective element cannot be completely eliminated. The SHAC Report suggested, however, that it could be further reduced by the use of a 'housing defects index'. Considerable work has been undertaken on this both north and south of the Border.

The official 'slum clearance returns' submitted by local authorities in 1954 and 1955 gave a total of 853,000 unfit houses in England and Wales and 113,500 in Scotland – a total of 966,500. In 1965 a new series of returns gave a total of 919,000 in spite of the fact that nearly $\frac{2}{3}$ million had been demolished in the intervening years. Of course, deterioration is a continuing process. Nevertheless, there is more than a suggestion that the official returns do not give a full picture. A study of the published 1954 returns (those for 1965 were not published) fully corroborates this view. Though some local authorities, such as Manchester and Liverpool included *all* the unfit houses in their estimate, others lowered their sights to what could be dealt with in a given period. To those who know Lancashire there is something odd in the fact that though 43 per cent of the houses in Liverpool were estimated to be unfit, the proportion in Oldham was 26 per cent; in Salford 24 per cent; in Bolton 10 per cent; and in Stretford 0·5 per cent. And the Glasgow figures of 17,000 in 1955 and 11,000 in 1965 clearly provide little indication of the true scale of that City's problem.

In the early 'sixties it came to be recognized by the central government that adequate national policies could not be formulated on the basis of statistics such as these. In England and Wales, with the very large expansion of the Ministry's statistical services, a national and a series of conurbation house condition surveys were mounted. A national house condition survey carried out in 1967, produced an estimated 1·8 million dwellings, compared with the official 1965 estimate of 820,000. Of these 1·8 million unfit dwellings, 1·1 million were in potential clearance areas and the remaining 700,000 needed to be dealt with individually by repair, closure or demolition. Additionally, some 113,000 dwellings were fit but in or adjoining potential clearance areas. These dwellings would be included with neighbouring unfit housing in clearance area action.

The survey also showed that unfit housing was less concentrated in the conurbations and in the north than had previously been assumed.

Nearly 4 million dwellings (a quarter of the total stock) lacked one of the major amenities and nearly 3 million did not have an internal WC.

Estimates were made of the cost of repairs required for all dwellings in the survey, assuming that they were to be retained in use for at least twenty years. Of the 13·7 million dwellings which were not unfit (and were outside potential clearance areas) some 3·6 million (26·5 per cent) needed repairs costing £125 or more and over 400,000 (3 per cent) needed repairs costing £500 or more.

No strictly comparable figures are available for Scotland, but the 1965 Housing Survey[20] estimated a total of 151,000 dwellings (9 per cent) which were either unfit or had a life of less than five years. The 1970 Clydeside Survey[21] (using the new 'tolerable standard') strongly indicates that this was a gross underestimate.

It would be tedious to continue examining this arithmetic of housing poverty: the main points are clear. First, there is a large proportion of the housing stock which is totally inadequate by present (let alone future) standards. Secondly, there is an undeniable need for major programmes of clearance, improvement and 'patching'.

SLUM CLEARANCE

Local authorities can require owners of houses which are unfit (or below the tolerable standard) to close or demolish them. Alternatively, they can compulsorily acquire the houses and undertake the demolition themselves. The former is more usual with individual houses; the latter with areas containing a number of houses (the sites of which are, in any case, frequently required for redevelopment).

Clearance Areas (England)

Any area containing two or more houses can be dealt with under the *clearance area* procedure if the houses are unfit or badly arranged, and if the local authority are satisfied 'that the most satisfactory method of dealing with the conditions in the area is the demolition of all the buildings in the area'. Before declaring a clearance area the local authority must also satisfy themselves that the persons to be displaced from residential accommodation can be adequately rehoused. Usually this is interpreted as meaning that the local authority is able to rehouse the displaced families: indeed it is often referred to as an 'obligation to rehouse'. In fact, however, a local authority is statutorily required to provide accommodation only in so far as suitable dwellings do not already exist. There are parts of the country where there is no great shortage of housing and where a significant number of displaced families do rehouse themselves: this applies particularly in the case of those owner-occupiers who receive full market value compensation for their houses. Nevertheless, the majority of displaced families are in fact rehoused by the local authority. (Local authorities have no such statutory obligation in relation to families displaced by demolition or closing orders, but in practice they accept a moral obligation to do so.)

To be included in a clearance area a house must be unfit or dangerous or injurious to health, but it need not be incapable of being made fit at reasonable cost. Other buildings – factories, schools, shops: indeed, *any* building – can also be included so long as they are so badly arranged as to be 'dangerous or injurious to health'.

Having declared a clearance area the local authority proceeds to secure clearance either by making an order for the demolition of the buildings by the owners – a *clearance order* – or by purchasing the properties and undertaking the demolition themselves. If a clearance order is made, ministerial approval is required, and all buildings included in the area solely because of 'bad arrangement' must be excluded. In other words the *order* must apply only to unfit houses. In practice, clearance orders are usually made only for small groups of houses where the local authority are not intending to redevelop the site. The majority of clearance areas are dealt with by way of a compulsory purchase order on the site as a whole. Even where the local authority are not intending to undertake the redevelopment this procedure has the particular advantage that the whole clearance area – not solely the unfit houses – can be purchased, as well as adjoining land which is needed for the satisfactory development of the area.

It is useful to know the jargon which is used in relation to clearance areas. Maps have to be prepared as part of the formal procedure for submitting proposals to the Secretary of State. On these, different categories of property have to be identified either by hatching and stippling or by colour. The names of the colours are frequently used as a shorthand description of the different categories of property. Thus, *pink* houses are those which are unfit for human habitation; *pink hatched yellow* are buildings included because of their bad arrangement; and *grey* properties are those which, though not in either of the other categories, are needed for the satisfactory re-development of the cleared area.

This categorization is important for two reasons. First, the compensation which an owner receives for his property will depend upon whether or not it is 'pink'. If it is he normally receives only cleared site value; if it is not he will receive market value for the site with the house on it. Secondly, the matters about which the local authority have to be satisfied vary. With a 'pink' house they must be satisfied that the house is unfit according to the criteria set out in the Housing Act. These in fact make no reference to the effect of the conditions on the health of the occupants – though objectors commonly use the argument that there is no evidence that their houses cause ill-health. With 'pink hatched yellow' properties it is legally necessary to prove that there is danger to health. This is difficult to do, at least in a manner which would be acceptable to a logician. The cynic might legitimately comment that all this is a legal fiction which – though relevant to nineteenth-century conditions – is now quite archaic. Nevertheless it is accepted that severe lack of light and air space; narrow, cramped courts, yards and alleys; and similar overshadowed and congested buildings do fall within the legal definition. In practice these conditions are commonly found in conjunction with internal inadequacies which render the house unfit. So far as 'grey' properties are concerned the only matter at issue is whether their acquisition is reasonably necessary for the satisfactory redevelopment of the areas. It is not necessary to prove that it is *impossible* to achieve a layout without them. It is sufficient to show that acquisition is reasonable.

Recently, rather more than 50,000 houses in or adjacent to clearance areas have been demolished in England and Wales each year. (A further 15,000-20,000 have been closed or demolished outside clearance areas.) In Scotland, the average has totalled around 17,500.

Housing Treatment Areas (Scotland)

Until the passing of the Housing (Scotland) Act, 1969, Scottish legislation closely mirrored the English. The 1969 Act introduced some major changes. As already explained, the concept of 'unfitness' was abandoned in favour of the standard of tolerability (though it is unlikely that this will make a significant difference in the immediate future). Further, a new, flexible bundle of powers was provided with the innovation of *housing treatment areas*.

A housing treatment area is one in which the greater part of the houses do not meet the tolerable standard. Having defined such an area the local authority can then demolish all the buildings (as in an English clearance area), improve all the houses which are below the tolerable standard (as in an English improvement area), or demolish some and improve the remainder.

A full discussion of these new powers and guidance on their use is to be found in Bulletin 2 of the New Scottish Housing Handbook, *Slum Clearance and Improvements* (HMSO, 1969).

Slum Clearance and Improvement 1955-70

| | Houses demolished or closed | | | Improvement grants approved | | |
	England and Wales	Scotland	Great Britain	England and Wales	Scotland	Great Britain
1955–59	213,402	61,545	292,947	219,068	16,051	235,119
1960–65	303,621	62,569	366,190	610,778	21,989	632,767
1965	60,666	15,534	76,200	122,993	6,333	129,326
1966	66,782	16,650	83,432	107,720	7,569	115,289
1967	71,152	19,087	90,239	113,142	7,307	120,449
1968	71,586	18,768	90,354	114,216	13,679	127,895
1969	69,233	17,847	87,080	108,938	14,951	123,889
1970	67,804	17,345	85,149	156,557	23,400	179,957
Total 1955–70	924,246	229,345	1,171,591	1,553,412	111,279	1,664,691

IMPROVEMENT POLICY

House improvement policy was first introduced in 1949 but it was not until 1954 that it got under way and not until 1969 that the policy shifted effectively from a concentration on individual houses to 'improvement areas'.

The policy operated (until the 1969 Housing Acts – the impact of which it is much too early to assess) largely by offering grants to owners who wished to improve their property. The objective has been to encourage owners to provide services and amenities in basically sound houses which are lacking the amenities which modern standards and aspirations demand. The justification for the spending of public funds on this is not only that living conditions are thereby improved, but also that unless old houses are modernized they will deteriorate into slums which then need to be cleared and replaced at public expense. The responsibility for making these grants lies with local housing authorities, though three-quarters of the cost is borne by the Exchequer. The grants are normally given on the basis of one half of the approved cost of the works, subject to a maximum limit. (Higher grants are temporarily given in development and intermediate areas – thus including the whole of Scotland.)

Improvement Areas

By the early 'sixties it came to be accepted that far more emphasis was needed on *areas* as distinct from individual houses. A MHLG circular of 1962 asked local authorities to take the initiative in securing the improvement of whole streets or areas. The 1964 Act went further, and gave local authorities powers to declare 'improvement areas' within which a limited degree of compulsion could be used against landlords.

The 1964 provisions were cumbersome in the extreme. This was the result of attempting to provide the maximum safeguards for owners and tenants, and the maximum opportunity for voluntary improvements. The powers were given with reluctance and only because of the urgent need to speed up the rate of improvements and because of the widespread feeling that some element of compulsion was required. But not only were the powers cumbersome: they were also ineffective and did not really enable an authority to secure the improvement of an area as a whole. The provisions related essentially to 'houses in areas' rather than areas which contained houses. The 1969 Housing Act is designed much more with the total environment in view. Local authorities in England and Wales are given power to declare *general improvement areas* within which the aim is to help and persuade owners to improve their houses not only by grants and advice but also by improving the environment. In the words of the White Paper *Old Houses into New Homes*, 'whole areas and streets cannot be brought up to proper standards unless something can be done for the environment, as opposed to the interiors of the houses'. The new concept of 'improving the area' encompasses a coherent set of powers, together with an Exchequer grant for such improvements as the provision of children's play spaces and parking spaces, planting trees, and traffic regulation.

In Scotland, these powers are incorporated in those relating to the *housing treatment areas* outlined above.

At the same time, improvement grants were substantially increased and provision was made for improved rent-controlled properties to be transferred to the 'fair rents' system.

Of particular significance is the emphasis in the 1969 Acts on voluntary co-operation with those who live in an area which is subject to an improvement policy.

There has been only limited experience of areat improvement, and Departmental guide-lines are necessarily very broad. In selecting areas, emphasis is to be placed on the potential of an area, the basic attractions of the area or its location, the attitudes of its residents and the need for public action. The last point is interesting and is an example of the way in which thinking is developing towards a more sensitive basis for policy. The intention is that public action should be concentrated on sensitive spots where the maximum benefit can be obtained. A MHLG circular (*Circular 65/69*) talks of avoiding areas which are 'too good' or 'too bad':

'A too good area could be one which is already attracting considerable money into renovation, and where any further encouragement by public funds would not only be unnecessary but might well lead to a drastic change in the social composition of the area. A too bad area is more difficult to define; but it is necessary always to keep in mind that area improvement is not an alternative to slum clearance.'

More recently, increasing emphasis has been placed on the use of systematic surveys. These are to be modelled on the Conurbation Housing Surveys. To date these have concentrated on physical factors, but given the mounting realization of the importance of 'citizen-participation', it is to be hoped that techniques for facilitating this will be developed.

Between 1955 and 1960, a total of 1,664,691 improvement grants were approved in Great Britain.

Deferred Demolition

Finally, mention needs to be made of the deferred demolition procedure. This is relevant only in the biggest cities with the most acute problems where (as the SHAC Report noted in relation to Glasgow) on the one hand, no conceivable rate of clearance would be adequate, yet on the other hand, full improvement of a large number of houses would be totally uneconomic.

Introduced in 1954, this procedure allows local authorities to acquire houses and to undertake essential repairs and the minimum improvements required to render the houses 'adequate for the time being'. In England, a total of 88,000 houses for deferred demolition was planned in the first five-year programme and, of these, 32,000 were in Birmingham, 11,560 in Hull and 20,000 in Lancashire.* In Scotland, local authorities' proposals over a three-year period for deferred demolition totalled a mere 452.

Deferred demolition is not a popular policy – particularly in Glasgow where it is most needed: local authorities seldom like to

* No later figures have been published. A large number of the Birmingham houses were purchased under the (now repealed) provisions of the Town and Country Planning Act, 1944.

be cast in the role of 'slum landlords'. But, in the words of the SHAC Report:

'. . . *irrespective of the cost* the policy of "patching" is essential. Families cannot be allowed to live in intolerable conditions without any improvement whatsoever. It needs to be stressed that even if the rate of clearance of unfit houses were doubled it would still be a lifetime of a child before all the houses at present unfit were cleared'.[43]

REFERENCES AND FURTHER READING

Comprehensive Redevelopment
1 Burns, W., *New Towns for Old*, Leonard Hill, 1963.
2 MHLG, *Town Centres: Approach to Renewal*, Planning Bulletin No. 1, HMSO, 1962.
3 MHLG, *Town Centres: Cost and Control of Redevelopment*, Planning Bulletin No. 3, HMSO, 1963.
4 MHLG, *Parking in Town Centres*, Planning Bulletin No. 7, HMSO, 1965.
5 MHLG, Circular 53/67, *Civic Amenities Act, 1967*, HMSO, 1967.
6 MHLG, Circular 54/67, *Contributions by Developers towards the cost of Parking Facilities*, HMSO, 1967.
7 MHLG, *Historic Towns: Preservation and Change*, HMSO, 1967.
8 MHLG, Circular 12/68, *Local Government Act, 1966 – Sections 7 and 8: Grants to Local Authorities in respect of Comprehensive Redevelopment and Public Open Space* (with Annex: *Explanatory Memorandum on Planning Grants*), HMSO, 1968.
9 MHLG, Development Control Policy Note 3, *Industrial and Commercial Development*, HMSO, 1969.
10 MHLG, Development Control Policy Note 5, *Development in Town Centres*, HMSO, 1969.
11 Ministry of Transport, Roads Circular 1/68, *Traffic and Transport Plans*, HMSO, 1968.
12 Sharp, E., *The Ministry of Housing and Local Government*, Allen & Unwin, 1969.
13 Tetlow, J. and Goss, A., *Homes, Towns and Traffic*, Faber, Revised Edition, 1968.
14 Town Planning Institute, 'Central Area Development', *Journal of the Town Planning Institute*, Vol. XLVI, No. 7, June 1960.
15 Tweddell, N., 'Partners in Urban Renewal', *The Cubitt Magazine*, Winter 1963/64.
16 Winterbottom, D., *Planned London* (Town Planning Institute Conference Handbook, May 1969), Town Planning Institute, 1969.

Inadequate Housing
17 Central Housing Advisory Committee, *Our Older Homes: A Call for Action* (Denington Report), HMSO, 1966.

18 Cullingworth, J. B., *Housing in Transition*, Heinemann, 1963.
19 Cullingworth, J. B., *Housing and Local Government*, Allen & Unwin, 1966.
20 Cullingworth, J. B., *Scottish Housing in 1965*, HMSO, 1967.
21 Cullingworth J. B. and Watson, C. J., *Reports on a Household Survey and a House Condition Survey in the Central Clydeside Conurbation*, HMSO, 1971.
22 Department of Health for Scotland, *Slum Clearance: Summary of Proposals by Local Authorities*, Cmd. 9685, HMSO, 1965.
23 DOE, *Area Improvement Notes:*
    1. *Sample House Condition Survey*, HMSO, 1971.
    2. *House Condition Survey within a Potential General Improvement Area*, HMSO, 1971.
    3. *Improving the Environment*, HMSO, 1971.
24 Duncan, T. L. C., *Measuring Housing Quality: A Study of Methods*, University of Birmingham, Centre for Urban and Regional Studies, Occasional Paper 20, 1971. (Distributed by Research Publications Services Ltd.)
25 Greater London Council, *The Condition of London's Housing: A Survey*, GLC, 1970.
26 Hallmark Securities Ltd, *The Halliwell Report*, published privately, 1966.
27 MHLG, *Slum Clearance: Summary of Returns by Local Authorities*, Cmd. 9593, HMSO, 1955.
28 MHLG, Circular 42/62, *Improvement of Houses*, HMSO, 1962.
29 MHLG, *Report of the Committee on Housing in Greater London* (Milner Holland Report), Cmnd. 2605, HMSO, 1965.
30 MHLG, *The Deeplish Study: Improvement Possibilities in a District of Rochdale*, HMSO, 1966.
31 MHLG, *Barnsbury Environmental Study*, MHLG, 1968.
32 MHLG, 'House Condition Survey, England and Wales, 1967', *Economic Trends* No. 175, May 1968.
33 MHLG, *Old Houses into New Homes*, Cmnd. 3602, HMSO, 1968.
34 MHLG, Circular 63/69, *Housing Act, 1969*, HMSO, 1969.
35 MHLG, Circular 64/69, *Housing Act, 1969: House Improvement and Repair*, HMSO, 1969.
36 MHLG, Circular 65/69, *Housing Act, 1969: Area Improvement*, HMSO, 1969.
37 MHLG, Circular 68/69, *Housing Act, 1969: Slum Clearance*, HMSO, 1969.
38 MHLG, Design Bulletin 19, *Living in a Slum: A Study of St Mary's, Oldham*, HMSO, 1970.
39 MHLG, Design Bulletin 20, *Moving out of a Slum: A Study of People Moving from St Mary's, Oldham*, HMSO, 1970.

40 SDD, *The Older Houses in Scotland: A Plan for Action*, Cmnd. 3598, HMSO, 1968.
41 SDD, The New Scottish Housing Handbook, Bulletin 2, *Slum Clearance and Improvements*, HMSO, 1969.
42 SDD, Circular 54/1971, *Improvement of Houses*, SDD, 1971.
43 Scottish Housing Advisory Committee, *Scotland's Older Houses*, HMSO, 1967.
44 Taylor Woodrow Group, *The Fulham Study*, published privately, 1963.

Chapter XII

REGIONAL PLANNING

REGIONAL THINKING

At present there is no executive machinery for regional physical planning in Britain. There is a large number of agencies undertaking responsibility for particular services and development on a regional scale, but there is no organization responsible for the co-ordinated programming, development and control. Nationalized utilities and hospitals, regional departments of government departments, large private firms, operate on a regional basis*; there is a host of regional advisory and consultative councils, and committees; and there is an increasing number of *ad hoc* and rather loose organizations of local authorities and others dealing with such diverse matters as further education, industrial development and sport. Finally, there is now the regional economic planning (advisory) machinery originally established under the aegis of the Department of Economic Affairs, and the very new Passenger Transport Authorities established in a number of the major conurbations.†

Thus though there is no regional planning system, there are many regional planning machines. In this chapter attention is focused on regional economic and physical problems and the development of machinery to deal with them.

A number of strands can be identified in the development of thinking on regionalism. Two are of particular relevance in this book – the physical planning and the economic planning strands. Some account of the former from the local end has already been given. It is now necessary to supplement this with an outline of the situation as it has developed from the centre.

* As does the Water Resources Board. For an account of the development of national and regional planning of water resources see Sharp, E., *The Ministry of Housing and Local Government*, Allen & Unwin, 1969, pp. 105–17, the Annual Reports of the Water Resources Board and the Wilson Report on *The Future Management of Water in England and Wales*, HMSO, 1971.

† On Passenger Transport Authorities, see Chapter IV.

At the end of Chapter II some stress was laid on the lack of a regional tier of planning between local authorities and the central departments. This lack did not seem (and was not) as important in the mid-'forties as it appeared when population growth, economic growth, increased personal mobility, a rising standard of living and a host of other related factors conspired in the 'fifties to increase pressures on land and the machinery of land planning control. In any case it was not possible to go further at the time. For a period the framework of regional advisory plans (particularly in the London Region) had to suffice. These had an impact: they enabled some broad planning objectives to be communicated to and, more important to be acknowledged by, local planning authorities. Informal arrangements, professional contacts and a generally shared planning philosophy also helped.

By the end of the 'fifties, it became clear that something more was needed. Development plans had become hopelessly out of date due to cumbersome procedures and the great change in the underlying forces with which they were supposed to cope. Furthermore, the disbandment of the regional organization of the Ministry of Housing in 1954–6 had (according to the former Permanent Secretary to the Ministry) the opposite effect to that intended. 'There was a strong feeling at headquarters that the divisions did not know their regions or their authorities as well as they should; and that it would be better if headquarters staff could be enabled to devote more time to travelling out. It was thought that the abolition of the regional organization would improve Whitehall's knowledge of, and contacts with, the North, the Midlands, the East and the South-West to the benefit of all; and that officers and representatives of local authorities might be encouraged to come more frequently to Whitehall as they had done in pre-war years. It did not come off.'[28] And so the problems changed in character and increased in complexity at the very time when the central department was in insufficient touch with local government.

REGIONAL STUDIES

The turn of the tide came in the early 'sixties in three areas for three different reasons. In 1962 a Northern Housing Office of the Ministry was opened in Manchester to assist the large programme of slum clearance and redevelopment in the North and North-West. In 1963 another regional office, with both housing and planning functions, was set up in Newcastle in connection with the 'Hailsham Plan' for the North-East, to which there was a clear political commitment. Probably of greater importance was the beginning, in 1961, of a series of regional studies. These resulted from the awareness in the Department of the inadequacy of the development plans and land allocations to meet the rising pressures for development. These studies started, in traditional manner, as 'regional conferences' and 'land studies' undertaken jointly by officers of local authorities and the Department. In the South-East and the West Midlands these developed into new-style regional studies covering unprecedentedly large areas.

The *South-East Study* was published in March 1964 and included regionally based proposals of a kind and on a scale which had not been seen since the wartime and immediate post-war period of optimistic planning. New cities (*sic*) were suggested in the South-ampton-Portsmouth area, the Bletchley area (later to become Milton Keynes) and the Newbury area. New towns were considered for Ashford and Stansted. Large-scale expansions were proposed for Ipswich, Northampton, Peterborough and Swindon. Consultants were appointed to consider, with the local authorities concerned, many of these proposals.

The next clearly identifiable step in this period of intense examination and thinking came with the decision of the Labour Government in 1964 to set up regional economic planning machinery. The trend towards this was already in evidence. Early in 1964 the President of the Board of Trade was made responsible for 'trade, industry and regional development'. The White Paper, *South-East England*, outlining the Government's reaction to the *Study* was published jointly by the Department and the Board. Indeed, the *South-East Study* was the only one to bear the imprint of the Ministry of Housing and Local Government. Before the next studies were completed (on the West Midlands and the North-West) the Department of Economic Affairs had been set up (taking over the regional development division of the Board of Trade). During its lifetime (1964–9) the DEA had responsibility for the direction and publication of regional studies. (This now rests with the Department of the Environment.)

REGIONAL ADVICE

There are ten Regional Economic Planning Councils – eight in England and one each in Wales and Scotland. These Planning Councils are advisory bodies and consist of a Chairman and about twenty-five Members all appointed by the appropriate Secretary of State. The Members are appointed as 'individuals having a wide range of knowledge and experience of their regions': they are not delegates or representatives of particular interests. The Councils' main functions are 'to study and advise on the needs and potentialities of their regions and on the development of a long-term planning strategy for their regions, and to advise central government on aspects of national policy which have a bearing on regional development'.

Alongside each Council is a Board consisting of senior civil servants from the main government departments concerned with regional planning. In the English regions, the Chairmen of the Boards are all senior officials of DOE. The functions of the Boards are 'to co-ordinate the regional economic planning work of Departments, and to co-operate with the Economic Planning Councils in developing the long-term planning strategies for the regions.'

The functions of this regional advisory machinery were officially stated in 1965 as being:

  (i) to work out broad objectives for each region and so provide a comprehensive framework within which decisions in particular sectors can be taken;

 (ii) to advise on the formulation of national policies where these can significantly affect the regions;

(iii) to advise on the application in the regions of national policy;

(iv) to stimulate interest within each region and build up a common approach within each region to its problems.

To date the work might be described as being 'regional stocktaking'. The primary objective has been to assemble the facts and figures relating to the regions which can form the basis for an overall assessment and for a broad regional strategy. Attention has been concentrated on preparing 'studies' on the lines of the *South-East Study*. The first two were published in 1965 for the North-West and the West Midlands.* Both of these were undertaken by 'a group of officials from Government Departments concerned with regional planning', and were 'referred' to the Planning Councils for the respective regions (without any commitment on the part of Government to the studies' findings or to the proposals which might be made by the Councils). Following the establishment of the Regional Councils, further studies were undertaken and published. Unlike the earlier two, these are reports by the Councils themselves. But they are not 'regional plans'; indeed they both specifically disclaim any pretension to be. As the foreword to the East Midlands Study puts it, they are attempts 'to present to the public an account of the region as it is, and as it is changing; it draws attention to problems and opportunities, with an indication of what is involved in them. It is hoped that the study will form an adequate basis for the public discussion out of which the main lines of the region's planning will

* A list is given at the end of this chapter.

emerge; until adequate opportunity for that discussion has been provided it would be presumptuous to go further.'

This approach stems from two important factors. First, the essential information and research needed for an adequately based system of regional planning is lacking. Secondly (and this would still be of crucial importance if the former inadequacy were rectified), the Regional Councils have no executive powers and no authority over either the central government or local authorities. They 'represent' the regions only in a very indirect way. They have to tread warily between the sensitive toes of Whitehall and the much more sensitive toes of Town Hall. It could hardly be expected that they would rapidly resolve the conflicts between the constituent local authorities (and particularly between town and county) which have for so long frustrated attempts to plan on any scale other than that circumscribed by local authority boundaries. Essentially the Regional Councils constitute an experiment in forging new, and wider, loyalties – loyalties to a region rather than to a locality. The studies and reports are thus not sets of policies agreed by the regions and submitted to the central government for consideration and action; rather are they the interim findings and thoughts of a group of individuals with experience of and interest in the regions, submitted to all concerned (Government at all levels, and public and private bodies) as a first exercise in regional thinking.

What then is the function of the regional studies? Probably the clearest statement is to be found in the report of the South-West Economic Planning Council, significantly entitled *A Region with a Future: A Draft Strategy for the South-West*:

'It has come to be recognized that it is too soon in the experience of regional planning to aim at achieving a set of Government-approved plans for all regions which will neatly dovetail with each other and which, in numbers of population, distribution of manpower, growth and location of industry, scale and disposition of public investment, etc., will in aggregate coincide with the forecasts, intentions and capabilities envisaged by the Government for the economy as a whole. The immediate aim should be for each Council to provide themselves with a "regional strategy" by which recommendations can be made on decisions affecting their regions which cannot wait, and advice be given immediately on the implications for their regions of national and local policies.'

The truth of the matter, however, is that the present regional machinery is a temporary makeshift which will be superseded when action is taken on the report of the Royal Commission on Local Government.

Two important points need to be stressed. First, the Councils have no executive powers whatsoever: they can comment or rant and rave but they can *do* nothing – they are purely advisory bodies. Secondly, the creation of the Boards in no way affects the existing powers and responsibilities of local authorities and central government departments. Advice and co-ordination: these are the essential functions of the Councils and the Boards.

THE EMBRYONIC REGIONAL PLANNING MACHINERY

Though it would be difficult to establish a clear causal relationship, the regional economic planning machinery has probably stimulated the coming-together of local authorities in loose groupings on a regional scale. Typically these have been termed – in an ungainly but innocuous way – 'standing conferences'. In some regions these have operated independently of (if not aloofly from) the regional planning councils. In others it has been possible to achieve close collaboration.

Thus in the West Midlands yet another *West Midlands Study* is being carried out by the Standing Conference of Local Planning Authorities. This is a purely local government undertaking: it is quite independent of the West Midlands Economic Planning Council, though advice is being rendered by the regional staffs of central government departments. At the other extreme is the South-East Joint Planning Study Team which reported in 1970. This was commissioned in May 1968 *jointly* by the then Secretary of State for Economic Affairs, the Minister of Housing and Local Government and the Minister of Transport, and by the Chairmen of the Standing Conference on London and South-East Regional Planning (a body which dates from 1962) and the South-East Economic Planning Council.

In Scotland, the Scottish Economic Planning Board (set up, like the English Boards, in 1965) was preceded by the Scottish Development Group (set up in 1963). The White Paper on the Scottish Economy 1965–7 was based on analysis of five broad sub-regions: Central Scotland, the Highlands, the Borders, the South-West and the North-East. In an attempt to bridge the gap between the responsibility for 'planning' and execution, the Scottish Office encouraged the establishment of sub-regional 'Local Consultative Groups'. (In the Highlands there is also the Highlands and Islands Development Board set up by statute in 1965 with the objective of stimulating the economic and social development of the seven crofting counties.)

In their evidence to the Royal Commission on Local Government in Scotland, the Regional Development Division of the Scottish

Office stated that one of the purposes of these Local Consultative Groups was 'to create a new sense of participation in national planning; but more specifically they are designed to create an awareness of the problems and potentials of the sub-regions looked at as coherent units, and to promote co-operation among all concerned within the sub-regions'. They warned, however, that it remained to be seen how well the Groups could cope with 'internal tensions' within sub-regions. Particular difficulty was experienced in even establishing a Group to serve Central Scotland which has particularly intractable planning problems of a sub-regional character.

What was termed 'a significant step forward' was, however, made in 1970 when a West Central Scotland Plan Steering Committee was established. This is representative of central government, local government and industrial and economic expertise in the region. Its remit is to prepare and keep up to date an advisory economic and physical plan for West Central Scotland which will serve as a guide to local planning authorities in preparing their development plans. Though the Committee is advisory, the Secretary of State for Scotland, through his power to approve or modify local authority development plans, 'can require these plans to conform with any regional plan which he accepts as part of his policy'.

This very explicit statement of intention is characteristically Scottish, though whether the results are any different from those in the English system is debatable. Perhaps it is simply that in the smaller country of Scotland the presence of central government is more apparent. Be that as it may, there is a trend in both countries (when the local political situtations allow) for regional plans to be prepared jointly by local and central government.

At the sub-regional level in England, however, recent years have seen the growth of studies undertaken collaboratively by local planning authorities.

It would be tedious to continue this exploration of the wide variety of attempts that have been made to come to terms with regional planning problems within a hopelessly out-dated system of local government. If the effort that has been expended during the later 'sixties in preparing plans is indicative of potentialities for execution, this augurs well for the reorganized local government of the future.

THE DEVELOPMENT OF ECONOMIC PLANNING POLICIES

Employment and economic change lie at the heart of regional planning. This, indeed, was the starting-point for the Barlow inquiry twenty-five years ago. Post-war industrial location policies

have been directed towards reducing unemployment in the development areas and restraining new industrial building in 'congested'
areas. This has been the interpretation given to the phrase 'a proper
distribution of industry'. This has, in the main, been regarded as a
social policy running alongside, but not supporting economic
policies:

'We should start from the assumption that the economic and industrial expansion of the country should proceed freely in response
to growing and changing consumer demand, and that it should
proceed on the principle of the most effective use of our national
resources. . . . This principle of the most effective use of our resources
must clearly be mitigated in some cases by Government action to
deal with certain social consequences which the nation does not
regard as acceptable.'*

During the 'sixties, however, there was an increasing awareness
that a maldistribution of employment had serious economic effects
on the national economy. The 1963 Report of the National Economic
Development Council on *Conditions Favourable to Faster Growth*
provides a good illustration of this new thinking:

'The level of employment in different regions of the country varies
widely, and high unemployment associated with the lack of employment opportunities in the less prosperous regions is usually thought
of as a social problem. Policies aim, therefore, to prevent unemployment rising to politically intolerable levels and expenditure to this
end is often considered a necessary burden to the nation, unrelated
to any economic gain that might accrue from it. But the relatively
low activity rates† in these regions also indicate considerable labour
reserves. To draw these reserves into employment would make a substantial contribution to national employment and national growth.'

This argument, it should be noted, was put forward not by town
planners but by economists. It differs very markedly from the
traditional type of economic argument; and it rejects the idea that
the long-term solution to regional economic decline lies in migration
to the prosperous areas. Apart from the social cost of large-scale

* The President of the Board of Trade (Mr R. Maudling) on the opening of the
Second Reading Debates on the Local Employment Bill, *H.C. Debates*, Vol. 613,
Col. 32, November 9, 1959. See also Select Committee on Estimates, Session
1955–6, *Development Areas*, House of Commons Paper No. 139, HMSO, 1955.
  † An 'activity rate' is defined as the proportion of civilian employees –
employed plus registered unemployed – in a given population age-group.

migration that this would involve, there are two other significant objections. First it would add to the problems of congestion in the South-East and the Midlands – problems which are already straining to the utmost the machinery of town and country planning. Secondly, it would be quite impracticable for these prosperous areas to absorb the required number of migrants. Furthermore, if the less prosperous regions were allowed to run down, their future problem would become even more difficult to solve. The aim should be to employ a regional development policy which would aim at achieving self-sustaining regional growth. It is here that the relationship between economic planning and town and country planning is most clearly seen: potential industrial developers are concerned not only with labour supply and good sites, but also with adequate services, educational provision, and so on. In short, if industrialists are to be attracted to the less prosperous regions then these regions have to be made both economically and socially attractive. In the words of the White Paper on *The North-East*: 'even generous assistance to enterprise may not be fully effective unless it is backed by faster progress in making towns and villages more pleasant, in improving communications, and in removing scars on the industrial countryside.'

The problems can thus be seen as a compound of the economic and the social. The promotion of industrial activity has to be accompanied by a modernization of the general environment. This is not merely a question of providing a 'bait' to industrialists: it is also a matter of economic efficiency – 'to ensure that the scale of the public services and facilities match the needs of a modern society'. The problem is in part one of historical legacies: the regions where economic growth is comparatively slow are the regions where there is a concentration of physical obsolescence. Indeed, some observers have spoken of a geographical division of the country into two nations – separated roughly by the River Trent. The 'Fortunate Regions' of the South have a high level of employment, a large amount of private investment, a high standard of health, a relatively high standard of social service and social amenity. On the other hand, the 'Unfortunate Regions' of the North, of Wales and of Scotland – the boom areas of the coal age – have an enormous legacy of obsolete social capital, a slower rate of economic growth, an accompanying higher rate of unemployment, a poorer standard of health and social service, and a not unrelated outward migration of population.

More detailed studies would show that the image of the two nations is overdrawn and false in many respects, but the essential point is valid: the regions with a slow rate of economic growth have acute environmental problems which are difficult to cope with in the context of their relatively low level of economic activity and which in turn present obstacles to an increased growth rate. It is for this reason that so much emphasis is now being given to improving 'infrastructure'.

Nevertheless, it does not follow that all existing towns and settlements should be modernized. Some areas have lost their economic *raison d'être* and have little or no potentiality for growth. In any case, a policy of promoting growth is most effective when it is applied to carefully selected areas where the potentialities are particularly good. Since 1960, industrial location policy has been mainly aimed at relieving high unemployment in development districts. This was a major departure from the previous policy of promoting growth more generally in regions. The 'selection' of development districts was made, however, on the basis of unemployment rates. The application of the 'growth point' idea, on the other hand, involves selection of the basis of potentialities:

'Better results might be secured for the slowly expanding regions as a whole by identifying their natural growth points and seeking to attract industry to them. Within the bigger areas a wider choice of location than at present would be available to incoming firms. This would increase the likelihood of attracting a larger number and a greater variety of firms, and of stimulating the development of industrial complexes. Firms would then benefit from the presence of kindred industry. These complexes and other places especially attractive to industry could be developed into growth points within the less prosperous regions. It could be expected that the benefit of new growth in any part would repercuss fairly quickly throughout the region.'[20]

The two regional programmes for Scotland and North-East England represented the first essays in comprehensive regional planning by central government. Their importance lies not so much in the actual proposals made, but in the advance in thought and policy which they represent. They (like the Welsh report, *Wales: The Way Ahead*) do, however, differ from succeeding reports – or 'studies' as they are typically called. They involved a degree of Government commitment which is notably absent from their successors, even when they have been prepared by central government. (The 'official' preface to *The South-East Study* underlines that its main purpose is to 'provide a basis for discussion'; the point is rubbed home even more clearly in the preface to *The West Midlands* regional study where it is stated that the Government 'are not in any way committed by the Study Group's findings'.)

The point is, of course, that regional planning is not simply a matter of planning *within* a region. It has to take place within a framework of national policies which can be translated into decisions about the allocations of resources *between* regions. The White Papers on Scotland and the North-East proposed increases in public service investment which would have involved (for 1964–5) Scotland receiving 11 per cent of the Great Britain total (for a country with less than 10 per cent of the population) and the North-East receiving 7 per cent (with $5\frac{1}{2}$ per cent of the population). These proposals were drawn up on the basis of a political assessment of the needs of these regions, but clearly there are problems in continuing with this approach for all regions.

THE 'INTERMEDIATE AREAS'

Indeed, as aid to the development areas has increased, there has been mounting political pressure from 'intermediate areas' (or 'grey areas', to use the more popular term). It was this pressure which led to the setting up of the Hunt Committee, whose report, *The Intermediate Areas*, was published in April 1969. The terms of reference of this committee were 'to examine in relation to the economic welfare of the country as a whole and the needs of the development areas, the situation in other areas where the rate of economic growth gives cause (or may give cause) for concern, and to suggest whether revised policies to influence economic growth in such areas are desirable and, if so, what measures should be adopted'.

The Committee quickly found that it was no easy matter to judge the presence and severity of 'causes for concern'. In the present state of regional knowledge and analysis, political judgment has a very large role to play. Nevertheless, a brave and useful attempt was made. The major 'cause for concern' was 'slow economic growth ... where it is associated with unused or under-used labour resources, low earnings, a concentration of industries with a declining labour force, poor communications and a run-down physical environment making areas unattractive for new economic growth, and net outward migration'. Their chosen criteria were:

(*a*) Sluggish or falling employment ⎫ as the major indicators
(*b*) A slow growth in personal incomes ⎬ of slow growth.
(*c*) A slow rate of addition to industrial and commercial premises – as indicating a low level of industrial and commercial investment and a slow rate of economic growth.
(*d*) Significant unemployment – as the most obvious measure of wasted human resources.

(e) Low or declining proportions of women at work – as indicating a particular under-use of resources, especially in areas with a tradition of female employment.

(f) Low earnings – as throwing some light on the efficiency of the use of labour and as one of the factors relevant to the economic opportunity of individuals.

(g) Heavy reliance on industry whose demand for labour was growing slowly or falling and was likely to continue to do so – as an indication of vulnerability to economic change resulting in possible under-utilization of labour resources.

(h) Poor communications
(i) Decayed or inadequate environment, including dereliction
} as material to slow growth in the recent past and to the potential for growth.

(j) Serious net outward migration – as a pointer to the danger of accelerating decline, and as a summing up of the reactions of individuals to a complex of social and economic factors such as the local range of employment opportunities, educational and social activities and the state of the social and physical environment.

They concluded that the severest problems were undoubtedly in the development areas and that there was not a clear-cut and well-defined category of 'intermediate area'. Rather were there 'symptoms of concern' present to a varying extent and a varying degree in different parts of the country. Nevertheless, they felt that the North-West and Yorkshire & Humberside stood in the greatest need of a new impetus and recommended special assistance for these regions, and more limited assistance to the Notts-Derbyshire coalfield and to North Staffordshire.

In recommending help to such a large area of the country (containing a fifth of the population of Great Britain) there was no suggestion that the 'growth-area' policy should be abandoned. On the contrary, the Committee were simply following the logic which underlay the setting up in 1966 of broad development areas in place of the former narrower and relatively scattered development districts, chosen on the basis of high unemployment:

'As a result of inducements being made available to industry throughout these wider areas, industrialists are not tied to locations of greatest need, which may not be the most viable long-term locations for industry.'

It followed that the recommended aid might go to relatively prosperous parts of an intermediate area, but this is in principle no different from the position in the development areas.

This, however, is to ignore the political difficulties. Any aid to intermediate areas which is effective in increasing new industrial development must (at least in the short run) have an effect on the development areas. As the Hunt Committee ruefully point out at the beginning of their report, 'the supply of mobile industry available to stimulate economic growth is, taken as a whole, insufficient at present to meet the needs of the development areas and overspill towns, let alone areas of slow growth. We recognize that remedial measures for areas of slow growth may hold back progress elsewhere.'

The Government's reaction was that the selection of areas to be given assistance to industry must be governed strictly by 'criteria of need', in particular the level and character of unemployment, the rate of outward migration and the scope for industrial growth. On this basis seven intermediate areas have been defined: North-East Lancashire, Yorkshire coalfield, North Humberside, Notts-Derby coalfield, South-East Wales, Plymouth and Leith.

THE REGIONAL POLICY DILEMMA

Throughout this continuing debate on the allocation of resources between regions there has been little attention paid to the impact on planning within regions – except in very broad, generalist terms such as that the movement of industry from London and the West Midlands will 'relieve congestion'. The Hunt Committee, however, did discuss as a 'possible cause for concern' the flow of industry to overspill areas in the South-East, East Anglia and the West Midlands, and in particular the difficulties being experienced by Telford New Town.

The essential argument here is that the high level of development area incentives is jeopardizing the overspill programme for London and the West Midlands and throws into question the viability of the future programmes which are based on the premise that the transfer of employment from the two conurbations will be on a substantially increased scale. The three Economic Planning Councils (South-East, East Anglia and West Midlands) all put up a case for a relaxation of i.d.c. control and additional finance inducements in overspill areas. The Hunt Committee favoured the former but not the latter. Conurbation firms should, in their view, be allowed to move to an overspill location provided that the Board of Trade (now the DTI) has advised the firm of the incentives and attractions of the development areas and provided that the movement is within the planned growth programme of the overspill area. Financial inducements, on the other hand, 'might divert a much needed amount of new work away from areas of high unemployment'.

But is it possible to implement current regional physical planning strategies within the context of the present economic policies of giving priority to development areas? If there is not sufficient mobile industry for the areas of high unemployment and for the overspill areas, something has to give way. Nowhere is this clearer than in the West Midlands.

It is here that we see the unresolved dilemma of present regional policies. Regional planning means different things to central and local government. As Senior has put it, 'what *central* government means by "regional planning" is primarily the correction of economic imbalance *between* one "region" and another; and it is only with reluctance that central government is reconciling itself to the fact that this purpose – crucial to its central function in the economic field – necessarily involves the making of investment decisions *within* "regions" on a territorial as well as a functional basis. What *local* government means by "regional planning", on the other hand, is primarily the expression of national policies in terms of a comprehensive long-term strategy for economic and physical development *within* each provincial-scale "region", in the context of which local planning authorities can work out meaningful structure plans for their own areas.'[25]

This gap cannot be bridged until there is a regional planning machine designed for the job. At present central government can channel (or block) resources to regions, but there is no machinery for rationally distributing resources *within* regions on the basis of a comprehensive strategy. The Department of the Environment has a role and powers quite inadequate for this; and in any case, it is not a proper task for central government – it is essentially a regional matter. Any plan involves the submerging of some interests in favour of others. At national level the priority given to development areas is a clear case in point. But at the regional level there is no system for determining priorities. Each local authority has the interests of its ratepayers at heart and development needed for a wider benefit is jeopardized. Thus (for instance), if a conurbation authority sees industrial overspill as having undesirable effects on its rateable value and a potentially good overspill authority sees development as an intolerable local burden, an overspill policy is killed at birth, even if it is in the wider interests of the region as a whole. To quote Senior again:

'Any plan which seeks to guide development in the interest of the region as a whole must call for the concentration of investment in particular parts of it and the prevention of development in others. But so long as the region is divided between different implementing authorities, one of them is bound to find that it is being called upon to bear more than its share of the cost and get less than its share of the benefit of giving effect to particular provisions of the overall plan: if this were not so there would be no need for such a plan. And it would be not only altruistic, but positively undemocratic, for that authority thus to subordinate its own ratepayers' interests to that of its neighbour's ratepayers. It is quite unreasonable to expect a wrongly organized local government structure to behave as it would automatically tend to do it were it rightly organized, when the wrong organization automatically produces a different incidence of the costs and benefits of acting in the interest of the region as a whole.'[25]

Until the appropriate machinery is devised, regional planning will remain largely a central government activity concerned with 'balance' and the location of major investments, The library of regional and sub-regional studies will increase, but effective co-ordinated action will be impossible to achieve.

REFERENCES AND FURTHER READING

1 Board of Trade, *Industrial Development Act, 1966: Annual Reports*, HMSO.
2 Board of Trade, *Investment Grants: Annual Reports*, HMSO.
3 Board of Trade, *Local Employment Acts: Annual Reports*, HMSO.
4 Central Office of Information, *Regional Development in Britain*, COI Reference Pamphlet No. 80, HMSO, 1968.
5 Central Statistical Office, *Abstract of Regional Statistics*, HMSO, annual.
6 Council of Europe, *Regional Planning: A European Problem*, 1968.
7 DEA, *The Development Areas: A Proposal for a Regional Employment Premium*, HMSO, 1967.
8 DEA, *The Development Areas: Regional Employment Premium*, Cmnd. 3310, HMSO, 1967.
9 DEA, *Economic Planning in the Regions*, HMSO, 2nd Edition, 1968.
10 DEA, *The Task Ahead: Economic Assessment to 1972*, HMSO, 1969.
11 Economic Commission for Europe, *Regional Physical Planning*, United Nations, 1966.
12 Greater London Council, *Greater London Development Plan: Statement; Report of Studies; 'Tomorrow's London'*, GLC, 1969.
13 Hammond, E., *An Analysis of Regional Economic and Social Statistics*, University of Durham, Rowntree Research Unit, 1968.
14 Hemming, M. F. W., 'The Regional Problem', *National Institute Economic Review*, No. 25, August 1963.
15 Hillman, J., *Planning for London*, Penguin Books, 1971.
16 *The Intermediate Areas* (Hunt Report), Cmnd. 3998, HMSO, 1969.
17 McCrone, G., *Regional Policy in Britain*, Allen & Unwin, 1969.
18 Mackintosh, J. P., *The Devolution of Power*, Penguin Books, 1968.
19 Masser, I., 'Methods of Sub-Regional Analysis: A Review of Four Recent Studies', *Town Planning Review*, Vol. 41, No. 2, April 1970.
20 National Economic Development Council, *Conditions Favourable to Faster Growth*, HMSO, 1963.

K

21 Needleman, L. and Scott, B., 'Regional Problems and the Location of Industry Policy in Britain', *Urban Studies*, Vol. 1, No. 2, November 1964.
22 Richardson, H. W. and West, E. G., 'Must We Always Take Work to the Workers?', *Lloyds Bank Review*, January 1964.
23 *Royal Commission on the Distribution of the Industrial Population: Report* (Barlow Report), Cmd. 6153, HMSO, 1940.
24 Royal Commission on Local Government in England, Vol. 1, *Report* (Redcliffe-Maud Report), Cmnd. 4040, HMSO, 1969.
25 Royal Commission on Local Government in England, Vol. 2, *Memorandum of Dissent by Mr D. Senior*, Cmnd. 4040–1, HMSO, 1969
26 Royal Commission on Local Government in England, Vol. 3, *Research Appendices*, Cmnd. 4040–11, HMSO, 1969.
27 Select Committee on Estimates, Session 1955–6, *Development Areas*, H.C. Paper 139, HMSO, 1955.
28 Sharp, E., *The Ministry of Housing and Local Government*, Allen & Unwin, 1969.
29 Smith, B. C., *Regionalism in England*, 3 Volumes:
    Vol. 1: *Regional Institutions: A Guide* (1964)
    Vol. 2: *Its Nature and Purpose 1905–1965* (1965)
    Vol. 3: *The New Regional Machinery* (1965)
    Acton Society Trust.
30 Smith, B. C., *Advising Ministers: A Case Study of the South-West Economic Planning Council*, Routledge & Kegan Paul, 1969.
31 Smith, P. M., 'What Kind of Regional Planning? A Review Article', *Urban Studies*, Vol. 3, November 1966, pp. 250–7 (a review of the North-West and the West Midlands regional studies and the 1966 White Paper on the Scottish economy).
32 Town and Country Planning Association, *London under Stress*, 1970.
33 Water Resources Board, *Annual Reports*, HMSO.

OFFICIAL REGIONAL AND SUB-REGIONAL
STUDIES AND PLANS

SURVEYS BY CENTRAL GOVERMENT OFFICIALS
The South-East Study 1961–1981 (1964)
The West Midlands: A Regional Study (1965)
The North-West: A Regional Study (1965)
The Problems of Merseyside: An Appendix to the North-West Study (1965)

REPORTS BY ECONOMIC PLANNING COUNCILS
Challenge of the Changing North (1966)
A Review of Yorkshire and Humberside (1966)
The East Midlands Study (1966)
A Strategy for the South-East (1967)
A Region with a Future: A Draft Strategy for the South-West (1967)
The West Midlands: Patterns of Growth (1967)
The North-West of the 1970s (1968)
Halifax and the Calder Valley (1968)
Huddersfield and Colne Valley (1969)
Opportunity in the East Midlands (1969)
Doncaster: An Area Study (1969)
The Plymouth Area Study (1969)
South-East Kent Study (1969)
Yorkshire and Humberside: Regional Strategy (1970)
The West Midlands: An Economic Appraisal (1971)

COMMAND PAPERS
Central Scotland: A Programme for Development and Growth, Cmnd. 2188 (1963)
The North-East: A Programme for Development and Growth, Cmnd. 2206 (1963)
The Scottish Economy 1965-70, Cmnd. 2864 (1966)
Wales: The Way Ahead, Cmnd. 3334 (1969)

REPORTS OF THE CENTRAL UNIT FOR
ENVIRONMENTAL PLANNING
Humberside: A Feasibility Study (1969)
Severnside: A Feasibility Study (1971)

REPORTS OF THE SOUTH-EAST JOINT PLANNING TEAM
Strategic Plan for the South-East (1970)
Studies: Vol. 1: Population and Employment
Vol. 2: Social and Environmental Aspects
Vol. 3: Transportation
Vol. 4: Strategies and Evaluation
Vol. 5: Report of Economic Consultants Ltd.

SUB-REGIONAL PLANNING STUDIES
Leicester and Leicestershire Sub-Regional Planning Study (1969)
Nottinghamshire and Derbyshire Sub-Regional Planning Study (1969)

Teeside Survey and Plan (1969)
North Gloucestershire Sub-Regional Study (1970)
Coventry-Solihull-Warwickshire: A Strategy for the Sub-Region (1971)

SCOTTISH REPORTS
Lothians Regional Survey and Plan (1966)
Grangemouth-Falkirk Regional Survey and Plan (1968)
The Central Borders: A Plan for Expansion (1968)
Tayside: Potential for Development (1970)
A Strategy for South-West Scotland (1970)

Chapter XIII

THE PLANNERS AND THE PUBLIC

PUBLIC ACCEPTANCE, SUPPORT AND PARTICIPATION

Town and country planning, land values, compulsory acquisition and the like present problems which, if they are to be adequately dealt with, demand a high degree of political sophistication and education on the part of the public. Yet to the 'man in the street' town and country planning is largely seen as a system of apparently arbitrary and irksome controls. Of course, this stems in part from the fact that much of contemporary planning is regulative – and there is a natural tendency to forget or to fail to see the real gains that have been made in, for instance, protecting the countryside from unsightly advertisement hoardings.

'The underlying purpose in the control of development (against the background of an approved Development Plan) is to secure that development takes place in the right places at the right time, and to stop it where it would be wrong. The public judge the success, or otherwise, of this control by what they see in town, village or country-side. What they do not see is what has been stopped by wise control of development. These cases are buried deep in the files of planning authorities and of the Minister. They did not materialize in brick and concrete to destroy or debase the urban or rural scene.'[7]

But the issue goes much deeper. Planning proposals are generally presented to the public as a *fait accompli,* and only rarely are they given a thorough *public* discussion. There is, of course, the machinery for objection and appeals, but, as will be shown in this chapter, this is a quasi-judicial process which is limited to a restricted range of interested parties. Furthermore, the general attitude to this system is far less favourable than to the normal judicial system. In any case the important point is not that the scope for registering 'objections' is limited, but that planning requires active 'citizen-participation', or at least public support and goodwill. Yet there is a very real divorce between 'the planners' and 'the planned'. There are several factors here. An important one is the effect of planning decisions on land values. Advance knowledge of planning proposals can markedly affect the value of the land concerned. This may lead to land speculation or to premature objections on the part of owners who expect to be adversely affected. As a result a planning department often has to operate under a veil of secrecy. This can only serve to increase public suspicion. Strangely this situation is itself in part the result of previous lack of public support. Though by no means the full explanation, there can be no doubt that the divorce between planners and the public is one of the factors which has led to the curious half-dismantled planning legislation which we now have – what Lord Holford has called 'a set of spare parts'. It must be axiomatic that compensation for acquisition of land or restriction on its use must be at a level which is publicly acceptable. This is so not merely on grounds of equity but also because 'inadequate' compensation will arouse such opposition as to inhibit public authorities from using their powers. This was the position under the 1947 Act. Each amendment of this Act has been designed to remove further injustices. But injustices still remain and will continue to do so until a scheme is devised which will at one and the same time be adequate for achieving planning objectives and prove publicly acceptable.

The point is basically a simple one: the planners cannot effectively move too far ahead of public opinion. This is not merely a matter of 'public relations': it is also one of leadership and community participation. This is to be seen clearly in the field of community improvement. 'Citizen-participation' may not be necessary for the successful development of a central area multi-level shopping precinct, but it is essential for the improvement of a decaying 'twilight' residential area. In view of the enormity of the British problem of rehabilitating sturdy yet obsolescent housing areas it is strange that so little thought has been given to the potentiality which could be realized if the interest and energy of the general public could be enlisted. Comparisons with the United States are striking. In Britain there is a remarkable acceptance of and reliance on Government; the Americans are less trusting and the curious result is a greater degree of 'grass-roots' democracy. This may not be as effective as United States Government hand-outs suggest, but so far as residential renewal is concerned there have been some dramatic successes. The British approach usually provides a choice only between private profitable redevelopment and subsidized municipal activity, and neither have, until recently, paid much attention to the twilight areas surrounding town centres.

The issue is not, of course, restricted to town and country planning. Similar problems exist in relation to the social services, to the nationalized industries, and indeed to any form of public or private monopoly or near-monopoly. It goes to the root of democratic government in modern industrial society; and it thus leads far from the central questions which form the subject matter of this book. All that can be attempted here is a discussion of a selection of relevant topics.

APPLICATION FOR PLANNING PERMISSION

Nearly 450,000 applications for planning permission are made each year to local planning authorities in Britain, of which about 85 per cent are granted. This enormous spate of applications involves great strains on the local planning machinery which, generally speaking, is not adequately staffed to deal with them and at the same time undertake the necessary work involved in preparing and reviewing development plans. Yet full consideration by local planning staffs is needed if planning committees – the elected members who have the responsibility for granting or refusing applications – are to have the requisite information on which to base their decisions. The importance of this is underlined by the fact that planning committees often have remarkably little time during a meeting in which to come to a decision. Agendas for meetings tend to be long: an average of five to six minutes for consideration of each application is nothing unusual, and in some cases the time may be as little as two minutes.[11] It cannot, therefore, be surprising that in a large proportion of cases (in the bigger authorities at least) the recommendations of the planning officer are approved *pro forma*. This may, of course, result in part from the harmonious relationship which commonly exists between local authority representatives and their officers; and, in any case, lay members tend to accept the technical expertise of their officials, while, on the other hand, the officials well know the minds of their political masters. Yet the point remains that both the elected representatives and the planning officials are hard pressed to cope with the constant flood of applications. Several important implications follow from this. First, and most obvious, is the danger that decisions will be given which are 'wrong' – i.e. which do not accord with planning objectives. Secondly, good relationships with the public in general and unsuccessful applicants in particular are difficult to attain: there is simply not sufficient time. Thirdly, this lack of time corroborates the view of many (unsuccessful) applicants that their case has never had adequate consideration: a view which is further supported by the manner in which refusals are commonly worded. Phrases such as 'detrimental to amenity' or 'not in accordance with the development plan', and so on, mean little or nothing to the individual applicant. He suspects that his case has been considered in general terms rather than in the particular detail which he naturally thinks is important in his case. And he may be right: understaffed and overworked planning departments cannot give each case the individual attention which is desirable.

This, of course, is not the whole picture. For instance, individuals who may wholly agree with a general planning principle will tend to see it in a different light when it is applied to their own applications. 'The man who has his home in one part of a green belt and owns what an estate agent would call "fully ripe building land" in another part, is as vociferous in relying on green belt principles to oppose building near his home as he is in denouncing the extreme and ridiculous lengths to which those principles have been carried when he is refused planning permission on his other land, and frequently he seems to achieve this without any conscious hypocrisy.'[8] This normal human failing is encouraged by the curious compromise situation which currently exists in relation to the control of land. On the one hand it seems to be generally accepted in principle (as it definitely is in law) that no one has a right to develop his land as he wishes unless the development is publicly desirable (as determined by a political instead of a financial decision). On the other hand, though the allocation of land to particular uses is determined by a public decision, the motives for private development are financial – and the financial profits which result from the development constitute private gain (though subject to capital gains tax). This unhappy circumstance (which is discussed at length in Chapter VI) involves a clash of principle which the unsuccessful applicant for planning permission experiences in a particularly sharp manner. It follows that local planning officials may have a peculiarly difficult task in explaining to a landowner why, for example, the field which he owns needs to be 'protected from development'.

Nevertheless, the success which attends this unenviable task does differ markedly between different local authorities. The question is not simply one of the great variations in potential land values in different parts of the country or in the relative adequacy of planning staffs. Though these are important factors there remains the less easily documented question of attitudes towards the public. All that can be said is that in some local authorities a great effort is made to assist and explain matters to an applicant, whereas in others the impression one gains is that of a bureaucratic machine which displays little patience and no kindness towards the individual applicant who does not understand 'planning procedures'.

DELEGATION TO OFFICERS

The 1968 Planning Act, which is discussed more fully later in this chapter, makes provision for the delegation to officers of planning decisions. This is in line with the recommendations of the Maud Report on *Management of Local Government*, the Mallaby Report on *Staffing of Local Government*, and the report of the *Management Study on Development Control*.

The background to this is that 70 per cent of all planning applications are of 'a simple nature'. The *Management Study on Development Control* found that a large proportion of these 'simple' applications were determined by a committee or by the council without presentation of details, without discussion and in accordance with the recommendations of the officers. They concluded that very many development control applications are already effectively delegated to officers for decision but are required to go through a formal procedure of ratification by a body of members. This creates unnecessary work for the local authority and unnecessary delay for the applicant.

Consideration was given to the possibility of a system which allowed for *approvals only* to be issued by a planning officer on certain clearly defined classes of application:

(*a*) Construction of one house in a residential area.
(*b*) Construction of blocks of private garages.
(*c*) Changes of use not conflicting with the development plan and not requiring advertising.
(*d*) Erection of temporary buildings and extension of existing temporary permissions.
(*e*) Construction of vehicular access on other than trunk roads.
(*f*) Construction of extensions to existing residential properties.

It was estimated that this would reduce by up to 50 per cent the number of cases needing to go to committee, 'would save committee time for more important work, would save a considerable amount of administrative work and time and would speed up the issue of decision notices to applicants'.

The Mallaby Committee added that greater delegation would provide more attractive and challenging official careers, and thus stimulate recruitment. In this way a better service would be rendered to the public.

The 1968 Act goes further than the proposals of the *Management Study*. It enables local authorities to delegate decisions on all kinds of planning application except those for listed building consent. The power is entirely discretionary: it is for local authorities to decide which officers, if any, should be given delegated powers and for which kinds of application. A decision of an officer exercising delegated powers has the same standing as one given by the Council itself.

This streamlining at the local level reflects the principle underlying the new legislation – that the planning system should be so organized that decisions are taken at the appropriate level. Thus the Ministry is responsible for broad policy issues, the local authority for local plans, and officials for detailed administrative issues which do not warrant committee involvement. In this way a real attempt is being made to reduce the bureaucratic, cumbersome and unwieldy system which has been paralysing the machinery. The relationships with, and the service to, the public should improve considerably. But much will depend on the more subtle factors than formal rearrangements of power: an issue to which we return shortly.

MALADMINISTRATION AND THE OMBUDSMAN

Most legislation is based on the assumption that the organs of government will operate efficiently and fairly. This is not always the case, but, even if it were, provision has to be made for the citizen who feels aggrieved by some action (or inaction) to complain, have his complaint investigated and be satisfied that the investigation is impartial. As modern industrial society becomes more complex the pressures for a machinery of protest, appeal and restitution grow – as is evidenced in such widely differing fields as social security, race relations and press publicity.

At the Parliamentray level, the case for an Ombudsman was reluctantly conceded by Government, and a Parliamentary Commissioner for Administration was appointed in 1967. The Commissioner has not so far found a single case of 'bias or perversity' on the part of the civil service and he reports that he is satisfied that the problems which exist concern 'defective administration' rather than 'maladministration'. In 1968 he reported on 374 cases and found 38 cases where there had been elements of maladministration which had led to some measure of injustice.[17]

There is no doubt about the relief experienced at central government level by the innocuousness of the Commissioner's findings. More important, there has resulted a more favourable attitude to the need for an Ombudsman for local government.

The activities of local government impinge upon the daily life of citizens more frequently and more directly than those of central government. The new local authorities which emerge from the reorganization of local government will undoubtedly (whatever plan is adopted) be larger and more powerful than most existing authorities. They will also inevitably be more remote, especially if, following the trend towards more efficient management, councillors concern themselves more with policy formulation and less with personal cases. This is particularly the case with town and country planning where there are now the powers for the delegation of decisions to officials.

As these trends continue, the character of local government will change and many issues of policy (not only within the field of 'town and country planning') will be seen for what they are: not technical issues to be settled by professionals but political issues to be settled by politicians responding to political processes, albeit with professional advice.

PLANNING APPEALS

An unsuccessful applicant for planning permission can, of course, appeal to the Secretary of State, and as pointed out in Chapter III, a large number do so. Each case is considered by the Department on its merits. This allows a great deal of flexibility and permits cases of individual hardship to be sympathetically treated. But at the same time it can make the planning system seem arbitrary – at least to the unsuccessful appellant. Although there has been a recent trend towards the setting out of certain broad policies, the general view in the Department is that a reliance on precedent could easily give rise to undesirable rigidities. 'Conditions vary so fundamentally from case to case and from one part of the country to another that it would be impossible, if not wrong, to draft rules that would hold good uniformly. The basic problem is that a variety of factors operate in a planning case; the art of making a decision lies in the striking of a proper balance. Under the circumstances, there is little that the Department can do beyond listing those factors which it considers crucial, and expressing rules of thumb which will help select those which should preponderate.'[11]

Other issues relevant to this view are the traditional local-central government relationship (in which local authorities are considered as equal partners in the processes of government) and the particular character of town and country planning in this country. The flexibility of the development plan, the wide area of discretion legally allowed to the planners in the operation of planning controls, and the very restricted jurisdiction of the courts necessitates a judicial function for the Department. But this function is only quasi-judicial: decisions are taken not on the basis of legal rules as in a court of law or in accordance with case-law, but on a judgment as to what course of action is, in the particular circumstances and in the context of ministerial policy, desirable, reasonable and equitable. By its very nature this must be elusive, and the unsuccessful appellant may well feel justified in believing that the dice are loaded against him. The very fact that appeals are heard by ministerial 'inspectors' and (probably) in the town hall of the authority against whose decisions he is appealing do not make for confidence in a fair and objective hearing. The contrast with the court is striking:

'The usual complaint of the civil litigant is not that his case is not fairly and impartially heard and determined, but that, owing to the complexity of the system, the delay and expense are excessive. The views of the planning applicant, except when he is successful, are quite different. He rarely complains of the cost (though quite often of the delay) but frequently takes the view that the inquiry or hearing was nothing more than an opportunity for him to "let off steam".'[8]

It is not easy to suggest what can be done to improve this situation. Keeble, in his book *Town Planning at the Crossroads*, has argued that the basic fault lies in the inadequate and sketchy nature of town plans, as a consequence of which a very large proportion of planning applications relate to development which neither complies nor conflicts with the plan (e.g. a small group of shops in a residential area). In his view the preparation and approval of detailed plans would reduce both the work in dealing with applications and the number of appeals – since a far larger proportion of intending developers would know what would be permitted and what would be rejected. This is precisely the opposite view to that expressed so cogently in the Planning Advisory Group's Report on *The Future of Development Plans*, and now embodied in the 1968 Town and Country Planning Act.

Unfortunately the problem is not merely that of the inadequate 'lead' given by development plans: there is the further point that many plans are out of date. Local planning authorities have been so overwhelmed with development control that a great number of them have been unable to devote the necessary time to keeping their plans in line with changing conditions.

But, of course, part of the expressed dissatisfaction comes from those who are compelled to forgo private gain for the sake of communal benefit: the objections are not really against procedures, and they are not likely to be assuaged by administrative reforms or good 'public relations'. They are fundamentally objections against the public control of land use – in particular, if not in principle.

PUBLIC INQUIRIES

Public local inquiries figure largely in both the approval of development plans and in development control. It is, however, important to appreciate the nature and purpose of these inquiries.

Essentially all inquiries are held to allow objections to be raised. An inquiry on a development plan does not aim to provide an adequate examination of its merits: it is an inquiry into objections. The inquiry is not a means by which a local authority seek to enlist public support for its plan: its very character (with its 'objectors' and 'witnesses') makes it inappropriate for this purpose. A good authority will do its utmost to inform the public and to obtain popular support; and it is usual for local authorities to attempt to meet objections – but all this is best done before the inquiry stage.

The nature of the inquiry involves the Department in more than merely considering the individual objections, which naturally usually relate to particular details of the plan rather than to its broad provisions. 'The public inquiry, therefore, has to be supplemented by an examination within the Department of such questions as whether the population for which the plan caters is in accord with probable developments; whether the allocation of land for various uses and purposes is sound and well balanced',[2] and so on. It follows that the Department can make substantial alterations to a plan. There is no legal requirement for a subsequent inquiry into such 'modifications', though 'where a proposal in a plan seems to the Minister misconceived but an alternative proposal would itself attract opposition, he has not infrequently deleted the proposal in the plan and asked for a new proposal to be submitted to him later, as an amendment of the plan. This enables him to hear objections to the new proposals before coming to a decision on it.' The Franks Committee thought that this was inadequate and maintained that it was desirable to introduce a procedure whereby those affected could express their views on all proposed modifications. This recommendation was accepted by the Government. A list of 'modifications' together with the reasons for proposing them is now sent to the local planning authority. These are then published and twenty-one days allowed for objections. The decision as to whether an inquiry should be held is taken by the Ministry 'on the circumstances of each case'.

Another change made following the Franks Report was the publication of inspectors' reports. This was a matter of considerable discussion during the proceedings of the Committee. One of the main arguments put forward by the Ministry of Housing opposing publication was that this would cause misunderstanding and embarrassment:

'The objection in principle that we would see to publication is that our inspectors really act in a dual capacity. They act first of all as the inspector who goes down to see the site and who, being a technical man, can give us an appreciation of the soundness of the authority's proposals; they hear the arguments and report to the Minister what took place, what impression it made upon them, what view they take of the site and so on. Then they make a recommendation and in that capacity they are acting as officers of the Department because their recommendation is essentially what should be the application of policy to the facts they found. That is why you can have identical facts but different decisions. They have got to be *au fait* with current policy and say what they think that the Minister, his policy being what it is, would wish to do in the particular case as they found it. We think that publication of the recommendation would cause embarrassment.'[2]

This passage clearly illustrates how a public inquiry is different from a judicial review. It is usual to apply the phrase 'quasi-judicial', but this is not very satisfactory, as the Franks Report implied. They saw the problem essentially as one of finding a reasonable balance between conflicting interests:

'On the one hand there are Ministers enjoined by legislation to carry out certain duties. On the other hand there are the rights and feelings of individual citizens who find their possessions or plans interfered with by the administration. There is also the public interest, which requires both that Ministers and other administrative bodies should not be frustrated in carrying out their duties and also that their decisions should be subject to effective checks or controls.'

The Franks Committee argued that inspectors' reports should be published, and this view was accepted by the Government. It is interesting to note that in the great majority of cases (on planning appeals) the Minister's decision has been 'broadly in line' with the recommendations of the inspector.

This is not the place to discuss all the issues relevant to these procedures: the interested reader is referred to the report of the Franks Committee. The immediate point is simply that neither the statutory provisions, nor the arguments on administrative inquiries, are concerned primarily with the encouragement of public participation in the planning process. To achieve this a local authority has to forge its own procedures. An account of the efforts of one (exceptional) authority is given later in this chapter. First, however, it is necessary to discuss the question of 'third parties'.

'THIRD PARTY' INTERESTS

The rights of 'third parties' – those affected by planning decisions but having no legal 'interest' in the land subject to the decision – were highlighted in the so-called Chalk Pit case.* This, in brief, concerned an application to 'develop' certain land in Essex by digging chalk. On being refused planning permission the applicants appealed to the Minister of Housing, and a local inquiry was held. Among those who appeared as objectors at the inquiry some were substantial landowners, including Major Buxton whose land was adjacent to the appeal site and was being used for agricultural and residential purposes. The inspector's recommendation was that the appeal should be dismissed, mainly because there was a serious danger of chalk dust being deposited on the land of Major Buxton and others in quantities which would be 'detrimental to the user of the land'; and that there was no present shortage of chalk in the locality. The Minister disagreed with the inspector's recommendations and allowed the appeal. Major Buxton then appealed to the High Court, partly on the ground that in rejecting his inspector's findings of fact, the Minister had relied on certain subsequent advice and information given to him by the Minister of Agriculture without giving the objectors any opportunity of correcting or commenting upon this advice and information.† But Major Buxton now found that he had no legal right to appeal to the courts: indeed he apparently had had no legal right to appear at the inquiry. (He only had what the judge thought to be a 'very sensible' administrative privilege.) In short, Major Buxton was a 'third party': he was in no legal sense a 'person aggrieved'. Yet clearly in the wider sense of the phrase Major Buxton was very much aggrieved, and at first sight he had a moral right to object and to have his objection carefully weighed. But should the machinery of town and country planning be used for this purpose by an individual? Before the town and country planning legislation any landowner could develop his land

* *Buxton and Others* v. *Minister of Housing and Local Government* (1960), 3 W.L.R. 866. The account given here of this case is based on a summary contained in *Public Law*, Summer 1961, pp. 121–8.

† This issue has been the subject of considerable discussion. See House of Lords Debates, Vol. 230, cols. 740–4, April 20, 1961, Vol. 231, cols. 35–76, May 8, 1961, *Annual Reports of the Council on Tribunals*, 1961, and 1962, HMSO, and *Public Law*, loc. cit.

as he liked, provided he did not infringe the common law which was designed more to protect the right to develop rather than to restrain it. The law of nuisance and trespass was not a particularly strong constraint on the freedom to use land. But, as the judge stressed, the planning legislation was designed 'to restrict development for the benefit of the public at large and not to confer new rights on any individual members of the public'.

This, of course, is the essential point. It is the job of the local planning authority to assess the public advantage or disadvantage of a proposed development – subject to a review by the Secretary of State if those having a legal interest in the land in question object. Third parties cannot usurp these Government functions. Nevertheless, it might be generally agreed that those affected by planning decisions should have the right to make representations for consideration by a planning committee.[23] The present position is that third parties have an 'administrative privilege' to appear at a public inquiry, but generally no similar privilege in relation to a planning application.

There is one group of exceptions to this. The Town and Country Planning Act of 1959 introduced a provision designed to give an opportunity for the public ventilation of objections to certain planning proposals of an 'unneighbourly' character. Such developments are advertised and objectors allowed to make written 'representations' to the local planning authority. If the planning application is granted there is no further opportunity for objections – however much the objectors may be affected. But, if the application is refused and the applicant appeals, the objectors have the normal privilege of appearing and being heard at the public inquiry. In short, the only new provision here is the requirement for publicity and the formal right to make representations. The types of development covered by these provisions are very limited – public conveniences, refuse disposal and sewerage works, slaughterhouses and theatres, dance halls, skating rinks, etc. It might be possible to extend this list somewhat (to include, for example, fish and chip shops and petrol stations), but to extend it to cover all applications would, quite apart from any objections on principle, lead to the danger of a breakdown in planning procedures. The machinery of planning is already overburdened with development applications and appeals. An extension of the opportunities for representations, objections and appeals would slow down procedures and make them dangerously cumbersome. This is a practical issue of importance, but the fundamental point is that it is the job of local planning authorities to assess what is publicly desirable. Measures designed to make the system open and fair are all to the good. Openness and fairness were two of the principles which the Franks Committee sought to apply to administrative tribunals and inquiries. Their third principle – impartiality – cannot be applied without qualification to planning procedures (as the Committee pointed out). If a local planning authority were merely a judicial body seeking to achieve a fair balance between conflicting private interests, many of the arguments for extending the rights of individuals to be heard and to object, could be accepted. But the local planning authority is not an impartial body: it is an agency of government attempting to secure what it believes to be the best development for its area. In short, it has a fundamentally political responsibility.

THE 1968 ACT AND PUBLIC PARTICIPATION

The 1968 Planning Act is a legislative landmark in the development of a new framework of planning designed to bring about a greater degree of citizen participation. The main stimulus for this has come, not from local authorities, but from the central government. Under the old development plan system the Department was becoming crippled by what a former Permanent Secretary has called a crushing burden of casework. The concept of ministerial responsibility has been shown to be inapplicable over the total field of development plan approval and appeals against planning decision. Not only is much of this work inappropriate to a central government department: its sheer weight has prevented the Department from fulfilling its essential functions – of establishing major planning policies. Under the new system much of the role of the Secretary of State as the ultimate court of appeal is to be devolved on to local authorities. His function will be to review and formally approve the broad outlines of local planning policies and, eventually to consider only those planning appeals which raise issues of ministerial policy.

The new system can be brought into full operation only when local government has been reorganized into units which are appropriate for the exercise of planning functions. But more than a reorganization of boundaries will be needed to make the system work: it demands a major change in the *practice* of local government. Citizen-participation is more than a desirable adjunct: it is an essential basis. If citizen-participation does not work, the system will collapse.

The 1968 Act provides only the barest skeleton of the new system – citizen-participation is much more than adherence to formal procedures. The Act merely provides that, in drawing up a structure plan a local authority must:

(i) give 'adequate publicity' to the report of the survey on which the plan is based, and to the policy which they propose to include in the plan;

(ii) provide publicity for their proposals and 'adequate opportunity' to enable representations to be made by the public;
(iii) take into account these representations in drawing up the
structure plan;
(iv) place the plan on deposit for public inspection, together with a
statement of the time within which objections may be made to
the Secretary of State;
(v) Submit the plan to the Secretary of State, together with a statement of the steps which have been taken to comply with the above
requirements, and of consultations which have been carried
out with 'other persons'.

A local plan is drawn up within the policy framework of an
approved structure plan and does not normally have to be submitted
to the Secretary of State for approval (though a copy has to be sent
to him and exceptionally he can direct that it 'shall not have effect
unless approved by him'). It follows the same procedure as a structure plan, but if there are any objections these are sent to the local
authority (not the Secretary of State) and are heard at a public
inquiry which is held by an independent inspector who reports to
the authority. The Secretary of State will not normally be concerned
with local plans (though he will presumably check that they do properly
reflect the policy approved in the structure plans).

At first sight it might appear that local authorities are to be
judges in their own case, particularly since there is provision for
inspectors to be appointed by local authorities. Indeed, much has
been made of this 'unfair judicial process'. But the fact is that the
process is not a judicial one: it is essentially administrative and
political. This is why citizen-participation is so crucial. If local
authorities do not succeed in carrying their citizenry with them the
new system will fail: public opposition will necessitate a move back
to the previous system.

THE SKEFFINGTON REPORT

Concern with – and even interest in – citizen-participation has not
been a particularly obvious strength of British local government
and it will be even more difficult to achieve with the large authorities
which are needed for effective planning. With little experience to
build on it was perhaps inevitable that the Government should
appoint a committee 'to consult and report on the best methods
including publicity, of securing the participation of the public at the
formative stage in the making of development plans for their area'.
The Committee was set up, under the chairmanship of the late

Arthur Skeffington (then Joint Parliamentary Secretary to the Minister of Housing and Local Government), in March 1968 and published its report *People and Planning* in July 1969.

The Skeffington Report made a number of rather obvious recommendations which do not carry us a great deal further, for example:

'people should be kept informed throughout the preparation of a structure of local plan for their area';
'local planning authorities should seek to publicize proposals in a way that informs people living in the area to which the plan relates';
'the public should be told what their representations have achieved or why they have not been accepted';
'people should be encouraged to participate in the preparation of plans by helping with surveys and other activities as well as by making comments'.

The mundane nature of many of the recommendations is testimony to the distance which British local government has to go in making citizen-participation a reality.

Unfortunately, the report does not discuss many of the really crucial issues, though passing references suggest that the Committee were aware of some of them. For instance, it is rightly stated that 'planning' is only one service 'and it would be unreasonable to expect the public to see it as an entity in itself'. The report continues: 'Public participation would be little more than an artificial abstraction if it became identified solely with planning procedures rather than with the broadest interests of people'. This has major implications for the internal organization and management of local authorities. So have the proposals for the appointment of 'community development officers . . . to secure the involvement of those people who do not join organizations' and for 'community forums' which would 'provide local organizations with the opportunity to discuss collectively planning and other issues of importance to the area', and which 'might also have administrative functions, such as receiving and distributing information on planning matters and promoting the formation of neighbourhood groups'.

What is conspicuously lacking in the whole debate on citizen-participation is its political implications. The Skeffington Report noted that it was feared that a community forum might become the centre of political opposition: but the only comment made was 'we hope that that would not happen; it seems unlikely that it would, as most local groups are not party political in their membership'. The issue is not, however, one of *party politics*: it is one of local policies, pressures and interest. Citizen-participation implies a transfer of some power from local councils to groups of electors. It is power which is the crucial issue – not in any sinister sense, but simply in terms of who is to decide local issues. The Department does not want to be concerned with these (except where they have ramifications over a larger front: hence central approval of structure plans). This will be a matter of intimate concern for local councillors – and officials as well.

The transfer of considerable statutory powers from central to local government will show only too clearly that planning is essentially a political process – a fact which has been confused by the semi-judicial procedures with which the Department has been so preoccupied.

None of this is to argue that the philosophy underlying the new legislation is misplaced: far from it. The intention is to demonstrate that the real problems of citizen-participation and local democratic control go far deeper than issues of formal procedures, of social surveys and public exhibitions. If the new system works it will have a major impact on British political processes; and it will not be confined to 'town and country planning'.

Curiously, it was not the Skeffington Committee but the Seebohm Committee (in their Report on *Local Authority and Allied Personal Social Services*) which highlighted another related issue (and one which the proposed community development officer would particularly face):

'the participants may wish to pursue policies directly at variance with the ideas of the local authorities and there is certainly a difficult link to be forged between the concepts of popular participation and traditional representative democracy. The role of the social worker in this context is likely to give rise to problems of conflicting loyalties. The Council for Training in Social Work suggest in evidence that if community work is to be developed by the local authority, then the authority "will need to recognize the fact that some of its staff may be involved in situations which lead to criticism of their services or with pressure groups about new needs. The workers themselves will need to be clear about their professional role and this will depend upon their training and the organizational structure within which they work." . . . Participation provides a means by which further consumer control can be exercised over professional and bureaucratic power.'

A further problem in citizen-participation is that of determining how representative are the views expressed by participating citizens. As the Skeffington Report implies, the views of 'the non-joiners and inarticulate' are as important as those of 'the actively interested and organized'. And as American experience shows, citizen participation can lead to strong demands to keep an area 'white', to exclude public authority housing, and to safeguard local amenities at a high cost to the larger community. It is not every community which is best placed to assess its needs in relation to a wider area.

Finally, reference needs to be made to the tricky problem of planning blight. The best way of avoiding this is to maintain the utmost secrecy until definite plans can be presented to the public as a *fait accompli*. Obviously this is not easy to reconcile with a greater degree of citizen-participation.

There is no easy answer to this. Indeed, the Skeffington Committee were probably right in saying that 'some increase in planning blight may have to be accepted if there is to be increased participation by the public'. Whether the compensation provisions for planning blight are adequate is another matter.

In the British scene it is likely that citizen-participation will be noteworthy for its gradual growth rather than its excesses. The essential ingredient is a concern on the part of elected members and professional staffs to make participation a reality. Here the experience of Coventry (which is now extensively documented in the Skeffington Report) is useful.

CITIZEN-PARTICIPATION: THE COVENTRY EXPERIENCE

'*Dear Citizen,*

The Planning of Coventry

An important task carried out by Coventry Corporation is town planning. Its aim is to ensure that the city shall have beauty and character, and be a convenient place in which to live and work. A plan was prepared in 1951 but a new plan is now being prepared to take into account changes that have taken place during the last ten years and those which are necessary for the development of Coventry during the next twenty years.

The Corporation is anxious that there should be the widest participation of citizens in the formulation of the new plan.'

So started a letter sent by the Coventry Planning Department to community organizations and head teachers in the City. Public meetings were held in every ward, and local residents were invited to give their views on what was needed to be done in their localities. These were chaired by local people who were recognized as being independent of local politics. Elected representatives of the ward together with members of the Planning Committee and planning officials, attended each meeting. The Committee member explained the objective of the meeting and the official outlined the specific projects scheduled for the area in which the meeting was held. Members of the audience were then invited to ask questions on the plans and to make suggestions. A record was kept of all the items mentioned at each meeting and forwarded to every member of the Council and the chief officers.

These meetings attracted a great deal of public interest. Altogether twenty-eight meetings were held between September 1961 and February 1962 and were attended by about 1,100 people. Support was forthcoming from several organizations in the City, particularly the district Ratepayers' Associations, who themselves promoted discussions on planning problems and public improvements.

The full report of the meetings ran to over 200 foolscap pages. Major proposals were considered for incorporation in the Review of the Development Plan. Minor items were submitted to the appropriate Committee and a sum of £8,000 was earmarked to enable work to be carried out quickly on small schemes.

The type of proposals made is illustrated by the following extracts from the Report:

'Attention was drawn to the considerable amount of kerb-side parking in the Charterhouse area by tradesmen's vans and vehicles by workers in the BTH factory. It was suggested that the Council should provide parking facilities in the area in order to get these vehicles off the road. A large area at the top of Gosford Street was suggested for clearance in order to provide parking facilities.

'It was suggested that Gosford Green should be preserved as an amenity feature in the redevelopment schemes for the area.

'Attention was drawn to the bad state of street lighting in Far Gosford Street and in other small streets in the area. Concern was particularly expressed regarding those streets which carry a substantial volume of traffic.

'Concern was expressed at the number of gable-end type of houses which were being built on the Ernesford Grange Estate. Criticism was made of their boxlike appearance.

'Attention was drawn to the waste land in the vicinity of Churchill Avenue. Residents wanted to know whether the Corporation had any proposals for this, and it was thought that it was suitable for the building of garages.

'A children's playground was very badly needed in the Stoke Aldermoor area. An offer to raise money was made from members of the Stoke Aldermoor Social Club if the City Council would provide the land for the playground.'

In addition to the Ward Meetings, local associations were asked for their observations on, for example, deficiency of public buildings, lack of public services, visual untidiness, vandalism and the reconstruction of the city centre. Head teachers were invited to seek the ideas of school children on the planning of the city – particularly playgrounds, sports facilities, youth clubs and so on.

The annual 'Welcome to Citizenship Exhibition' was supplemented by a letter from the Planning Officer asking for ideas on the future planning of the city. (This exhibition is held for all who reach the age of majority and become eligible for entry on the Electoral Register, and is aimed at explaining and illustrating the work of the various departments of the Corporation.)

Finally, an exhibition of future plans for the city was mounted in the Planning Office and the public were invited to enter an 'Ideas Competition', for which five prizes were awarded.*

The success of this venture would need independent appraisal. There were certainly difficulties. The lessons which the city learnt were:†

(i) There is a tendency for people to become aligned with protest organizations before they have considered the full implications of a proposal within the totality of the Plan, thus inhibiting rational assessment of policy.

(ii) Modifications to meet objections, or compromises, can create equally important and often greater objections from those subsequently affected by the modification. (The 'sounder' the original proposal the greater are these objections likely to be.)

(iii) The processes of consultation and participation inevitably result in a lengthening of the administrative processes. Decision making is even further removed from the analysis of data. Even a continual review will not eliminate this.

(iv) The complexity of technical evidence (e.g. traffic data, analysis and assignments) presents problems of explanation and communication. There clearly has to be a professional assessment of the relevance and interpretation of complex technical data.

(v) It is essential that pressure groups (e.g. an amenity organization or ratepayers association) are not assumed to be representative of public opinion. Such a pressure group may make representations to expedite action which may be in the interests of one particular locality, or one particular element in environmental

* Further details will be found in Appendix 3 to the Skeffington Report.

† I am grateful to Mr Terence Gregory, the City Architect and Planning Officer of Coventry, for the following.

planning; but when such action is viewed within a total programme of priorities for the city as a whole, it may be premature
or completely unjustified.
(vi) Participation and consultation are essential, but they do not
and cannot result in everyone being satisfied, if only because
some interests are mutually exclusive.

Finally, and somewhat sadly, though the Coventry venture
aroused a great deal of interest it became very clear that 'the majority
of the public are largely apathetic towards planning issues or are
content to leave matters in the hands of the authority, provided that
they themselves are not affected by proposals'.

What is significant in Coventry's approach was that they were not
attempting to forestall 'objections' to firm plans, but seeking public
participation in the planning process. It is noteworthy that the
Coventry planners regard this as a vital and essential part of their
work. There are at least three benefits to be gained.[24] First, there is
the negative aspect of calming opposition and thus easing the
problems of the planners. More important is the question of ascer-
taining the wishes of the electorate. This is by no means a simple
matter. Wishes may cancel each other out, they may be contradictory,
impracticable or completely utopian. And, in any case, the local
authority must itself act as guardian and interpreter of the common
good. Nevertheless, in so doing it should maintain a close relationship with the public it serves. Though ideally it should demonstrate its value of political leadership, it must always ensure that
it does not get too far ahead of public opinion. On the other hand,
a progressive authority can interpret its role in such a way as to exert
a very considerable influence on the formation of public opinion.

Thirdly, an approach to planning which welcomes and encourages
citizen-participation is a good thing in itself. In spite of the lip-
service which is given to this, it is unfortunately true that citizen-
participation is often regarded as a time-consuming and fruitless
frill. This is far from being the case: if democratic planning is to cope
with the mounting problems of a complex industrial and land-
hungry society, it is essential that the public image of the planners
should be improved. There is, of course, a definite limit to which
'government by participation' can replace 'government by consent',
but an authority which can take the public into its confidence and
enlist its support will thereby become a more effective planning
agency. This demands a completely different outlook on the part of
many planning authorities. To illustrate, at the 1963 conference of
the Town and Country Planning Association a vice-chairman of
one planning committee argued that though it was possible, it was

also extremely difficult to obtain any useful advice from the average citizen group: 'Your local planner needs not to be a sensitive ear listening to the Townswomen's Guild or the Chamber of Commerce and this, that or the other. He needs to be a single-minded steam-roller'. In the final analysis, the real problem is to find the balance between the advantages of increased public consultation and participation and the need for a reasonable speed in planning procedures. This might be achieved by defining the occasions on which consultations can produce the maximum benefit. If this is not done, the danger is that the planning machine might become so bogged down with citizen-participation that its effectiveness and efficiency would be seriously harmed.

Citizen-participation cannot be effective unless it is organized. This, of course, is one of the fundamental difficulties. Though a large number of people may feel vaguely disturbed in general about the operation of the planning machine (and particularly upset when they are individually affected), it is only a minority who are prepared to do anything other than grumble. The minority may be growing, and with the general rise in educational levels we can hope that it will continue to do so. It has to be recognized, however, that citizen-participation will, as far as can be seen, always be restricted: 'The activity of responsible social criticism is not congenial to more than a minority. Most of us for most of the time are content to remain complacently acquiescent in our social niche. . . . The activist, the social critic, the reformer will always be a small section of any society. Their activities require not only extra effort which few are willing to expend, but also the ability to criticize and organize which comparatively few possess.'[1]

The minority is, nevertheless, an important one, and as the success of the Consumers' Association and similar bodies has shown, it can be instrumental in activating widespread interest and support (even if this stops short of actual participation). A little official encouragement might have surprisingly widespread effects. At the local level this could be on the lines suggested by the Coventry experiment. At the national level it might take the form of government financial assistance towards the administrative overheads of a central agency – as is done with the Civic Trust and the National Federation of Housing Societies. But the leadership role and concern for wider community interests must always remain the reponsibility of the local authority.

IN CONCLUSION

The debate on citizen-participation (like that on local government reorganization and regional devolution) raises the fundamental question of whether the machinery of government is deploying its resources in the most effective way. The issue is important not only in the interests of the mental health of the central administration, but also because their over-commitment with detailed aspects of planning and issues which are of purely local concern means that there are insufficient human resources left for a consideration of the broader planning issues which should be their particular responsibility. Fogarty in his book *Under-Governed and Over-Governed* has put this argument in general terms. Ministers, top managers and trade union leaders he argues, 'have over-committed themselves to settling detailed problems, and as a result have left themselves with too little time and energy to deal competently with the broader issues of overall government and management. By doing so they have also defeated even their immediate purpose and have made it harder to find sound solutions to problems of detail.' Town and country planning 'has fiddled with details. But it has succeeded neither in promoting timely action over such major features of regional development as the reshaping of the older conurbations or the building of new motorways, nor in creating a satisfactory urban landscape in newly developing areas, nor in bringing home to people in particular localities what they themselves might do to improve their neighbourhood amenities on the lines of the well-known schemes of the Civic Trust.'

The argument does not have to be accepted in full for its major point to be appreciated. Now that regional planning is beginning to move into the realm of practical politics, it is becoming increasingly important to reduce the amount of effort consumed by details. Broad regional policy-making is a more fitting task for central government than considering appeals on the design of suburban bungalows. It is in this context that the question of public support and citizen-participation needs to be considered. In the long run it may well prove to be a fundamental issue in adapting the planning machine to meet the problem of the second half of the twentieth century. The issue is now recognized at central government level and it is entering the debate on local government reorganization. The 1968 Planning Act represents a bold step towards a realignment of political forces in the field of town and country planning. If it succeeds it will not stop there.

REFERENCE AND FURTHER READING

1 Broady, M., 'Social Change and Town Development', in *Planning for People*, National Council of Social Service, Bedford Square Press, 1968.
2 Committee on Adminstrative Tribunals and Enquiries (Franks Committee): *Minutes of Evidence and Memoranda Submitted by Government Departments*, Vol. 2, HMSO, 1956.
3 Committee on Local Authority and Allied Personal Services, *Report* (Seebohm Report), Cmnd. 3703, HMSO, 1968.
4 Committee on Public Participation in Planning, *People and Planning* (Skeffington Report), HMSO, 1969.
5 Council on Tribunals, *Annual Reports*, HMSO.
6 Coventry City Council, *First Quinquennial Review of the Development Plan: Report on Ward Meetings*, September 1962.
7 Essex County Planning Department, *Development Control Procedures*, May 1963.
8 Grove, G. A., 'Planning and the Applicant', *Journal of the Town Planning Institute*, Vol. 49, May 1963, p. 130.
9 Hill, D. M., *Participating in Local Affairs*, Penguin Books, 1970.
10 Keeble, L., *Town Planning at the Crossroads*, Estates Gazette, 1961.
11 Mandelker, D. R., *Green Belts and Urban Growth*, University of Wisconsin Press, 1962.
12 MHLG, *The Future of Development Plans*, HMSO, 1965.
13 MHLG, *Management of Local Government* (Maud Report), HMSO, 1967.
14 MHLG, *Management Study on Development Control*, HMSO, 1967.
15 MHLG, *Staffing of Local Government* (Mallaby Report), HMSO, 1967.
16 National Commission on Urban Problems, *Building the American City*, US Government Printing Office, 1969.
17 *Parliamentary Commissioner for Administration, Second Report*, H.C. Paper 129, Session 1968/69, HMSO, 1969.
18 Rees, I. B., *Government by Community*, Charles Knight, 1971.
19 Reynolds, J. P., 'Public Participation in Planning', *Town Planning Review*, Vol. 40, No. 2, July 1969, pp. 131–48.

20 Robson, W. A., *The Governors and the Governed*, Allen & Unwin, 1964.
21 SDD, Circular 49/71, *Publicity for Planning Proposals*, SDD, 1971.
22 Select Committee on the Parliamentary Commissioner for Administration, Session 1968–9, *Report*, H.C. Paper 385, HMSO, 1969 (MHLG Evidence, pp. 112–21).
23 Silkin, Lord, 'Third Party Interests in Planning', *Report of the Proceedings of the Town and Country Planning Summer School, 1962*, Town Planning Institute, pp. 40–9.
24 Slayton, W. K. and Dewey, R., 'Urban Redevelopment and the Urbanite', in Woodbury, C. (editor), *The Future of Cities and Urban Redevelopment*, University of Chicago Press, 1953.
25 Wraith, R. E. and Lamb, G. B., *Public Inquiries as an Instrument of Government*, Allen & Unwin, 1971.

ERECTION OF HOUSES ON AN EXISTING ESTATE WHERE
FURTHER DEVELOPMENT WAS UNDESIRABLE

'The appellants applied for permission for the erection of ten pairs of semi-detached houses on a site which was situated 1½ miles from a borough in a southern county and which formed part of an existing housing estate erected just before the war.

The estate consisted of some sixty houses which had been built on either side of the one estate road, which jutted straight out into the countryside from a trunk road. Surrounding land to the south, east and west was agricultural. Westwards along the main road there was a small group of houses, a public house and a restaurant. Opposite the junction of the estate road and the main road was a factory, and a little to the east, where the main road crossed a railway, were some six or seven cottages.

The appellants' proposals represented the completion of the estate road in the manner originally permitted by the pre-war planning authority. The Council gave permission for the erection of two of the houses in order to fill undeveloped plots between existing houses, but considered that any extension of the development would be undesirable.

The Council stated that the development was permitted in 1938 as part of the area then zoned for residential development, but that it had since been found advisable to re-plan in order to give effect to the proposals of the Greater London Plan. They contended that the proposal would be harmful to farming interests, since the extension of the estate southwards would sever a considerable area of agricultural land lying to the east and west of it; development would also add to the potential dangers of a very busy trunk road. While the Council considered that the development was unrelated to any existing or proposed development area, the appellants contended that the development, already carried out, together with that to the east, provided a well-sited and suitable community area, and that there was nothing to suggest that the area should not be satisfactorily completed.

The Minister agreed with the Council that the estate was an undesirable type of development, since it was an intrusion of housing into purely agricultural land and some distance from the nearest shops, schools and other necessary services. In those circumstances. he considered that, while infilling could be justified, any extension of the estate should not be permitted and he upheld the Council's decision.'*

DEVELOPMENT IN RESIDENTIAL AREAS†

'(1) The North Birmingham Branch of the British Legion proposed to use for their headquarters, a large three-storey Victorian house at 31 Trinity Road, Birmingham. They said that their present head-quarters in a neighbouring street had been compulsorily purchased by the Council and were to be demolished with other adjoining properties to make way for Council flats. The Council would not extend the lease or provide other accommodation, and the branch was faced with extinction after thirty-four years. They had been offered the appeal premises, which were ideal for their purposes, only after countless inquiries. The ground floor would be used for social purposes, the first floor as committee rooms, and the top flat as living accommodation for a caretaker.

The Council acknowledged the good work done by the appellants, but said that the premises were suitable for living accommodation, either for single family occupation or for conversion into three to four flats. There was an acute shortage of houses in the city and the loss of this accommodation was unjustified.

The Minister thought that the house was well suited to the needs of the appellants, and that it would be unfortunate if the branch had to close for lack of premises. Since they had to leave their present building because it was required for redevelopment, he came to the conclusion that they ought to be given permission for the proposed development.

The appeal was allowed.'

'(2) Beginning in 1907, the appellants had developed on garden suburb lines an estate of fifty-four acres at Harborne. The estate contained shops, a club building with the company's office, tennis courts, and a dance hall about 63 feet long by 30 feet wide. The appellants said that they would have liked to retain the hall as a social centre, but its use had declined steadily in recent years. Largely owing to an increase in rates and the opening of another hall with better transport facilities which had taken away business, it was running at a loss, and they therefore sought to change the use of

* Ministry of Housing and Local Government, *Bulletin of Selected Appeal Decisions, No. XI*, September 1952, pp. 4–5.

† These two cases are taken from Ministry of Housing and Local Government, *Selected Planning Appeals, Second Series, Volume 1*, June 1959, pp. 22–3.

their hall to professional offices. There would be no change in the external appearance of the building and the tenant would be carefully selected. There was no question of other applicants as the rest of the estate consisted of small houses. Residents in the vicinity did not object to the proposed change: some of them had complained of the noise when dances were held.

The Council said that this was a pleasant residential area and the intrusion of commercial uses should be resisted for the sake of local amenities. The hall was designed and built for social purposes, and its conversion to an office would mean the loss of a very useful social centre.

The Minister said that he appreciated the difficulties confronting the appellants, but the introduction of the proposed office use into this pleasant residential areas would affect amenities, and he considered that he would not be justified in allowing it without considerably more evidence than had yet been offered that the hall could no longer serve a useful social purpose or be run without loss.

The appeal was dismissed.'

Appendix II: A Note on Changes in Planning Organization and Policy 1971–1973

Since the fourth edition of this book was prepared, in August 1971, major changes have taken place in the institutional framework of planning. Typically less dramatically there have also been shifts in planning policy. It is the purpose of this note to outline some of the more important of these.

At the time of writing (December 1973), local government re-organization in England and Wales was well under way: the new councils had been elected and are to take over from existing authorities in April 1974. In Scotland, a more far-reaching reorganization has been embodied in the Local Government (Scotland) Act, 1973. This will come into full operation in 1975.

The main lines of the legislative changes are now clear, though it will be some time (especially in Scotland) before the implications, particularly for the operation of the planning system, are apparent. Structure planning has started south of the Border, but in Scotland it has been postponed until the new authorities come into being. English experience so far has been disappointing, and some lessons have been learnt by the Scots who have made major changes in the system before it has been introduced. Both countries, however, are experiencing a major increase in planning applications and appeals. As a result, new measures are being introduced to 'streamline' the planning process.

At the same time, policies in relation to urban renewal and restructuring are placing increasing emphasis on improvement (as distinct from clearance) and on public transport (as distinct from motorways for private transport).

Citizen participation in the planning process is receiving increasing emphasis, extending (in England) to road planning. Its importance is highlighted by the new structure planning system, where it is intended largely to replace the public inquiries which were such a significant part of the former development plan system. Moreover, parish councils in England, and community councils in Wales and Scotland are being, or will be, established to represent local views and to undertake limited action on behalf of local communities.

Greater emphasis is also being placed on environmental protection, on making 'polluters' bear a greater share of the costs which they impose on the wider community, and on compensating individuals who are adversely affected by environmental pollution (a term which now has a wider meaning than was the case a few years ago).

These are the issues which have been singled out for discussion in this note. The discussion is necessarily selective and in summary form, though lists of new publications and references are given as a guide to further reading.

LOCAL GOVERNMENT REORGANIZATION IN OUTLINE

England

The Redcliffe-Maud Commission recommended fifty-eight all-purpose authorities for the whole of England outside four conurbations. One of these, Greater London, had already been reorganized on a two-tier system in the mid-sixties. For the other three (centred on Birmingham, Manchester and Liverpool) the Commission recommended a two-tier system of metropolitan and metropolitan district authorities.

The Local Government Act of 1972 rejected the unitary system, and established a two-tier system of counties and districts throughout the country. In six areas there are metropolitan counties (Greater Manchester, Merseyside, South Yorkshire, Tyne and Wear, West Midlands, and West Yorkshire) with a total of 35 metropolitan districts. Outside these metropolitan areas are 39 counties and 296 districts.

All these authorities have planning powers. The counties have responsibility for strategic planning issues while the districts have responsibility for local plans and the administration of development control. Additionally, parish councils can claim to be consulted on planning applications affecting their area.

Wales
Local government reorganization in Wales has reduced the number of local authorities from 181 to 45. In place of 13 counties, 164 districts and 4 county boroughs is a complete two-tier system of 8 counties and 37 districts. In addition there are to be community councils – the Welsh equivalent to the English parishes.

The division of responsibility for planning is broadly the same as in England.

Scotland
The Wheatley Commission recommended that the 4 Counties of Cities, 21 large burghs, 176 small burghs, 33 counties and 196 districts of Scotland should be replaced by a two-tier structure of 7 regional and 37 district authorities. With some modifications, this general structure was accepted by the Government. Following amendments made by Parliament (particularly the addition of Fife as a separate region and the exclusion of several districts around Glasgow from the Glasgow District), the Local Government (Scotland) Act, 1973 provides for a two-tier system except in the three island areas of Orkney, Shetland and the Western Islands (which become 'most-purpose' authorities).

There are 9 regional and 53 district councils. Together with the three island authorities there are thus 65 local authorities of which 49 have planning powers.

The fact that, unlike the situation in England, not all local authorities have planning powers is a result of the difficulties of devising a local government structure for those parts of the country which cover a large area but contain few people. By allocating planning powers in these areas of scattered population to the regional authority it was possible to increase the number of districts (and thereby also reduce their enormous geographical size).

There are thus three different types of area:

(i) in the Central, Fife, Grampian, Lothian, Tayside, and Strath-clyde regions planning is divided between regional and district authorities;

(ii) in the Borders, Dumfries and Galloway, and Highland regions, planning is allocated to the regions: the districts have no planning functions. These three regions are termed 'general planning authorities';

(iii) in the three island areas of Orkney, Shetland and the Western
Islands there are no districts: there is thus only one local
authority which undertakes the functions of both a regional
planning authority and a district planning authority. These
authorities are termed 'islands areas' (not regions) and are
designated as 'general planning authorities'.

In effect therefore there is a two-tier planning system in six
regions and a 'general' planning authority system elsewhere. The
former include nine-tenths of the population of Scotland.

The regions vary greatly in size and one – Strathclyde – with a
population of 2½ million, has nearly half the country's population.

Community councils are to be established in accordance with
schemes to be submitted to the Secretary of State by district and
islands authorities. It is not, as yet, clear what powers these will have.

Local Government Reorganization: Further Reading

Bristow, S. L., 'The Criteria for Local Government Reorganization
and Local Authority Autonomy', *Policy and Politics*, Vol. I, No. 2,
pp. 143-62.

DOE, Circular 74/73, *Local Government Act 1972, Town and Country
Planning: Co-operation between Authorities*, HMSO, 1973.

DOE, Circular 112/73, *Local Government Reorganisation in England:
List of Orders, Government Department Circulars etc.*, HMSO,
1973.

Eddison, T., *Local Government – Management and Corporate Planning*, Leonard Hill, 1973.

Eddison, T., 'Organization and Management in Scotland: The
Paterson Report Examined', *Town and Country Planning*, December 1973, pp. 549-50.

Greenwood, R., Smith, A. D. and Stewart, J. D., 'Corporate Planning and the Chief Officers' Group', *Local Government Studies*,
No. 1, October 1971, pp. 5-17.

Greenwood, R. and Stewart, J. D., 'Corporate Planning and Management Organization', *Local Government Studies*, No. 3, October
1972, pp. 25-40.

Jones, G. W., 'The Local Government Act 1972 and the Redcliffe-
Maud Commission', *Political Quarterly*, April/June 1973.

Long, J. and Norton, A., *Setting up the New Authorities*, Charles
Knight, 1972.

*The New Scottish Local Authorities: Organisation and Management
Structures* (Paterson Report), HMSO, 1973.

Richards, P. G., *The Reformed Local Government System*, Allen &
Unwin, 1973.

Stewart, J. D., *Management in Local Government: A Viewpoint*, Charles Knight, 1971.

Stewart, J. D., 'Developments in Corporate Planning in British Local Government', *Local Government Studies*, No. 5, June 1973, pp. 13-29.

Study Group on Local Authority Management Structures, *The New Local Authorities: Management and Structure* (Bains Report), HMSO, 1972.

Functions Removed From Local Government

One of the major reasons for reorganizing local government was to make it better able to carry out its functions. It was even hoped that some functions which had been transferred to *ad hoc* bodies could be brought back into the local government system. Paradoxically, three major functions are being taken away from local government (by separate legislation) – the personal health services, water supply and sewage disposal. Personal health services are being 'unified' under *ad hoc* area health committees and boards (together with hospitals), while the functions of river authorities, water undertakers, sewerage and sewage disposal authorities have been transferred to *ad hoc*

The New Local Government Structure

LONDON

Greater London Council
|
32 London Boroughs

ENGLAND OUTSIDE LONDON

6 Metropolitan Counties	39 Counties
35 Metropolitan Districts	296 Districts

WALES

8 Counties
|
37 Districts

SCOTLAND

Regions		*Islands*
6 Regional Planning Authorities	3 General Planning Authorities	3 General Planning Authorities
37 District Planning Authorities	16 District (not planning authorities)	

regional water authorities. On the latter see J. McLoughlin, *The Water Act 1973*, Sweet & Maxwell, 1973; DOE, *A Background to Water Reorganization in England and Wales*, HMSO, 1973; and DOE, *The New Water Industry: Management and Structure*, HMSO, 1973. For Scotland see *The Water Service in Scotland: Report of the Scottish Water Advisory Committee*, HMSO, 1972.

THE NEW PLANNING SYSTEM UNDER LOCAL GOVERNMENT REORGANIZATION

In England and Wales, the new planning system has been introduced in advance of the reorganization of local government. It is thus now necessary to adapt it to the new local government system. The Local Government Act, 1972 (Schedule 16) provides the statutory framework, and DOE Circular 74/73 offers guidance on how working arrangements between counties and districts should be evolved.

County and District Responsibilities
The legislation allocates responsibility for structure plans to the counties, while responsibilities for local plans and most matters of planning control are allocated to the districts. The essential feature of this division of responsibility is that the counties have the statutory responsibility for establishing and maintaining the general strategic policies within their areas, while the districts bear the main general responsibility for the character of development within their individual areas. However, planning cannot be so neatly divided: it is (to quote Circular 74/73) 'an interrelated process and this will need to be reflected in the arrangements made between authorities'. Statutory provisions requiring counties to consult districts on structure plans, or to certify that a local plan conforms to an approved structure plan, and such like are legalistic devices which are of far less importance than the working relationships which are established between counties and districts. These working relationships, by their very nature, must be a matter for local authorities to devise. Nevertheless, the Local Government Act provides for a specific procedure 'designed to promote effective co-operation in the planning field and to minimize delay, dispute and duplication'. This is the requirement for the preparation of a *Development Plan Scheme*. Following consultations between the county and its constituent districts, a document must be prepared (and submitted to the Secretary of State) setting out the allocation of responsibility and the programme for the preparation of local plans.

This could be the object of considerable controversy. Theoretically, it provides a legal opportunity for a county council to seize the power to undertake responsibility for local plans (though the district could appeal to the Secretary of State). But the objective is precisely the opposite: to secure a constructive and sensible relationship in plan-making between counties and districts which is appropriate to individual circumstances.

There is no parallel statutory provision for a *Development Control Scheme*, though the Secretary of State has advised that 'informal' (i.e. non-statutory) schemes should be drawn up in every area. The legislation clearly allocates responsibility for development control to districts, except in the case of 'county matters'. These include applications concerned with mineral workings, with development in national parks, and with developments which would conflict with county policy. The last (which is spelled out in some detail – if not clarity – in Section 32 of Schedule 16 to the Local Government Act) is obviously the most problematic. On the one hand it could be seen as a sensible way of giving counties reserve powers; on the other hand it could be used as a means of removing large areas of power from districts to a county.

It is, of course, too early to say how this will work out. One planning officer has nicely referred to the situation as 'a delicate balancing act',* while others have thought it more appropriate to call it 'a two-tier *double entendre*' and have stressed the difficulties which have arisen in the two-tier system which has operated in London since 1965.† Certainly the London experience cannot be considered encouraging, but it is not readily apparent how comparable London is with anywhere else.‡

Nevertheless, there is clear cause for concern at the length of time which may be needed to effect the change-over to the new structure planning system. A report of the Standing Conference on London and South-East Regional Planning§ has underlined this: 'it would be

* J. Dean, 'County Matters', *Built Environment*, December 1973. This issue of *Built Environment* is largely devoted to issues relating to development control.

† W. McKee, 'A Two-Tier *Double Entendre*', *Built Environment*, December 1973.

‡ See W. McKee, *op cit.*, for a brief discussion. Extended analyses of the working of the reorganized London local government are to be found in D. Foley, *Governing the London Region: Reorganization and Planning in the Sixties*, University of California Press, 1972; and G. Rhodes, *The New Government of London: The First Five Years*, Weidenfeld & Nicolson, 1972. For a detailed study of problems of housing policy and administration in London following reorganization see J. B. Cullingworth, *Report to the Minister of Housing and Local Government on Proposals for the Transfer of GLC Housing to the London Boroughs*, published by MHLG (now DOE), 2 vols, 1970; and the reports of the Action Group on London Housing (obtainable from DOE).

§ Standing Conference on London and South-East Regional Planning, Report LRP 2125, *The New Development Plan System*, March 1973.

optimistic to expect authenticated full plan cover, by structure and local plans, to emerge in more than a few places until the early 1980s and complete cover of the region not until the 1990s, unless major changes in the present direction of events can be engineered.... Such long time scales negate the plan-making effort, for experience in the south-east is that the pace of change is such that as the plan is being prepared and argued over, so events are invalidating the bases of the plan.'

The Report recommends a time-table for completing 'plan cover' over the south-east. Additionally it makes a number of proposals for speeding up and simplifying plans and procedures:

(i) that plans might be so presented as to distingish between proposals for positive implementation by the authorities; and (the more general case) the context against which the authority will manage the demographic, economic, social and development pressures which in fact emerge;

(ii) that written statements be limited to the fundamentals of the structure of the areas concerned and to matters directly within the control of the authorities;

(iii) that presentation separate out existing proposals and policies, already statutorily authorized, which are to be carried over intact into the new plan, and which are not for reconsideration and re-debate;

(iv) that in limiting consideration to certain matters requiring priority, initial submissions of structure plans might note other matters which will be dealt with in subsequent submissions;

(v) that work on local plans proceed concurrently with work on structure plans or in time for key local plans, in particular, to be adopted when structure plans are adopted.

These proposals would need significant legislative changes before they could be put into effect but, even so, the report concluded that they did not go far enough. A wide-ranging and 'fundamental review of the purposes and nature of development plans' was proposed.

It must be a matter for real anxiety that a new planning system introduced to overcome the shortcomings of the previous system should attract such criticism and proposals for radical change. Some changes have, in fact, already been made by the Town and Country Planning (Amendment) Act, 1972. This provides for joint structure plans to be prepared and submitted by two or more local planning authorities and, more significantly, replaces public inquiries on structure plans by 'examinations in public'.

*The Examination in Public**

Whereas a public inquiry is concerned with the hearing of objections (see pp. 301 ff. above), the examination in public is an investigation of selected matters affecting the Secretary of State's consideration of a structure plan. Though the rights of individuals to object to a structure plan (and the duty of the Secretary of State to consider all objections) are maintained, there is no longer any right for objectors to present their case at an inquiry. The examination will deal with only those matters which the Secretary of State considers need examining in public. Moreover, he will determine who shall participate in the examination (whether or not they have made objections or representations).

This is a major departure from traditional practice. Its rationale is far more than the negative one of avoiding lengthy, time-consuming and quasi-judicial public inquiries. It is related essentially to the basic purpose and character of a structure plan. A structure plan will not set out detailed proposals and, therefore, will not show how individual properties will be affected. It will deal with broad policy issues: the examination in public will focus on these and on alternatives to those set out in the plan. These will include such matters as the future level and distribution of population and employment; transportation policies; and availability of resources for major proposals of the plan.

But the examination will not deal with all the key policy issues. Only those on which the Secretary of State needs to be more fully informed by means of discussion at an examination will be selected. In short, the examination is intended to assist the Secretary of State in determining his views on the plan and in arriving at his decision.

The matters needing examination are most likely to arise from clashes between the proposals of a plan and those of a neighbouring area or wider regional and national policies. Additionally, major inconsistencies within the plan or issues on which there is unsettled controversy may be the subject of examination.

The issues selected will be published in advance (together with a list of those selected to participate). There will be an opportunity for written comments on these to be sent to the Department but, though the Secretary of State has power to add to the list of issues or participants, major changes are not envisaged since the selection will have been made on the basis of the contribution which the examination of the selected matters can make to his decision on the plan.

* See DOE Circular 72/72, and *Structure Plans: The Examination in Public*, DOE 1973. (Inexplicably, the latter document is not on sale through HMSO but can be obtained only from DOE.)

The examination will be carried out typically by a panel with an independent chairman. The chairman has the discretion (both before and during an examination) to invite additional participants.

This new procedure is as yet untried (though, at the time of writing, preparations for the first examination in public – on the Coventry Structure Plan – were in hand). It is fraught with difficulties, particularly since there is likely to be considerable criticism from any objectors who are excluded from participation in the examination. In this connection it is important to stress that the examination is envisaged as only one part of the process by which the Secretary of State considers the plan, while the plan itself is only part of the total planning process. Of crucial importance in this process is the extent to which effective citizen-participation has taken place in the preparation of the plan. This is a statutory requirement (see pp. 305–6 above) and, in submitting a structure plan to the Secretary of State, a local planning authority must include a statement on publicity, public participation and consultations. The selection of matters for examination will be closely linked to the effectiveness of the public participation which has been achieved. The hope is that public participation will highlight the crucial issues on which alternative policies need to be examined.

National Parks*

Under the Local Government Act, planning functions in a national park are largely allocated to county councils which must establish a National Park Committee to carry out these functions. There are, however, exceptional provisions for the Lake District and the Peak District: here new Planning Boards are to be set up.

For each national park, a National Park Officer must be appointed (after consultation with the Countryside Commission). A National Park Plan must be prepared (by April 1977) setting out the policy for the management of the park and 'the exercise of the functions exercisable' in relation to the park.

A number of functions are, however, to be carried out by district councils concurrently with a park committee or board (e.g. tree preservation, treatment of derelict land, public access, and the provision of country parks). Moreover, there is provision (subject to the agreement of the Countryside Commission) for arrangements to be made with district councils to carry out any of the functions of a committee or board on an agency basis.

How all this will work out is, at the time of writing, unclear.

* DOE, Circular 63/73, *Local Government Act 1972: Administration of National Parks*, HMSO, 1973.

THE NEW SYSTEM IN SCOTLAND

The new local government organization in Scotland (which comes into effect in 1975) has already been outlined. The Scottish Local Government Act, however, introduces new planning provisions which are significantly different from those south of the Border. Some may be attributed to the much more thorough-going nature of the Scottish local government reorganization; others may legitimately be attributed to a canny move to avoid some of the difficulties which can be expected in the English system (and which have been highlighted in the report of the Standing Conference on London and South-East Regional Planning).

The three major changes in planning legislation are the introduction of 'regional reports', an amendment of the mandatory provisions relating to structure plans, and a provision under which local plans can be prepared in advance of structure plans.

Regional Reports
Some of the Scottish regions are far larger than is appropriate for a structure plan. Nevertheless, there is a need for a policy plan to cover the whole of the area. This need is met by the innovation of the 'regional report'. But the opportunity has been taken to make this a flexible feature of the new planning system. Though it may indeed relate to the whole of a region, the legislation enables it to be used to serve a variety of purposes. It may be used to provide a basis of discussion between the Secretary of State and a region about general development policy; it may provide a basis of guidance for the preparation or review of structure plans; and, in the absence of a structure plan, it may serve as a guide to district planning authorities and developers on planning policies. A regional report may cover the whole or only a part of a region. Moreover, it may be restricted in its scope to particular issues.

In striking contrast to structure plans, there is no formal procedure for the preparation, submission or approval of a regional report. The only requirements are that a regional report shall be based on a survey, that affected local authorities shall be consulted, that it shall be submitted to the Secretary of State (who shall 'make observations' on it) and that it shall be published (together with the Secretary of State's observations).

Though the Secretary of State will not formally approve or amend a regional report, planning authorities will be required, in their planning practice, to 'take account' of both the report and of the Secretary of State's 'observations'.

The Secretary of State will also be able to direct a regional or planning authority to submit a regional report and, in default, to prepare a regional report himself.

Structure Plans for Parts of an Area

As originally envisaged, structure plans were to be single plans covering the whole area of the authority responsible for its pre-paration. Though there was provision for a structure plan to be submitted by instalments, the assumption was that these would eventually build up to a single plan which would then be kept up to date as a whole. This concept is radically changed by provisions introduced in the 1973 Local Government Act. Regional and general planning authorities will be able to prepare structure plans for different parts of their areas. The intention here is that the regions should be divided into areas which, by virtue of their geography and cohesion in terms of socio-economic structure and the pattern of communications, form natural structure plan units. Moreover, it will no longer be necessary for all parts of a region to be covered by structure plans.

The significance of this change is more striking when it is appre-ciated that, with the introduction of regional reports, there will be three (not two) levels of planning: regional, structure and local. It is unlikely that all three will be necessary in all areas. It is much more likely that regional reports and structure plans will be seen as alternatives. At the least, there will be the possibility of a flexible approach which the English system denies.

Given this loosening-up of the procedures for large-scale planning it is not surprising that changes have also been made in relation to local plans.

Local Plans

Local plans were conceived as detailed elaborations of proposals sketched out as matters of broad policy in a structure plan (see p. 102 above). This concept is abandoned in the 1973 Act: 'every general and district planning authority shall, as soon as practicable, prepare local plans for all parts of their district'. Thus local plans are to be mandatory and are to be prepared as soon as possible and thus (probably typically) in advance of a structure plan.

The only qualification to this is in cases where a structure plan (or a regional report) is under way and would have a significant impact on the area to be covered by a proposed local plan. Effect is given to this by requiring a district planning authority to obtain the consent of the regional planning authority to the preparation of a local plan. This consent is not to be unreasonably withheld and the district will have the right of appeal to the Secretary of State. (In line with the current emphasis on avoidance of formal proceedings, there would not be a public inquiry: the Secretary of State would decide the matter as simply as possible and his decision would be final.) This procedure, of course, does not apply to general planning authorities since they are responsible for regional, structure and local plans.

Local plans remain the responsibility of the districts (except in the areas of general planning authorities) and therefore are subject to 'approval' only by the authorities who prepare them – unless they are 'called in'. This may be done either by the Secretary of State or by the regional planning authority. Again there is machinery for appeal but no public inquiry.

The 'call-in' power of regional authorities is a new one. The circumstances in which this can be used are set out in the 1973 Act and are:

(i) when a local plan is urgently required to implement the provisions of an approved structure plan, and the district planning authority concerned have failed to adopt an appropriate local plan: *or*

(ii) when the district of more than one district planning authority is likely to be affected by the local plan in question; *or*

(iii) when the local plan does not conform to a structure plan approved by the Secretary of State; *or*

(iv) when the implementation of the local plan will render unlikely the implementation of any other local plan relating to their district.

Development Control
Development control is a district or general planning authority function but, as in England, certain powers are allocated to the upper-tier authority. The powers of the region are, however, not as far reaching (or set out in detail) as in the case of the English counties. Moreover, there is no reference to 'county matters'. The Scottish provisions simply supplement the powers previously exercised solely by the Secretary of State by a power of regional planning authorities to call in applications where:

(i) the proposed development does not conform to a structure plan approved by the Secretary of State; *or*

(ii) the proposed development raises a new planning issue of general significance to the district of the regional planning authority.

This power is exercisable only in cases where the application is not called in by the Secretary of State himself.

Planning appeals will continue to be lodged with the Secretary of State, but regional planning authorities will be notified of all appeals and have the right to take part in the appeal proceedings. Regional planning authorities will also be informed of proposals for revocation, modification and discontinuance of use orders and can make representations or objections on them to the Secretary of State. Finally, they will have default powers to make such orders themselves if they think that an order is necessary to prevent 'material prejudice' to an approved structure plan.

These powers of a regional planning authority in relation to development control are essentially rights of intervention to give effect to regional planning policies. They are defined in straightforward terms (avoiding the complexities of the English legislation). In all cases there are simple rights of appeal to the Secretary of State to enable him to resolve any disputes between a district and a region.

Countryside Planning

Countryside responsibilities, rather confusingly, 'shall be a general, regional or district' function. This overlap of function is deliberate and presumably implies that regions shall meet regional needs while districts meet district needs.

There are no national parks in Scotland and thus no need for the revised administrative arrangements embodied in the English 1972 Act.

Land Resource Use in Scotland

A massive study of *Land Resource Use in Scotland* was undertaken by the Select Committee on Scottish Affairs during 1971–2. (Its report and evidence were published in five volumes, under this title, by HMSO: H.C. 511 (i) to (v), October 1972.)

The Committee concluded that there was a need to improve the system of land use planning, particularly at the national level. They argued that there should be a national structure plan for Scotland, embodying a national industrial strategy; that 'a more integrated and comprehensive view of urban land use' was required to improve the quality of the urban environment and that it was necessary to bring together in closer consultation all the bodies responsible for individual land uses in the countryside. New machinery was proposed for these purposes:

(i) a top level working party to recommend the content of a structure plan for Scotland, including a national industrial strategy with a system of advance zoning and acquisition of land for industrial purposes;

(ii) a Commission for the Urban Environment to advise on urban environmental standards and how they may be achieved;

(iii) a Land Use Council drawn from individuals of high standing and long experience to act as a central forum for discussion of rural land use and to make recommendations to the Government;

(iv) a Land Use Unit of professional planners to give advice to Ministers on present land use options and to warn of future difficulties.

This emphasis on institutional innovations was largely rejected by the Government. (See *Land Resource Use in Scotland: The Government's Observations on the Report of the Select Committee on Scottish Affairs*, HMSO, Cmnd. 5428, 1973.) In particular, 'decisions in both development planning and development control must continue to be taken by elected representatives: no appointed body, however eminent its members, ought to be invested with powers which conflict, or seem to conflict with this principle'. The Government's view was that the shortcomings identified by the Select Committee could be rectified by making better use of the existing machinery (which, in any case, was about to undergo extensive reorganization) and by two significant additions to it: a Standing Conference of Regional Authorities and a Standing Committee on Rural Land Use.

The Select Committee's review extended over a wide field – from citizen participation to derelict land, from Muirburn to the designation of further new towns, and from information systems to planning manpower.

It is self-evidently impossible to deal with this enormous range of issues in a short note, but the interested reader is referred to Volume I of the Select Committee's Report (H.C. 511 (i), 1972) and the Government's observations in the White Paper of 1973 (Cmnd. 5428).

STREAMLINING THE PLANNING MACHINE

In 1970 there were 360,936 planning applications in England and Wales. In 1971 the number rose to 404,455, and in 1972 to the unprecedented figure of 547,927. A similar 50 per cent increase was experienced in Scotland. At the same time, the number of planning appeals increased: in England and Wales, from less than 9,000 in 1970 to over 14,000 in 1972. Both trends continued in 1973.

This unforeseen situation has developed at the very time when local authorities are also facing the problems of reorganization and of the introduction of structure planning. The pressure is thus for some 'streamlining' of the planning machine, even to the extent of introducing a *deemed approval* for applications which are not decided within the statutory two months' period. (It is unlikely that this would be an effective way of expediting procedures: it is more likely that it would lead to wholesale refusals and consequent appeals.) The DOE have increased their inspectorate to deal with appeals and have issued advice (in Circular 142/73) on a wide range of administrative matters related to planning applications. They have also appointed Mr G. Dobry QC to undertake a rapid review of the development control system. His terms of reference are:

(i) 'To consider whether the development control system under the Town and Country Planning Acts adequately meets current needs and to advise on the lines along which it might be improved, bearing in mind the forthcoming redistribution of planning functions between local authorities, and the new system of structure and local plans.'

(ii) 'To review the arrangements for appeals to the Secretary of State under the Planning Acts, including the right of appeal and the handling of appeals in the Department of the Environment, and to make recommendations.'

There is no specific mention here of the still mounting public concern about 'the environment' and pressures for more – and more effective – public participation (though Circular 142/73 refers to both). A revised development control system will need to take these demands into account. Whether effective and acceptable proposals for a revised system can be elaborated in the six months which the Dobry review has been given remains to be seen.

For a list of the questions which Dobry has prepared in connection with his review see *Built Environment*, December 1973. See also DOE Circular 142/73, *Streamlining the Planning Machine*, HMSO, 1973, and T. Hancock, 'A Trojan Mule', *Town and Country Planning*, December 1973, pp. 542-4. *Planning Applications for Industrial Buildings* are dealt with in DOE Circular 30/72 which bears this title (HMSO, 1972). Statistics on planning decisions are published annually in DOE, *Statistics for Town and Country Planning, Series I, Planning Decisions: Statistics of Decisions on Planning Applications*, HMSO. (Series II relates to floor space in industrial, shopping, office and other uses, while Series III relates to population and households.)*

* Note: Since this was written, Dobry has presented an interim report: DOE *Review of the Development Control System: Interim Report*, HMSO, January 1974.

PROTECTION OF THE ENVIRONMENT

Conservation

The Town and Country Planning (Amendment) Act, 1972 introduced government grants and loans for 'preservation or enhancement of character or appearance of conservation areas'. It also provided powers for the control of the demolition of unlisted buildings in conservation areas. Details are given in DOE Circular 86/72, *Town and Country Planning (Amendment) Act 1972: Conservation*, HMSO, 1972.

A broad statement of government policy on conservation was given by Lord Sandford in the 'quality of life' debate in the House of Lords on January 31, 1973:

'We need full and firm conservation policies. Past and present conservation work has concentrated upon areas of exceptionally important landscape and historic townscape. Steps are taken to conserve buildings of high architectural merit or historic importance. But the new approach must be broader than this. It can be realised within the present plan-making procedures. It should take account of the growth of public opinion in favour of conserving the familiar and cherished local scene. It should also have care for the conservation of existing communities and the social fabric, wherever public opinion points clearly towards it. Conservation of the character of cities ought more strongly to influence planners at all stages of their work; conservation of the character of cities should be the starting point for thought about the extent of redevelopment needs; and conservation of the character of cities should be the framework for planning both the scale and the pace of urban change.'

Four implications of this are spelled out in DOE, Circular 46/73, *Conservation and Preservation: Local Government Act 1972*.

First, the new local authorities must have fully adequate arrangements for professional advice. The Local Government Act, 1972 gives the Secretary of State powers to issue directions to local authorities whose arrangements he considers to be inadequate.

Secondly, 'there must be imaginative although not necessarily costly provision for the enhancement of conservation areas, not least in preparing for European Architectural Heritage Year'. In addition to the normal grants now available under Town and Country Planning (Amendment) Act, 1972, a once-and-for-all grant of £150,000 has been announced (for England and Wales) over the period 1973–5 'for those conservation schemes, carried out in connection with European Architectural Heritage Year, which are in conservation areas not considered to be outstanding'. Grants made under this scheme are termed 'Heritage Year' grants.

The European Architectural Heritage Year has been designated (for 1975) by the Council of Europe – thus illustrating the fact that increased concern for the environment is by no means a British phenomenon. The objectives are 'to awaken the interest of the European peoples in their common architectural heritage; to protect and enhance buildings and areas of architectural or historic interest; to conserve the character of old towns and villages; and to assure for ancient buildings a living role in contemporary society'. (See DOE Circular 86/72, *op. cit.*)

The third implication is that 'there must be dissemination of practical information for councillors and others on ways in which the environment can be improved'. (On this see DOE, *New Life for Old Buildings*, HMSO, 1971 and *New Life for Historic Areas*, HMSO, 1973.)

Finally, 'there should be full co-operation with like-minded amenity bodies'. (See Civic Trust, *Pride of Place*, published by the Trust.)

Lorries and the Environment

Mention can also be made here (though it is equally relevant to the section on Transport) of the environmental impact of the lorry. On this see H.C. Debates, November 29, 1972; DOE Circular 57/63, *Lorries and the Environment*, HMSO, 1973; DOE Circular 115/73, *Long-Distance Lorries: National Network of Secure Parks*, HMSO, 1973; D. Sharp, *Living with the Lorry: A Study of the Goods Vehicle in the Environment*, Freight Transport Association and Road Haulage Association, 1973; Greater London Council, *Traffic and the Environment*, GLC, 1972; and the *Heavy Commercial Vehicles (Controls and Regulations) Act 1973*; DOE, *Lorries and the World We Live In*, HMSO, 1973; also references quoted in the section on Transport.

Protection of the Environment Bill

Chapter VIII of this book carries the same title as that of a Bill presented in the House of Lords in November 1973 (see H.L. Debates, Vol. 347, November 27, 1973). Following a series of reports by the Royal Commission on Environmental Pollution and other bodies (selectively listed below) and heightened public concern – the Bill 'makes further provision with respect to waste disposal, water pollution, noise, atmospheric pollution and injurious substances; and for purposes connected with the matters aforesaid'.

The Bill is a complex one and, of course, may be amended during its passage through parliament. Hence no attempt is made here to summarize its provisions, but one illustration can be given. The Bill provides for the designation of 'noise abatement zones' in which local authorities will be able to control noise levels. Local authorities will also be able to control the noise on building and demolition sites. Particularly noteworthy are the new powers for enforcement and review. For example, an offender can be fined for every day on which the offence continues. The powers to regulate levels of noise (and pollution) enable standards to be changed without the need for fresh legislation.

There is now a virtual library of material on the protection of the environment. References listed below are only a selection of the more recent publications:

Central Office of Information, *Towards Cleaner Air: A Review of Britain's Achievements*, HMSO, 1973.

DOE, *Report of a River Pollution Survey of England and Wales 1970*, HMSO, Vol. I 1971, Vol. II 1972.

DOE, *Report of a Survey of the Discharges of Foul Sewage to Coastal Waters of England and Wales*, HMSO, 1973.

Friends of the Earth, *Evidence to the Committee on Mineral Planning Control*, FOE, June 1972.

Noise Advisory Council, *Neighbourhood Noise: Report by the Working Group on the Noise Abatement Act*, HMSO, 1971.

Noise Advisory Council, *Aircraft Noise: Flight Routeing Near Airports*, HMSO, 1971.

Noise Advisory Council, *Traffic Noise: The Vehicle Regulations and their Enforcement*, HMSO, 1972.

Porter, E., *Pollution in Four Industrialised Estuaries: Four Case Studies Undertaken for the Royal Commission on Environmental Pollution*, HMSO, 1973.

Royal Commission on Environmental Pollution, *Second Report: Three Issues in Industrial Pollution*, Cmnd. 4894, HMSO, 1972.

Royal Commission on Environmental Pollution, *Third Report: Pollution in Some British Estuaries and Coastal Waters*, Cmnd. 5054, HMSO, 1972.

Scottish Development Department, *Towards Cleaner Water: Report of a Rivers Pollution Survey of Scotland*, HMSO, 1972.

Solicitors' Ecology Group, *Ecology: The Lawyer's Role?*, published by the Group, 34 South Molton Street, London W1, 1972.

Wain, P., *Spring Cleaning Britain* (derelict land), Bow Group, undated.

Warren Spring Laboratory, *National Survey of Air Pollution 1961-71*, 2 vols, HMSO, 1972.

TRANSPORT PLANNING AND URBAN RENEWAL

Urban Motorways Committee

In July 1972, the report of the Urban Motorways Committee was published (DOE, *New Roads in Towns*, HMSO, 1972). This Committee was established, under the chairmanship of Sir James Jones, with the following terms of reference:

(i) to examine present policies used in fitting major roads into urban areas;

(ii) to consider what changes would enable urban roads to be related better to their surroundings, physically, visually and socially;

(iii) to examine the consequences of such changes, particularly from the points of view of:

    (*a*) limitations on resources, both public and private;

    (*b*) changes in statutory powers and administrative procedures;

    (*c*) any issue of public policy that the changes would raise;

(iv) to recommend what changes, if any, should be made.

The Committee were supported by a full-time team of officials who had the responsibility for a series of research studies and for the preparation of material on problems and procedures. Their report was published separately (*Report of the Urban Motorways Project Team to the Urban Motorways Committee*, HMSO, 1973).

The Committee's main recommendation was that 'the planning of new urban roads should form an integral part of planning the urban area as a whole and that indirect costs and benefits of building urban roads should be looked at with the same care as the direct cost and movement benefits'.

The first part of this recommendation led (in conjunction with an unpublished review of compensation law) to the White Paper, *Development and Compensation – Putting People First* (Cmnd. 5124, 1972) and the land Compensation Act, 1973 (which applies to Scotland as well as to England and Wales).* The second led to a new system of transport grants and the introduction of Transport Plans and Programmes. (These have been elaborated for England and Wales, but it is expected that the Scottish system will follow the same lines.)

The major emphasis in the first of these changes is on giving a greater priority to the social and human implications of road and other types of public development. As the White Paper put it:

* The Scottish provisions were re-enacted in the Land Compensation (Scotland) Act, 1973.

'The Government believe the time has come when all concerned with development must aim to achieve a better balance between provision for the community as a whole and the mitigation of harmful effects on the individual citizen. In recent years this balance in too many cases has been tipped against the interests of the individual. A better deal is now required for those who suffer from desirable community developments. . . . The answer is not to stop community developments that would make life more comfortable, convenient and pleasant. To do that would simply deprive many people of the opportunity of a better environment. The answer must be to plan new development so as to minimise the disturbance and disruption they can cause and to improve the compensation code to alleviate any remaining distress.'

But to talk of 'desirable community developments' begs the issue, and the very pressures which led to the review of road planning procedures and compensation have also led to a more searching attitude to development proposals. Thus the question is no longer how best to develop a road, but whether a road is needed at all, and whether it is not better to allocate the resources to public transport. This was a main theme of the Expenditure Committee's Report on *Urban Transport Planning* (H.C. Paper 57, 3 vols, HMSO, December 1972), and arose not only from an appreciation of the physical consequences of major urban highways and their effects on the communities through which they pass, but also from a growing awareness of the wider distributional consequences of current transport policies and the social significance of personal mobility. (See the *Report*, paragraphs 25 and 59–61; and the evidence of Meyer Hillman, pages 235–50; also M. Hillman *et al.*, *Personal Mobility and Transport Policy*, PEP Broadsheet 542, 1973.) The Committee went so far as to recommend that policy should be directed towards promoting public transport and discouraging the use of cars for the journey to work in city centres. Government policy is moving in this direction, but the current emphasis is on comprehensive planning (through the *Transport Policies and Programmes* – the TPPs) which will cover the whole transport field: roads, public transport, parking, traffic management and the movement of goods. (See *Government Observations on the Second Report of the Expenditure Committee: Urban Transport Planning*, Cmnd. 5366, HMSO, 1973; and DOE Circular 104/73, *Local Transport Grants*, HMSO, 1973.)

An interesting illustration of the mounting pressures is provided by the inquiry into the Bromsgrove section of the M42. Though DOE had widened the scope of their provisions for 'Participation in Road

Planning',* their 'statement of case' for this road included the warning that:

'The Government's policy to build these new motorways will not be open to debate at the forthcoming inquiries; the Secretary of State is answerable to Parliament for this policy. But objectors will be free to argue, if they so wish, that the M42 Bromsgrove section and M40 Warwick section should not be built upon the line at present proposed by the Secretary of State. . . .'

But after considerable objection to this, the offending passage was withdrawn, and it was agreed that objectors would be 'in no way debarred from presenting any argument that they consider relevant'. (See *Transport 2000*, Autumn 1973.)

It is not only in relation to roads that public opinion (or, at least, articulate public opinion) and government policy is changing: the same applies to slum clearance and urban redevelopment. Recent White Papers (and legislation promised for 1974) explicitly accept that 'in the majority of cases it is no longer preferable to solve the problems arising from bad housing by schemes of widespread, comprehensive redevelopment'. The English White Paper continues:

'Such an approach often involves massive and unacceptable disruption of communities and leaves vast areas of our cities standing derelict and devastated for far too long. Regardless of the financial compensation they receive [sic], many people suffer distress when their homes are compulsorily acquired. Increasing local opposition to redevelopment proposals is largely attributable to people's understandable preference for the familiar and, in many ways, more convenient environment in which they have lived for years. Large-scale redevelopment frequently diminishes rather than widens the choice available to people in terms of the style of houses, their form of tenure and their price.'

(This quotation is from *Better Homes: The Next Priorities*, Cmnd. 5339, HMSO, 1973. The Scottish White Paper was entitled *Towards Better Homes: Proposals for Dealing with Scotland's Older Housing*, Cmnd. 5338, HMSO, 1973. Earlier White Papers were published in 1973: *Widening the Choice – the Next Steps in Housing*, Cmnd. 5280; and *Homes for People – Scottish Housing Policy in the 1970s*, Cmnd.

* See the DOE 'Consultation paper' with this title (published by DOE in March 1973) and the paper of the same title (published by DOE in July 1973). Regrettably neither is obtainable through normal booksellers or from HMSO, but copies can be obtained direct from DOE, 2 Marsham Street, London SW1.

5272. See also Tenth Report from the Expenditure Committee: *House Improvement Grants*, H.C. 349, June 1973; and Liverpool Shelter Neighbourhood Action Project, *Another Chance for Cities: SNAP 69/72*, Shelter, 1972.)

Three major principles arise from this rapid survey: that individuals should be better compensated for the harmful effects of development, that they should have a greater say in decisions affecting their lives, and that a greater emphasis should be placed on improvement (e.g. of public transport, housing and the environment) and a lesser emphasis on redevelopment.

These principles are in process of being incorporated in new legislation but (at December 1973) only one Act had been passed: the Land Compensation Act. The following discussion is therefore restricted to this.

The Land Compensation Act 1973
The law relating to compensation is inevitably complex, and no summary of the 1973 Act can be adequate. Greater detail (and hence accuracy) is to be found in DOE Circular 73/73, *Land Compensation Act 1973*, HMSO, 1973; DOE Roads Circular 44/73, *Land Compensation Act 1973: A New Approach to the Planning and Design of Roads* (obtainable only from DOE); and, for Scotland, SDD Circular 84/1973, *Land Compensation (Scotland) Act 1973* (obtainable only from SDD).

The provisions of the Act can usefully be discussed under the five headings which relate to the five main parts of the Act.

(i) *Compensation for depreciation caused by use of public works*: this creates a new statutory right to compensation for a fall in the value of property arising from the use of highways, aerodromes and other public works which have immunity from actions for 'nuisance'. The depreciation has to be caused by physical factors such as noise, fumes, dust and vibration and the compensation is payable by the authority responsible for the works. The use of new roads or runways are thought to be the most likely to give rise to such depreciation.

(ii) *Mitigation of injurious effect of public works*: there is a range of new powers under this heading, e.g. in relation to sound insulation; the purchase of owner-occupied property which is severely affected by construction work or by the use of a new or improved highway; the erection of physical barriers (such as walls, screens or mounds of earth) on or alongside roads to reduce the effects of traffic noise on people living nearby; the planting of trees and the grassing of areas; and the development or redevelopment of land for the specific purpose of improving the surroundings of a highway 'in a manner desirable by reason of its construction, improvement, existence or use'.

(iii) *Provision for benefit of persons displaced from land*: of particular significance here is the introduction of Home Loss Payments as a mark of recognition of the special hardship created by compulsory dispossession of one's home. Since these payments are for this purpose they are quite separate from, and are not dependent upon, any right to compensation or the new 'disturbance payment' which is described below. Logically they apply to tenants as well as to owner-occupiers and are given for all displacements whether by compulsory purchase, redevelopment or any action under the Housing Acts.

Additionally, there is a general entitlement to a Disturbance Payment for persons who are not entitled to compensation, and local authorities are given a duty 'to secure the provision of suitable alternative accommodation where this is not otherwise available on reasonable terms, for any person displaced from residential accommodation' by acquisition, redevelopment, demolition and closing orders, etc. This provision goes a long way towards implementing the recommendation on rehousing obligations of the Central Housing Advisory Committee. (See CHAC, *Council Housing: Purposes, Procedures and Priorities*, HMSO, 1969, Chapter 7.)

(iv) *Compulsory Purchase*: a number of changes are made in the law relating to the assessment of compensation. These are aimed at improving the provisions and meeting some particular problems. A right is also given to the advance payment of compensation.

(v) *Planning Blight*: important changes are made to the planning blight provisions. In particular the classes of land in respect of which blight notices may be served are extended, for example, to land affected by proposals in structure plans or local plans submitted to the Secretary of State, to new town areas covered by a draft or substantive New Town Designation Order, and to dwellings and other buildings within areas declared to be a clearance area (in Scotland, a housing treatment area).

Transport Policies and Programmes
'Transport Policies and Programmes' constitute an important element in the emerging new system in England and Wales. These TPPs will be statements of policies relating to all transport matters and a financial statement for the transportation element of structure and local plans. The new system also involves a new grant system (which replaces the existing specific grants for highway and public

transport expenditure). Details are given in DOE Circular 104/73, *Local Transport Grants*, HMSO, 1973).

The new system (subject to parliamentary approval of the necessary legislation) is proposed to come into effect for the financial year 1975-6. Its major purpose is to facilitate the consideration of transport problems comprehensively and in the wider context of land use planning. The 1972 Local Government Act (sections 202-3) places the duty on the new county councils to promote the provision of efficient and co-ordinated systems of public transport and the power to support them financially. (For Scotland see sections 150-1 of the 1973 Local Government (Scotland), Act.) Together with existing highway and traffic regulation powers, these new provisions enable county councils to develop and implement comprehensive transport plans. But the multiplicity of transport grants (at different rates, some payable to operators, others to local authorities) is not suited to the comprehensive approach envisaged and they are therefore being replaced by a new system (for which powers are provided in the Local Government Bill: if passed, this will become the Local Government Act 1974. It applies only to England and Wales).

The new system proposes that:

(i) as many as possible of the existing specific grants will be replaced by a new unified system covering current as well as capital expenditure, and public transport as well as roads;

(ii) part of the money at present distributed in these specific grants will be absorbed into the 'needs element' of the rate support grant;

(iii) the remainder will be distributed as a 'supplementary transport grant' for the year to each county whose estimated programme of expenditure exceeds a prescribed 'threshold' (this has still to be defined and elaborated);

(iv) on the basis of approved estimates capital programmes (loan sanctions) will be approved.

This system (which will take several years to come into full operation) represents a major shift in transport policy. Two particularly interesting features are, first, that grant will be based not on the actual cost of individual schemes (the traditional procedure), but on county programmes of estimated expenditure backed by a comprehensive statement of transport policies for the area. (This also allows a major reduction in detailed central government controls.) Secondly, financial support for public transport will be largely channelled through local authorities instead of being paid direct to operators.

It is in this financial context that TPPs assume an important operational status. They will be annual statements of policy which will form the basis for the supplementary transport grant and for loan sanctions. Detailed advice on TPPs is to be issued, but it will contain not only financial estimates for the year but also (*a*) a statement of the county's transport objectives and strategy over a ten to fifteen year period; (*b*) a five-year rolling programme for the implementation of the strategy; and (*c*) a statement of past expenditure and physical progress, and the extent to which objectives and policies are being met.

Further References on Transport

Beesley, M., *Urban Transport: Studies in Economic Policy*, Butterworth, 1973.

Casement, R., 'Urban Traffic: Policies in Congestion', *The Economist*, Brief No. 30, 1972.

DOE, *Getting the Best Roads for our Money: the COBA Method of Appraisal*, HMSO, 1972.

DOE, Circular 104/73, *Local Transport Grants*, HMSO, 1973.

Greater London Council, *Traffic and the Environment*, GLC, 1972.

National Old People's Welfare Council, *Age Concern on Transport*, NOPWC, 1971.

Society of County Borough Treasurers. *Public Transport in Urban Areas*, 1972.

Starkie, D. N. M., 'Transportation Planning and Public Policy', *Progress in Planning*, Vol. I, No. 4, Pergamon Press, 1973.

SHORTER NOTES

Population

Population projections continue to be revised downwards. Projections for the year 2000 made between 1960 to 1972 are as follows:

Base Year of Projection	*Projected Population in 2000*	
	England and Wales (thousands)	Scotland (thousands)
1960	55,646	6,348
1964	65,680	6,888
1968	60,211	5,944
1970	58,197	5,857
1972	54,687	5,571

For a fuller discussion than is possible here see the author's *The Social Framework of Planning*, Allen & Unwin, 1972, Chapter I, 'The Demographic Framework'; and the new annual publication of the Office of Population Censuses and Surveys, *Population*

Projections, HMSO. Reference can also be made to DOE, *Long-Term Population Distribution in Great Britain*, HMSO, 1971 (of which the final chapter is reprinted in *Planning for Change*, edited by J. B. Cullingworth, Allen & Unwin, 1972). The broadest official population study since the 1949 Royal Commission on Population is the *Report of the Population Panel*, Cmnd. 5258, HMSO, 1973. See also the Reports from the Select Committee on Science and Technology, Session 1970–1, *Population of the United Kingdom*, H.C. Paper 379, HMSO, 1971; and Session 1971–2, *Population Policy*, H.C. Paper 335, HMSO, 1972.

The increasing concern on 'the population question' is reflected in the appointment of the Lord President of the Council as the Minister responsible for co-ordinating future work on population matters (see H.C. Debates, December 18, 1973).

The 1972 Use Classes Order
A revised Use Classes Order came into operation in October 1972 (Statutory Instrument 1972, No. 1358). It takes account of increasing public concern about the freedom under the replaced Order to establish certain kinds of premises without 'development' being involved. Thus launderettes, cafés and restaurants are excluded from the definition of a 'shop' and a change to one of these uses (from, e.g. a fruit shop) now needs specific permission.

See pp. 82–3 above and DOE Circular 97/72, *The Town and Country Planning (Use Classes) Order 1972*, HMSO, 1972.

The 1973 General Development Order
The 1973 General Development Order (Statutory Instrument 1973, No. 31) consolidates, with amendments, the GDO 1963 and five subsequent amending orders. Details are given in DOE Circular 12/73, *Town and Country Planning General Development Order, 1973*, HMSO, 1973.

Development by Government Departments and Statutory Undertakers
At one time, development by government departments and statutory undertakers was either exempted from planning provisions or effectively beyond their reach (see p. 92 above). This privileged position has gradually been eroded. Development by government departments is now subject to new arrangements which are set out in DOE Circular 80/71 (replacing the 1950 Circular No. 100 of the Ministry of Town and Country Planning). The main changes are:

(i) Proposals for development by government departments will in general be given publicity in the same way as proposals for private development.

(ii) The extent to which departments will undertake development without consultation is redefined by reference to the kind of development permitted by the General Development Order.

(iii) Proposals to demolish or materially to alter buildings of special architectural or historic interest are brought formally within the system for the first time.

(iv) Proposals are subject to time limits on the start of development. (On this see also DOE Circular 71/72.)

For statutory undertakers a 'code of practice' has been drawn up and 'commended' to the statutory undertakers by the appropriate Ministers. See Appendix C to DOE Circular 12/73 *Town and Country Planning General Development Order 1973*, HMSO, 1973 or paragraphs 25–30 of DOE Circular 71/73, *Publicity for Planning Applications, Appeals and Other Proposals for Development*, HMSO, 1973.

The Coastline
The Countryside Commission proposed (see p. 212 above) that certain stretches of coastline of particular scenic quality should be designated 'Heritage Coasts'. While endorsing the underlying objective, the Government have decided that it is not necessary to introduce any new statutory designation procedure. Instead they suggest that the Commission should consider whether Heritage Coasts which are not already in a national park or area of outstanding natural beauty should be designated as the latter, and that the policies to be pursued in the Heritage Coasts should be incorporated (as appropriate) in structure and local plans. Pending the preparation of such plans, local planning authorities should prepare 'non-statutory interim plans'. (See DOE Circular 12/72, *The Planning of the Undeveloped Coast*, HMSO, 1972.)

Water Space Amenity Commission
Under the Water Act 1973 (which establishes regional water authorities in England, the Welsh National Water Authority, and a National Water Council) a Water Space Amenity Commission is to be set up. It will have the duty to advise the Secretary of State, after consultation with such bodies as the Countryside Commission and the Sports Council, on 'the formulation, promotion and execution of the national policy for water so far as relating to recreation and amenity in England'.

Neither the title of this body nor its objectives are expressed in language which could be called poetic, and it is unclear how its responsibilities relate to the bodies it is required to consult or the Waterways Board (which was originally to be abolished). The amenity and recreation provisions of the Water Act were substantially amended during the passage of the Bill through Parliament and it remains to be seen how they will work out.

(See *Fifth Annual Report of the Countryside Commission 1971-2*, HMSO, pp. 1-2; DOE, *The New Water Industry: Management and Structure*, HMSO, 1973; and M. Dower, 'Water and Recreation', *Town and Country Planning*, April 1973, pp. 211-12.)

The New Sports Council
Between 1965 and 1971, an advisory Sports Council operated under ministerial chairmanship. In the latter year it was succeeded by a new Council (now incorporated by Royal Charter), with executive functions and an independent chairman. Since 1972 it has had the function of administering central government grants to sport. The nine regional Sports Councils now have extended responsibilities. These are set out, together with details of the grant system in DOE Circular 1/73, *Provision for Sport and Physical Recreation*, HMSO, 1973.

Other References
Broads Consortium, *Broadland Study and Plan*, Norfolk County Council, 1971.
Colenut, R. J. and Sidaway, R. M., *Forest of Dean Day Visitor Survey*, Forestry Commission Bulletin 46, HMSO, 1973.
Countryside Commission, *Recreation News* and *Recreation News Supplement*, published by the Commission regularly.
DOE, *Provision for Sport: Indoor Swimming Pools, Indoor Sports Centres, Golf Courses*, HMSO, 1972.
DOE, Circular 12/72, *The Planning of the Undeveloped Coast*, HMSO, 1972.
DOE, Circular 1/73, *Provision for Sport and Physical Recreation*, HMSO, 1973.
Owen, M. C. and Duffield, B. S., *The Touring Caravan in Scotland*, Scottish Tourist Board, 1971.
Second Report from the Select Committee of the House of Lords on Sport Leisure, H.L. 193, 3 vols, HMSO, 1973.
Seeley, J. H., *Outdoor Recreation and the Urban Environment*, Macmillan, 1973.

Industrial and Regional Development
In March 1972, a White Paper *Industrial and Regional Development* (Cmnd. 4942) outlined the 'new measures to stimulate industrial growth and create confidence'. It was stated as a self-evident truth

that these had to be 'as clear, simple and certain in their impact as possible'.

The new measures were aimed at both national and regional industrial development and were designed to be complementary. The former took the form of improved tax allowances for investment in plant, machinery and buildings. The latter were in the form of grants. The separation of tax allowances (for national policies) and grants (for regional policies) allowed for independent administration: 'this will make for greater speed and simplicity, and industry will know clearly what help it can expect'.

The White Paper proposals were implemented by the Industry Act 1972. (In addition to the White Paper see the memorandum of DTI to the Expenditure Committee on *Regional Development Incentives*, H.C. Paper 327, HMSO, 1973.)

The national incentives had the effect of abolishing the previous differential incentive in favour of investment in the development areas. The new system of grants maintains the differential but changes its character. Whereas assistance under the Local Employment Act was available only for projects which provided employment, grants under the Industry Act ('regional development grants' – graded according to the respective needs of the main types of assisted area) are designed to assist modernization and rationalization – thus providing 'a major incentive for improving the efficiency and competitiveness of industry in the assisted areas'. Given this broader economic approach, regional grants have been made available not only to firms moving into assisted areas, but also to firms existing in these areas. (See further *Industry Act 1972: Annual Reports by the Secretary of State for Trade and Industry*, HMSO.)

Office Development

Details of policies in relation to the control of office development can be found in the Annual Reports of the Secretary of State for the Environment and the Secretary of State for Wales. (See, e.g. *Annual Report for the Year Ended 31 March 1973*, H.C. Paper 375, HMSO, 1973.) It should be noted that the relevant part of the Control of Office and Industrial Development Act is now consolidated in the Town and Country Planning Act 1971.

The 1970 White Paper, *The Reorganization of Central Government* (Cmnd. 4506) announced that the Government had decided to 'take a fresh look at the location of government work, and in particular at the possibilities of dispersing more of it from London'. The outcome was the Hardman Report (*The Dispersal of Government Work from London*, Cmnd. 5322, HMSO, 1973).

This has been the subject of considerable criticism because of its limited perspective on the issues involved. A notable critique (which understandably exhibits the very different perspective of those in West Central Scotland) is *The Unanswerable Case*, published by the Corporation of Glasgow (available, free of charge, from the Public Relations Officer, Corporation of Glasgow, City Chambers, Glasgow). At the time of writing no decisions had been taken on the Hardman Report.